Scots Who Made America

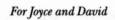

For Joyce and David

Scots Who Made America

Rick Wilson

BIRLINN

First published in Great Britain in 2006 by
Birlinn Ltd
West Newington House
10 Newington Road
Edinburgh
EH9 1QS

www.birlinn.co.uk

ISBN10: 1 84158 485 1
ISBN13: 978 1 84158 485 0

British Library Cataloguing-in-Publication Data
A catalogue record for this book is available
from the British Library

Typesetting and origination by Brinnoven, Livingston
Printed and bound by Cox and Wyman Ltd, Reading

Contents

Introduction   vii

AMERICA'S GREAT SCOTS

Henry St Clair (1398)	1
Captain Kidd (1645–1701)	6
John Witherspoon (1723–94)	12
James Craik (1730–1814)	17
James Wilson (1742–98)	21
John Paul Jones (1747–90)	25
Alexander Wilson (1766–1813)	32
'Uncle' Sam Wilson (1766–1854)	36
Archibald Binny (?–1838) and	
James Ronaldson (1768–1842)	39
James Gordon Bennett (1795–1872)	71
Allan Pinkerton (1819–84)	42
Andrew Carnegie (1835–1919)	50
Andrew Smith Hallidie (1836–1900)	59
John Muir (1838–1914)	63
Robert Dollar (1844–1932)	75
Alexander Graham Bell (1847–1922)	80
David Dunbar Buick (1854–1929)	89
Bertie C. Forbes (1880–1954)	95
Tommy Armour (1895–1968)	103
Harry Benson (1930–)	107
Hugh Grant (1958–)	113

THE SCOTTISH INFLUENCE

Alexander Selkirk (1676–1723)	119
William Cullen (1710–90)	124

James Small (1740–93) 129

John McAdam (1756–1836) 131

Robert Burns (1759–96) 134

Charles Macintosh (1765–1843) 140

Walter Scott (1770–1832) 143

Johnnie Walker (1800–59) 146

Alexander Bain (1811–77) 149

James Dewar (1842–1923) 153

Robert Louis Stevenson (1850–94) 155

Arthur Conan Doyle (1859–1930) 159

James Matthew Barrie (1860–1937) 163

Harry Lauder (1870–1950) 167

Alexander Fleming (1881–1955) 171

John Logie Baird (1888–1946) 175

Robert Watson-Watt (1892–1973) 178

Sean Connery (1930–) 181

Jim Clark (1936–68) 187

Tom Farmer (1940–) 191

Tony Blair (1953–) 198

Introduction

I could try to put this modestly, but that would be simply disingenuous. While I wish to avoid the impression of 'wha's like us' chest thumping, this book is an unashamed celebration of home-born Scots who have had an incalculable effect on the life and culture of the United States. Most of them ended up on those western shores, though some performed their magic from afar. Most are gone now, but a few are happily still with us.

I have not tried to be particularly objective – one person's objectivity often being quite different from another's – but have elected to profile especially colourful, imagination-capturing personalities in the fields of science, culture, engineering, publishing, literature, business and medicine. Neither have I felt limited by this or that period, in covering notable achievements from the (alleged) discovery of America by Scots nobleman Henry St Clair in the fourteenth century to the photographing of no fewer than ten American presidents by Harry Benson, a New York-based cameraman who often flies home to walk along his native Scottish beaches with old pals from his childhood.

I have, however, employed some criteria that have precluded our dwelling on the already much-covered impact of second, third and succeeding generations of Scottish-Americans. With that remit, the sky would have been the limit. I could have mentioned multi-millionaire John D. Rockefeller, who inherited Scottish blood from his mother; James Naismith, who invented baseball; James Monroe, the US president and great-grandson of a Scots Covenanter who arrived in the USA in chains; President Lyndon Johnson, whose family came from Dumfriesshire; Neil Armstrong, the first man on the moon, also descended from a Dumfriesshire family; Davy Crockett, the legendary adventurer of Scots descent; Walter, Arthur and William A. Davidson, co-founders of the Harley Davidson motorbike group, whose family hailed from Angus; billionaire tycoon Donald Trump, whose mother was born on the Isle of Lewis; Robert Barclay of Aberdeenshire roots, who was founding governor of New Jersey; and even Elvis Presley, also rooted in Aberdeenshire via a Presley who went to America in the early 1700s. So, in visiting the shores of Britain only once – en route to America from his army unit in Germany – Elvis did so aptly at Scotland's Prestwick Airport in 1960.

But from the McDonalds hamburger chain to the McDonnell Douglas aircraft company, Scottish blood runs through every vein of America, and the little land at the top corner of Europe can lay claim to having indirectly bred some of the most symbolic contributors to US society – sharp-suited entrepreneurs such as IBM builder Thomas Watson and Microsoft founder Bill Gates – as well as some of the more leathery and controversial Wild West figures, like Wyatt Earp, Jesse James and James Wilson Marshall, who started the Californian gold rush.

Indeed, 61 per cent of US presidents have had Scottish origins, and nine of the thirteen governors of the newly created United States of America were Scots. Everywhere you look in America there are fascinating traces of tartan – even on the dollar bill itself: the Scots typefounders Archbald Binny and James Ronaldson designed the dollar sign, while Scots-descended James Pollock became Director of the Mint at Philadelphia and was responsible for putting the phrase 'In God We Trust' on US money.

But it is not American-born Scots on whom I have focused this exercise, and neither have I insisted on US residency as a qualification for inclusion. Some big Scots names have impacted on America without being on the spot. Some have just spent some time there. So a fair part of the book focuses on 'influencers from afar', people such as movie star Sir Sean Connery, who have been much in demand, though not resident, in America. I have noted the magical effects of certain stay-at-home figures, such as Peter Pan creator J.M. Barrie and Crusoe-inspiring Scots sailor Alexander Selkirk. I have examined the life-changing temptations that emigration presented to Scotland's famous writers like Robert Louis Stevenson and Robert Burns, who, despite their subsequent impact on American culture, never quite made the break. I have acknowledged the significant impact that Scots-resident groundbreakers in radar, penicillin, television and refrigeration made on both sides of the Atlantic. And I have noted that other developments, such as the ever-popular mac raincoat and tarmac road surfacing, have been successfully exported into US life without the accompanying presence of their Scots inventors. I have even paid due heed to the regard with which Edinburgh-born Tony Blair is held in America.

But the bulk of this volume is devoted to the men who gave not just their talents but also their whole physical selves to America; whose work made them famous after their arrival on its shores. Obvious names like Andrew Carnegie, the weaver's son from Dunfermline who became the richest man in the world, and Alexander Graham Bell, well-named inventor of the telephone; as well as lesser-known characters like Andrew Hallidie, who invented the San Francisco cable car, or Alexander Wilson, the Paisley-born father of American ornithology.

Such human stars of the American element of the Scottish diaspora provide a clear illustration of just how actively creative immigrants can be. Indeed, Andrew Carnegie himself said: 'Without the Scots America would have been a poor show.' I would not go that far, but – particularly in the days of the Highland Clearances, when people were forced to make way for sheep (1790–1845) – there was a mutual enthusiasm for what each party had to offer. The Scots sought new opportunities and the Americans welcomed their industry, application and high standard of education. One American observer wrote: 'Of all immigrants to our country, the Scotch are always the most welcome. They bring us muscle and brain and tried skill and trustworthiness in many of our great industries, of which they are managers of the most successful.' These days, however, the tables could be turning, and Scotland may soon be tested as a host country of opportunity in much the same way that America has been.

Noting how the transfer of human ingenuity from one nation can energise another seems particularly relevant at this point in Scotland's history. For as relative independence has been returned to it through its own parliament for the first time in 300 years, so the debate about the virtues of imported human talent has opened up with a new intensity.

With Scotland's own five-million population static or falling simultaneously with the enlargement of the European Union, the question now is: would a brain-drain in reverse from the eastern countries be welcomed? Would immigrants and their energy be appreciated in the same way that Scots and their talents have been allowed to flourish in the land of the free?

There must be little doubt that the Scots, of all people, will record the answer 'Yes' to that. Time, in any case, will tell.

Women readers may be disappointed that all the personalities covered in the book are men. This is largely because at the point of the biggest explosion of Scottish emigration to the USA – after the 1707 Act of Union between Scotland and England and before female rights began being properly asserted in the late twentieth century – it was, like it or not, a man's world. A few names of enterprising women were considered but they were so few that I suspect the charge against me then would have been 'tokenism'. Let's trust that, a century from now, there will be opportunities aplenty for the publishing of such a book focused on the exported achievements of Scottish women.

But for the moment, I celebrate the Tartan Titans, the Scotsmen who shaped America.

I am grateful to friends and colleagues who have helped with this project, particularly journalists Jack Webster and Jim Gilchrist, and my eagle-eyed wife Alison, who can spot an errant comma from a mile away.

America's Great Scots

Henry St Clair (1358–1400)

He led, Columbus followed

Could it possibly be true that America was discovered by a Scots nobleman almost a century before Christopher Columbus? It is a beguiling proposition that captivates a growing number of today's natives of Caledonia, the more familiar they become with the story and evidence of Sir Henry St Clair and his medieval meanderings.

One compelling piece of evidence is to be found on Edinburgh's doorstep today, in a fascinating ancient place redolent of medieval intrigue and mystery just south of the city: a finely hewn building like a miniature cathedral where pagan and Christian traditions live a little uneasily side by side.

This is the well-preserved fifteenth-century Rosslyn Chapel – described by its caretakers as a 'jewel in stone' – whose elevated but secluded position near the rolling foothills of the Pentlands is not only beautiful but dramatically illustrative of the difference between Scotland then and now. Why? Simply and mundanely because of its proximity to the hugely popular Edinburgh outlet of the Swedish IKEA furniture group.

Only a few miles apart, both powerful symbols taken together show just how ages and ever-evolving cultures have radically changed the Scots. But they have one thing in common: they can really pull in the crowds – albeit of acutely different kinds of people. The chic-but-cheap store daily attracts hundreds of materialistic home-improvers happily absorbed into the Scandinavian furnishing trend that has flooded almost every corner of every household in the land; the chapel is a magnet for more spiritual and cerebral types like historians, students of religion and mystics . . . joined relatively recently by the Hollywood actor Tom Hanks and waves of international book and movie fans keen to take in and sense the denouement scene of Dan Brown's blockbuster novel and film, *The Da Vinci Code*.

What they behold is a compact, filigreed masterpiece of the stonemason's art that defies description – at least by some, such as

1

a lost-for-words author called Britton who, in his 1812 *Architectural Antiquities of Britain*, said the chapel would be found 'curious, elaborate and singularly interesting, impossible to designate by any given or familiar term', its 'variety and eccentricity not to be defined by any words of common acceptation'.

But should they start to study the detail of the elaborately carved interior, a visitor's already dazzled eye might settle on the pattern of repeated bulbous shapes that make a sweeping lower border to the arch over one of the chapel windows. These have been identified as American maize, which should not have been known in Britain when the chapel was founded in 1446 by William Sinclair, the third earl of Orkney.

If the American continent was only found by Columbus in 1492, and even if the chapel took another forty years to complete, how did these representations manage to appear in Scotland? It is only logical to conclude that someone with a connection to Rosslyn must have made the transatlantic voyage before that date; and the common assumption is that that person was William's grandfather, Sir Henry St Clair, sometimes described as 'Prince' Henry because of his royal connection. The current earl of Rosslyn, who has written an informative introductory book about the chapel for visitors, simply asks: 'Is it possible that knowledge [of the plants] brought home by Prince Henry passed to his grandson?'

But for many Scots who look askance at the annual celebration of the Genoese navigator's 'discovery' of America, there is very little doubt that, having crossed the Atlantic at the head of an impressive fleet, the Scottish knight set foot on the rugged shores of Nova Scotia, near to what is now Guysborough, on the Feast of the Trinity in 1398. And they see it as quite natural that his grandson William should have immortalised that early transatlantic voyage in stone at the chapel in the family estate of which he was the baron.

But Henry St Clair was not just the baron of Rosslyn. He was known by many other grand titles: knight, of course, and Lord Chief Justice of Scotland, Admiral of the Seas, and First Prince [or Earl] of Orkney – the last bestowed upon him by King Haakon of Norway, who endowed him with 200 strategically located Scottish islands over which he reigned all-powerful, more like a king than a prince. But he is also thought to have been the legendary figure known as 'Glooscap' among the Micmac Native American Indians whose folklore is said to describe his ships as 'islands with trees growing on them'.

To begin, however, at the beginning . . .

What we know of the story is largely thanks to chronicles of a sixteenth-century Venetian, whose namesake and forebear, Nicolò Zeno, was sailing round the north coast of Scotland when, after being shipwrecked off the Faroe islands, he was rescued and befriended by a local chieftain. Was this St Clair? That point is not clear, but gratefully wishing to help the chief in his endeavours, the Italian summoned his brother Antonio from Venice and together, in 1393, the two skilled shipbuilders led a successful mapping expedition to Greenland. Nicolò died the following year, but Antonio stayed on to make another expedition in 1398, this time almost certainly with Sir Henry.

Known as the *Zeno Narrative*, the story of St Clair's voyage to North America was written by the 'new' Nicolò Zeno a historian and prominent citizen, in 1558. His claimed sources were letters written by the original Nicolò, and his brother Antonio. Antonio's letters (as given in the *Narrative*) also refer to a book he had written that described in detail the lands they visited, and they included a map of the islands and countries of the North Atlantic.

But why was such an ambitious expedition mounted? The St Clairs were linked to the once-powerful Knights Templar, some of whom had fled to Scotland after they were outlawed, and it is speculated that the journey was intended to find and found a Templar colony far from their hunters' eyes. Formed during the Crusades, the Knights Templar were a wealthy band of warrior-monks who had become the most feared soldiers of Christendom – until, after two centuries of unrivalled power in Europe and the Holy Land, they were abruptly suppressed by King Philip IV of France and proclaimed open to arrest over most of Europe on charges of heresy, blasphemy and obscenity. Scotland was one of only two European countries – the other was Portugal – where the order was not proscribed by the Pope. It was seen as their last refuge from persecution; but was it far enough away from the rest of Europe?

In any case, some records say bluntly that Sir Henry sailed from Orkney 'with Templar funding', and it was certainly with a big and well-equipped force that he did so. No fewer than twelve ships set off with what seemed indeed remarkably like a colonising 300-strong company – of Templar knights, soldiers, sailmakers, armourers, carpenters and farming monks – complete with Venetian Pietro cannon.

Sailing via Shetland, they first reached Newfoundland from where, after making an unsuccessful attempt to land, they pushed on south through vicious seas – losing no fewer than five ships – to Nova Scotia. The remaining ships must have been struggling by the time they got there, and readers can surely draw their own conclusions from the fact that, in 1849, two brass Venetian naval cannon of the late fourteenth century were dredged up off the shore of Louisburg harbour on Nova Scotia's Cape Breton Island.

In any case, perhaps in an attempt to cut his losses, it was in Nova Scotia that Sir Henry is said to have sent most of his fleet back to Orkney while he and his shore party spent more then a year exploring the new land and making the acquaintance of the Micmac Indians.

So the story goes. But what evidence is there? It is largely anecdotal, but it is intriguing nonetheless. Along with other tribes in the surrounding regions, the Micmacs have a legend of a white 'prince' who came from across the sea and met their people at Pictou, which has been identified as the second landfall of the expedition. Said to have been wise and kindly, he apparently showed the Indians the European styles of fishing, hunting and plant cultivation. The lore also records that the white prince travelled in 'a great stone canoe', also described as 'a floating island with trees growing out of it', which surely evokes the picture of a European sailing ship with high masts.

These and other native American peoples are also said to have referred in their folklore to the landfall of a vessel 'like a bird with a broken wing' and still act out the arrival of a foreign hero called 'Glooscap', a name reckoned by some to be the Indians' version of Earl Sinclair. And according to Jim Gilchrist, a Scots writer who has done considerable research into the subject, 'ethnologists say that it was around this period that the natives of the area started fishing with nets, European-style, rather than with lines, while others point to Gaelic and Norse words assimilated into the vocabulary of the Algonquin and other native peoples'.

It is also told that when Sir Henry took his leave of his new-found admirers after his mutually enriching year among them, his intention was to be heading for home. A sudden storm blew up, however, and drove him south to Massachusetts, which was the catalytic moment that meant he was to set foot in what we now know as America almost a century before Columbus. Shortly after his landing there, it is recorded in the *Zeno Narrative*, they climbed a hill where his close companion and cousin, the Templar Knight Sir James Gunn of Clyth, suddenly died – either from heat exhaustion or by being beaten in a fight. And it is here that further compelling evidence of the landfall begins to emerge.

There has since been discovered, roughly scratched out of a rock at Prospect Hill in Westford, Massachusetts, the unmistakable effigy of a fourteenth-century knight holding a sword – dated between 1375 and 1400 – and a shield which was identified by a former Lord Lyon, the Scottish authority on crests, as being from the Gunn family.

Sir Henry may even have reached as far south as Rhode Island, where some evidence suggests that he and his men could have built Newport Tower, a two-storey circular stone needle which, say researchers, is definitely European – rather than native American – and has architectural features that owe something to the medieval church towers of Scotland's northern isles.

If all this is true (and it has to be said that there are many dissenters, even in Scotland), it would be touching and apt for Sir Henry to have left such an impact over the centuries; for he was undoubtedly a man of great courage, achievement and presence. Indeed, his Venetian companion Antonio Zeno is recorded as saying that 'if ever there was a man worthy of immortal memory, it is this man'.

While the time and place of Sir Henry's death remain a mystery – some say his remains were brought to Rosslyn Chapel to be buried among the other St Clair knights who lie there – those words would surely have made a suitable epitaph for the enterprising Scot who (probably) 'discovered' America for the Europeans.

Note. 'The whole business of "discovering" countries is, of course, somewhat subjective,' says Jim Gilchrist. 'High-profile explorers get recorded in the history text books, others "discover" places without posterity noting the fact. Thus, ten years after his "discovery" of America, Christopher Columbus received a letter from some English merchants alleging that he knew perfectly well that they had already been there for fish.'

Captain Kidd (1645–1701)

The reluctant pirate

When we talk of pirates and their dastardly deeds, the name Captain Kidd is sure to come quickly to mind. How does the image go again? An evil-looking, lank-haired man with knife gripped between rotting teeth, a red headscarf roughly stained with skull-and-crossbones, the quick flash of evil in the one eye not covered by a patch, and a less-than-pleasant bodily odour. Those who don't see Captain Kidd as the archetypal bad guy of the seven seas are rare, for he was so successfully demonised in a propaganda exercise that, over the three centuries since his body was trussed up to rot on the oak gibbet at Tilbury after his hanging in London, succeeding generations of readers have swallowed the story. Right up to the present day. And the story's essence is that, in the days of mean ship-raiding swashbucklers, he was the meanest of them all.

Interesting idea, pity it's not the truth.

There are, admittedly, many things that we don't know about Captain William Kidd, such as his age when he was so crudely dispatched to meet his maker in 1701 – many accounts of his life say he was born in 1655, others say his birth year was 1645. All are agreed that he was born in Scotland, but there is considerable disagreement about where.

Several accounts say he came from Greenock, the west coast port near Glasgow, but others suggest that he was in fact from the east coast, and that his place of birth was actually Carnock 'near Dundee'. It depends what is meant by 'near', of course, for there is no Carnock in the immediate vicinity of Dundee, though there is one very close to Dunfermline in Fife – the county south of the River Tay, on whose northern bank Dundee sits.

The distance between Carnock and Dundee is some fifty miles, and as Kidd lived much of his life in New York and often referred to Dundee as his provenance, perhaps that was just his shorthand for the convenience of others who may have heard of the city but not the

6

village. From that faraway standpoint, they would not have considered the city-to-village distance so great.

There is more in favour of the east. At a hearing in the High Court of the Admiralty in 1695 he gave his age as forty-one and his place of birth as Dundee. The surname Kidd is popular in Fife but relatively rare on Scotland's west coast. His father is listed as a seaman, which explains why one of the chronicles of the day (the *Newgate Calendar*) called him a man 'born to sea'. The exhaustively researched book *The Pirate Hunter* by Richard Zacks simply calls him 'Captain Kidd of New York City and Dundee'. But the clinching fact for this writer is that Kidd affectionately named his black cabin boy 'Dundee'. Anyone who knows the Scots and their little geographic loyalties knows that no one from the west coast would be inclined to put sentimental store on anywhere in the east, or vice versa.

The west coast author Sandra Macdougall, who claims William Kidd for Greenock – 'although there are no local records confirming this fact' – in her book on famous people from Inverclyde's past, will no doubt take issue with this conclusion, especially as my own attempts at finding evidence of his birth in pretty little Carnock also drew a blank. Neither the local church minister nor the nearest library at Oakley had heard of the link. But both were intrigued and, as you read this, might still be burrowing excitedly into their records. So might Lizz Mogg, senior teacher at Carnock School who has chronicled the village's history. 'Captain Kidd came from here?' she exclaimed. 'That really would be something to update my book with. The children would love that.'

Carnock is certainly near enough to big water – the Firth of Forth is visible four miles away – to have weaned a famous sailor. And it is old enough to feel like his cradle. A handful of simple cottage-style buildings, it nestles in the dale of the Carnock Burn three miles north-west of Dunfermline. Said to have been named after St Caranoc, a disciple of St Ninian, it has a parish church built in 1840; but nearby in the old kirkyard stand the ruins of the original twelfth-century parish church and the fine gravestone of John Row, minister of the parish and the Church of Scotland's first historian, who died in 1646. Thus would two famous lifelines have crossed in the village – if William Kidd was indeed born in Carnock in 1645.

It can't be denied that his early career was obscure, and all accounts of his colourful life are plain on that point. But what they all also agree on is that, however he spent his early years at sea – buccaneering or privateering – by the time he surfaced on the record in 1689 as a legitimate privateer for Great Britain against the French, he had learned how to cultivate important people and was himself something of a gentleman.

In other words, he was nothing like the clichéd wild man still pictured by so many people. Indeed, it is questionable whether William Kidd was ever a pirate at all, so much of his fate resting as it did on the sometimes-difficult distinction between that word and the word privateer (having government permission to attack enemy ships on the understanding that the spoils will be shared).

In any event, he was as much a well-to-do merchant as he was either of these. While the sea was in his blood and he always felt drawn back to it, he owned considerable property in New York, married a rich widow there, was very well connected in the city all the way up to the governor, and wore – in his only known contemporary portrait – a gentleman's fashionable long wig.

There is, though, a decidedly sharp adventurer's glint in his eye, and there is no doubt about the fact that he was something of a magnet for trouble. A Scot who lorded it over Dutch, English and American crew members was never going to be popular and when he captained a privateer ship, *Blessed William,* commissioned in 1689 to protect the English colonies in the Caribbean against French attacks, his crew mutinied and left him stranded on the island of Antigua.

Not a bad place to be stranded, some might argue, but he made his way back to New York where he could have settled quietly into an elite business life. Adventure still called, however, and by 1695 he was on his way to London to take a contract as a privateer commanding the 237-ton, 34-cannon *Adventure Galley* with orders to attack and loot any (then enemy) French ships.

The *Adventure Galley* had not gone far on her journey to New York and then on to the Red Sea – to capture any ship belonging to a country at war with England – when she was relieved of much of her crew by a Royal Navy squadron desperate to replace sailors lost to scurvy: a right that it had by law against any ship flying an English flag.

Scraping the bottom of the barrel in New York, a frustrated Captain Kidd added more crew – probably with piratical tendencies – then set sail for the Indian Ocean on his mission to clear the sea there of pirates, though there was probably an unspoken understanding between him and his scheming backers, who included Richard

Coote, the earl of Bellomont and other nobles (such as the king), that he would also consider any enemy ships with valuable cargo fair game.

Mutinous muttering began again as months went by and Kidd's failure to take a prize ship meant that, under the terms of the privateer's contract, there would be no pay for the crew. They pressured Kidd to turn pirate and attack anything, and after he refused to plunder a becalmed Dutch ship they had sighted, a row broke out in which he killed gunner William Moore by hitting him violently over the head with a bucket.

Then, finally, in February 1698, Kidd took his most valuable prize – an Indian-owned ship, the *Quedah Merchant*, which carried a treasure trove of a cargo worth some £710,000 and had French papers making her a legal target under Kidd's privateer terms. She was renamed *Adventure Prize* and her cargo of silk, muslins, sugar, calico, iron and saltpetre seemed set to enrich her captors and their backers. But there was a snag . . . or two.

It did not look like it, but luck was turning against Kidd just as abruptly as politics in London. He had been away from there for nearly two years and in that time there had been a dramatic change in attitude towards piracy and privateering. Officialdom now wanted to pursue only legal trading procedures. And complicating things further was the fact that the *Quedah Merchant* belonged to an influential Armenian merchant who demanded that the East India Company, the English trading company in the East Indies, make restitution.

Having thus offended England's commercial establishment, William Kidd was denounced as an 'obnoxious pirate' and murderer. All the circumstances were crowding against him, as they had done from the moment his crew had forced him over the privateering edge. He had become very bad news, as the enemies of his backers used him to discredit the Whig party to which many of his powerful friends belonged. Soon, his friends distanced themselves from him too.

When Kidd got full appreciation of his plight, he ran for New York where he thought his influential friends, including the governor, would attest to his innocence. He made his way to Block Island, where he began negotiations through his contacts in New York to gain a pardon for his actions, claiming he had been forced into piracy by his crew. But it didn't work. He was captured in July 1699, jailed, then sent to England aboard the frigate *Advice,* to stand trial and incidentally become a political pawn to bring down powerful men in the government.

The trial started on 8 May 1701, and despite his protests that he was not prepared for it and could prove, given time 'to get my evidence ready', that he was only a privateer, it was completed the next day. He was not a man of particular guile and his bluntness could grate in a well-oiled courtroom, but he fought hard and straightforwardly for himself. A small exchange from the trial went like this:

Kidd to character witness Colonel Hewetson: 'Do you think I was a pirate?'

Hewetson to the court: 'I know his men would a gone a-pirateering and he refused it, and his men seized upon his ship.'

And in a letter protesting his innocence he wrote: 'I must be sacrificed as a pirate to salve the Hon'r of some men who employed me . . .'

William Kidd was nonetheless found guilty of multiple piracies and murder (ironically committed when trying to stamp down piracy in his crew) and sentenced to hang on the gallows on 23 May 1701. But he did not do so in total sobriety – 'he was inflam'd with Drink', said his attending priest – or with convenient good grace. The rope broke on the first attempt, granting him another ten minutes of life before it was replaced. At that moment, it was later reported, Kidd sobered up and asked those around him to send his love to his wife and daughter back in New York and said his greatest regret 'was the thought of my wife's sorrow at my shameful death'.

An accurate report? Why should he have felt shamed if he was not guilty, as he had protested? William Kidd may not have been an angel but he was a victim of heavy politics, rich men's plotting and a set of cruel circumstances. If he was a pirate, he was probably an unwilling one. Certain items could have helped his case. But strangely, his logbook was burned and the papers that might have proved his innocence disappeared in Lord Bellomont's hands.

During his career, at least the recorded part of it, Kidd had never seen the need to return to his native Scotland. But that he remained a proud Scot was evidenced by his disparaging reference in one letter to 'their' justice. Then, as now, England and Scotland had distinctly different justice systems.

Certainly, he had no reason to hold the English Establishment in high regard. All his life he had been used as a scapegoat by those more politically powerful than he, and now, even in death, there was no mercy – only humiliation. The Scottish captain's corpse was tarred and suspended and displayed to rot in an iron cage on the dock at Thames estuary for several years as a warning to would-be pirates, and a grim welcome to seafarers arriving in England's main port.

For him, every strategy of self-defence had failed; even the letter to the Tory speaker of the House of Commons in which he offered the government £100,000 worth of his 'lodged goods' if he were allowed to lead a ship to them. His offer fell foul of more pressing business that day, but it has never been forgotten since.

Captain Kidd is believed to have buried much of his treasure from the *Adventure Prize* in several places, and while some of it was found during his life or shortly after his death, the largest deposit is thought to be still for finding, and even today, as author Richard Zacks reminds us, that promise prompts 'treasure hunters to dig holes all over New England, the Caribbean and Madagascar'.

Imagine if the cards had fallen more fortunately for William Kidd. He could have made his way back to his 'lodged goods' and bellowed out a last laugh to reverberate all the way back to Carnock. But it was not to be.

John Witherspoon (1723–94)

Princeton president, freedom fighter

Yester is not a bad name for the East Lothian parish where John
Witherspoon was born, in the manse of the little towered kirk
that sits neatly atop the rise of pretty Gifford village. Not a bad
name – evocative as it is of 'yesterday' – because at first glance almost
everything here seems to have stood still for centuries. Many of the
venerable gravestones clustered about the white-walled church are
infirm, weather-worn and leaning, adding to the general feeling that,
on entering the village, you have entered another, earlier age.

Save for the occasional modern shop nestled between them, the
modest sandstone houses that line the village's few streets would seem
to have changed little since the young Witherspoon grew up here,
where his father preached in the early 1700s. But appearances can
be deceptive. Unexpectedly elegant interiors and the occasional fine
car parked outside betray a 21st-century reality: that such precious
olde worlde village atmosphere now comes at a price, making this
special place on the River Gifford – a tributary of the Tyne – one of
the hottest property spots in the general vicinity of the hottest of
them all, Edinburgh.

John Witherspoon has to be its other claim to fame.

Having learned that the church's exterior boasted a plate to
the memory of this Scots minister who found fame by becoming
president of Princeton University and a signatory of America's
Declaration of Independence, this writer repeatedly circled the old
churchyard getting steadily more puzzled while failing to find the
tribute supposedly erected in 1955 by the St Andrew's Society of the
State of New York.

But just as I stepped into the body of the village to seek help from
the locals, a reflected sun-ray sparkled into my eye, as if to say, 'I'm
here' and, thus pulled back almost magnetically, I saw, behind a
small expanse of grass, the head-high bronze plate on an old stone
wall across the Haddington road from the church. And as I read

the inscription, the image of the old minister seemed to look on approvingly . . .

In honoured memory of the Reverend
JOHN WITHERSPOON, D.D., LL.D.

Only clergyman to sign the American Declaration of
Independence. The first Moderator of the Presbyterian General
Assembly in America, and President of Princeton University. Born
in the manse of Yester, Gifford, Feb 5th, 1723

'. . . The States of America may hand down the blessings of peace
and public order to many generations.'

Property values would not have much interested the self-denying Witherspoons. As minister of Yester parish, the father passed on to the son not just his piety and fluent literacy but also a love of simple tastes. Which was probably already in the genes, for they were lineally descended from the formidable ascetic reformer John Knox, whose prayers made Mary Queen of Scots – she once said – 'more afraid than of an army of ten thousand men'.

Like that ancestor and his own father, John Witherspoon was also to become a renowned preacher whose reputation would carry his career to great heights. After initially exercising his keen mind in his schooling at Haddington, he went to Edinburgh University at fourteen and made a big impression in the theological hall before completing his studies at twenty-one and going straight into preaching in the parish of Beith, in the west of Scotland, where he was held in high regard by his congregation. From there, he went to Paisley, near Glasgow, where he won over the affections of a new and larger congregation.

By all accounts, Dr Witherspoon was a compelling preacher. But he was not just a pulpit thumper; his merits as an author were much appreciated, and an admirer said of his writings that 'to every serious and intelligent reader, they discover an uncommon knowledge of human nature, and a deep and intimate acquaintance with the holy scriptures'.

Somehow, this tall, dignified gentleman managed to combine duties as a devoted pastor with his increasingly ambitious literary efforts – one of which really set the heather on fire in 1753. 'Anonymous' it may have claimed to be, but his was suspected to be the pen behind the satire, *Ecclesiastical Characteristics,* which stung the Church of

Scotland as it identified the shortcomings of some of its ministers. It was the talk of the coffee houses – as was its follow-up, *A Serious Apology* [for the *Characteristics*] in which Dr Witherspoon admitted writing the *Characteristics*.

Three years later he published, from Glasgow, his acclaimed essay *Connexion Between the Doctrine of Justification by the Imputed Righteousness of Christ, and Holiness of Life*. This was followed by a still more celebrated work, *A Serious Inquiry into the Nature and Effects of the Stage*, and in 1764 he went to London to oversee publication of his *Essays on Important Subjects* – a three-volume collection of essays already sporadically published in Scotland.

Unsurprisingly, all this publishing activity spread his reputation far and wide, and soon he was fighting off 'please join us' invitations from congregations in Dublin, Dundee and even the Scottish church in Rotterdam. His attachment to Paisley was too strong to break for any of these, but – with his fame having even crossed the Atlantic – something completely different soon came along which was sufficiently appealing for him to leave not just Paisley but his beloved Scotland.

This was an invitation from the trustees of the College of Princeton, New Jersey (now Princeton University), to become their president. Sympathising with his wife's fear of sailing and of leaving friends and family behind, he at first declined, and indeed he could well have profited from sticking to that decision, for a rich relation offered to make him his heir if the call were ignored. On rethinking things, however, Mrs Witherspoon steeled herself and Dr Witherspoon changed his mind, leaving behind not just great sadness among his Paisley people but, according to one chronicler, 'a sphere of great respectability, comfort, and usefulness'.

He and his family – three sons and two daughters – landed safely in America in August 1768, and in the same month he was inaugurated as the sixth president of the College of Princeton. The excitement of having acquired a man of such erudite reputation to be an intellectual leader in this corner of America caused an immediate fillip not just to the number of students but to the college's funds, which had not been overly healthy at a time when it depended upon contributions rather than state support. And as its finances began to flourish, with new contributions recorded from Virginia to Massachusetts, so did the college's reflected reputation. And the early faith in Dr Witherspoon proved not to have been misplaced. Soon, he had wrought a total revolution in the instruction system practised before his arrival, boosting the study of mathematical science and natural philosophy, bringing in 'all the most liberal and modern improvements of Europe', and making changes in every department of instruction, from history to law, while personally passing on many of the principles of good taste and good writing.

Said to be 'the most companionable of men' with a good sense of humour, his natural facility for governing was a bonus much admired by many of his students who sought to copy, and even emulate, such leadership skills. During his administration the college achieved a national reputation that it has preserved to this day. The number of high achievers who studied under him during his twenty-six-year tenure at Princeton is impressive. They included: US President James Madison, Vice-President Aaron Burr, nine cabinet officers, twenty-one United States senators, thirty-nine members of the House of Representatives, twelve governors, six members of the Continental Congress, three Supreme Court Justices, thirty-three state and federal judges and thirteen college presidents.

But there was another, high-achieving John Witherspoon. It was when the start of the American Revolutionary War caused the college's officers and students to be broken up and dispersed in 1776 that he appeared in a new and surprising public guise – not so much the divine philosopher as the thinking civilian. Incurring the severe displeasure of his friends back home in Scotland, where he was called a 'rebel and a traitor', he embraced and expounded America's case for independence and, receiving a totally different reaction from his American friends, was sent by them as a representative of the people of New Jersey, to the Congress of the United States.

His opinion on all the great issues was valued and he was a true and outspoken champion of his new country's right to independence. Those who opposed his viewpoint were liable to feel – at least – the sharpness of his wit. When one claimed the land was not yet ripe for independence, Dr Witherspoon replied scathingly: 'Sir, in my judgement the country is not only ripe, but rotting.'

Another example of his quick wit was seen in the tale of the rather slow messenger sent to convey the news of the British Army's surrender to General Gates at Saratoga. The aide took so long to reach Philadelphia to impart the vital intelligence, that when he finally arrived, he was told that it had reached the city three days before. As it was customary to offer such a messenger a gift from

Congress, a fine sword was proposed – at which point Dr Witherspoon rose to amend the motion by substituting a pair of spurs.

Amusing or not, the six-foot Scot never forgot that first and foremost he was a solemn clergyman – the only one, indeed, to sign the Declaration of Independence; and a month before doing so, he preached regretfully of 'all the disorderly passions of man' and asserted that only God could turn conflict to good.

When the question of American independence was settled in early 1783, Dr Witherspoon resumed his college duties for a couple of years before paying a short visit to Britain to refresh old friendships. Feelings about his loyalties were still running high, however, and the trip was not a great success. After some preaching sessions in Paisley he said his final fond farewells and returned to America to wind down into retirement. But not before he contributed significantly to the organisation of a newly independent and national Presbyterian Church, opening its first General Assembly in 1789 with a sermon, and presiding until the election of its first moderator.

In domestic life, Dr Witherspoon was an affectionate father and husband, having been married twice – latterly when he was seventy and the young lady only twenty-three. This did not mean, however, that he was particularly young for his age; indeed, his health was fragile and, after losing his sight for the last few years of his life, he died on 15 November 1794.

His spirit lived on at Princeton, however, and in the following century another learned Scot – James McCosh, from Ayrshire – took over the baton as the college's eleventh president. The latter's impact was also impressive during his twenty-year tenure, and in what was (almost) a remarkable conjunction of dates, he died on 16 November 1894, exactly a century and a day after Dr Witherspoon.

James Craik (1730–1814)

The first president's doctor

They were born not far apart in years, and even less so in geography, where we are talking mere metres. Indeed, if their age difference had been a bit smaller than seventeen years, they might have grown up as young friends playing among the same woods and gentle coastal hills. And they had more than the same root in common. Both famously 'went native' on making acquaintance with America, both also shipped out of Scotland in the mid-1700s, and neither ever looked back, each writing himself indelibly into the history of the new United States. The rather more famous one – John Paul Jones – became the celebrated father of the American navy (see page 25); but the other well-known emigrant son of Kirkbean was also a man of remarkable achievement.

James Craik was the son of Robert Craik, a British MP and laird of Arbigland – a sizeable family estate on the north bank of the Solway Firth in placid, low-lying Dumfriesshire – where John Paul Jones' father was the gardener.

Born in 1730, Dr Craik was educated to be a surgeon in the British Army, taking a medical degree from the University of Edinburgh, but ended up as Physician General of the United States Army and as the personal physician to George Washington, first president of the United States, by whom he was called 'my old and intimate friend'.

The Scots doctor even had the debatable honour of being on duty at the deathbed as he and a colleague strove to save the president's life in 1799. But to arrive at this trusted position in the eyes of such a great statesman had not been so long and challenging a journey as one would imagine. They were firm friends within a few years of Craik's arrival on American soil.

He had set off for the Caribbean to work as an army surgeon in 1751 but, intrigued by the lure of a nascent America, soon moved on to that land to set up a medical practice at the frontier village and military base of Winchester, Virginia. From there he was drawn – as surgeon of the Virginia Provincial Regiment, latterly commanded by Washington – into the American phase of the French and Indian war between France and Britain, and it was during this campaign that the lifelong friendship between him and Washington took root.

On duty in the ill-fated advance against Fort Duquesne in 1755, Craik found himself in the thick of the battle in which the British were routed by the French and their Indian allies; indeed, he dressed the wounds of the doomed General Edward Braddock on the field and tended him until his death the next day, when the then 23-year-old Washington, as senior surviving officer, read a funeral tribute over his body.

Craik then went with Washington to Winchester, where, between 1755 and 1758, the latter was in command of provincial forces charged with protection of the Virginia and Maryland frontier from hostile Indian forces until the final fall of Fort Duquesne on 25 November 1758, in which the bold young leader played a glorious part.

The Indians' faith in the invincibility of the French thus punctured, their raids ceased and Dr Craik resigned from the army, moving to Maryland, where he bought a plantation at Port Tobacco, set up a medical practice, and built an impressive home for his new bride, Marianne Ewell, great-aunt of General Richard S. Ewell of the Confederate army.

But the Scot and Washington remained steadfast friends. And it was around this time that the two men's loyalty to Britain began to come under severe strain as domestic peace proved less promising than they had hoped.

Washington's peace plan was to manage his Mount Vernon lands well and build a happy home life within his marriage to the attractive widow Martha Dandridge Custis; but along with other planters, he began to feel frustrated, exploited and infuriated by British merchants and British regulations.

Then suddenly, while so volubly resisting the mother country's trading restrictions, he was catapulted into the role of Commander-in-Chief of the Continental Army when attending the Second Continental Congress as a Virginia delegate in Philadelphia in May 1775.

Meanwhile, Dr Craik had been taking an active part in a meeting of Charles County citizens at Port Tobacco in which resolutions were adopted protesting against the blockade of Boston and pledging aid in commercial reprisals against the British.

It looked inevitable that the two friends would soon be back on the warpath, both having come to similar conclusions about revised political allegiances.

Dr Craik joined the American army in 1777 when Washington offered him a position as a medical officer, and he rose rapidly through the ranks during the Revolutionary War. In 1780 a reorganisation of the medical department made him the senior of four, holding the title of Chief Hospital Physician and Surgeon. He was active in disclosing the conspiracy of 1777 to remove the commander-in-chief, and in 1781, as director-general of the hospital at Yorktown, he was present at the surrender of Cornwallis after the siege there, when Cornwallis's entire army marched out with its band playing 'The World Turned Upside Down'.

But the Scot's elevation to the US army's very top medical position was not to be – until after the war. Having left in 1783, he had returned to private practice, this time in Alexandria, Virginia, and looked settled for life – until in 1798 Washington, now the former first president, was summoned from retirement to command the army in a threatened war with France. Now in a strong position to have all of his conditions accepted, he named Dr Craik for his chief medical officer, and the Scot was appointed Physician General on 19 July of that year.

In the event, the feared war never materialised but Dr Craik's association with George Washington continued quite literally to the end – when, as the ex-president's private physician, he was called to Mount Vernon to diagnose the old man's final illness and treat him till his last hours on 14 December 1799.

Dr Craik, still the army medical chief, found the 68-year-old Washington to be suffering from 'cynanche trachealis', a throat-restricting infection now called streptococci cellulitis.

As attending physician, the doctor's account of the death read:

He was fully impressed at the beginning of his complaint, as well as through every succeeding stage of it, that its conclusion would be mortal; submitting to the several exertions made for his recovery, rather as a duty, than from any expectation of their efficacy. He considered the operations of death upon his system as coeval with the disease; and several hours before his death, after repeated efforts to be understood, succeeded in expressing a desire that he might be permitted to die without further interruption.

But the president had not forgotten his old friend. A great honour was paid to the Scot in Washington's will, when he wrote: 'To my compatriot in arms, and old and intimate friend, Dr Craik, I give my bureau (or, as the cabinet makers call it, tambour secretary), and the cabinet chair, an appendage of my study.'

Dr Craik himself died in Fairfax County, Virginia, on 6 February 1814.

James Wilson (1742-98)

Creator of the US presidency

Few people in his native land have heard of James Wilson, but he was one of the most important Scots ever to settle in America. For when the new nation was being moulded, he was instrumental in shaping the still-enduring structure of its presidency. A big achievement without doubt, so why so little recognition for it?

While he was conspicuously intelligent and a brilliant speaker deserving of a significant place in history on both sides of the Atlantic, could his reputation have fallen foul of his undoubted character flaws? His abundance of brainpower and personal ambition were matched only by his lack of personal control in matters of investment risk-taking and/or gambling. Enough to have him airbrushed out? It's debatable, so he was probably the least understood and most underrated of America's founding fathers.

One of seven children, born in 1742 to a Presbyterian farming family in Fife, Wilson was always a clever man, having attended no fewer than three Scottish universities – Glasgow, Edinburgh and St Andrews – the last being nearest to his home village of Carskerdo. The plan was that he would join the Church of Scotland ministry, but the death of his father forced him to abandon his studies and rethink his intended trajectory.

Like many of his countrymen at the time, he was less than enamoured of Scotland's relatively recent surrender of its free nationhood to 'the union' and couldn't wait to take off to another place where independence was rising against that force rather than yielding to it. So, resolved to add his undoubted promise to the promised land, he sailed for America in 1765, but confident as he was, even he could not have guessed at the catalytic role he was to play, as a signatory of the Declaration of Independence and member of the Constitutional Convention of 1787, in the new country's foundation.

With the help of letters of introduction, he soon became a

tutor – and recipient of an honorary MA degree – at the College of Philadelphia, Pennsylvania, and was hailed as the best classical scholar ever to hold such a position; yet he did not hold it long. Taking a sudden interest in the study of law, he was admitted to the bar within two years of his arrival. Soon, he was practising in a couple of smaller towns before settling back in Philadelphia.

Meanwhile, he had truly 'gone native', supporting the revolutionary struggle for American liberty with an impressive zeal. Indeed, it was said that he had become American at the moment he landed on the western shore, and a powerful tract he published – *Considerations on the Nature and Extent of the Legislative Authority of the British Government* – bluntly challenged British parliamentary authority over America, asserting that, as the colonies had no representation within it, parliament could have no power over the colonies.

As an increasingly prominent lawyer, he signed the Declaration of Independence in 1775 as a member of the Second Continental Congress – after some weeks' hesitation, caused by the fact that he represented the Middle States, where opinions differed on the crucial matter of independence. But his eventual signing committed Pennsylvania to an independence vote.

He reached the pinnacle of his career as a member of the celebrated convention of 1787, which gathered in Philadelphia for no less a task than forming the Constitution of the United States. There, his influence on the Committee of Detail was formidable and his powers of oration and passion of delivery were much commented upon.

Being such a fluent and compelling speaker, he helped define great points of principle in the formation of the new government when, for instance, delegates considered important points such as the amount of power the executive should have or the best means by which to elect the executive. And when they discussed whether presidential power should be in the hands of a single individual or shared by several people, Wilson moved it should consist of the former. After he had put his case with his usual fluency, arguing that conflicts would be more easily avoided if there were only one executive, who could be carefully watched by Congress and answerable to it, a lengthy silence ensued. But the other framers finally yielded to his view and decided upon a single president.

Wilson, who was practically alone among the Founding Fathers in advocating direct election of the single-person executive, later said: 'The president is the dignified, but accountable magistrate of a free and great people. The tenure of his office, it is true, is not hereditary; nor is it for life: but still it is a tenure of the noblest kind.'

Though the president would enjoy many powers, the framers were anxious to avoid the reign of a tyrannical one – and so proposed a system of checks and balances. Such as: the 'chief' would be ineligible for re-election, could be impeached and convicted by the Supreme Court, and could have his/her actions checked by two-thirds of both Congressional houses. Several adjustments were made to the proposals in the final days of the Convention, and the executive office evolved into its current form.

Was Wilson happy with that? When the state convention of Pennsylvania assembled to ratify the federal constitution, he confessed to it:

> I am not a blind admirer of this plan of government, and there are some parts of it which, if my wish had prevailed, would certainly have been altered. But, when I reflect how widely men differ in their opinions, and that every man (and the observation applies likewise to every state) has an equal pretension to assert his own, I am satisfied that any thing nearer to perfection could not have been accomplished.
>
> If there are errors, it should be remembered that the seeds of reformation are sown in the work itself, and a concurrence of two-thirds of the Congress may, at any time, introduce alterations and amendments. Regarding it, then, in every point of view, with a candid and disinterested mind, I am bold to assert, that it is the best form of government which has ever been offered to the world.

Among the powers granted to his single-person executive were commander-in-chief of the armed forces, the authority to grant pardons and reprieves, the ability to veto legislation, the power to make treaties with other nations, and the power to appoint judges.

There was a certain irony in the last point, as Wilson had high hopes of being appointed Chief Justice of the Supreme Court as a reward for his service in the formation of the federal government. But in the event, the first president, George Washington, appointed him only an associate justice in 1789.

Wilson was tall, dignified and graceful, but he was no paragon. He had borrowed heavily and gambled aggressively throughout his life. And after his wife died in 1786, he fell into an ill-advised land speculation deal, which so financially compromised him that he spent some time in a debtors' prison while still serving as a judge. Indeed, he continued in that role until his death in 1798, while on circuit duty at Edenton, North Carolina.

He was fifty-six and left six children from the first of his two marriages.

John Paul Jones (1747–90)

US naval hero, British pirate

Down by the sandy shore at Carsethorn, all you can see today that evokes the tears and fears of the busy, long-gone era of the sailing ship are a few posts of black, rotting wood that once supported a great jetty jutting out into the Solway Firth. Sit beside them for a while and you can almost hear the excited chatter of ghosts; the ghosts of thousands of Scots who took their families and their dreams this way out to the New World.

The high-masted ships came in the other way too, of course, bringing exotic cargoes from far-off lands, so that the great triangle of water that cleaves its western way between Scotland and England was for many years a bustling, fascinating thoroughfare of water-borne traffic.

In the mid-1700s, when lands and alien cultures were still being discovered in a great adventure even more intriguing than today's exploration of space, the romantic lure of the sea and its mysteries must have been hard to resist, especially if you enjoyed a view of the Firth like that of the young John Paul (who added the Jones later). As he looked at it in wonder from the south-facing windows of his parents' cottage at the nearby Arbigland estate – where his Fife-born father was the gardener – the water and its promising passport to an exciting future seemed almost to lap at the door; in fact, it was barely a mile off. Indeed, Carsethorn was near to him in more ways than one, being literally central to his life, almost equidistant from his home and his school at Kirkbean; so he spent much of his time around the port and its traffic in a form of play that was to have a significant influence on his life.

William Craik, the Arbigland estate owner's son, once recalled how John Paul 'would run to Carsethorn whenever his father would let him off, talk to the sailors and clamber over the ships' and would teach his playmates to manoeuvre their little boats 'to mimic a naval battle, while he – taking his stand on the tiny cliff overlooking the roadstead – shouted shrill commands at his imaginary fleet'.

It was his grooming for the adult responsibilities that were to come sooner than even he had hoped or imagined. It was not surprising that the romantic pull of the sea seduced the boy, but who could have guessed that he would have risen to become a captain by the tender age of twenty-one . . . and eventually, the victorious Admiral John Paul Jones of the American Revolution, often called the founding father of the American Navy (though marked down as a fearful pirate in the land of his birth). Yet his early, formative days left an indelible mark on him. He was famed in later life not just for his achievement of rank and swashbuckling deeds of daring but also for dramatic pronouncements that had a ring of playground bravado about them. Such as . . .

'I wish to have no connection with any ship that does not go fast, for I intend to go in harm's way' – when responding in 1779 to a French invitation to buy a captured British ship in Brest harbour.

'I have not yet begun to fight' – at the vicious Battle of Flamborough Head, when it initially looked as if superior British firepower would prevail and he was thus invited to 'strike' (lower his flag in surrender).

Facing out across the Solway Firth to the English Lake District, the flat curve of coastal land at Arbigland is sandy, with sparse vegetation. Inland a little, dropping away from the wings of the old Georgian house, azaleas and rhododendrons flourish alongside the gardens. This is where, in the still-standing white-painted small cottage at the end of an avenue of pines, John Paul was born in 1747. It has changed little on the exterior, apart from bearing a wall plaque that reads:

Commodore John Paul Jones, Illustrious Naval Hero of the American Revolution, Born here July 6, 1747. This tablet was placed in his memory by the Naval Historical Foundation and the Army and Navy Chapter of the Daughters of the American Revolution both of Washington DC, United States of America. AD 1953.

But changes have taken place in and around the cottage since Jack and Primrose Dougan – last of the estate workers to live there – left in 1990.

Primrose used to receive spontaneous visitors who made the pilgrimage to the remote cottage. Interviewed in the 1980s, she said: 'Most of them are American or ex-navy and most of them don't have a clue what they are coming to see. So it's often a disappointment when they discover it's still just a private cottage instead of a museum.'

That state of affairs was attended to in 1993 when the cottage became the centrepiece of the John Paul Jones Museum (with an outbuilding as a supporting shop), established with the help of private donations. Although some might argue for keeping such a house lived in, the glossed-up concept tunes in well with modern thinking – on audio headsets, visitors can hear the story of life in the cottage as told by the great man's 'mother' – while still evoking the atmosphere of John Paul Jones' time there, as the middle child of a family of seven.

The two-roomed cottage is furnished in the style of the 1700s, and in an extension built in 1831 by an admiring US navy lieutenant there is a reconstruction of the great cabin of the *Bonhomme Richard*, the ship John Paul Jones led into the blazing Flamborough Head engagement in 1779. But it is the cottage's small windows to the water that fascinate above all.

'If you stand at these windows, you can see why John Paul got the call,' said last resident Primrose. 'He was bound to go down to the shore and watch the ships going by. No wonder he didn't want to stay.'

In fact, he was thirteen when he crossed the firth to the English port of Whitehaven, signed up for a seven-year seaman's apprenticeship, and set off on the Barbados–Virginia run in a ship called the *Friendship*. He was a quick and willing learner, picking up skills and sophistication wherever he could. While that first ship was in port at Fredericksburg, Virginia, he spent much of his time learning navigation, and no doubt took on board (literally) some sartorial tips and creations from his older brother William, who had emigrated there to thrive as a tailor.

Despite being less than tall, John Paul had a handsome, well-defined face with strong nose and high cheekbones, and he always took pains to be well turned out. No one could have better personified the saying that 'clothes make the man'. It was perhaps another of his romantic views of the seafaring life: that the captain should have some theatrical flair and look good in his uniform. And he expected similar standards from his officers. 'When we went to dine with him, we were obliged to appear in the great cabin with our best clothes on,' one wrote, 'otherwise we were sure not to meet a favourable reception from him.'

When it came to career and love life, this philosophy certainly did him no harm. He was blessed with robust health too, and when fever gripped a ship on which he was serving, killing its captain and mate, he was forced to take command, bringing it safely home and so launching his career as a captain at the remarkably tender age of twenty-one.

But despite the fact that he had just washed his hands of the 'abominable' slave trade after serving as mate on two 'blackbirders', this developing gentleman was not always a gentle soul, and his quick temper – while giving him the necessary edge as a leader – would often get him into unfortunate scrapes. Two of these involved deaths of seamen, the first – of which he was acquitted – alleging excessive punishment with the cat-o'-nine-tails; and although suspicion would stick to him like a limpet, the second was more serious and prompted him to change not only his name but also his country of residence – and, probably in consequence, his sense of national loyalty.

It was in 1773, after having been in command of the West Indian ship *Betsy*, that he was accused in the West Indies of having put fatally to the sword the ringleader of a mutinous dispute over wages ('a brute of thrice my size'). Sensing local feeling against him and reckoning the chances of a fair trial remote, John Paul made his escape to Virginia, using first the name of John Jones and later John Paul Jones, probably to set him apart from the many Welshmen of that name in the area. As the American Revolution began to boil up and his letters revealed growing loyalty to the colonists, he surfaced again a couple of years later when – as a Scot and no great believer in Great Britain anyway – he offered his services to the Continental Navy being formed by Congress, and was appointed a first lieutenant.

The ragbag American Navy was beginning with but six extant ships and thirteen frigates on the drawing board, and soon – as he distinguished himself as lieutenant of the *Alfred* and later captain of the *Providence* – his professional advice on the drafting of naval regulations became highly valued. With a direct clash between Britain and her colony looming, his skills as a seaman were at a premium. But he preferred practice to theory.

A life of action was what this wiry swashbuckler wanted, and while enjoying the burgeoning executive role his growing reputation was giving him, he was soon out at sea again, getting 'in harm's way'.

Jones believed that any navy formed by the colonists could be most effective by avoiding head-to-head confrontation and seeking and striking the Royal Navy's weak spots. In June 1777 he was appointed captain of the *Ranger* and sailed for France – where he forced the

French to salute the American flag in a harbour for the first time – before embarking on an audacious direct attack on a British town.

Because he knew it so well – and also knew response to such an action would be exaggerated by the British – he decided to raid the port of Whitehaven, from which he had sailed as a ship's boy in 1760. After taking and capturing some small ships in the Irish Sea, the assault turned out to be a messy, half-hearted affair – while he knocked out the port and set fire to some colliers, a number of his men chose to go to the pub, having won no loot to speak of. But the psychological impact was immense. Had the Royal Navy been asleep? This was the first raid on an English port since the Dutch Admiral de Ruyter raided the Thames and Medway in 1667. Britain was plunged into turmoil and, as some locals had recognised the commander, his name hit the headlines and his demonisation grew some more.

Operationally, John Paul Jones was proving to be a painful thorn in old Albion's side. Pledged to destroy British commerce in the North Sea, as captain of the *Bonhomme Richard* – a French East Indiaman he had converted into a warship – he led a squadron of seven ships into Edinburgh's Leith harbour in August 1779, intending to capture the port and extract a £50,000 ransom. The ill-prepared defenders were quaking with fear, but the American attackers were foiled by a gale that blew them back out to sea.

Not much more than a week later, however, the *Bonhomme Richard* was making big trouble again – this time by engaging in the bloody confrontation for which John Paul Jones is most remembered: the Battle of Flamborough Head.

Circling south of Newcastle with the intention of cutting off London's winter coal supply, Jones' squadron – trailing a string of captured vessels – sighted off Scarborough a forty-one-strong convoy protected by the fifty-gun *Serapis* and the sloop-o'-war *Countess of Scarborough*. Seriously outgunned, John Paul Jones nevertheless calculated that he would have to deal with the warships to get his hands on the merchantmen, and so fearlessly lashed his ship alongside the *Serapis* and simply began to slug it out for four hours, watched by crowds of fascinated onlookers lining Flamborough Head.

It was early in this battle that he was invited to surrender but famously replied: 'I have not yet begun to fight.'

Fearing damage to itself, the *Serapis* could not use its superior fire power at such close quarters to best effect, and slowly but surely the muskets and hand grenades of the *Bonhomme Richard* cut down the *Serapis*' crew.

A witness aboard Jones' ship, Midshipman Nathaniel Fanning, recalled the captain's impressive demeanour in the heat of the boarding action:

> Captain Jones ordered the sailing master, a true-blooded yankee whose name was Stacy, to run our jib boom into *Serapis*. Jones at the same time cried out 'Well done, my brave lads, we have got her now; throw on board the grappling irons and stand by for boarding.' Jones assisted Mr Stacy fasten the end of the enemy's jib stay to our mizzen mast, where he checked him for swearing by saying 'Mister Stacy, it is no time for swearing, you may by the next moment be in eternity'.

Though great losses were sustained on both sides – over half of the two ships' crew members died or suffered dreadful burns – in the end, it was the British captain, Pearson, who surrendered to the American ship – ironically, just before it sank like 'a battered raft', according to one chronicler.

And Fanning recalled:

> The captain of the *Serapis* gave repeated orders for one of his crew to ascend the quarter deck and haul down the English flag, but no one would stir to do it. They told the Captain they were afraid of our riflemen . . . the Captain therefore ascended the quarter-deck and hauled down the very flag which he had nailed to the flag staff little before the commencement of the battle; and which flag he had at that time, in the presence of his principal officers, swore he would never strike to that infamous pirate John Paul Jones. Thus ended this ever memorable battle, after a continuance of a few minutes more than four hours.

It was indeed a memorable battle. It has been described as 'a naval combat the like of which has never been fought before or since', and Jones' dramatic victory was the high point of a career that made a spectacular contribution to the American War of Independence, while also making him a feared and hated pirate figure in his own land.

From then on, however, his career slipped slowly downhill. Though in 1781 Congress passed a vote of thanks to him for 'sustaining the honour of the American fleet' and he spent the last years of the war advising on the establishment of the navy and the training of naval officers, oddly he seemed to be more honoured by other countries as he grew older. He became the toast of Paris, being awarded the Order of Military Merit by Louis XVI, and, in a political secondment recommended by Thomas Jefferson, he was made a rear admiral in the Russian navy by Empress Catherine II. After prevailing in a battle against the Turks, he wrote: 'I am delighted with the courage of the Russians, which is more glorious because it is without show off'.

After returning to Paris in 1790, he was struck by pneumonia and died at the age of forty-five, before he could learn that he had been appointed US Consul in Algiers. He was buried in an unmarked grave in a cemetery for foreign Protestants and forgotten about.

Better late than never, however, the USA eventually came to recognise fully the little Scot's significant influence in founding its navy, and in the early summer of 1905 four American cruisers, *Brooklyn*, *Tacoma*, *Chattanooga* and *Galveston*, crossed the Atlantic to France on a special mission – to bring back for President Theodore Roosevelt the American hero's body that had been buried outside the walls of Paris more than a century before. In 1913, he was laid to rest in a grand Napoleon-style sarcophagus in the crypt of Annapolis Naval Academy.

And forty years later another great warship crossed the Atlantic on his behalf – the one that carried the plaque to grace the wall of his birth-cottage. The name of the vessel? The USS *Paul Jones*. The ghost of the little ship-watcher of Arbigland would have been inordinately proud of that.

Alexander Wilson (1766–1813)

Ornithologist extraordinary

During his twenty-eight early years in Scotland Alexander Wilson revealed only slight shadows of the driving curiosity and drawing talent that would one day make him – through his classic nine-volume *American Ornithology*, published from 1808 – the recognised father of American ornithology.

Born in 1766 and growing up in the weaving town of Paisley, not far from Glasgow, he displayed no particular interest in his Scottish feathered friends, although he was conspicuously creative, trying desperately to emulate the rampant poetic success of Robert Burns, seven years his senior. Indeed, what little success as a poet 'Sandy' Wilson did have was registered by a comic ballad titled 'Watty and Meg', which was published anonymously but ironically thought by many to have been written by Burns – who, equally ironically, is said to have praised it.

The son of an illiterate but intelligent distiller who encouraged his education, Wilson was apprenticed as a weaver but did not pursue that trade with any enthusiasm, opting instead to produce a veritable mountain of verse, which – according to one critic – needed assiduous gold-panning to find 'the few pieces that are really good . . . like modest little poppies that have caught the bright colours of the sunlight and the freshness of the dewdrop, but are overlooked in the great field of dry stubble'.

Like Burns, the slight but handsome Wilson was also given to writing satire, but perhaps could not command the required forgiving elegance, for in 1792 some of his poetic comments on the unfair treatment of weavers by their bosses landed him in trouble with local manufacturers, and led to a fine, the enforced burning of his offending poems, and a short term in jail.

Generally speaking, life in Scotland did not promise much for Sandy Wilson as he approached thirty, and he knew it. Never financially successful at publishing his own verse, which he vainly peddled around, and unwilling to commit his artist's heart and soul to the weaver's sedentary existence, he was virtually penniless and almost hopeless when he heard the siren call of the young United States and reckoned he had nothing to lose by answering it. In July 1794, he raked up enough money to buy deck space for himself and a nephew on an American ship bound for Delaware from Belfast.

It was an inspired move. While his nephew set off in search of a farm to develop, the heady freedom of America immediately became the wind beneath the wings of Sandy's creativity. His well-practised writing skill was more appreciated in Pennsylvania where, after dabbling in copperplate printing, he became a weaving teacher with a regular wage and decided to take drawing lessons. At first, he struggled, but when he attempted the delineation of birds, he soon acquired a technique that not only impressed his teachers but overtook them. His success in this prompted a sudden enthusiasm for ornithological work, and with encouragement from the naturalist William Bartram, whom he had befriended, he first mentioned 'making a collection of all our finest birds' in letters to friends in 1803.

So fired was he by this inspiration that he decided to release himself again – to draw, research and write on birds, with the highly ambitious aim of depicting every species in North America. The decision was truly the start of something big: an obsession that was to make him, but also literally to kill him, at the cruelly young age of forty-seven.

After setting up a dollar-a-day page-engraving deal with a publisher, in 1804 Wilson armed himself with sketching materials, notebooks, guns, a horse, a parrot and a messianic sense of mission, then plunged into the swamps and undergrowth to travel over 10,000 miles through the eastern USA observing and recording the previously unrecorded.

He published his first volume of *American Ornithology* in 1808. Enthused by the acclaim it received, he said he was now 'fixing correspondents in every corner of these northern regions, like so many pickets and outposts, so that scarcely a wren or a tit shall be able to pass along, from York to Canada, but I shall get intelligence of it'.

But Sandy Wilson drew most of the birds himself, and for the rest of his life wore himself down by rough-travelling widely, bird-spotting, note-taking, drawing and collecting subscribers for his book's successive volumes. He found travels over treacherous terrain often arduous, once recalling a 'howling wilderness' where he was challenged not just with dysentery but with

> the most horrid swamps I had ever seen . . . covered with a prodigious growth of canes and high woods, which together, shut out almost the whole light of day for miles. The banks of the deep and sluggish creeks, that occupy the centre, are precipitous, where I often had to plunge my horse seven feet down, into a bed of deep clay up to his belly; from which nothing but great strength and exertion could have rescued him; the opposite shore was equally bad, and beggars all description.

And he wrote to his brother David:

> Since February 1810, I have slept for several weeks in the wilderness alone, in an Indian country, with my gun and my pistols in my bosom; and have found myself so reduced by sickness as to be scarcely able to stand, when not within 300 miles of a white settlement, and under the burning latitude of 25 degrees. I have, by resolution, surmounted all these and other obstacles, in my way to my object, and now begin to see the blue sky of independence open around me.

His second *Ornithology* volume was published by late 1810, and Wilson – now celebrated as an important American ornithologist, naturalist and illustrator – then dedicated himself to publication of the third and fourth volumes in 1811, the fifth and sixth in 1812 (when he became a member of the Society of Artists of the United States) and the seventh in 1813.

It was in that year that things became particularly difficult, as volumes eight and nine made exceptional demands on his body and soul. Planning now to focus on water birds, Wilson and his friend George Ord made a four-week journey into New Jersey's Great Egg Harbour, a trip that plainly weakened him, and when he returned to find himself (after a workers' dispute) doing much illustration-colouring alone, by mid-August he was exhausted and stricken again by dysentery. He died ten days later, during the writing of his ninth volume, and some accounts say he drowned in pursuit of a rare bird.

Wilson's short life was nevertheless a fulfilled one, despite its unpromising beginnings. Not only were several species of bird named after him – Wilson's Plover, Wilson's Phalarope, Wilson's Warbler and Wilson's Storm-petrel – but he garnered many an honour to be proud of. He was elected a member of the American Philosophical Society and other learned bodies. His reputation spread not only in America, but throughout Europe, and few crowned heads did not subscribe to the *American Ornithology*. He is now regarded as the greatest American ornithologist prior to Audubon.

As a driven perfectionist, he would have been eternally grateful to know that volumes eight and nine were still published, thanks to the hard finishing work of George Ord, who saw them both completed by May 1814. And although the whole work fell short of Wilson's original plan to document every American feathered thing, it illustrated 268 species of birds, 39 of which had not previously been described, and was highly respected throughout the whole of thinking society – though it never made him rich. Wilson nonetheless achieved his own American dream by realising his pledge to himself – 'to raise some beacon to show that such a man had lived'.

Yet he felt he owed it all to the encouragement of his father. In February 1811, he wrote:

> The publication of my *Ornithology*, though it has swallowed up all the little I had saved, has procured me the honour of many friends, eminent in this country, and the esteem of the public at large; for which I have to thank the goodness of a kind father, whose attention to my education in early life, as well as the books then put into my hands, first gave my mind a bias towards relishing the paths of literature, and the charms and magnificence of nature. These, it is true, particularly the latter, have made me a wanderer in life; but they have also enabled me to support an honest and respectable situation in the world, and have been the sources of almost all my enjoyments.

Wilson's mother died when he was ten but his father survived him by three years.

'Uncle' Sam Wilson (1766–1854)

The United States personified

For many Americans the ideals encompassed in his name give him an almost god-like status. Soldiers die for him, athletes run for him, and families metaphorically embrace him as a kind of permanent, if abstract, super-president. But even in Europe and many other parts of the world the image of Uncle Sam – essentially as portrayed in Flagg's famous portrait on the 'I Want YOU' army recruiting poster from the First World War – is the ultimate symbol of US conscience and culture. So much so that in some faraway places with extreme views it is not uncommon to see his effigy being carried shoulder high or consumed in flames, depending on the point of view being expressed about America.

But what were the origins of this revered badge of American-ness? We know that they were human, and even Scottish, just as we know too that the man himself was never a caricature like the one we now know – a tall, white-goatee-bearded figure with intense eyes, top hat, striped pants and red, white and blue star-spangled suit – thanks to the inventiveness of artists and cartoonists.

No, it is safe to believe that Samuel Wilson looked nothing like that universal image of Uncle Sam. But how did a clean-shaven man with Scottish roots come to be the provenance of the universal symbol of America in general and the US federal government in particular?

It is here that we have to come clean. An essential criterion for selection of the names featured in this book has been that they were born in Scotland. We know that Sam Wilson was born of parents from the south-western Scottish port of Greenock – Edward Wilson and Lucy Francis – and that he was the sixth of their thirteen children. Not being certain of when they got on the boat for the New World, however, we are tempted to believe that Sam might have been conceived in Scotland. In this exceptional case, I respectfully ask the benefit of the doubt!

In any case, Samuel was born on 13 September 1766, in Menotomy (now Arlington), Massachusetts, and at fourteen moved with his family to Mason, New Hampshire, where he was eventually to meet his young sweetheart Betsy – an army captain's daughter – for whom he was moved to fire up an entrepreneurial career that would provide her with the comfortable life her beauty deserved.

To that end, he would try anything once. At the age of twenty-two, he and his brother Ebenezer walked through deep snow 150 miles to Vanderheyden (now Troy), New York, where – by rolling up their sleeves in a typically Scottish fashion – they contrived to find themselves in demand as apple-tree sellers, brickmakers and then remarkably successful meat-packers. Betsy must have been a very patient girl, for it was not until Samuel was thirty-one – and she twenty-four – that he felt his financial circumstances could finally do her proud. He returned to Mason, married her, and romantically swept her back to Troy in a jingling sleigh.

While she was busy having four children, Samuel's meat-packing business went from strength to strength – daily slaughtering upwards of 100 cattle and packaging them into barrels also made by the firm, which even had its own ships and jetties lining the Hudson River. But the Big Contract was still to come . . . and with it, the Big Name.

In 1812, although the revolution was over, the British were meddling in American trade and had to be stopped. When the resulting mini-war began, the US Army asked Wilson not only to supply meat for its troops in the northern states but also to act as a beef and pork inspector. As part of the deal, the barrels that made up large shipments of meat to the Army were stamped 'US', and it was during this time – when few people understood the relatively new combination of initials – that some kind of verbal exchange took place, which would lead to Samuel Wilson's name giving birth to the Uncle Sam concept.

As a well-liked boss, Samuel had already become known as 'Uncle Sam' to many of his employees. So when – according to one version of the story – a visitor asked a Troy dock worker the meaning of the stamped letters on the meat barrels, the latter's joking reply, referring affectionately to his employer, was: 'Uncle Sam!'

This tale has the joke travelling well – first to the army's receiving station at East Greenbush, where the soldiers, not knowing Sam Wilson, thought the name was new slang for the US government and quickly adopted it. And the idea spread at the same pace as the barrels crossed the country; so that all the government's property was soon popularly considered to be Uncle Sam's.

Another account says that the legend was born earlier, with some help from Samuel Wilson himself. On seeing people looking curiously at the large letters 'US' on the front of a relative's store in Troy, he is said to have answered their unspoken question by telling them that they meant 'Uncle Sam' – and that he was that very person! And the adoption of his self-nickname spread like wildfire from there . . .

Whichever tale was true (and perhaps the truth was a bit of both), it was always an amusing idea that seemed to appeal to people's sense of humour and belonging.

There is no doubt that it added even more to Samuel Wilson's popularity as he himself – as well as the government – became commonly referred to as 'Uncle Sam'. And soon, the nickname began to appear in print as meaning the country. Legendary status did not begin to take root, however, until after Wilson's death on 31 July 1854. And although the legend was eventually made official when the House of Representatives unanimously approved a resolution establishing his grave as a national shrine; and although President John F. Kennedy signed a resolution in 1961 officially establishing him as the original Uncle Sam, his gravestone at Troy's Oakwood Cemetery reads simply:

SAMUEL WILSON
Died July 31, 1854
Aged 88 Years

Archibald Binny (1763–1838) and James Ronaldson (1768–1842)

Makers of the dollar sign

In the Lawnmarket, a couple of hundred yards down the Royal Mile from Edinburgh's celebrated castle, is a venerable four-storey townhouse called Gladstone's Land – a high, handsome building and the oldest surviving example of the city's Old Town dwellings, dating from the mid-1600s. It is open to the public as a tourist attraction, so Riddle's Court is not hard to find. It is just across the cobbled Lawnmarket street, directly opposite the famous old house.

But why would we want to find Riddle's Court? There should be a clue in the eye-high metal plaque that meets the visitor at the mouth of the tunnel-like close that leads to a dark little square where tall stone walls, wood-canopied stairs, dungeon-type gate and a low weather-worn doorway take you instantly into another, earlier century.

But, no. Like many of the similar 'explanatory' signs placed at such points in the city's most-visited area, the plaque teases more than it tells:

Riddle's Close and Court

In Close lived David Hume before settling in James' Court;
in Court beyond, Baillie MacMorran banquetted in his
house James VI and his Queen and Danish nobles.

There is no mention there, or in the courtyard, of Archibald Binny, who lived there for three years before he emigrated to America in 1795.

But why should there be? Who was Binny and what did he do that he should be honoured with his name on such a wall-plaque? If the minimal records of his achievements are to be believed, it was he – and his partner James Ronaldson, about whom even less is known – who first forged into type the globally recognised American dollar sign.

Although they both came from Edinburgh and one-time baker Ronaldson was already a businessman in Philadelphia when punch-cutter Binny arrived there, it seems they had not known each other in Scotland; but when they met on the far side of the Atlantic they clearly delighted in their shared heritage and hit it off pretty quickly. For within a year of Binny's arrival they were combining their technical and business talents to set up the first American type foundry. Called simply Binny & Ronaldson and based in Philadelphia, it was an immediate success, ending America's dependence on Europe in typographical matters. Today the company is still remembered for having produced, in 1809 and 1812, the first American type specimen books – *A Specimen of Metal Ornaments* and *A Specimen of Printing Types*, respectively.

But it is also credited with nothing less than the first typeset design of the dollar sign, most conspicuously in Updike's *Printing Types: Their History, Forms & Use,* which states that 'in 1797 the Philadelphia foundry of Archibald Binny and James Ronaldson offered for sale the first dollar marks ever made in type'.

It would not have been before time. Up to then, there had been some confusion about the currency of the young country that emerged from the war of independence that began in 1775 and ended in 1783. Before 1775, the nation's monetary system was in disarray, and Congress decided to clarify it by backing all its legal tender with the most commonly circulated coins – Spanish coins minted in the New World. Americans then began trading with the 'Spanish milled dollar' as they shed the British pound . . . though not quite.

For while the word dollar itself comes from the German thaler (the name of a large European silver coin) and the US symbol for it seems to owe more to the Spanish peso, the latter's positioning before, rather than after, the designated amount is a lingering echo of the pound.

Contrary to some popular opinion, the now-accepted dollar sign is not a deliberate placing of a narrow letter 'u' over a letter 's' as an abbreviation for Uncle Sam or the US. Its origins are rather more complex.

The credit for the written – rather than typographical – interpretation of the sign is given by many to one Oliver Pollock, an Irish immigrant who became a wealthy plantation owner in New Orleans, then part of the Spanish Empire, and penned his business in pesos, which he abbreviated by intertwining 'p' and 's' so that the result looked like an 's' with two lines through it.

This habit was adopted by one of his most important contacts, Congressman Robert Morris, financier of the American Revolution, and seemed to catch on more generally, evolving into the dollar symbol that is used today.

But coming soon after the moment that Binny and Ronaldson's design was conceived, the appearance of the dollar sign in print – in a 1797 book by Chauncey Lee – signified the acceptance of the stylised dollar sign as a purely American symbol. And there is little doubt that the two enterprising Scots were responsible for that.

Somebody had to do it, as they say. But what prompted them? Were they inspired by being based in the same city as the US 'Mother Mint', which had come into being in 1792? Were they encouraged by executive nudging? A message from the top? Suffice to say that they were obviously respected enough to enjoy the appreciation of the then-former President Thomas Jefferson, whose help they were not afraid to enlist in sourcing antimony (used in metal type-casting) when an international trade dispute had interrupted supplies. As a champion of homegrown American industry and admirer of the typefaces of Binny & Ronaldson, which had become the most popular in the USA, Jefferson was only too happy to help find them a new source in France.

Such patronage can be rewarding in more ways than one, and both Scots retired as rich men. Ronaldson, who died in 1842, was described as a philanthropist in later life, and Binny, who died in 1838, had retired to a 5,000-acre plantation on St Mary's River – which he called Portobello, after his sandy birthplace on the Forth estuary on which the Scottish capital stands.

He clearly remembered Edinburgh fondly, though the favour was not returned: Edinburgh largely failed to remember either him or his business partner.

James Gordon Bennett (1795–1872)

The man who made the news

To those for whom Gordon Bennett is something more than a name –
an expression of astonishment perhaps, or a phrase synonymous with
outrageous behaviour – the sight of the peaceful Scottish village
of Newmill must be unexpectedly serene. Could this simple little
place of a few dozen square-built granite cottages, a population of
under 400, and an environment straight out of a dream entitled
'rural peace and quiet', possibly have been the cradle of the man
who took New York's blood-and-guts publishing world by storm and
spawned a namesake rogue of a son who would make even more of
an international impact?

Relieved only by a pub, a post office and a clock tower, the otherwise
monochrome Banffshire village hugs the full quarter-mile length of
its main street and is embraced in turn by rolling sheep-dotted hills,
arable fields and a shaded valley where piled-up regiments of barrels
await the lucrative liquid gold of Chivas Regal and other famous
whiskies produced in Keith, two miles away.

The handsome, centrally situated clock tower built in 1923 and
dedicated to the memory of local men who fell in the First World
War is Newmill's most notable landmark. Driving past it going south,
you catch a glimpse of Hill Street, pushing up to the hills on your
right. Much of it has retained its venerable stone-built character but
halfway along on the left are several newish houses, one of which has
replaced the modest cottage where the first James Gordon Bennett
was born.

Is there any evidence of this today? Nothing. No plaque, no little
garden, no acknowledgement of any kind. So perhaps the most
remarkable thing about Newmill is that its most famous son has been
emphatically, and probably deliberately, forgotten.

No one in the village today seems to want to talk about him (or his
son). It is not known what his parents did for a living, though it was
'surely something agricultural', one villager volunteers reluctantly,

adding that they must have been relatively well-off to spare a bright son to attend Aberdeen University. Though he had actually intended to train for the Roman Catholic priesthood, in the event his higher education was to serve as a launch pad for a spectacular career abroad. But there is no memory of his ever having come home in a similar way to Scots near-neighbour and fellow US publishing tycoon Bertie Forbes (see page 95). Was it this strange forgetfulness that caused the villagers to conclude that the feeling was mutual – and virtually airbrush him out of their folklore?

If they are remembered at all, the two Bennetts' names tend to fuse in people's memories and, if they don't, the younger one has left such an indelible splash of colour that he is still a preferred subject of controversy. To this day, the son's reputation commands scant respect in the village as – so goes the tale – he was invited by the war memorial committee to contribute to the building of the clock tower and never troubled himself to respond. What more could you expect from such a spoiled brat? This is perhaps an unfair charge, however, as the tower was built five years after James Gordon Bennett Jnr died, in 1918, after a lifetime of high living.

But it was Bennett the elder who put all the hard groundwork into the creation and development of the *New York Herald* as a significant root of the ubiquitous *International Herald Tribune,* the only truly global newspaper, which, in a hugely challenging Paris-based publishing exercise, today has thirty print locations around the world for daily distribution to a quarter of a million buyers in 185 countries.

Bennett senior had acquired a taste for writing at university after his abortive education for the priesthood, and resolved to become a journalist. In pursuit of this, he crossed the Atlantic at twenty-four in the spring of 1819 and while doing a variety of jobs over the next ten years, from teaching (in Nova Scotia) through something menial in book publishing (in Boston) to being a correspondent and associate editor for the *New York Enquirer* and the *Morning Courier,* he began to acquire another taste: for being in command of his own career through ownership. It started with his launch of *The Globe* in 1832, which, despite being short-lived, was a valuable learning process. By 1834 he was beginning to get the idea that perhaps it was not wise to depend on political patronage when launching a paper while doubling as a proprietor and chief editor of the Philadelphia-published *Pennsylvanian.* But it was in 1835 that he really began to spread his wings . . .

That was when he changed the face of American journalism from a cellar in New York. At the age of forty, with just $500 as working capital, he launched *The New York Herald,* the paper that was to make him famous. The first four-page issue of the one-cent publication claimed to eschew 'all politics' and pledged itself to survive on – rather than subsidies from politically interested parties – advertising and circulation, the last of which would demand bizarre stories that might be characterised as 'juicy' today; so that passing people would be curious enough to dig into their pockets. That meant crime and society scandals, lurid illustrations, scurrilous charges, tales of monsters – anything weird and wonderful, indeed, that would capture the public imagination.

But Bennett the journalist was no one-trick pony. The newsman in him demanded that he focus on newsgathering even while developing new editorial techniques that invited wider readership. Therefore, alongside all the offbeat offerings came new ideas and new investment in new ways of covering serious news. During the Civil War the paper had a staff of no fewer than sixty-three war correspondents. On 13 June 1835, it published the first Wall Street financial article to appear in any US newspaper; in December of that year it printed a vivid account of the great fire of New York; and the following year it covered the Helen Jewett love-nest murder, the first such case to be featured in American journalism.

No, he was not cut out for the priesthood.

Bennett the audacious liberal publisher was financially shrewd, interested only in what would sell, and untroubled by moral considerations. This broad-minded approach proved a huge commercial success. So much so that his most desired source of funding thankfully emerged as planned – impressive annual profits for reinvestment. And as these began to blossom and confidence in the product grew, the crassness of his early 'pop' philosophy began to moderate with fresh thinking gradually adding new dimensions. Thus *The Herald* pioneered many innovations in modern journalism, including illustrated news stories, establishment of a team of European correspondents, joint founding of the Associated Press news agency, introduction of a society department, first major use of the telegraph for reporting of a long political speech; the list went on. It all led to a highly successful and profitable news empire, which, by the time it was handed over to Bennett's son in 1867 – five years before the old man's death – was registering annual profits of $400,000.

A rival newspaper greeted news of his death in 1872 with the comment that his character was 'defective' and his career 'a conspicuous example of prosperous infamy'. It went on: 'Visit him, and you would see before you a quiet-mannered, courteous, and good-natured old gentleman on excellent terms with himself and with the world, but . . . that region of the mind where convictions, the sense of truth and honour, public spirit, and patriotism, have their sphere, was in this man mere vacancy.' It considered 'unfortunate' the fact that his newspaper survived him. But it hadn't seen nothin' yet . . .

The younger James Gordon Bennett, born in 1841 with such a silver spoon in his mouth, went out of his way to become an outrageous playboy who conducted the paper from his yacht in Europe; who is said to have spent $30,000,000 of the *Herald*'s earnings; who gave rise to the 'Gordon Bennett!' near-expletive by flying an aeroplane through an open barn; who drove so recklessly he tipped out Winston Churchill's mother; and who appalled the family of his fiancée by urinating in their open fireplace after getting drunk.

The eccentric and capricious Bennett was fond of sports, especially of yachting, and established the James Gordon Bennett cup as a trophy in international yacht races and similar cups for balloon and aeroplane races. Whether or not these are considered good things, he did manage a couple before he expired. In 1869 he sent reporter Henry Stanley on the trail of Dr David Livingstone to register a memorable world exclusive that is still talked about today. He opened *Herald* soup kitchens for the poor during the economic panic of 1873–74, and in 1877 he began the forerunner of what is now the *International Herald Tribune* in Paris. But some said this was merely an 'ego' exercise and things were not looking so good at home. In the face of intense competition in the newspaper wars of the 1890s, *The Herald* began to decline and Bennett's absence in Paris did not help. Three years after he died in France in 1918, the ailing *Herald* merged in 1922 with the New York *Tribune,* thereby creating the famous international title (recently taken over by *The New York Times*).

In New York City's Herald Square today, an elaborate monument honours the two Bennetts. But at the time of writing there were still no plans to build one in Newmill, Banffshire.

Allan Pinkerton (1819–84)

The first private eye

On the face of it, the extremely humble beginnings of Allan J. Pinkerton would not seem to have qualified him for the amazingly colourful career and grand roles he enjoyed in later life – as the world's first-ever private eye, dogged pursuer of legendary outlaws, and confidant of America's most admired president, Abraham Lincoln.

The founder of the famous detective agency that still bears his name, Pinkerton was truly a man of many parts; and when all these parts were drawn together, the sum became either a remarkably complex person or a somewhat confused one. On the professional front he was a cooper, a prolific author and a highly accomplished investigator – the expression 'private eye' comes from his agency's logo that depicts a large, open eye above the line 'We Never Sleep'. At various points in his life, he was seen as a drunkard, a defender of truth and liberty, a left-wing troublemaker, an employers' puppet, a patriot, a traitor, a fugitive from the law, an idealist and an adventurer.

Perhaps the last word describes him best, for he managed to turn every stage of his adult life into an adventure of one kind or another. Everywhere he went, in every pond he paddled, he made waves.

And neither was he born into calm waters, when his parents lived in close proximity to the River Clyde that cleaves through Glasgow like a giant sword blade. As Scotland's biggest city, Glasgow is today a vibrant, confident place, which has tackled its historic social problems with a resolve born of a modern awareness that the reputations of its worst neighbourhoods – such as the squalid Gorbals, now comprehensively renewed – were tarring the rest of the city with their dirty brush.

It has been a lot to live down, for when Pinkerton was born in the Gorbals on 25 August 1819, it was a forbidding place indeed: a web of dark, crime-ridden narrow streets where drunkenness, chronic diseases, unplanned children and prostitution were rife, and where murderers (often in the shape of body-snatchers) lurked round every corner. But in a paradoxical way, that formidable scenario probably gave the young Pinkerton a head start in the matter of crime solving, for he must have grown up with an intimate knowledge of human weaknesses. Not only that: his father William was a police sergeant who, until his untimely death, presumably added considerably to Allan's early store of experience.

Having once recalled the excitement at home when his mother brought home 'a precious egg' as a rare treat for her hungry family, no doubt the young Allan also understood the part poverty played in the grim mix of human conditions that surrounded him. And that might also have explained his early motivation to champion the downtrodden.

'Downtrodden' was something he knew about. Born in a crumbling second-floor flat above a corner shop in Muirhead Street, near the spot where the imposing Central Mosque now stands, Allan and his brother Robert were the second brood of William – by his second wife Isabella, a handsome mill girl who also took on his five children from his previous marriage.

Reality and responsibility slammed down on Allan long before adulthood, when his father was killed during a political rally that broke out in a city square – and so the imperative for his heartbroken mother became cash earning by the family for the family. Not that Allan's first job brought in much more than grief. He became a pattern-maker's apprentice and worked night and day in a sweatshop for a pittance. But as his later life would prove, he was nothing if not an enterprising lad, and soon – by the age of twelve – he had acquired another, better, job as a cooper and quickly became pretty good at barrel making.

The carrot-haired rabble-rouser was also good at soap-box oratory, and little did he know it then, but the first skill was to serve him well for the start of a new life in the New World, while the second would provide the spark to launch him away.

That came when his boundary-pushing instinct got him into trouble as a militant member of the Chartist Movement that fought for 'freedom' of the working classes. When he began to advocate physical conflict in speeches to men from the cooperage floor, the authorities took a dim view. Learning that his name was on the King's Warrant list, he was forced to become a fugitive, lie low and weigh up his limited options.

Inevitably, the New World beckoned, promising him a new life and a clean slate; but he wasn't going anywhere without the love of his life, Joan Carfrae, from Edinburgh. She agreed readily to his proposal, but did she know what she was taking on? She certainly got a taste of it the day they were married in March 1842. No sooner had they taken their vows than word came that soldiers were on their way to arrest Allan. And so began – as they were smuggled aboard a Canada-bound ship the next morning – the couple's long life of drama and adventure.

The first alarming scene was the ship's approach to land – in a violent storm – four weeks later. The vessel was blown 200 miles off course and foundered on a reef off Nova Scotia. The newlyweds lost everything they owned in the submerged hold, but luckily not their lives, as they abandoned ship into a lifeboat. It was a close-run thing, though, as on reaching land the rescued passengers were greeted by trinket-hunting Indians, and Mrs Pinkerton was relieved of her wedding ring – after her husband was persuaded by the captain not to risk his life by fighting for it. So the newlyweds began their life together with only the clothes they stood up in, and a few silver coins in Allan's waistcoat pocket.

It would not be so for long, however. Even as the rescue ship that retrieved the stranded passengers passed down the St Lawrence Seaway separating Canada from the USA, new ideas were forming. They heard tempting tales of a fast-growing town called Chicago on the western edge of Lake Michigan. In an age when everything was transported by barrel, Pinkerton reckoned such a booming metropolis would surely welcome his skills as a cooper, and so decided against their original plan of settling in Quebec in favour of the USA instead. In the event, diverted perhaps by the familiar name from home, they settled – after a short stay in Chicago when he made some seed money as a cooper at Lill's Brewery – in a little 'Scottish' town called Dundee north-west of the city. There, they started a much-needed firm, Pinkerton's One and Original Cooperage of Dundee, which soon employed ten men.

Demand for his barrels, which were better and cheaper than those of competitors, was increasing at an impressive pace as customers appreciated their quality and the boss's occasional willingness to exchange his product for theirs. And with the birth of the Pinkertons' first child – William, who was to be followed by twins Robert and Joan – it looked as if they were becoming firmly established domestically and professionally.

Politically, he was feeling pretty satisfied too, as a local leader in the slavery-abolition movement who managed to be both outspoken and covert in his sympathetic activities, working with an underground railroad (by using his cooperage as a 'station') that brought slaves in from the south and up to Canada.

He liked the idea of covert action, but little did he suspect that it was about to seduce him completely. Allan Pinkerton would soon find out that – even more than his barrel-making skills – Chicago would appreciate his as-yet-undiscovered qualities as a detective.

The catalytic moment that revealed his latent talent for detection came in 1846 when, to supplement his dwindling stock of barrel hoops, he made a boat trip to a small, woody island in the Fox River, several miles from Dundee. 'It was commonly supposed that the island was uninhabited,' wrote Sigmund A. Lavine in his book about the Scot, 'but Pinkerton, a most observant individual, noticed that the grass and bushes were bent back, making a path from the shore. Curious, he followed it, and in a thick stand of trees found a campsite that appeared to be used quite frequently.'

Curiosity became suspicion. After he informed the local sheriff and was deputised to help him in this case, both men kept a nightly watch on the spot for five nights, and on the fifth were rewarded with a stunning coup – their arrest, at gunpoint, of a twelve-strong gang carrying spades and sacks full of the kind of counterfeit money that had been spreading uncontrollably around northern Illinois.

Impressed by his success on this case, and by his bravery during the arrests, local businessmen hired Pinkerton to watch for more counterfeiters, and again he registered several successes, not least by putting himself at risk as part of a 'sting' operation.

Seeing that he could also make money at a business he relished, Pinkerton was hooked, and barrel-making quickly lost its appeal. As his reputation grew in Chicago, he literally rolled out the barrels and moved his family back there to accommodate more case-solving offers by the Treasury Department and the Cook County Sheriff's Department, which asked him to find the kidnappers of two Michigan girls. He tracked down and shot one of the abductors, adding a 'biggie' to his record-breaking number of arrests in 1848 and earning himself a full-time position as deputy sheriff. He also became Chicago's first police detective in 1850. He kept on taking freelance commissions, however, and business was so good that by the end of that year he felt the time was right to set up the North-Western Police Agency.

Later to be renamed The Pinkerton National Detective Agency, it was soon also to be known as a highly professional, uncompromising private outfit whose agents would not flinch at the most difficult assignments and would never give up until they got their man (or woman). Its tenacity became legendary among the criminals of Chicago, who, having overwhelmed the regular police, would now quake in their shoes when they heard they were on the Pinkerton target list.

His agency hired no one but the best. His operatives were clean, honest and upstanding with 'vigour of body', but tough-minded and nobody's fool. They were thoroughly vetted and cleverly chosen. Indeed, the agency employed Kate Warne, America's first female private eye, who could get into places male detectives couldn't. The agency's methods were also clever . . . and original. Disguise and infiltration proved effective in case-solving, and although primitive by modern standards, an innovative 'rogues' gallery' – filed photographs to identify criminals – was a breakthrough in the battle against crime; for meticulous research was the essential foundation of Pinkerton's success, along with patient surveillance and often-dangerous undercover work.

In the general atmosphere of lawlessness that prevailed at the time, when the west's expansion was fuelled by gold- and cash-laden trains pushing across often-hostile open country, the post office and the railroads became the agency's biggest clients, and Pinkerton's main work consisted of hunting down railroad thieves such as the notoriously vicious Reno Gang.

But there were also 'security' jobs to be done and one can't help but wonder how the old Chartist firebrand reconciled his past with his agency's investigative work in the area of union activities: he was seen to be responsible for keeping unions out of various trades in the Chicago area for years, and 300 of his agents played an infamous part in the restraint of protesting workers at the Homestead steel plant of fellow-Scot Andrew Carnegie (see page 50). That has proved a lot for both men to live down in the pages of history. And yet, and yet . . .

Perhaps the workaholic Pinkerton was just too busy building his booming business to appreciate the irony of such matters; for another 'security' job, the biggest imaginable, was won at least in part by his abolitionist sympathies (which extended to him and Joan making their fine house in Adams Street busier with fugitives than was his Dundee cooperage). This drew him to the attention of President-elect

Abraham Lincoln who hired his agency for bodyguard services. Just as well; for what then transpired was, without much doubt, Allan Pinkerton's finest hour . . .

As the Civil War boiled up, executives of the Philadelphia, Wilmington and Baltimore Railroad called him in to investigate rumours that secessionists were planning to blow up train ferries on the Susquehanna River. The detective disguised himself, adopted a southern accent and insinuated his way into the company of the suspects – one of whom, in a drunken slip of the tongue, revealed that something much bigger was being planned.

The plot, thus uncovered by Pinkerton, was to assassinate the president as he passed through Baltimore on Saturday, 23 February 1861, on his way from Philadelphia to Washington to take his oath of office and deliver his inaugural speech in front of the unfinished Capitol on 4 March.

Pinkerton requested an urgent meeting between himself and the president in Philadelphia, and there the detective spoke words that made the politician blanch with shock: 'We have come to know, Mr Lincoln, and beyond the shadow of a doubt, that there exists a plot to assassinate you. The attempt will be made on your way through Baltimore, the day after tomorrow.'

The Scot suggested that the president should accompany him directly to Washington that very night; but Lincoln felt too obliged to go through with speeches in his next day's schedule. After that, however, he pledged to follow Pinkerton's advice – and duly did so, by changing his travelling times and passing through Baltimore at night.

Although the move probably saved his life, Lincoln was ridiculed by his enemies for his 'undignified' nocturnal trip to the capital, and was sufficiently stung to express some regret about it later. But with the Civil War breaking out that same year, he was impressed and grateful enough to enlist Pinkerton's help as a spy against the Confederacy. He responded well, with valuable information on rebel supplies, defences and conspirators. And it was an honour indeed when he was appointed Chief of the Secret Service. Though by consensus this turned out to be an example of the Peter Principle in practice – he was clearly rather out of his depth at that level – it was quite a way to rise for the poor boy from the Gorbals.

Indeed, intertwined as his name was with the presidency and all the infamous banditry of the Wild West, the story of Allan Pinkerton's life reads like a Hollywood movie script – or perhaps several. Apart from running to earth four members of the Reno Gang (who were then lynched by vigilantes), he became famed for his dogged pursuit of many legends of the Wild West including the Hole in the Wall Gang, the James Brothers (Jesse and Frank), who returned the compliment by making Pinkerton their number-one murder target, and Butch Cassidy and the Sundance Kid, who always seemed to be one step ahead of Pinkerton agents armed with photos and drawings of the pair.

The elusiveness of Butch and Sundance – vanishing, ultimately, on a South American trail that went cold – was part of their Hollywood-acknowledged sophistication, for Robert Le Roy Parker (Butch) and Harry Longabaugh (Sundance) considered a raid to have been successful not only if it delivered the goods (with the help of inordinate amounts of dynamite) but also came off 'clean', involving no loss of life and no molestation of passengers.

The Molly Maguires were something quite different. An Irish group who claimed to support and defend the interests of their immigrant fellows in the grim coalfields around Pennsylvania, they became a violent secret society who robbed, murdered and spread terror on a massive scale. Into this poisonous stew a brave Pinkerton agent was dropped – a 29-year-old Irishman James McParland, who at great risk to himself, infiltrated the organisation in the time-proven Pinkerton way, befriended its leadership, was instrumental in their arrest, then gave courtroom evidence that sent no fewer than twenty of them to the gallows as a just punishment for all their appalling atrocities. His heroism was hailed by one newspaper as 'one of the greatest works for public good that has been achieved in this country and this generation', but few were surprised by the success, for it came down to the much-acclaimed quality of Pinkerton's people. Even bandits acknowledged it, and in *The Molly Maguires*, one of the books he wrote (about the pursuit of the gang) in yet another career, Pinkerton outlined his expectations of a good private eye: 'The detective should be hardy, tough and capable of laboring, in season and out of season, to accomplish, unknown to those about him, a single absorbing object . . . able to distinguish the real from the ideal moral obligation, and pierce the veil separating a supposed from an actual state of affairs.'

When hiring agents, Allan Pinkerton warned them that he was a hard man who ran his company with an iron hand: 'I am self-willed and obstinate. I must have my own way of doing things.' But it could not be quite as simple as that. The one character strand that ran through all his complexities was surely a deep sense of romance, if not sentimentality.

When he approached retirement and began to pump out a long string of books dramatising his agency's exploits, it was more than an exercise in self-justification. He had a real taste for the adventure-packed frontiers of young America, and he knew he was a significant part of them. He would never forget his beloved Scotland, however, and even as he approached the end of his life, he was building a grand house called The Larches for which larch trees were shipped from Scotland to line the driveways.

When Pinkerton passed away in 1884 his agency, with its branches in Chicago, New York and Philadelphia, was taken over by his sons Robert and William, who continued its movement from detective work to security and protection.

His gravestone in Chicago's Graceland Cemetery reads:

In memory of
ALLAN PINKERTON
Born in Glasgow, Scotland
April 15th 1819
Died in Chicago, Illinois
July 1st 1884
Aged 65 years

A FRIEND TO HONESTY AND A FOE TO CRIME

Devoting himself for a generation to the prevention and detection
of crime . . . he was the founder in America of a noble profession
in the hour of the nation's peril. He conducted Abraham Lincoln
safely through the ranks of treason to the scene of his first
inauguration as president. He sympathised with, protected and
defended the slaves and labored earnestly for their freedom. Hating
wrong and loving good, he was strong, brave, tender and true.

Today the still-thriving company has almost 40,000 employees. In 2000 it celebrated 150 years of service by donating to the Smithsonian Institute in Washington a vast archive of materials, which included once-secret documents on Jesse James, the Hole-in-the-Wall Gang, and Butch Cassidy and the Sundance Kid.

Wherever they and their tenacious old pursuer are now, it would not be surprising to learn that they were still giving each other a hard time.

Andrew Carnegie (1835–1919)

Man of steel, heart of gold

To stand in the tiny, low-ceilinged room where Andrew Carnegie was born in 1835 is to shiver with the realisation that life can deliver some truly unexpected results. It is almost impossible to take in that, from the small wooden box-bed in the darkest corner of the modest weaver's cottage in Moodie Street, Dunfermline – a place that knew real economic alarm, if not sheer poverty – a lad of such simple birth could have grown up to become the richest man in the world. That would be more than adequate achievement for anyone; but Andrew Carnegie, the keen-eyed elder son of handloom weaver William Carnegie and his wife Margaret, also became the world's greatest philanthropist.

That is an easier thing to say than to actually appreciate, of course, and my own means of appreciation came in dramatically physical form when, in the days of telex, I was setting up a feature on the great man for the *Scotsman Magazine* and asked the Carnegie Dunfermline Trust to send a list of the libraries he had funded. There were 2,811 of them in all, and the strip of paper that accommodated the typed list of names stretched from one end of the rather long magazine office to the other. I gasped with amazement – for I realised that, in the days when a million really was a million, the $60,000,000 he had injected into these widely distributed symbols of humankind's instinct for self-improvement represented only a fraction of his spending budget. At his death in 1919 every US state had at least one Carnegie-built library, Britain and Ireland had 660, Canada 156, New Zealand 23, South Africa 13 . . . and so it went until Singapore, with 1. Scotland alone has 147.

But his philanthropy extended well beyond libraries to the establishment of a remarkable range of trusts and foundations in the USA, Britain and Europe. He also set up schools, colleges, teachers' pensions and church organs, and financed – 'to hasten the abolition of international war, the foulest blot upon our civilisation' – the building of the International Court of Justice in The Hague, known as the Peace Palace. Not to mention the museums, institutions and concert halls that still bear his name, from the 600-seat Carnegie Hall in his home town of Dunfermline to the world-famous 2,804-seat Carnegie Hall in New York. Many minor Scottish artists have been known to boast that 'I once filled the Carnegie Hall' – not exactly lying while impressing listeners, but also failing to say that the experience was in Fife, Scotland, and not Manhattan!

Scotland in general benefited, too, from the millionaire's enduring fondness for his native land, as he endowed its universities with large bequests aimed at paying for the fees of the students. Having become a millionaire by thirty-three and worked to about double that age consolidating his fortune, Andrew Carnegie's final years were much concerned with the *purpose* of the accumulation of wealth and self-analysis around that question. By 1900 he was able to outline his thought-out principles when he published *The Gospel of Wealth,* the key points of which he put like this:

> The man of wealth thus becoming the mere trustee and agent for his poorer brethren, bringing to their service his superior wisdom, experience and ability to administer, doing for them better than they would or could do for themselves . . . The man who dies thus rich, dies disgraced.

So – determined not to die disgraced in his own eyes – from the turn of the twentieth century he went about the business of shedding his wealth with the same energy that he had put into acquiring it. The only difference was that he couldn't finish the task – of distributing the allocated $350,000,000 – and had to pass it on to a range of trusts, despite help being offered from all corners. Indeed, even as he arrived on a return visit to Britain in 1901, he found his fellow-countrymen anxious to help him get rid of the money. Newspapers carrying ads from the makers of Mother Siegel's Syrup with a competition inviting readers' ideas on 'how Mr Carnegie should get rid of his wealth'. There were no fewer than 45,000 suggestions.

Devoted as he was to his home town in Scotland and to 'improving the masses', he showered the people of Dunfermline with gifts that still survive and thrive today – not just the Carnegie Hall, but also the town library and two swimming baths. There are other monumental reminders of Carnegie all over the town, such as Lauder College, a well-regarded place of learning founded in 1899 as a tribute to 'the man to whom I owe the most'– his beloved uncle, George Lauder, who played a large part in augmenting the basic education he received at Mr Martin's School in Rolland Street, and taught him to use his memory. There is also a fine statue of Carnegie in the town's green and leafy Pittencrieff Park, not far from his birth cottage, and the story of how he saw that special place given to the people has a delicious element of poetic justice. More of which later . . .

But the town's most poignant reminders of the great man are the well-preserved birth cottage, all that remains of the street of weavers' houses that he knew as a boy, and the now-attached Andrew Carnegie Birthplace Museum which was given in 1928 by his then-widow Louise to display the hundreds of tributes and gifts he received from all over the world.

In stark contrast to this younger companion building and its grand role, the simple cottage recreates the poor atmosphere of the weaving family's home in the 1840s. It is dark and wooden and in one of the two rooms on the ground floor there is a real Jacquard loom, representing the pair that used to clack away making damask linen on that floor. And upstairs, where the family lived, there is only one room, with a table and old grated fireplace – ahead of you as you enter – and two framed box-beds lined along the right-hand wall. It is believed Andrew was born in the bed in the far corner, where there is now a small window (but wasn't in his day). It is a tiny room, perhaps three by four metres, and it is hard to imagine that from here the world was changed so significantly.

Go back downstairs, on the short twist of wooden staircase where the small Carnegie feet once scampered, and in the reception area you may well find visitors from every part of the world, or at least their signatures, in the address book. Walk further into the museum itself and there, under glass, you will find an older visitor book from the cottage, lying open at the entry of one particularly important visitor . . . Andrew Carnegie himself. It reads: 'Andrew Carnegie, Skibo, Sept 27th, 1909. First visit to my birthplace. The humble home of honest poverty, the best heritage of all when one has a heroine for a mother.'

The Skibo address referred to his Scottish home – the magnificent Skibo Castle on the Dornoch Firth in Sutherland, which he and his wife bought, restored and enlarged in 1898. It became their much-loved Scottish retreat, though nowadays, having passed out of the

Carnegie family, is also famous for having hosted the star-studded wedding of pop star Madonna in 2001.

But how did the little weaver's son grow from that simple cottage to such a fabulous home and the worldwide fame and incredible fortune that accompanied it?

Misfortune came first. For his father, William, the cottage served as home and factory, but as Andrew approached his teens, industrial times were changing. The development of power looms meant the days of cottage hand-weavers were numbered, and throughout the 1840s the pressures on Dunfermline's damask linen manufactures became increasingly intense – until the day William had to announce despairingly to his elder son: 'Andra, I can get nae mair work.'

Supporting the family was then down to Andrew's 'heroic' mother Margaret, who earned that subsequent tribute in the cottage visitor-book by sewing shoes at night and running a shop by day. But it was a hard life offering little future, and the grim winter of 1847–48 was the last straw, bringing the Carnegies to the brink. Hope, then, seemed to lie across the ocean.

Margaret's young sisters, Annie and Kitty, had married and moved to Pennsylvania in 1840, and although they had not found the life easy, their letters home had suggested that the USA offered many more opportunities than dreary, depressed Dunfermline. After much agonising, it was decided that the family should try to earn a share in the prosperity of the New World.

In his book *My Own Story,* Andrew recalled that, after the decision was taken, 'my father's sweet voice sang often to mother, brother and me' . . .

> To the West, to the West, to the land of the free
> Where the mighty Missouri rolls down to the sea
> Where a man is a man even though he must toil
> And the poorest may gather the fruits of the soil

Depressed it may have been, but Dunfermline, ancient capital of Scotland sixteen miles north of the current capital Edinburgh, remained a beautiful place to Andrew and one that proved hard to leave. A sale of the Carnegies' house-factory goods and equipment designed to fund their journey proved 'most disappointing', he recalled, and £20 had to be borrowed from a friend before they could set off from the town in the omnibus that ran along the coal railroad to Charlestown. 'I remember that I stood with tearful eyes looking out of the window until Dunfermline vanished from view, the last structure to fade being the grand and sacred old Abbey. And during my first fourteen days of absence my thought was almost daily as it was that morning: "When shall I see you again?" '

They crossed to the west coast and set sail from Glasgow in a converted whaler. And despite his sadness, the young Andrew – he was twelve – kept a firm hand on his five-year-old brother Tom as they breathed in the vivid new experiences of the fifty-day voyage and the 'bewildering' sights and sounds that met them in New York.

Arriving in Pittsburgh in mid-August 1848, after a long, crawling trip from New York via the Erie Canal and Lake Erie, they took a house at Rebecca Street, Allegheny, and William Carnegie returned to work as a handloom weaver making table-cloths 'which he had not only to weave but afterwards, acting as his own merchant, to market himself, selling from door to door' – before again being defeated. Disillusioned by returns that were 'meagre in the extreme', he was forced to take a job in Blackstock's cotton textile mill.

Andrew got a job there too, starting his working life as a bobbin boy at $1.20 a week, before moving to Hay's bobbin factory where, for $2 a week, he tended the steam engine, fired the boiler and, being a conspicuously luckier fellow than his father, managed to be in the right place at the right time when the boss found himself without a clerk. Andrew was asked what his penmanship was like and given a test. 'The result pleased him,' Andrew recalled, and the boss was even more pleased to find the quick-minded young Scot was also good at figures.

He was growing in confidence, and success with another job opportunity – as a telegraph messenger boy for the O'Reilly Telegraph Company – sent him 'wild with delight'. He wrote: 'From the dark cellar running a steam engine, begrimed with coal dirt, I was lifted into paradise, yes, heaven, as it seemed to me, with newspapers, pens, pencils and sunshine about me . . . I felt that my foot was upon the ladder and that I was about to climb.'

He was right there. While also bettering himself in his spare time – by means of the scheme set up by a well-meaning Colonel James Anderson to allow working boys to read books from his private library on Saturday afternoons – Andrew worked hard to become a top telegraph boy, and to this end he became one of the few people in America capable of deciphering Morse telegraph messages by ear. This remarkable skill did not go unnoticed, and in February 1853, he was appointed personal telegraph operator and confidential secretary to Thomas A. Scott, Superintendent of the Pittsburgh Division of the Pennsylvania Railroad Co., at the impressive salary of $35 a month.

Andrew Carnegie was stocky and cherubic of face, with a glint of steel in his eye. While not conventionally handsome, he kept getting himself noticed through his intelligence and initiative. When a rail network failure disrupted systems in his chief's absence he displayed formidable powers of organisation and averted disaster by taking sole charge; a move that did his career no harm at all.

With the sad death of Andrew's father at fifty, Thomas Scott became something of a new father figure to him. It was he who was to lay the foundations of Andrew's formidable fortune when, in 1856, he advised the lad to purchase shares in the Adams Express Company. On later receiving his first dividend cheque (barely eight years after arriving in the USA), Andrew exclaimed: 'Eureka! Here's the goose that lays the golden eggs.'

He wrote: 'I shall remember that cheque as long as I live . . . It gave me the first penny of revenue from capital – something that I had not worked for with the sweat of my brow.'

Under Scott's wing Andrew advanced rapidly in the company and by 1859 he himself had become the Pittsburgh Division superintendent and was able to employ his brother Tom as his personal assistant.

Soon, another fortuitous moment arose that combined Andrew's interest in the railroad with his new-found interest in investment. He was approached by T.T. Woodruff, inventor of the sleeping car, and was so impressed by his inspiration that he put it to Mr Scott – who agreed to test a built vehicle and urged his young protégé to take up the one-eighth interest in the carriage company offered to him by the inventor. Andrew borrowed the $1,250 investment from the bank, and it was quickly repaid from dividends, as the sleeping cars were a big success, bringing him an annual income of $5,000.

This was heady stuff. There was no stopping him now. He threw himself wholeheartedly into moneymaking through many such shrewd investments of small sums, and quickly became wealthy while still working for the Pennsylvania Railroad Company. The Chartist child of Dunfermline was all set to grow into the Capitalist father of America, but not before being seconded to help Washington organise the Union military telegraph service during the Civil War.

When that conflict ended, he quit the rail company to devote all his energy to his expanding business interests, which, by 1865, were giving him an annual income of $50,000. And his cherubic side was not always in evidence as he applied a fast-growing, often aggressive business expertise to oil, railway construction and financing, bridge building, telegraphy, iron and steel.

With the post-war economy expanding and railroads pushing out all over the continent from coast to coast, he invested in companies making related products such as rails, bridges and wheel axles, and quickly saw the potential in a new British system for the mass production of steel. He invested in the process, and so the American iron age became the age of steel, starting with his Edgar Thomson Steel Rail Mill, named in honour of its first customer, president of the Pennsylvania Railroad Company.

The superior qualities of steel, as opposed to iron, proved all-conquering and there was no looking back. But personal tragedy was to spoil Andrew's dreamlike progress, when his mother and brother died within a few days of each other in 1886. At fifty-one, he recovered from that double blow, and from his own bout of typhoid, to marry Louise Whitfield, daughter of a New York merchant, the following year. They soon had a daughter – named Margaret after his mother –and Louise quickly became 'more Scotch' than Andrew, encouraging him to buy a home for them in the Highlands of Scotland, which was when Skibo was welcomed into the family.

It was while they were in Scotland in 1892, when all seemed to be going well personally and professionally – with his web of steel interests now largely consolidated into the Carnegie Steel Company – that the infamous Homestead Affair put an indelible blot on his proud record of good, if paternalistic, relations with the working class. As a child of that class, he had, despite his acquired wealth, felt an affinity with it; but it became apparent that the feeling was not mutual when the workers at Homestead – one of four steel plants that came under the umbrella of the new company – went on strike after management–union talks on wage rates broke down. All hell broke lose, with the executive left in command locking out the workers and getting himself shot twice ('but not dangerously'), 300 Pinkerton agents employed to protect the plant being attacked and beaten by the strikers, and 8,000 state militia being called in to restore order.

Though he did not return to intervene personally, Andrew Carnegie was left with a bitter taste in his mouth from this ugly episode, in which several men were killed, and he later wrote with clear regret:

'Nothing I have ever had to meet in all my life, before or since, wounded me so deeply. No pangs remain of any wound received in my business career save that of Homestead. It was so unnecessary.'

His conscience was much troubled by this affair, and while steel continued to pour from his company's furnaces to the extent of their making almost half of America's requirement by the end of the 1890s, he became increasingly aware of the responsibilities of his ever-growing wealth and developed a compulsion to return it to the people in some way as he came closer to retirement.

The critical moment came in 1901 when the Carnegie Steel Company was sold for $480,000,000 and amalgamated with other steel companies to become the United States Steel Corporation; Andrew Carnegie's personal share was $360,000,000 and, when the deal was done, the organising financier, Junius P. Morgan, shook his hand and said: 'I want to congratulate you on being the richest man in the world.' It was at this point that Carnegie realised the struggle to accumulate riches had come to an end . . . and that the heavier, more responsible task of sharing them had begun.

In all, what he gave away before he died in 1919 – and was buried in New York's Sleepy Hollow cemetery in a grave marked by a Celtic cross of stone quarried near his beloved Skibo – represented almost $3 billion in today's values. And still it goes on: his given-away fortune continues to fund education and research, and the combined incomes of the trusts and foundations he established enables them to spend over $150 every minute 'for the improvement of mankind'.

Despite his despair at the First World War and his own failing health towards the end, he died a well-fulfilled man. For his was the perfect rags-to-riches story. Within it, however, was another story that gave him the greatest gleeful satisfaction of all. Dunfermline never lost its pull on him. 'What Benares is to the Hindoo, Mecca to the Mohammedan, Jerusalem to the Christian, Dunfermline is to me,' he once wrote. And when he was a boy he looked upon the town's Pittencrieff Glen – or Park, as it is now known – as a leafy haven where the chance to play would have been pure paradise. But he was barred from the place because he was related to families who campaigned against the owning laird in favour of the town's rights to the park for the people. Andrew Carnegie regarded it as one of his greatest triumphs that, in 1902, he was able to buy the park for £45,000 and thereby become himself Laird of Pittencrieff – 'the happy possessor of the grandest title on earth in my estimation' – and see it handed over to trustees to bring 'sweetness and light into the monotonous lives of the toiling masses of Dunfermline'.

The intense satisfaction he felt at the 'true romance' of this development – that he should 'arise and become the agent for conveying the Glen to the people of Dunfermline forever' – was more than adequately expressed by the man himself: 'This is the crowning mercy of my career! I set it apart from all other public gifts. Truly the whirligig of time brings in some strange revenges.'

It truly does . . .

Andrew Smith Hallidie (1836–1900)

Inventor of the cable car

It was his witnessing of a heart-stopping incident that inspired Andrew Smith Hallidie to invent the horseless cable car, which, to this day, encapsulates the magic of 'the city by the sea' to virtually the same degree as its acclaimed Golden Gate.

Who can imagine San Francisco, America's fairest city, without its colourful, clanking cable cars crawling up, and clattering down, its picturesque but mountainous streets? And who can forget that so-evocative line – 'Where little cable cars climb halfway to the stars' – in Tony Bennett's classic song 'I Left My Heart in San Francisco'?

But in 1869 the image of the city's horse-drawn streetcars was a deal less magical as the horses struggled bravely to pull the carriages up those challenging gradients. One cold morning in that year, the 33-year-old Hallidie saw several such horses in distress as they lost their footing on the frosty street.

He recalled the moment in a later report to the Mechanics' Institute:

> I was largely induced to think over the matter [of inventing a horseless cable car] from seeing the difficulty and pain the horses experienced in hauling the car up Jackson Street, from Kearny to Stockton Street, on which street four or five horses were needed for the purpose – the driving being accompanied by the free use of the whip and voice, and occasionally by the horses falling and being dragged down the hill on their sides, by the car loaded with passengers sliding on its track.

This enterprising Scot, who had emigrated from London to the United States at the age of sixteen with his Dumfriesshire parents – engineer-inventor Andrew Smith from Fleming and Julia Johnstone from Lockerbie – had good reason to believe that he could come up with something that would put an end to such alarming incidents, while simultaneously improving the city's sluggish transport system.

Taking after his clever father, he was also an engineer-inventor, and one of his many mining experiences in America had inspired him to develop mechanical solutions with wire rope, a field in which Andrew Snr held several patents. Drawing on these, the young Andrew – who had adopted his surname in honour of his uncle, physician to Queen Victoria – solved a problem at a quartz mill, for instance, where cars brought rock down a hillside with the help of gravity and went back up for refilling via rope which lasted just two months. He proposed making a wire rope system to replace it, and the owners were delighted to find that this rope lasted for two years.

Having taken the principle of that system back into the city, where he established a manufacturing plant and saw demand for his product grow in mining and bridge-building contexts, it was as a successful businessman that he was inspired to set about the cable car enterprise 'with the view of obviating these [horse-drawn] difficulties and for the purpose of reducing the expense of operating street railways'.

His plan was to have streetcars propelled by underground cables – or a 'rope railway', as he called it – when he announced his intention in the *Sacramento Record* in 1870.

How would it work? Put simply, the cable car would be hauled by a long, steam-powered cable moving slowly in a loop beneath the street surface and between the rails. But the devil was in the detail, and it was not only a complicated concept to get up and running, it was also a nail-biting one.

Expensive too. Hallidie himself contributed all the spare capital he had – $20,000 – and while design and construction were undertaken, more backing had to be rustled up (mainly from three reluctant friends), a site identified and surveys made for the first test (Clay Street), and a franchise received from the city – which demanded that a test run take place no later than 1 August 1873. 'I devoted all my available time to the careful consideration of the subject,' he later recalled.

But the deadline turned out to be almost impossible to meet. Every day the engineering challenges seemed to be more difficult, and everyone on the construction team was aware that all rights would expire if no cable car were running by the first day of August. On the eve of that day, several exhausted men worked through the night to make the unlikely dream a reality, and they must have felt a deep glow of satisfaction when at last they heard the engine starting to take up the slack of the cable as the grip car was put in place.

Some accounts say that the first actual travelling test did not take place until the following day (though the city did not void the franchise) but a plaque dedicated to Hallidie on the lower terrace of Portsmouth Square, near Clay and Kearney, reads:

> Site of eastern terminus first streetcars in world propelled by cable.
> Commenced operation August 1, 1873. Ceased February 15, 1942.
> Invented and installed by Andrew S. Hallidie . . .

Some accounts also say that, when the car was ready to run down to the foot of the mist-shrouded Clay Street, Hallidie's gripman took one look down the steep hill and, being paralysed by trepidation, refused to operate the car – so that the inventor himself had to spring to the levers. Those watching from the top saw the car disappear into the mist, and learned later to their considerable relief not just that the bottom had been reached safely but that 'the damned thing works'.

It was 5 a.m. As the town was asleep, there were no cheers; but there were strong, silent handshakes and broad smiles among the working team. The horseless cable car had been born.

A month later, a regular service was started with the Clay Street line, and although the system was slow to gain acceptance and ridiculed at first as 'Hallidie's folly', it steadily grew to be a huge popular and financial success, with 600 cars eventually carrying passengers around 120 miles of city streets, and making the doggedly innovative Scot a very rich man in the process.

That in itself might have been reward enough, but Andrew Smith Hallidie could look on in considerable satisfaction as similar cable railroads were adopted by Los Angeles, New York, Chicago, Kansas City, St Louis and Philadelphia.

And you have to wonder if the pioneer – who died in 1900 – is not still wearing a quiet smile. Might he still be watching, from somewhere high above the highest San Francisco hill brow, as – despite setbacks and threats like earthquakes and repeated modernisation proposals – the cars go on and on, protected by the sheer popular affection and enthusiasm that they evoke?

There have been changes, of course. In the early 1980s the present cable car system underwent a two-year-long programme of renovation. But the people of San Francisco have fought many battles to stop their historic streetcars being totally replaced by modern transport, and the result is that forty examples of two types remain, on which natives and delighted tourists can still shake, rattle, bump and grind over ten miles of undulating track.

A favourite position for them is riding precariously on the outer running boards. Which is how they know you have to hang on tight to this unique machine – physically as well as metaphorically.

John Muir (1838–1914)

Father of the national parks

> When I was a boy in Scotland I was fond of everything that was wild, and all my life I've been growing fonder and fonder of wild places and wild creatures. Fortunately, around my native town of Dunbar, by the stormy North Sea, there was no lack of wildness . . . with red-blooded playmates, wild as myself, I loved to wander in the fields to hear the birds sing, and along the seashore to gaze and wonder at the shells and seaweeds, eels and crabs in the pools among the rocks when the tide was low; and best of all to watch the waves in awful storms thundering on the black headlands and craggy ruins of the old Dunbar Castle when the sea and the sky, the waves and the clouds, were mingled together as one.

Since the lean, bearded, grown-up John Muir wrote these poetic lines to boyhood memory, nothing much has changed around the rugged coastal shoulder of south-east Scotland on which Dunbar sits. The ancient town may have acquired some new homes and modern shops, but the salty, rocky places of its seashore, where the young John played in the 1840s, still embrace and placate the wild waves that stir where the North Sea joins the Firth of Forth. And though the well-used harbour walls have been repaired here and there, in contrast to the ravaged and lowering remains of the nearby sandstone castle, you can still sense the old fishing community's timeless nearness to nature.

It was here that John Muir's formidable sense of wonder and curiosity about the natural world was awakened; a sense that made him a champion of the environment long before that word acquired its current significance; a sense that powered him around the globe long before aircraft criss-crossed it with ease. Indeed, carried by the wind, the energetic, multi-talented Scot became a truly well-travelled man who could have put any modern peripatetic business executive to shame. Not only did he emigrate from Scotland to Wisconsin while still a boy; as his passion for the study and protection of the God-given environment grew, a fascination with glaciers attracted him to Alaska, a need to know about forests drew him to Australia and Africa, and a driving curiosity about exotic lands in general drove him as far as China and Japan.

He passionately believed that the glory of nature had to be protected from man's avarice and indifference when profitable industry was all that seemed to matter. 'The battle for conservation will go on endlessly,' he wrote. 'It is part of the universal battle between right and wrong.'

Yet wherever he went on his great odyssey through life and geography, John Muir's modest home town in Scotland never lost its place in his heart. Once, after walking 1,000 miles across America, he smelled the sea on the wind. When he was a day's trek from the Gulf of Mexico, he wrote, 'a wind blew upon me from the sea . . . and the Firth of Forth, the Bass Rock, Dunbar Castle and the wind and rocks and hills came upon the wings of that wind, and stood in as clear and sudden light as a landscape flashed upon the view by a blaze of lightning on a dark night'.

And in the fond, proud way that John Muir remembered Dunbar no matter where he wandered, the town now remembers him. For another significant thing that has remained unchanged in that venerable place thirty miles south of Edinburgh is the facade of the three-storey house at 126 High Street where he was born on 21 April 1838. It is still a square unremarkable building, sitting shoulder-to-shoulder with its neighbours in a street that has held its historical integrity; but it has been painted white and its deteriorated interior fabric stripped to create a light, airy and superbly designed visitor attraction in the form of 'a stunning interpretative centre highlighting the work and achievements of this remarkable man'. Established in response to a new awareness that relatively few Scots had ever heard of Muir (while in America his writings are as celebrated as those of his fellow Scots Robert Burns and Robert Louis Stevenson), the centre graphically presents records of his global travels in written and drawn sketches of places, flora and fauna, while generally paying tribute to the farmer, inventor, botanist, explorer, naturalist, writer and conservationist who became 'the father of the US National Park system'.

Of course, there is no shortage of tributes to the man in America, where over 340 historic sites – parks, woods, mountains – comprising over 80 million acres of wild land cared for by the National Park

Service, have been named in his honour. They include the John Muir Memorial Park near the Muir homestead at Fountain Lake, Wisconsin; the John Muir Wilderness and John Muir Trail in the High Sierra; the Muir Woods and Muir Beach near San Francisco; the Muir Glacier and Mount Muir in Alaska . . . the list goes on and on. His later home at Martinez, California, is designated The John Muir National Historic Site 'in recognition of his campaigns and books that celebrated America's natural heritage'.

Until lately, it had been quite different in what was a relatively indifferent Scotland. But now the very existence of various Muir-inspired bodies and initiatives which helped East Lothian Council bring about the Dunbar visitor centre – the John Muir Birthplace Trust, John Muir Trust and local John Muir Association – represents a fair indication of today's changing perception of a now-more-famous son at home. And just across the High Street, there is a relatively new, handsome statue of John as a boy setting a bird to flight. To the west of Dunbar, there is also the John Muir Country Park, eight miles and 1,760 acres of 'unspoiled nature'. Not to mention the John Muir Way, a pathway developed to provide a continuous coast-hugging path linking East Lothian with Edinburgh.

The significance of the Dunbar spark that ignited the famous man's future fire should not be understated, but the catalytic moment came when John, the eleven-year-old first son and third child of the seven-strong brood of grain merchant Daniel Muir and Anne Gilrye, was hard at homework with his nine-year-old brother David one evening in 1849. Their well-to-do father had been unable, it seemed, to find a compatible context for his intense religious beliefs in Scotland, and so had decided to join the Disciples of Christ sect in America. It was for very different reasons that John was pleased about that decision, and later he recalled the thrill of the moment when it was put to him: 'One night, when David and I were at Grandfather's fireside solemnly learning our lessons as usual, my father came in with news, the most wonderful, the most glorious, that wild boys ever heard. "Bairns," he said, "you needna learn your lessons the nicht, for we're gan to America the morn." '

Why was the news so 'wonderful and glorious' when John loved Dunbar so much? If a note sent from a Scottish visit back to daughters in America some forty-four years later was anything to go by, he was no doubt feeling relief that he would no longer have to suffer the singularly brutal regime of a Scottish schooling:

July 12, 1893

Hello Midge, My Sweet Helen

Are you all right? I'm in Scotland now, where I used to live when I was a little boy, and I saw the places where I used to play and the house I used to live in. I remember it pretty well, and the school where the teacher used to whip me so much, though I tried to be good all the time and learn my lessons.

It was not anticipation of America being a 'schoolless and bookless wilderness' that so enthused John as he, David and their thirteen-year-old sister Sarah set sail from Glasgow with their father, leaving the eldest sister Margaret and the three youngest of the family to follow on with their mother after a farm and comfortable house had been found. Reading was an important impulse, but he hated being obliged to perform on pain of stern punishment and hoped that his new life across the Atlantic would at least see the end of the double pressure of his despotic father and harshly strict school. And indeed, that proved the case, according to his first impressions (recorded later in life) of the Fountain Lake Farm virgin land bought by his father:

This sudden splash into pure wildness – baptism in Nature's warm heart – how utterly happy it made us! Nature streaming into us, wooingly teaching her wonderful glowing lessons, so unlike the dismal grammar ashes and cinders so long thrashed in to us. Here, without knowing it, we were still at school; every wild lesson a love lesson, not whipped but charmed in to us. Oh, that glorious Wisconsin wilderness!

True to plan, then, the homestead was found in 'glorious' Wisconsin, and the rest of the family sent for; but the establishment of home and farm required much hard labour, and father Daniel then seemed to transfer his harshness in education to his sons' physical work. He pushed and beat the boys hard, even denying them a doctor when they buckled with illness, but John at least had other diversions – whenever he could, he would wander into the country to study the flora and fauna, and his enthusiasm for book-learning remained strong.

He was also something of a carpenter and, to satisfy his father's diktat that he should not stay up reading late at night, he came up with an ingenious invention that tipped him out of bed at an early hour to maximise the day and allow for more reading. Installed in his bedroom in the family's log cabin, it consisted of a home-made wooden clock that, on reaching the requested time, set off an alarm mechanism that, in turn, activated a cross-bar to push his bed (and his body) into a vertical position.

As he showed such an imaginative talent, it looked to family and friends as if he might become an inventor; but he himself was not sure about a career direction. He had done enough reading to enter the University of Wisconsin, where he dipped into chemistry, geology and botany, emerging in 1863 still without a clear idea of how to employ his hard-won education and ingenious, if butterfly-like, mind.

The answer came to him by accident – literally. In 1867, while working at a carriage parts shop in Indianapolis at the age of twenty-nine, he suffered a blinding eye injury that was to change his life. When he regained his sight a month later to his great relief, he resolved – by seeing the world through even more appreciative eyes than before – to devote himself to observing, recording and protecting the beauty of nature. And so began his years of travelling that would take him from North and South America (including Panama and Cuba) to Australia, Africa, Europe, China and Japan; but it was closer to his adopted American home that he registered his greatest triumphs.

He walked 1,000 miles, for instance, from Indianapolis to the Gulf of Mexico, observing 'fields, mountains and forests' and keeping a day-by-day journal, in which he discussed animals and plants, geological formations and forests, people and his deeper thoughts. Other arduous walks and climbs, initiated to understand the geography of unmapped areas, took him to Nevada and Utah, to the north-west and to Alaska, and as he went he filled some seventy books with sketches and observations. In California, where he eventually settled, he was captivated by the Yosemite Valley and the Sierra Nevada, where he found living glaciers in the High Sierra, and proposed their role in sculpting entire mountain ranges over vast stretches of time. His theory that the Yosemite Valley had been so formed was laughed at by the famous Californian geologist Josiah Whitney ('What does a sheep herder know about geology?') but proved correct by Louis Agassiz, the father of glaciology.

Muir never lost his sense of awe at nature's power and complexity, just as he never lost his Scottish accent or the influence of his strict Scottish upbringing. When he wrote, the language of the King James Version of the Bible – which he was compelled by his father to learn virtually by heart – rang through his sentences with a certain drama. He was not conventionally religious, but his father gave him a sense of his own destiny and conviction in his message, and his word power was compelling. His fine turn of phrase could inspire and influence. Example: 'When we contemplate the whole globe as one great dewdrop, striped and dotted with continents and islands, flying through space with other stars all singing and shining together as one, the whole universe appears as an infinite storm of beauty.'

Realising that his pen was probably mightier than anything else he could think of to bring about responsible care for the natural world, Muir started his writing career seriously in 1874, and by the end of it he had had 10 major books and over 300 articles published.

Encouraged by the respected editor Robert Underwood Johnson, he fought through magazine columns to bring to public attention the devastation of mountain meadows and forests by cattle and sheep – 'the hoofed locusts', as he colourfully called them – and by 1890 an act of Congress created Yosemite National Park, which would further protect the area from the devastating effects of farming. He was also involved in the creation of Sequoia, Mount Rainier and Grand Canyon national parks and he laid the foundations for the creation of the National Park Service.

There were essential pauses in his driven life, of course. He married the daughter of a Polish immigrant, Dr John Strentzel, and bought from his father-in-law part of a fruit farm. From 1881 to 1891 he worked hard to establish this as a viable business, eventually earning enough to look after himself, his wife and two daughters – before resuming his travels and the non-stop campaigning that was to win over public opinion and a succession of presidents and defeat the lobbying of the timber barons.

Muir fought hard to save the giant redwoods of California, and in 1892 he and some supporters founded the Sierra Club environmental organisation 'to do something' – in his words – 'for wildness and make the mountains glad'; and as its first president, he led the battle to enlarge the protected boundaries of Yosemite Valley. Today the club continues to do important conservation work, and is now the premier conservation body in the US with more than 600,000 members.

Muir's advocacy of national parks culminated in the highest power in the land being converted to his cause. In 1901 he published a book, *Our National Parks*, which brought him to the attention of Theodore

Roosevelt, and in 1903 the president – persuaded by Muir to come camping – visited the conservationist in Yosemite where, over four days that were catalytic to the president's mindset, they discussed plans and ideas for the many conservation programmes which he subsequently undertook

Could the lad from Dunbar ever have imagined pulling such influential strings of power? Not then, perhaps. But the level of his success in the fullness of life can be gauged from the fact that, under his influence, Roosevelt's first years of office were marked by the establishment of no fewer than sixteen new national parks, taking in 148 million acres. But that was only the beginning. During his lifetime John Muir also influenced presidents Wilson and Taft as they designated more than 50 national parks, 200 national monuments and 140 million acres of National Forest.

But the depth of his energy and commitment was staggering, even – and especially – as he approached the end of his life. As we are told in the introduction to his book *John Muir's Last Journey*, for over forty years he kept alive the dream that he might yet journey to the 'two hot continents' to study their richly biodiverse flora and fauna. And so, just three years before his death, he set off in 1911 on an epic trip that would have daunted many a man half his age (he was seventy-three). Leaving from New York and travelling alone, he embarked with enthusiasm on his eight-month, 40,000-mile voyage to South America and Africa. He first went 1,000 miles up the Amazon, then down the Atlantic coast and across the continent to the Chilean Andes before re-crossing the pampas to Buenos Aires, Argentina. From there, he sailed east and travelled through south and central Africa and to the headwaters of the Nile, before returning to New York via the Red Sea, Mediterranean and North Atlantic. It was a gigantic, life-maximising journey inspired by a gigantic curiosity that the world must still be grateful for.

When he died at the age of seventy-six in a Los Angeles hospital, the lad from the seashore of Dunbar had left an immeasurable legacy to mankind.

After his death, Roosevelt wrote of him in 1915:

His was a dauntless soul. Not only are his books delightful, not only is he the author to whom all men turn when they think of the Sierras and northern glaciers, and the giant trees of the Californian slope, but he was also – what few nature-lovers are – a man able to influence contemporary thought and action on the subjects to which he had devoted his life. He was a great factor in influencing the thought of California and the thought of the entire country so as to secure the preservation of those great natural phenomena – wonderful canyons, giant trees, slopes of flower-spangled hillsides . . . our generation owes much to John Muir.

Muir has been voted 'Most Famous Californian of All Time' and appeared on two US postage stamps. Truly a man of many parts, in all senses of the expression, he lived a life filled to the very brim, with so much left over for the edification of succeeding generations in perpetuity. To the roles of farmer, carpenter, inventor, philosopher, botanist, climber, geologist, explorer, naturalist, writer and especially pioneer of conservation, we could fairly add the phrase 'all-round visionary genius'.

He more than deserves the last word . . .

They will see what I mean in time. There must be places for human beings to satisfy their souls. Food and drink is not all.

Robert Dollar (1844–1932)

Grand Old Man of the Pacific

What more apt surname could a self-made Scots-American millionaire have? It is almost as if Someone Up There had decided Robert Dollar's fate at birth, though it is conceivably more likely that the name's provenance was the picture-postcard town of Dollar about twenty miles across the Forth River from the bigger central-belt town of Falkirk, where he was born in 1844. And like Andrew Carnegie, his fellow Scots-born millionaire, Dollar came to consider that the mountains of dollars he acquired during his long lifetime – largely and ultimately through his ocean-going fleet of steamships – were somehow rather vulgar if kept to himself; and so, in an echo of Carnegie's end-of-life generosity, he gave at least $1 million away (when a million was a million) and among the gifts he scattered on both sides of the Atlantic were several impressive ones for his home town: swimming baths, a park, a set of church chimes, a fountain and the book-stock for the town library.

Today, that library – the building of which was funded by Carnegie – remembers both men's benevolence with a large brass plaque on an interior wall, while Dollar's many letters of negotiation about his books donation ('it will all be paid in a few days') are treasured by its staff. But few people in Scotland now seem to even know the name that ranged so conspicuously over the world's oceans, emblazoned as it was across the hulls of Dollar Steamship Company ships – whose smokestacks carried the not-so-subtle logo of a large dollar sign. An obvious device, yet one that 'Captain' Dollar had doubts about . . .

His love–hate relationship with money was clearly evident in a letter he wrote to a friend:

> In this world all we leave behind us that is worth anything is that we can be well regarded and spoken of after we are gone and that we can say that we left the world just a little bit better than we found it. If we can't accomplish these two things then life, according to my view,

has been a failure. Many people erroneously speak of a man when he is gone as having left so much money. That, according to my view, amounts to very little.

Which of his Falkirk contemporaries could have guessed, however, that the humbly born lad who once confessed to having 'practically no education' would have grown into the elegant, confident shipping magnate who strode across the world stage and mixed with presidents and kings as he became known as 'the Grand Old Man of the Pacific'? He even had the enviable honour of being portrayed on *Time* magazine's cover in March 1928.

But, perhaps a touch ironically, the way he grew in stature owed more than a little to the simple trade that defined his upbringing in Falkirk, where his father William ran a sawmill. Robert and the rest of the family – his mother Mary and two brothers – were accommodated in a house above the building, which was later demolished to make way for new housing, though that sadness seems to have been compensated for by the birth of Dollar Avenue.

Wood-processing being the business he knew, it sustained Robert when at fourteen – after the death of his mother – he emigrated to Canada with his father in 1858 and started work as a cook's boy in a lumber camp. By 1866 he was camp foreman and, in 1871, he bought his first piece of timberland. Broadening his scope, he then moved to Michigan, and, in 1888, to California where he opened an office in San Francisco and set up home with his wife Margaret in San Rafael. By 1893 Dollar had a mill and lumbering business at Usal in Mendocino County, and shortly after, at the age of fifty, embarked on his second career – in shipping.

But how did that come about? Frustrated at finding his lumber deliveries to be at the mercy of unpredictable schedules operated by unreliable shipping companies, he acquired in 1895 a vessel of his own to transport his products from the Sonoma coast to San Francisco.

The steam schooner *Newsboy*, which had been owned by the recently bankrupted Navarro Mill, proved a shrewd investment and, as it began to effect improvements in his operation's efficiency, it simultaneously awakened the beginnings of his steamship line. He continued buying vessels to ship lumber, and by 1901 had bought his first large steamer and established the Dollar Steamship Company.

It was the start of something big. Being internationally minded,

Dollar had an instinctive feeling about Eastern promise – the potential market across the sea – and decided to make a test-run with one of his ships, which was memorably successful. He thus became the first to transport American lumber across the Pacific to the Orient, and his frequent subsequent trips to the Far East convinced him of the need for development of foreign trade across the Pacific. Each year he increased the number of ships carrying lumber and freight to Japan, China and Singapore. But that bold, successful strategy was not just a matter of international prestige. There were two winning commercial angles to it. One was the signal it sent to encourage leaders of various other American industries to explore Asia as an exciting new market; the other was the incalculable boost to his own Dollar Steamship Company, which was to boast, by 1930, the largest fleet of cargo and passenger liners that ever operated under the US flag.

Dollar became such a respected name in Asia that, by the First World War, his word alone was enough 'collateral' to allow the US government to commission the construction of ships in China to the value of $30 million.

But he not only became a pioneer and leader of American trade with the Orient, he also developed a round-the-world cargo service in 1920, which was followed in the mid-1920s by the purchase of seven 'President' ships owned by the US government; the acquisition of the Pacific Mail Steamship Company and its trans-Pacific routes; and the inauguration of a round-the-world luxury passenger service that was the first to publish scheduled departure and arrival times.

And what luxury! With a history of travelling extensively on his own ships on business – he made eight circumnavigations of the world and over forty trips to the Orient – Dollar was supremely qualified to commission the construction of two of the largest ocean liners ever built in the United States – the *President Hoover* and *President Coolidge* – with which he impressed even himself. When he boarded the former on 6 August 1931, he gasped: 'The ship is a wonder!'

He was not wrong there. Each ship carried 988 passengers in super-plush accommodation, and how they were pampered, not least by the attentions of a crew of 324. There were phones in every room, stunning art deco furnishings, outdoor pools and even gymnasiums.

The luxury and elegance of these two vessels were in stark contrast to the hard time of the Great Depression, which lasted until the Second World War. And although the Dollar Line lasted through it, when it came to an end it was plain that the effect had taken its toll. Fortunately, Robert Dollar did not live to see the collapse of his dream: the scrapping of the *President Hoover* in 1937 after she ran aground near Hoishoto Island; the arrest of the *President Coolidge* in San Francisco the following year for an unpaid debt of $35,000; his family's passing of the line's ownership to the government in return for a cancellation of its debts; and the renaming of the company to American President Lines – whereby a white eagle replaced the famous dollar signs on its funnels.

A true workaholic, Dollar had remained active in the business until several weeks before his death at the age of eighty-eight on May 16, 1932. Control of the company went to his sons, but A. Melville Dollar died several weeks after his father, and J. Harold Dollar in 1936. R. Stanley Dollar then headed the company until his death in 1958. Today, what remains of the family business consists primarily of lumber operations.

But it was a blaze of global glory while it lasted. During it, Dollar amassed a fortune of $40,000,000 and was rated number 88 in a survey of the wealthiest 100 men in the US – not a bad conclusion for a poor immigrant from Scotland who became an astute American businessman with remarkable vision. Throughout it all, he made several trips back to his home town of Falkirk – where he enjoyed being noticed and followed by admiring groups of children who reminded him of his own childhood – and back in America a particular source of pride for him was his grand house in San Rafael, which he bought in 1906 and named Falkirk (and which today houses the Falkirk Museum).

It is from here that we get a picture of his character, as described by his granddaughter, Grace Dollar Dickson Kleiser, who went to live there with her sister after their mother died in 1920. 'Grandfather sat at the end of the table and said grace before each meal,' she recalled. 'At festive occasions he would tell us a story about his life in the Canadian north woods and have us all spellbound and laughing. He had dark brown, very sparkling eyes and a white beard and you couldn't keep your eyes off him when he was talking. Although we heard the same stories over and over, we always asked him to tell them again.'

More than 3,000 people attended his funeral at the First Presbyterian Church just down the road from the house, and among friends and family were many foreign dignitaries, business associates and government officials. The US government even sent the giant airship *Akron* over the scene to drop flowers from the sky. Honorary pall bearers included the mayor of San Francisco and Governor James Rolph Jr of California, who said: 'Robert Dollar has done more in his lifetime to spread the American flag on the high seas than any man in this country.'

But Dollar did not make his exit without leaving a message to those who wished to do as well as he had. It came in the form of four simple instructions:

Do not cheat; do not be lazy; do not abuse; do not drink.

Alexander Graham Bell (1847–1922)

The man who rang the changes

In any competition to name one person who has changed the world more than any other, Alexander Graham Bell would have to be well worth putting your shirt on as a potential winner. That may be a big statement, but just think for a moment of the sweeping alterations in our way of life that this Scot's invention of the telephone has wrought. It was big enough back then, in 1876, when he made the momentous breakthrough; but even after conquering the challenge of worldwide communication – where before were only horses and sailing ships and an inadequate telegraph service – the telephone's development continues thunderously today, as new ideas are added to it virtually by the day, to feed an endlessly demanding and seemingly ever-young market.

Surprising, then, that the man's birth home in a handsome Georgian building just off Edinburgh's celebrated Princes Street is acknowledged by little more than a few words engraved into the one of the building's 32-inch-wide fluted fascia blocks:

Alexander Graham Bell

Inventor of the Telephone

Born here on 3rd March, 1847

Set to the left of its high, dark-green main door, the words draw little attention to the wood-panelled apartment in South Charlotte Street, on the corner of the classical Charlotte Square, where Alexander's parents – Eliza and Melville Bell – lived and worked; where they were more than a little interested in communication with and for the deaf, as his mother had seriously impaired hearing and his father and grandfather were elocution teachers specialising in that area.

To their surprise and delight, no doubt, the young Alexander chose not to rebel against family tradition in the predictable way of each new generation, but to embrace it with a lifelong fascination for deaf education and acoustics. And he brought to the exercise an invaluable something extra – an inventive mind capable of conceiving ingenious devices to facilitate laudable objectives.

The bearded man with his rich, rounded vocal tones may have been modest himself, saying some years after the world hailed his invention: 'I am sure that I should never have invented the telephone if I had been an electrician. What electrician would have hit upon so mad an idea? I must confess that, to this day, I don't understand how it is possible that someone can speak in Washington and someone else hear him at the foot of the Eiffel Tower.'

But only a few words on the wall? Where better, after all, than the Bell birth-house to create an Alexander Graham Bell Museum (of the history of telecommunications) to add to the Scottish capital's rich mix of money-spinning tourist attractions?

Its absence becomes even more bizarre when you consider that, but a few years ago, the house was actually owned by the very people who live by his invention as an industry – British Telecom.

Today, the company protests that during its year-long ownership it was seriously considering developing the property into a heritage centre. But several insurmountable problems got in the way – it was too small, it didn't lend itself to a large turnover of visitors (disabled access being difficult) and, most serious of all, BT found itself in deep financial trouble after the dot.com bubble burst and had to urgently divest itself of much valuable property.

Now, at time of writing, the recently refurbished building – acquired by property developers – is a series of 'small office suites' housing software firms and such like. No further mention of its world-famous earlier incumbent; no exciting exhortation to use the head and crank up something special.

To give BT its due, it has been instrumental in providing a large variety of fascinating artefacts for an impressive £1 million telecommunications permanent exhibition entitled 'Communicate!' and opened in October 2003 at the National Museum of Scotland in Edinburgh.

Bell's great-grandson, Hugh Müller, seventy-one, who made the journey from Nova Scotia for its official opening, said at the time: 'I think my great-grandfather would be very pleased. He always prided himself in being a Scot. When he went to Scotland for the last time he was given the freedom of Edinburgh and he told people that, of all the awards and honours he had, that was the one he prized the most.'

Showing the many different ways in which people have communicated over the centuries – from bongo drums, carrier pigeons and telegraph wires to the internet and the mobile phone – 'Communicate!' pays implicit tribute to the pioneering work of Scotland's telephone inventor, and is the only formal celebration of his achievements in Scotland. One of its champions argues: 'Some people might find this museum exhibition the most appropriate home for a Scottish tribute to Bell.'

But this writer is not convinced. Surely, the birth-house would have been more apt. Where a great, custom-made museum should naturally be, there is nothing.

Likewise in Elgin, in the northern county of Moray, where the teenage Alexander enrolled as a student teacher of music and elocution at Weston House. There is today no sign of his having been there. And it was an important, formative time in his life when, after teaching during the day, he learned in the evenings about electricity, became fascinated by telegraphy, and conducted experiments on the pitch of vowel sounds, even building a machine to produce them electronically.

Fine old Weston House was demolished in 1955, to be replaced by a car-sales garage, which has since become a branch store of a well-known electrical chain. And at no time has there ever been a public note on the site of the illustrious Scotsman's presence.

It is a different story in North America, of course, where he went at the age of twenty-three – first to Ontario – with his surviving family to recover from the tuberculosis that killed two of his brothers in 1870. Though it was not a big step from Canada to the USA, where he then took a job teaching deaf children in Boston, it would stay close to his heart, and vice versa.

On Cape Breton island, Nova Scotia, there is an Alexander Graham Bell National Historic Site on ten hectares of land. Overlooking Baddeck Bay and Beinn Breagh, Bell's second home, where much of his scientific work was pursued and where he and his wife Mabel are now buried, the centre commemorates and interprets his scientific and humanitarian work, illustrated by fascinating artefacts such as books, photographs, material from his archives, personal furniture and awards received during his lifetime.

A more-than-fitting tribute to a well-remembered man. But Bell's early professional sojourn north of the border lasted only a year. It was 'down south' in Boston, where he taught at a special day school for deaf children and became a renowned educator by opening classes to train teachers of speech to the deaf, that he began to lay the groundwork that would lead to the invention of the telephone.

Encouraged by a number of local scientists interested in acoustics, in his spare time he sought to combine his work for the hearing-impaired with his interest in invention, and began to believe with growing conviction that it might be possible for an electrified wire to carry the human voice over great distances. To this end, his keen ear helped him experiment with musical notes in trying to develop a device that would record the rising and falling of voice tones in speech. As he saw there was little difference in the harmonics, he realised speech transmission must be within reach.

It was during this time, when he was also professor of vocal physiology and the mechanics of speech at Boston University, that he determined to move on through inventions of the phonautograph (a device for converting sound into visible traces) and the multiple telegraph (increased capability for the dot-and-dash system) to the 'speaking telegraph' itself.

He was encouraged in this by the entry into his endeavours of Tom Watson, a skilled electrician who seemed to understand his ideas and was capable of developing devices to support them. The two men were to become one of history's most legendary partnerships – reminiscent almost of Sherlock Holmes and his 'elementary' Watson – and, as their goal came tantalisingly close, Bell gave up teaching to focus all his considerable brainpower and energy on reaching to grasp for his holy grail. By 1874, he had worked out the principles for electronic transmission of speech; by mid-1875, Bell and Watson proved that a fluctuating current could carry sounds as a whole variety of them were transmitted through their wires; and by 7 March 1876, Bell had got his patent for the invention he called the 'telephone'.

How does it work? Simply described, it is a system that converts sound, specifically the human voice, to electrical impulses of various frequencies and then back to a tone that sounds like the original voice. To some degree Bell's work on it reflected that of the German Johann Philip Reis who, in 1864, nearly solved the problem of long-distance talk by constructing an apparatus capable of transmitting music – but not the spoken word; and it cut across the bows of American Elisha Gray who had been doing similar work to Bell's. Indeed, both Bell and Gray filed for a patent on their designs at the New York patent office on February 14 1876, with Bell beating

Gray by only two hours! Although Gray had built the first steel diaphragm/electromagnet receiver in 1874, he did not master a workable transmitter design until after the tireless Bell – who had slaved over various types of mechanism year after year. But there were many legal challenges.

To the highly principled Bell, every lawsuit was an assault on his integrity. 'He took it very personally,' Hugh Müller, his great-grandson, told the *Scotsman* newspaper on his 2003 visit to Scotland:

> His lawyers would tell him not to worry about it, not to react, but he found that very difficult. He was a man of very high integrity. What really bothered him was when people thought he was stealing ideas, that he had been fraudulent. He was a product of the Victorian age, not necessarily religious, but of very tight morals. After the lawsuits about the telephone he didn't write on a scrap of paper without first dating it.

Court battles over his patent went on for almost two decades, and although all were eventually resolved in his favour, Bell must have wondered to himself if it had not been granted a touch prematurely. For it was not until 10 March 1876, three days after his Gray-beating green light, that the famous verbal request that was to become possibly the most recorded one in human history, was sent out over the wire from one room to another, and was clearly understood by the recipient, Tom Watson.

The many reports of that moment have produced, like Chinese whispers, various versions of the immortal words spoken, and there have been dramatised accounts of the reaction such as 'Watson dropped the receiver and rushed with wild joy across the hall to tell Bell the glad tidings' – so here, just for this record, is the event as told through the horse's mouth, from the pages of Bell's experimental notebook for that fateful day. It began with a drawing of his latest, most refined instrument:

> The improved instrument shown in Fig 1 was constructed this morning and tried this evening. P is a brass pipe and W the platinum wire, M the mouth piece and S the armature of the receiving instrument.
>
> Mr Watson was stationed in one room with the receiving instrument. He pressed one ear closely against S and closed the other ear with his hand. The transmitting instrument was placed in another room and the doors of both rooms were closed.

I then shouted in to M the following sentence: 'Mr Watson – come here – I want to see you.' To my delight, he came and declared that he had heard and understood what I had said.

I asked him to repeat the words. He answered, 'You said, "Mr Watson – come here – I want to see you." '

We then changed places and I listened at S while Mr Watson read a few passages from a book into the mouth piece M. It was certainly the case that articulate sounds proceeded from S. The effect was loud but indistinct and muffled. If I had read beforehand the passage given by Mr Watson I should have recognised every word. As it was I could not make out the sense – but an occasional word here and there was quite distinct. I made out 'to' and 'out' and 'further', and finally the sentence 'Mr Bell, do you understand what I say? DO-YOU-UN-DER-STAND-WHAT-I-SAY' came quite clearly and intelligibly. No sound was audible when the armature S was removed.

And so the telephone, that boon and blessing to mankind, was born. Among the many huge consequences of that historic moment was the burgeoning of telephone exchanges, the first of which was installed in Hartford, Connecticut, in 1877, and the founding of the Bell Telephone Company (later AT&T), which grew to be the world's largest phone company.

It is difficult now to appreciate the sense of wonder the invention engendered at the time; but at the back of one of my bookshelves I have found a musty volume of the *New Harmsworth Self-Educator*, published in the 1920s, that seems – in its introduction to the chapter entitled 'Transmission of Speech: Invention of the Telephone' – to capture the true impact and magnitude of the development. It reads:

Of the many inventions which distinguished the latter half of the 19th century, it is safe to say that none excited greater wonder and interest than that of the Telephone.

It was looked upon as the first step in the direction of realising the 'Arabian Nights' dream of a magic carpet – the brilliance of the conception cannot easily be realised.

For thousands of years men had been content to transmit their speech sounds over at most but a few hundred feet. In 1876 Graham Bell astonished the world by showing how the energy of sound vibrations could be transformed into electrical energy, transmitted along a wire at a speed approximating to that of light, and re-transformed into sound waves under conditions which seemed to annihilate all the pre-existing limits of time and space.

When we remember that sound in air travels at about 1,100 feet per second – a speed which would require over half an hour to traverse the distance between London and Glasgow [400 miles] and at the same time know that every day men converse between these towns as easily as if in the same room, we appreciate more fully the modern miracle of the telephone.

As has occurred with many other epoch-making inventions, so in this case all the necessary component parts were in existence, and only the touch of genius was required for a great forward step.

It must have been an indescribably exciting time in the life of the young Scot. Thanks to the stunning achievement of his 'touch of genius' at the tender age of twenty-nine, his professional and domestic future – on the brink of marriage, as he was, to one of his students, Mabel Hubbard – looked not just secure but remarkably bright in 1876. Indeed, Mabel's well-off father became a funding champion of Bell's system, and it is amusing from this remove to read the response he and his son-in-law got when they offered his patent to the Telegraph Company (which became Western Union) for $100,000 in 1876. Chauncey M. DePew, president of the company, had a committee investigate the offer and here is part of its report . . .

The Telephone purports to transmit the speaking voice over telegraph wires. We found that the voice is very weak and indistinct, and grows even weaker when long wires are used between the transmitter and receiver. Technically, we do not see that this device will ever be capable of sending recognisable speech over a distance of several miles.

Messer Hubbard and Bell want to install one of their 'telephone devices' in every city. The idea is idiotic on the face of it. Furthermore, why would any person want to use this ungainly and impractical device when he can send a messenger to the telegraph office and have a clear written message sent to any large city in the United States?

The electricians of our company have developed all the significant improvements in the telegraph art to date, and we see no reason why a group of outsiders, with extravagant and impractical ideas, should be entertained, when they have not the slightest idea of the true problems involved. Mr. G.G. Hubbard's fanciful predictions, while they sound rosy, are based on wild-eyed imagination and lack of understanding of the technical and economic facts of the situation, and a posture of ignoring the obvious limitations of his device, which is hardly more than a toy . . .

In view of these facts, we feel that Mr. G.G. Hubbard's request for $100,000 of the sale of this patent is utterly unreasonable, since this device is inherently of no use to us. We do not recommend its purchase.

For this astonishing lack of prescience, Bell got his poetic justice in the end – when in 1882 he acquired a controlling interest in Western Union!

But, back in 1876, the timing of his breakthrough couldn't have been better, with the Centennial Exposition in Philadelphia – to celebrate 100 years of US independence – coming up in June of that year.

Surprisingly, the stand displaying his groundbreaking invention was largely ignored – until a VIP recognised Bell himself, as the distinguished expert in speech training who had helped him in a training session at Boston University. This was the Brazilian Emperor Dom Pedro II, who came over to say hello then accepted an invitation to hear the inventor reciting Shakespeare over the telephone. 'Great heavens! The thing talks!' exclaimed the emperor, as heads all over the hall turned. From that point on, the telephone was the star attraction.

Bell could have been forgiven for being content with the success of his world-changing invention and being ready to take life rather more easily. But such a thought never crossed his mind. The following month, two days after forming the Bell Telephone Company, he married Mabel and they set out on a year-long working honeymoon in Britain to introduce the telephone there.

While he was to make a great deal of money on selling his interests to big business, Alexander Graham Bell was also a man driven to the end by his inventive impulses. The Bells had two daughters, Elsie and Marian, and eventually settled in Washington and Nova Scotia. But he never stopped experimenting and inventing. In 1881, he invented a probe to locate bullets in a body; in 1886 he sold his patents for making wax phonograph discs to open a place to carry out his work for the deaf; in the 1890s he conducted experiments with flying machines, earning his portrait a place on a US postage stamp between the Wright Brothers' heads; and so on it went.

Late in life, he told a reporter, who was clearly awed by his mental energy: 'There cannot be mental atrophy in any person who continues to observe, to remember what he observes, and to seek answers for his unceasing hows and whys about things.'

Interested in aeronautics and physics, he worked on a variety of projects as diverse as flying machines, metal detectors, automatic switchboards, hydrofoil designs and – after his new-born son Edward tragically died from respiratory problems – an early version of the iron lung. And all the while he remained a prominent advocate for new methods of teaching the deaf to speak and lip-read; for he saw himself, above all, as a dedicated teacher of the deaf.

For the rest of the world, of course, he would be principally remembered for his momentous invention of the device with which his name has now become almost synonymous. In 1915, in New York, he spoke to Watson in San Francisco, in celebration of the first transcontinental telephone link. And in a tribute that seemed to match the size of his achievement, when he died seven years later, the entire telephone service of the United States – something that simply didn't exist before the kindly Scot crossed the Atlantic – stopped operating for one minute in his honour.

David Dunbar Buick (1854–1929)

Who gave the car its name

You can't find No. 26 these days, and you can barely discern the vestigial shape of Green Street itself in Arbroath, the east-coast fishing port famed for its piquant smoked haddock and now-ruined abbey, where the Declaration of Arbroath (a model for the American Declaration of Independence) was signed in 1320. The one-time position of the little house in question can be vaguely perceived between the cluster of newish homes that have ambushed it and the wider outer circle of older houses built in the town's distinctive red sandstone – the same stuff, hewn by monks from the nearby shore's dramatic cliffs, that made that celebrated abbey. Indeed, in the absence of the house and its one-time neighbours, the only building that still holds the street's virtually vanished line is the little Victorian Milne masonic hall, on one of whose walls, just above head height, is the brass plaque I have been advised to seek out.

This intrigues me for two reasons: the first being that I grew up through babyhood only a few metres from this spot – with my back-bedroom in Lochlands Street well within dummy-throwing distance; the second being that, until recently, and in common I assume with most townspeople, I knew little of my famous fellow-toddler from this street. For many decades he had been something of a forgotten hero at home as well as in his adopted country of America.

In people terms, Arbroath had been known for being the home town of James Chalmers, who famously developed the adhesive postage stamp; for lawnmower inventor Alexander Shanks, and for the kilted entertainer Andy Stewart. But here was evidence that the little town just north of Dundee could boast yet another important son. The plaque, which was placed on the hall by a group of US car industry executives more than a decade ago to mark the hundred and fortieth birthday of the man who gave his name to the Buick automobile, reads:

David Dunbar Buick Sept 17, 1854–March 5, 1929. American motoring pioneer and founder of the Buick Motor Company of America, David Dunbar Buick was born at No. 26 Green Street, Arbroath, which lay approximately 90 metres north of this, the only remaining building to show the line of the original street.

Sponsored by the Buick Motor Division of the General Motors Corporation of America.

To accompany its unveiling, the Buick bosses brought along a brace of their most handsome cars – one from 1937 and one hot off the 1994 presses. They were put on display lined outside the hall for locals to gasp at in a cathartic moment of great local rediscovery – for although his story did not have a traditional happy ending as the person himself almost vanished out of the history books, paradoxically David Buick's name is one of the most enduring in automotive history.

It was only two years after he was born that his parents decided to up sticks from Arbroath and take the family to America. They settled in Detroit, where his carpenter father died three years later and his mother then worked in a candy store to support the family.

At the age of fifteen, David was hired by the Alexander Manufacturing Company, a Detroit fabricator of plumbing fixtures – where Henry Ford had also worked as an apprentice – and there he acquired and developed the inventive and tactile skills that were both to serve him well and lead him astray. He became a prolific engineer and inventor of many new applications – thirteen patents for valves, water closets, bathtubs and a lawn sprinkler, not to mention his ground-breaking process for heat-binding porcelain and wrought iron to make white bathtubs – and by 1882 he and an old school friend, William Sherwood, had taken over the plumbing business.

Buick & Sherwood, of which Buick was president, was successful and would undoubtedly have made them considerable fortunes, but . . . When he saw his first automobile, bathroom fittings were immediately a thing of the past for David Buick. Always an innovative thinker, and always more interested in making things than making money, he turned his attention to petrol engines and became so obsessed with developing them that tension began to play on the delicate business partnership with Sherwood, until it cracked under the latter's change-or-else ultimatum.

'Or else' it was. The company was sold in 1899 for $100,000 and Buick, then forty-five, used his share to form a new firm to build petrol engines for farm and marine use. The Buick Auto-Vim and Power Company, as he called it, was the cradle of a smart Buick prototype, which the cash-strapped David sold for $225 to its chief engineer, Walter Marr, in 1901.

That was a signal of how things were about to go. Buick's ambitions to build a great car were driving him on, but he did not have deep enough pockets to match them, as his company's name was constantly changed to reveal his burning intent.

In 1902 it was transformed into the Buick Manufacturing Company – where the famous Buick valve-in-head engine was designed. Indeed, so advanced did his designs become that the Buick Motor Car Company – formed the following year – was overspent before it began, and did not have an easy birth. It completed fifty experimental cars at $1,200 each before selling any, and often had to be saved from financial failure by optimistic believers such as Walter Marr and Buick's businessman friend Ben Briscoe, who believed in Buick's hands-on talents but was wary of his business abilities. His patience with the Scot often grew thin, and he once said the Buick story 'is so fraught with romance that it makes the Arabian Nights tales look commonplace'.

And the terms of the new firm's organisation would haunt Buick all his life. It was capitalised with $100,000 in stock – $300 for Buick and $99,700 for Briscoe. As president, Buick could gain control of all the stock if he repaid Briscoe $3,500 he owed him within four months. If he couldn't, he would forfeit all interest in the company. In what he probably reckoned was a smart move, Buick sold the company before the deadline – to Flint Wagon Works, which was looking for a way into auto manufacturing and was impressed by his car, settled his corporate debts, and embraced both the Buick set-up and its name.

But while Buick became entangled in what was actually a bad bargain with the new owners, the Buick Motor Company was moved from Detroit to Flint. He became secretary of the new car works and was allotted 1,500 shares but would not receive the stock until his dividends paid off his personal debts.

Meanwhile, the show had to go on, and a catalytic moment for the fledgling car giant came in the summer of 1904, when the first Flint-built pre-production Buick was taken on a test run to Detroit and back by Walter Marr and Buick's son Thomas. Here is a contemporary account of that historic drive in the Model B . . .

They started out on Saturday, July 5, 1904, at 1:15pm from Flint's
Sherman House Hotel on a 90-mile route to Detroit via Lapeer. A
rear-bearing failure caused them to spend a night in Lapeer. They
arrived in Detroit on the Sunday, the *Flint Journal* reporting that 'the
distance from Pontiac to Birmingham was covered in ten minutes'.
They bought car license No. 1024 Monday and headed back to Flint
Tuesday. Driving in a steady rain through the small towns of Pontiac,
Oxford and Lapeer, Marr averaged more than 30mph. 'The roads were
deep in mud every mile of the way,' Marr said. 'I did the driving and
[Tom] Buick was kept busy wiping the mud off my goggles'.

In one town they were challenged to a race by an electric car, but
the Buick 'showed them the way', Marr said. 'We went so fast at another
time that we could not see the village's 6mph sign. At one place, going
down a hill, I saw a bump at a bridge too late to slow up. When I hit
it I threw in all the power and landed over it safely in the road. Buick
was just taking a chew of tobacco when a lump of mud as large as a
baseball hit him square in the face, filling his mouth completely. We
were plastered with mud from head to foot when we reached Flint.

Marr drove his first Flint Buick directly to the office of the *Flint
Journal* on his return. 'The machine made the run without a skip,'
he boasted. 'It reached here in the best of condition. We took the
hills handily with our high-speed gear and the machine sounded
like a locomotive.' Back at the plant, Marr told the directors: 'Well,
we are here.'

The test was so successful that the order was given to start
production immediately, and by the end of the year, thirty-seven
Model B Buicks had been built. But the company ran into financial
trouble again – and turned to prominent local entrepreneur William
C. Durant, a horse-drawn carriage builder who didn't particularly
like automobiles . . . until he saw how the Buick could climb hills and
run through mud like no other car he had ever seen.

Once Durant made the decision to switch (from) horses, there was
no going back. The Buick's success was assured. Few people could
raise money and interest in a product like 'Billy' Durant, and when
he went to the 1905 New York Auto Show he took orders for 1,000
Buicks before the company had built 40.

None of which was particularly good news for David Buick,
personally or professionally. As a non-commercial animal with
little interest in company politics, he began to lose out dramatically.

Like Henry Ford, Durant knew the motor industry's future lay in speeding up production and cutting assembly costs. But Buick was a craftsman who saw each new car as a unique piece of work. His role in the business declined rapidly until he finally lost the manager's title to Durant in early 1906. The company was clearly not big enough for both of them, and one would have to go. Buick sold his stock to Durant for $100,000 – stock that would soon be worth $115,000,000.

So in 1906, at the age of fifty-two, David Dunbar Buick severed all his links with the company he had started, and returned to Detroit with his wife and son. He had been involved in the making of only 120 Buicks and, after a while, the only vestige of his input was his name, which continued to suit the car as its technology advanced with the company's growing strength. In 1908, Durant acquired Cadillac and Oldsmobile to form General Motors – which, as it grew towards today's global conglomerate, then took in Chevrolet (1918), Britain's Vauxhall (1926) and Germany's Opel (1929).

By 1923 Buick production had reached 100,000 units a year, a figure that has risen steadily until now – when there is a 300-acre complex employing 20,000 people producing 350,000 cars a year.

It is a remarkable and romantic story, but it ended less than sweetly for David Dunbar Buick. Forgotten and impoverished, in the last years of his life the automobile pioneer held a series of low-paid jobs. When he was found in 1928 by the young reporter Bruce Catton – who later became a Pulitzer-Prize-winning historian of the American Civil War – the once dapper bespectacled executive had become 'a thin, bent little man' working behind the information desk as an inspector at the Detroit School of Trades. He was described as having, at seventy-four, grey hair, a slight frame and a deeply lined face, but bright and cheerful eyes.

In his talk with the reporter, he was candid about the way his life had worked out and seemed nevertheless to be looking forward. He was not to know that less than a year later, on 5 March 1929, he would die of colon cancer complications in Detroit's Harper Hospital.

In that same year, while he couldn't afford to keep a telephone in his home, let alone buy one of the automobiles that bore his name, General Motors produced 196,104 Buicks, making it the sixth most popular car line in the United States. Eight years later, GM adopted the Buick family crest as the logo for the car line. To date, the Buick name has been stamped on over 25 million cars.

But in his talk with Catton, Buick was neither bitter nor regretful. In response to a question comparing what had gone before with his current situation, he said: 'I'm not worrying. The failure is the man who stays down when he falls – the man who sits and worries about what happened yesterday, instead of jumping up and figuring what he's going to do today and tomorrow. That's what success is – looking ahead to tomorrow.'

David Buick was not alone in ending in a destitute state. Perhaps he allowed himself an ironic smile when he learned, wherever he was, that Billy Durant eventually lost control of GM and ended up running a bowling alley in Flint.

The Buick name has lived on, however, in the handsome badges of sophisticated state-of-the-art models that cruise across America today, and it has come to mean guaranteed quality and luxury.

Come to think of it, the car-crazy boy from Arbroath might just have been happy with that.

There is still a Buick living in Arbroath who has a strong relationship with the car company. Eric Buick, an industrial cleaning contractor, was keen to find out if he was related to the Buick founder – and, after some research in the early 1990s, was saddened to find that he wasn't.

That didn't stop him making friends with the company's executives, however, and it was at his suggestion that they came over to fix and unveil plaque the DDB plaque in 1994.

'I told them I thought it was a shame that David Buick was not commemorated at his birthplace and their PR man Larry Guston responded quickly with a bit of a challenge,' he recalls. 'If I could come up with a good idea, they would come up with the funding.'

Eric did . . . and they did.

So strong is his relationship with Buick that he was invited by his company contacts to attend the record-breaking 'Buicktown centenary gathering of the cars' at Flint, Michigan, in July 2003.

Eric still feels he might one day find some living relatives of the auto pioneer. 'His grandson, David Buick II, died in the late '80s and, on the face of it, that seems to have marked the dying out of the family name. But I'm still researching and I live in hope . . .'

He feels David Buick had 'a pretty rough deal', being pushed out of the firm early.

Bertie C. Forbes (1880–1954)

Founder of Forbes Magazine

If you care to look for them, there are many pearls of wisdom attributed to Bertie C. Forbes, some of them pertinent to living in general ('Jealousy is a mental cancer' or 'The truth doesn't hurt unless it ought to') and some with particular reference to the decent conduct of business ('A shady business never yields a sunny life' or 'Real riches are the riches possessed inside'). But the one aphorism that seems to have particular relevance to the unfolding of his own thoroughly fulfilled life is: 'To make headway, improve your head.'

He might easily have added 'and use it', because using his head was what the remarkably enterprising Scot seemed to do from the moment he was born in 1880 – the sixth of the ten children of Agnes and Robbie Forbes, a modest tailor and ale purveyor in the small farming community of Whitehill in the parish of New Deer, Aberdeenshire.

It is tempting, while telling such rags-to-riches tales, to overuse the word 'poor' in characterising the parents or offspring; but I suspect even the little Bertie Forbes knew the word could not apply to him – his early life may have been hard, with little on the table and an often-chilly mile walk to school and back every day from his cottage home known as the Cunnyknowe, but his earthy agricultural environment was rich indeed, characterised by rolling fields of oats, glossy cattle and good fresh air.

He was a well-loved lad, too. But if you could ask him now what he considered his greatest blessing, he would doubtless answer with the name of one man. It would not be that of a US president or any of the famously rich people he met in later life; it would be that of Gavin Greig, a man who was the very embodiment of the legendary idea (now sadly faded) of a 'guid Scots education'.

This enlightened, erudite man was not only a respected playwright, poet, composer and collector of the region's folk songs but also the headmaster of the little school at Whitehill where he taught the three Rs – reading, writing and 'rithmetic – and the classics with equal dedication and passion to the simple country children in his charge.

Some, of course, were less simple than others. And as a man of letters himself, Greig sensed and encouraged an aptitude for words and hungry curiosity that he saw in the keen young Bertie Forbes. So when an exciting opportunity presented itself in class one day, the teacher was not surprised to see Bertie stick up his hand in instant response. Dauvit Scott, publisher of *The Peterhead Sentinel* local newspaper, was on the look-out for a printer's devil, and had asked Gavin Greig to announce his requirement in class to the older children.

There was no doubt in Bertie Forbes' mind that this chance, which he immediately related to his interest in writing, was a golden one. And so, with his eager response taken positively, he set off at the age of fourteen on the long journey to be a publisher himself – and one of America's most important ones. It is intriguing to wonder now, with hindsight, at the catalytic significance of that small moment, when the first seed of America's most prestigious business and financial magazine was sown.

Headquartered on New York's Fifth Avenue, a few blocks from the Empire State Building, *Forbes Magazine* quickly grew into something of an institution, the American business person's long-established 'bible' – full of intelligent, conscience-searching and respected features but perhaps best-known for its many periodic 'wealth' lists. Today, these include the Forbes 400, a list of the richest people in the United States; a list of the richest people in the world; and the Forbes 500, a list of largest companies taking into account market capitalisation, revenue, income and assets.

The magazine's own income and assets have been mightily impressive too over the years, making many of its prime family movers multi-millionaires. Not the least of them, of course, Bertie Forbes.

And it all surely began in the fishing port of Peterhead, not far from his family home. There, his first job might not have been the world's greatest, at a wage of a few shillings a week, but its importance in the great scheme of his life could not be underestimated. He spent three years typesetting there and acquired not just a vital grounding in technical understanding but a valued introduction to editorial work. Any veteran journalist will tell you how important these things used to be, and in the same breath will surely mention the *Dundee Courier* – long acknowledged as Britain's best in-at-the-deep-end training ground for journalists in the days before computers and formal training schemes.

And that was where Bertie went next, to be a fast-learning *Courier* cub reporter – who, while still in his teens, was transferred to Montrose, an important harbour town on the east coast between Aberdeen and Dundee, as boss of the branch office there.

So before he was twenty-one and on his way to new horizons at the turn of the century, Bertie had a formidable secret weapon under his belt – he was already a relatively tried and trusted journalist. Did he look it? Probably not. And that misperception, as we will see later, was something he relished having to counter with the surprising revelation of his skills when the right moment presented itself.

For many of the facts and memories in this chapter I am indebted to another man of letters from the Greig family, my old journalistic colleague Jack Webster, great-grandson of the great teacher. In his tender trade-choosing years Jack actually met Bertie on several occasions and was even encouraged into journalism by him – with satisfying results, it has to be said. For Jack, now in his seventies, has a distinguished career in national newspapers behind him and is quietly famous himself thanks to his finely written books, features and star-spangled interviews, which have included names like Charlie Chaplin and Bing Crosby. It is to him, then, that we turn for some unique memories of, and insights into, Buchan's formidable son:

'Bertie was in my granny's class at school and he always felt very much indebted to our family because of my great-grandfather,' recalls Jack.

> He just idolised Gavin Greig. In later life he said he thought Greig was a greater man than any of his great American pals like Henry Ford and John D. Rockefeller. This was because of the superb education he gave his pupils, turning them out not just with top-class English but also Latin and Greek and a real appetite for the world. They were incredibly well educated by the age of 14.

That included Bertie, of course. And when the Boer War stirred his appetite for worldly adventure, he left the *Courier* to set sail for far southern horizons. In Johannesburg the (later) great mystery writer Edgar Wallace, who had been a war correspondent and decided to stay on, was looking for help to revamp the post-war *Rand Daily Mail*. When he met Bertie Forbes he knew this was 'just the kind of guy he was looking for, a hard-working Scot prepared to get his jacket off'.

Eventually, Bertie became so trusted by Wallace he would be allowed to take over his columns as if he were the master himself.

'But he had another important string to his bow,' says Jack. 'Having developed an interest in golf, he would often be on the golf courses caddying for the big diamond merchants, and as he did so he would keep his ears open to learn about high finance from their conversation.' Though he was doing well on the new paper, Bertie decided that if he was going to be so interested in stocks and shares, the best city to be in was New York. And so, by 1904, he was waving Wallace goodbye and steaming off to another new life in the Big Apple.

> He had no contacts there. Nobody knew a thing about him. He tried to get a job but nobody would take him on. Who was this Scottish country bumpkin anyway? At twenty-four he was too old to be an office boy, and he probably wasn't experienced enough for a real editorial job. Seeing this problem of perception, Bertie offered to work for nothing, but the *New York Journal of Commerce* yielded and grudgingly admitted him to its humblest post for a few dollars a week.

With his feet thus under the table, Bertie began to push in articles, which were received – and published – with great approval and surprise. Which must have been very gratifying for the unknown country boy, who suddenly found himself rising quickly up the ladder so that, in next to no time, he was the paper's respected financial editor.

'Soon he was doing syndicated columns under different names, and at one of our meetings,' recalls Jack,

> I listened open-mouthed as he told me how William Randolph Hearst, the biggest newspaper tycoon in the world, was so keen to hire him he gave him a blank cheque to sign his own salary. He asked for a massive $20,000 and Hearst told him later that, although he had been prepared to pay much more, he had calculated that a Scot would under-estimate his own value.

By 1917 Bertie Forbes had become so famous as the most widely read financial writer in America that he decided to capitalise on his name by starting *Forbes Magazine*. To acquire much of the needed (borrowed) capital, he knocked on the Fifth Avenue door of the industrialist Charles Frick and won him over in a charm offensive. And once the magazine was up and running, he pulled no punches.

The very first issue reminded readers that 'business was originated to produce happiness, not pile up millions' and carried a column with the biblical exhortation 'With all thy getting, get understanding'. Indeed, he became known as 'the great humaniser of business' and, despite becoming a friend – and fellow-millionaire – of people like Henry Ford, Andrew Carnegie, John D. Rockefeller and Frank Woolworth, he practised an unusual morality in the magazine and would not pull back from criticising, say, Ford for slave-driving in his factories.

In time, however, as the magazine steadily grew in stature and financial stability between the two wars and between the great sprouting skyscrapers of Manhattan, Bertie Forbes found himself thinking more and more of his simple Scottish roots, and how he would like to honour the people from whom he came. And so, after he got himself established around the early 1920s, he started going back to Scotland every two years, and his picnics at Whitehill became something of an institution.

'The idea of Bertie coming always caused tremendous excitement in the parish,' recalls Jack.

> We weren't used to mixing with millionaires, and he always paid special attention to my family when he came back – my granny was still there, of course, and as I was the great grandson of his great hero, I got a bit more attention than most.
>
> I first remember him when I was a little lad, about 1935 or '37. He was quite Americanised by that time – a small, rotund, fairly typical cigar-smoking American, with gold-rimmed specs. But he wasn't long back before he was speaking with something of a Buchan accent again, with local words . . . the American nasal bit would gradually give way to the voice of the real Buchan boy.
>
> Then of course the war came so we didn't see him again until 1946, and by then I was 15 and keen to be a journalist. So he devoted a lot of time to encouraging me, thinking I suppose that he was paying back a debt to Gavin Greig. He told me stories about his friends like John D. Rockefeller and Frank Woolworth . . . and he aroused great excitement in me to be a journalist, though I was keen anyway by that time. All the stuff about his life in New York was fascinating . . . playing Saturday night poker games with Mrs Gershwin, mother of George, and me being a great Gershwin fan!'

In all, Jack Webster met Bertie Forbes five times after the war.

He would come over to our house in nearby Maud, two miles from Whitehill, and play poker with my father . . . and I'd just sit and listen. He would sit in our best room and just chat away over a cuppa – for which the best china was brought out – or a dram. He exuded tremendous personality. You could still see the wee butter ball of a Buchan boy in him, but you had to look through all these layers of American sophistication. He had just grown hugely in stature.

The millionaire's picnic two-yearly visits after the war started in 1946, and so then took place in 1948, 1950, 1952 and . . .

For the next one we shouldn't have been expecting him until '54. But word got around that he was coming for Christmas '53, and my mother – who was a bit intuitive – said 'That's very odd. I wonder why he's coming then, he's never been here at Christmas'. So he came and played Santa Claus for the kids, and visited our house as usual. But when he left in his big limousine with his chauffeur to drive back to Glasgow to catch his ship (he often came on the *Queen Mary*) I remember my mother saying: 'We're never going to see Bertie again.'

Indeed, the following May the millionaire publisher was found dead – lying on the floor of his office – by a night security man who wondered why his light was still burning. He had had a heart attack and died there and then, with a pen in his hand. So he would not have made it to Scotland for the summer of 1954.

Bertie had been editor-in-chief of *Forbes* until his death, though he was assisted in his later years by Bruce and Malcolm, the two oldest of the surviving four of his five sons (Duncan had been killed as a teenager in a car crash). Bruce took over the business, but within a few years, in 1964, he too had died – of cancer, in his forties. So Malcolm, the colourful third son, who had not been thinking about taking the helm, was called into service, and proved a godsend, as he developed Bertie's worthy company into a billion-dollar business.

In fact, Malcolm not only sorted out the company; he sorted out his father's position for eternity. The old man was buried in a New Jersey cemetery, but thirty-four years later Malcolm brought his body home to Scotland be re-interred in the old churchyard at New Deer. Jack Webster has a story to tell about that too . . .

Malcolm had asked me to help him bring back the old picnic tradition, and after the first revived one in 1987 I was driving him back to the airport when we passed New Deer cemetery. I said: 'Your ancestors are buried in there' and I could see his mind working . . .

When he got back to America, he summoned a family conference which then decided that Bertie would probably be happier back among his ain folk in New Deer. That was when he got on the phone and said: 'We've decided to dig up Dad and bring him back'. So in 1988 about 18 members of the family came flying in and we reburied Bertie in the old churchyard in New Deer just across the road from the village church, St Kane's, that he used to attend with his whole family, all ten of them.

I had a cord to lower him into his new grave. The coffin had been sent in advance. I can't remember if it came by sea, but it sat for some time in the potting shed of the village joiner, who was also the local undertaker.

Malcolm was a flamboyant man whose colourful lifestyle included lavish star-studded parties, motorcycling interludes with Liz Taylor, flying hot-air balloons, and an unsuccessful stab at New Jersey's 1957 gubernatorial election; and when he died in 1990, he left a fortune estimated at over $1 billion.

Times soon began to get relatively harder for the Forbes family, however, as much of that sum went on taxes, and the eldest of his four sons who took over, Malcolm Stevenson Forbes Jr (known as 'Steve'), spent an estimated $76 million on two unsuccessful bids for the Republican presidential nomination in 1996 and 2000.

It is no secret, of course, that such expenditures – combined with the advertising downturn that followed the Twin Towers catastrophe – prompted the organisation to pull in its belt a little and, at time of writing, Steve's brother Kip was mounting a big effort to shore up the family finances and was initiating a number of commercial ventures, including a wine label, jewellery and designer furniture.

Other measures designed to keep the family fortune intact included the selling of their father's collection of Fabergé eggs to a Russian collector, and the licensing of the company's business name for products ranging from calendars to furniture. But setbacks and challenges are what the Forbes dynasty has been always about, and it seems unlikely that its foundations can be seriously shaken now. Indeed, one can almost hear the ghostly voice of Bertie Forbes booming out across the Atlantic with another of his memorable advisory observations:

History has demonstrated that the most notable winners usually encountered heartbreaking obstacles before they triumphed. They won because they refused to become discouraged by their defeats.

Tommy Armour (1895–1968)

The one-eyed golf champ

> It is not solely the capacity to make great shots that makes champions,
> but the essential quality of making very few bad shots.

Many a frustrated amateur – and even professional – golfer will recognise the wisdom in that memorable quote by Tommy Armour, one of the few club-swinging Scots to really capitalise on the fact that he was born in the land that claims (although the Dutch might dispute it) to have invented the game.

This baker's son was, in fact, born in full view of a cemetery in Edinburgh's Balcarres Street, which skirts the vibrant shop-rich Morningside area, in a foursquare Victorian block, which must have appeared quite pristine when he entered the world on 24 September 1895. It looks a little worn at the edges today, with eight flats spread over four floors, but it could well be good for another 100 years.

And although he died in 1968, it looks as if Tommy Armour's reputation could also live on for a century or more. Already more than a half-century since the height of his fame, his name remains one of the more recognisable among golf aficionados largely because of the respected and sought-after range of golf equipment still marketed under its branding.

The resonance of the name also has much to do with the man's achievements, of course – as golfers always like to be associated with success – and the Silver Scot, as he was fondly known, registered a jaw-dropping list of these. He chalked up no fewer than twenty-five tour victories and three major championships: the 1927 US Open, the 1930 Professional Golfers' Association (PGA) Championship and the 1931 British Open (the first to be staged at Carnoustie, about seventy miles north of his birthplace – for which he returned from a new life in America). He was also made a member of the World Golf Hall of Fame, posthumously, in 1976.

But the most remarkable thing about his achievements was that he accomplished them with only one eye. How did that come about?

There was nothing too precious about golf in Scotland when he was growing up. In many places, especially near the undulating dunes and links immediately inland of the shores, it was still a game most people could participate in. There were public courses galore where youngsters could pay and play, and Tommy honed many of his skills while growing up with his full sight.

The First World War put a rude stop to his progress, however, when he was called up. After enlisting with the Black Watch, with which regiment he gained quite a reputation as a keen-eyed machine gunner, the Fettes College alumnus transferred to the Tank Corps in 1918, where he rose to staff major. In the heat of battle, however, he was blinded and badly injured in a mustard gas explosion, and surgeons had to add a metal plate to his head and left arm. During his convalescence, he regained the sight of his right eye and was understandably deeply relieved that he could – to some degree – take up his beloved game again.

But neither he nor his friends expected he could ever measure up, thereafter, to the performances of fully sighted players. Such an obvious disadvantage as having no sight in his left eye was almost certain to inhibit the development of his golfing career. But they were all surprised. While he certainly had to give himself a good deal more time to line up his shots, his game remained stunningly effective at home in Scotland after the war, and he was soon making his mark in amateur competitions, reaching the final of the Highland Open and taking second place in the Irish Open in 1919.

After winning the French Amateur the following year – the same year he married Consuelo Carrera, with whom he later had two children – Tommy decided to head for America, hoping to make his mark in the professional big-time there. It took him no time at all. On the transatlantic voyage he met the golfing legend Walter Hagen, who was returning from the British Open. By the time the two men disembarked in New York they were good friends, and Hagen soon helped the young Scotsman land a job as secretary of the Westchester-Biltmore Club in that city.

The Silver Scot went increasingly native in his adopted land. Though he represented Britain in 1921 in an informal match against an American team at Hoylake and played for Scotland against England in 1922, some four years later he was playing on the American team in a US-v.-Great Britain competition at Wentworth that some now consider to have been the 'unofficial' precursor of the Ryder Cup.

By 1926, he had become a US citizen after quickly establishing a reputation as an excellent player. But his playing career really took off in 1927, his fourth year as a professional, when he achieved seven tournament victories, including the Canadian Open and the highly prestigious US Open, in which he defeated 'Lighthorse' Harry Cooper in an eighteen-hole play-off, taking the title by three shots.

While still riding high, he went on to win the 1930 PGA and the 1931 British Open, becoming just the third golfer – after Jim Barnes and Walter Hagen – to take all three titles.

Other big wins included the 1929 Western Open (then considered a major) and two more Canadian Open titles. But things were not going so smoothly in his personal life: around this time he was going through a traumatic divorce from Consuelo Carrera to enable his marriage to Estelle Andrews, with whom he later had one son.

And painfully soon after he had registered his greatest triumphs, another trauma lay just around the corner. His putting began to let him down in the early 1930s, as he was increasingly afflicted with what he called 'the yips' – a jerky, nervous stroke – and he had a tough decision to make. Regretfully, he retired from major competitions in 1935 and decided to take up teaching full-time. This he did with considerable success, however, in Washington and New York in summer and Saratoga or Boca Raton, Florida, in the winter months.

His putting might have been his eventual downfall in competition but, having very strong hands, the Silver Scot was considered one of the finest iron players of his generation, though he himself considered his driving – to set up things nicely for the irons – was his strongest point.

When teaching, he worked not just with great golfers but with ordinary amateurs, charging some of the highest rates of the time: upwards of $50 a lesson. But many of his students appreciated his blunt Scottish style as he told them – among other things – to 'just knock hell out of it with your right hand'.

As he watched each pupil hit twenty balls, which he sharply analysed before asking for another twenty, he became almost as famous for his quotable sayings as for his golfing prowess. Example: 'Golf is an awkward set of bodily contortions designed to produce a graceful result.'

Indeed, the author Ross Goodner once recalled of him: 'At one time or another, he was known as the greatest iron player, the greatest raconteur, the greatest drinker and the greatest and most expensive teacher in golf.'

He may have been an expensive tutor, but he was a colourful, larger-than-life character who believed in giving value for money on all fronts. With his endless store of reminiscences and anecdotes told in a sharp, waspish style, he would keep students and co-players constantly entertained on the practice ground – or in the clubhouse – over the inevitable gin and tonic

He augmented his healthy income with a bit of betting, often on himself. He would challenge visiting golfers to matches for stakes of $50 or $100, and he would seldom lose.

Another lucrative sideline was the writing of best-selling how-to books. In 1953, he co-wrote *How to Play Your Best Golf All the Time* with Herb Graffis. It became a best-seller and was for many years the biggest-selling book on golf ever written. Six years later he brought out another must-read for serious golfers: *A Round of Golf with Tommy Armour.*

Both books are still widely available, and so the Silver Scot who lives on in memory has achieved another, more tangible form of immortality. His body may have gone – he died in New York on 11 September 1968 and was buried there – but his body of work lives on.

Harry Benson (1930–   )

Photographer of ten presidents

When Robert Kennedy fell to an assassin's bullet on 5 June 1968, one of the many newspaper photographers who found themselves almost literally on the spot was Harry Benson of the London *Daily Express*. Most of them seemed to seize up – 'out of respect for Bobby or something,' he recalls – but, as they were paralysed, he was galvanised. 'I thought to myself: "This is it, kid. This is what all your training and experience have been about . . . this is what you're in the business for. You can mess up tomorrow but not today, not now . . ." '

Benson's sensational monochrome pictures of the prone, dying Kennedy sprawled in his own blood swept around a shocked world, elevating the photographer in the process to global status. It mattered not that the hastily shot images were badly focused, claims Benson, suggesting that this even added to their drama, freezing the shock and confusion of the moment for posterity.

Kennedy had been on his way to the White House. He had won major primaries in Indiana, Nebraska and California. And on leaving a celebration in Los Angeles after his victory in the California primary was assured, he was shot in the back of the head at close range by the Jerusalem-born Jordanian Sirhan Sirhan, and died the following day. His gravesite in Arlington National Cemetery is near that of his brother, President John F. Kennedy.

JFK had also been photographed by Harry Benson – in rather happier circumstances – as one the many famous people to have filled the Scotsman's lens in studio conditions; and had his brother reached the Oval Office, he too would doubtless have had the pleasure of being benignly photographed by the talented man who was eventually adopted by *Life* magazine to capture memorable images of the great and the good for its readers and then, no doubt, the history books.

Happily ensconced in his favourite seaside hotel on Scotland's west coast, the cheekily handsome and smartly dressed Benson is the first to admit that representing such a highly regarded magazine, albeit

well-earned by his previous work, was his unique and enviable entrée
to the world of the rich, important and famous. And neither would
he deny that such a prestigious sponsor had given him an enviable
lifestyle, in which his first home is a luxurious apartment shared with
his Texan wife Gigi in New York's 73rd Street.

'Of course, with a name like *Life* behind you, all doors open like
magic,' he says; and indeed a roll-call of his photographic subjects
over the years sounds like a *Who's Who* of the last century . . . no fewer
than ten American presidents since Eisenhower, and many more
legendary names to conjure with such as Churchill, Beaverbrook,
Solzhenitsyn, Bobby Fischer, Norman Mailer, Dolly Parton, Liz
Taylor, Jack Nicholson, Roman Polanski and Michael Jackson. The
A-list goes on.

Regardless of how famous his subjects are, Harry Benson finds it
easy to strike up personal relationships with them. 'I'm not overawed
by anybody,' he says. 'You can't get Willie Nelson into a bathtub for
an absurd picture if you don't have a nice rapport with him.'

Perhaps it is a veteran's understanding of who makes the newsmakers
(that is, people like him) that keeps Benson singularly unimpressed
by such names, or by the things he has done. He has just had a 'big
show' in a Palm Beach museum, for instance; but big names and big
shows are his work. For pleasure, he prefers the company of old home
town buddies and returns to Scotland 'about once a week these days
to keep up old ties, eat fish and chips, and walk along the beach at
Troon, contemplating things'.

In fact, he visits about three times a year because he doesn't want
to forget the land of his birth, nor does he want it to forget him, and
often there's an exhibition in Edinburgh or a book being published in
Glasgow. Being at time of writing well into his seventies, with fifty-five
years of brilliant picture-taking behind him, perhaps he is anxious to
appreciate the basic values of human relationships after a lifetime of
looking for depth in the glittery world of celebrities. He found some
too, and with matter-of-fact acceptance that his is a trade like any
other, he now describes himself as 'a people photographer'.

The son of a curator of Glasgow Zoo ('I've always hated the caging
of animals'), he was born in the Knightswood area of the city before
being moved to Troon on the west coast 'within five days of my birth'.
His career got off to a racy start as a holiday camp photographer at
Butlin's in nearby Ayr, and the steps from there were logical if not as
rapid as the impatient and ambitious young man would have liked.

Weddings and fires are the staple stuff of local papers and it was in recording these that he learned his trade on the *Hamilton Advertiser*, Scotland's biggest weekly and once the local paper of the famous explorer of Africa, Dr David Livingstone: 'our darkroom used to be the chapel where he prayed on his way to his home at Blantyre'. About a dozen bleary-eyed night train trips to London with his portfolio finally landed him a job in the national *Daily Sketch*'s Scottish office, and that in turn provided the stepping stone to London when he was seconded for a while to its Fleet Street office.

The *Sketch* was ailing at the time, and the *Daily Express* booming. So how did he manage to change horses?

> I gatecrashed a top people's party which happened to be attended by Max Aitken [son of *Express* proprietor Lord Beaverbrook] and as I was snapping away, I heard he wanted to speak to me. I went over and introduced myself. He said he liked the way I was working, and if I gave him my number someone would call me. I did, but nothing happened. Then, about six months later, I saw him coming out of Caprice restaurant and said: 'Remember me?' He nodded and recalled my name as I added: 'I haven't heard from you'. He smiled, walked on, and said: 'You'll hear tomorrow.'

And he did. At the *Daily Express*, Benson was quickly seen to be a great photographer – and charmer – of people. So when The Beatles began their amazing transatlantic rise in the 1960s, the *Express* sent the Scot to accompany them and cover their every move. Inevitably, he became a good friend of the Fab Four and, as such, had access to many of their private moments – like their famous feathery pillow fight at the George V Hotel in Paris, of which he took some memorably happy snaps.

Benson recalls that John Lennon once even wrote a poem about him. 'Can you believe it? I just lost it. It didn't seem important at the time. I remember how it finished up – "and Harry, I want you always to have a happy Beatlebrook" – playing with the words Beatle and Beaverbrook.

> Ironically, many years down the line I found myself photographing the guy who shot and killed Lennon, Mark David Chapman, and he seemed to feel the need to apologise to me. When we met in prison he took me aside and said: 'I know he was your friend and I'd like to apologise to you for killing him.' What could I say? He seemed

genuinely sorry, but they'll never let him out. Celebrity killers are not well treated.

Like Lennon, Benson could not get America out of his blood. Like Lennon, he had chosen to stay in New York. Indeed, Benson was hooked on the place by the time the touring Beatles left him in America in 1964. 'After I'd had a few more stimulating years there, the *Express* editor told me I ought to come home and give someone else a chance, but I couldn't leave. America had been so good to me. In many ways, I'd have liked to have chosen Britain – especially Scotland – but the pull of America and its big, prestigious magazines was too strong.'

It was when he and the *Express* parted company that he started developing his contacts on such magazines, and the fact that he could eventually command thousands of dollars for a *Life* cover suggests he did so with no small degree of success.

Having now photographed every president in living memory, who is his favourite? He warns that his answer might surprise . . .

'Nixon,' he says.

Why?

Because the most interesting things happened to and around him, and they weren't all bad. They were often very good. He was strong on civil rights and opening up to China, for instance. And it's very hard in our business to dislike somebody who just allows you to do your job. I mean, if he had stepped out of line I'd have zapped him – and I did; some of my shots of him were not so flattering; but he was kind to me and helped my career a lot.

I was the only journalist allowed on the plane with him to San Clemente after his resignation and I spent a couple of days there with him. This was not the best time of his life. He was deeply humiliated. I was photographing him for *Life* and thanked him very much for giving me his time and patience under such trying circumstances. He just smiled wryly and said: 'Well, Harry, you've got to allow professional people the chance to do their job' – which was a very nice thing to say.

And his other favourites?

I found George W. Bush a good guy too. I was photographing him swinging a golf club outside the governor's mansion when he was running for president. I told him I'd become an American citizen and he just shrugged. But then it seemed to dawn on him. He pointed his club at me and said: 'That means you can vote, Harry . . . and I'm asking for your vote.'

It's very personal, as you'd imagine, when a presidential candidate asks you for your vote. But I said: 'Well, Governor, I'll see how it goes today.' And he laughed. We got along like a house on fire. But in general I don't really get too close to my subjects. I wouldn't say I was a friend, as such, because they might step out of line, and where would you be then as an objective journalist?

Often I don't pick up a phone after I've done a job because I don't want some big star saying to me, 'Hey, Harry, that picture of me in the bath, please don't use it . . .' I don't want to have to choose between my best shot and my new best friend.

Has he ever had a political influence on any of his famous sitters? He laughs:

I would hate to think so . . . I would hate to think that a little pipsqueak from Glasgow would have any say in world events. But I did discuss the war on drugs with Nixon – he was the strongest advocate of that – and also with Nancy Reagan. I told her I'd been to a few parties with famous movie stars and that they'd all been sniffing cocaine. She wasn't surprised. Disappointed maybe, but she wasn't naïve. She knew what went on.

Not surprisingly, Benson found the Reagans, as two former film stars, easy and professional in front of the camera:

I took them kissing each other for *Vanity Fair*. They were terrific – polite, and knew exactly what to do; and Nancy was quite the opposite of the painted doll everybody thought she was. She combed her own hair and came on the set with no make-up at all.

And Ronald Reagan used to tell funny stories. There's nothing worse than some big shot telling you a story that isn't funny and you have to laugh. But his were genuinely funny stories, not patronising jokes.

You get amusing moments too. Take John Kerry, who was the Democrats' presidential candidate at the time I photographed him. This guy with the war-hero image wanted to be captured for posterity looking macho on his sparkling new Harley-Davidson. But I'd taken only about five shots when it started to rain and he started complaining: 'Oh, I'm getting wet . . . I'm getting wet . . . we can't go on anymore'.

His aides said I should follow him to his next stop, where he was meeting senior citizens indoors, but I said no, I wasn't interested in senior citizens, and in any case the few shots I'd taken turned out fine.

Next thing I know I'm going though airport security and my cellphone rings. It's Kerry himself – phoning to apologise for looking such a wimp, afraid of a little rain. He could laugh at himself at least, and I thought that was OK, and it was nice that he called personally.

We journalists do rub shoulders with famous – and infamous – folk. Almost literally. I mean, take Sirhan Sirhan, who killed Bobby Kennedy. I was standing right next to him when he did it. Sometimes when you tell these things it sounds like you're really bullshitting, but they are all truths . . . just part of the job.

Though he has lately used the 'people photographer' label for convenience, Harry Benson doesn't like to be pigeon-holed. He points out that he has also done 'starvation in the Ogaden, the IRA on manoeuvres, Russian prisoners-of-war in Afghanistan, the Iraq war, and lots of stuff like that, because I'm also a photo-journalist'.

It is vital, he says, for a good photographer to be multi-dimensional.

I'll do high fashion for French *Vogue* as soon as anything else. Some photographers are caught off-base if they have to work outside their strengths. You shouldn't stay just in your most comfortable area. You've got to come out and work on your weak sides, too . . . keep challenging yourself. But in the end, all I want is a good picture.

The last comment sums up Harry Benson precisely. Despite his place in American photographic history and his obviously ambivalent feelings about home – is it Scotland or New York? – he is essentially an uncomplicated, hard-working picture-taker. From his wallet he produces a print of his latest famous subject and shows it with almost boyish pride. Yes, it's a good picture, you concede; and he's happy, if a little puzzled, about how he can get along so well without the artist's mystique.

But his Scottish west-coast humour defines his sense of perspective. 'My last book was rather unpretentious,' he says with a small laugh. 'I think I'll try to make the next one pretentious.'

And his final laugh is explosive: 'As I've said hundreds of times, I don't know what I'd have done if I'd had to work for a living.'

Hugh Grant (1958–)

Controversial GM crops boss

Love them or loathe them, there is no doubt that genetically modified (GM) crops can induce strong feelings in people. But however much he might be demonised by those who dislike his company's raison d'être, Hugh Grant – not the film star – is anything but satanic and often reveals to those who meet him a surprisingly sincere interest in agriculture and its possibilities.

Perhaps that should not be so surprising, given his background and education. The gentlemanly president, chairman and chief executive of the controversial Monsanto company was born in 1958, in Larkhall, fifteen miles south-east of Glasgow, right on the edge of the picturesque Clyde Valley where – in his words – 'coal and steel stopped and dairy farms began'. He earned a bachelor of science degree in agricultural zoology with honours at Glasgow University before going on to take a postgraduate degree in agriculture at Edinburgh University and a master's in business administration in England.

He now lives in St Louis, Missouri, which is also home to the headquarters of his company, which employs 15,000 people and records revenues of $5 billion. But as he travels the world from there – explaining the benefits of GM crops, as he sees them, to farmers from South Africa to China – Scotland remains his anchor. He comes 'home' regularly to visit friends and relatives; he is an international advisory board member of Scottish Enterprise; and he still speaks with a soft Scottish accent of which he is clearly quite proud. 'He is very measured and very careful,' says an acquaintance, 'but he is still very much a Scot.'

It is ironic, however, that the land of his birth – Britain, if not Scotland – has given one of the world's most hostile receptions to Monsanto's cause.

Those on his side believe that, as the earth's 6 billion population will double in fifty years, GM foods will help increase food production in the same given cultivation area. And genetic engineering can create plants that are resistant or tolerant to 'danger' factors such as disease, cold, insects, drought and even weed-killer. It can also change a crop's properties, reducing growing time, adding nutrients, making better taste.

But opponents have many concerns – the first being environmental. They argue that GM foods can cause harm to other organisms unintentionally and that in reality they will largely be used to feed the power and profits of agri-food corporations rather than alleviate Third World hunger.

Not that the lurid 'Frankenstein Food' headlines faze Hugh Grant. He is a patient man who is in it for the long game and said, in a *Financial Times* interview with Stefan Stern:

> You have to keep going. I don't like it much, but what I've learned is that you can't get too discouraged by some of the rogue headlines.
>
> There's the headline, and then you go to the letters page. It's changing. Seven years ago it was 'absolutely not'. Today, if you go to the letters page, there's a discussion . . .
>
> Companies like mine are in the process of learning to speak a language that people understand. I think that's more than high theory – I think that's how this is evolving.

Hugh Grant joined the company in 1981 as a product development representative in Scotland, and spent the first ten years there in a variety of European sales, product development and management roles. Being keen to see the world, he needed little persuasion to relocate in 1991 to St Louis as global strategy director of the agriculture division. In 1995, he was named Monsanto's managing director for the Asia-Pacific region, with responsibility for the company's agriculture, nutrition and pharmaceutical businesses in South-east Asia.

A succession of bigger executive jobs followed and each seemed increasingly to suit his instincts and education: in 1998 he was named co-president of the company's agriculture division, in which role he jointly oversaw global business operations and led the business and product strategy. As co-president, he reported to the president of Monsanto and was responsible for the operational and commercial performance of all agriculture division business units and brands worldwide.

In 2000, he became an executive vice president, and not long after that he was entrusted with the very top job. But he is not one to ensconce himself behind a gigantic desk and issue orders from there. As a lad he grew up on the edge of rural Scotland and learned to appreciate the joys of fresh air. So he likes to be on the road – the world's highways and airways anyway – spreading his message to all who will listen.

He may or may not win the argument, but he will have enjoyed himself trying.

'There were two passions for me,' he told the *FT*, with reference to his early life. 'I was really intrigued by the idea of getting the chance to work outside, rather than being chained to a desk – a bit naïve, maybe – and the other was the chance to travel, to see the other parts of the world. I've been very lucky. Agriculture is a global industry and it happens outside.'

The Scottish Influence

Some Scots have impacted on America and its culture without actually living there. Here are a few of them . . .

Alexander Selkirk (1676–1723)

The original Robinson Crusoe

Just how indelibly the romantic tale of Robinson Crusoe has imprinted itself on the American imagination was illustrated by the modern movie version – *Castaway* – which updated Daniel Defoe's much-loved 1719 classic through the acting talent of Tom Hanks, playing a Fed-Ex engineer marooned after a plane crash en route to Malaysia.

We all dream of such a telling experience – of being left alone on a desert island with only our initiative to keep us alive – and wonder how we would fare if stripped of our layers of civilisation. Hanks' Chuck Noland almost loses his mind but survives for four years by spearing fish, extracting his own teeth, treasuring a picture of his girlfriend, creating a buddy called Wilson from a volleyball and lashing together a rough getaway raft.

It was not so different in the early eighteenth century when such an experience really happened, not to a fictional Robinson Crusoe, but to a real person: Alexander Selkirk, a sailor from the little Fife coastal town of Lower Largo on the north bank of the Forth estuary.

His story was every bit as exciting as the Crusoe one – which was probably based on his experiences after an assumed (but unrecorded) meeting between him and author Defoe – but there were some essential differences. Whereas Crusoe's story had the hero being shipwrecked, adopting a native servant as Man Friday and living for twenty-eight years on his tropical island, Selkirk's experience was shorter and sharper. He actually asked to be let off his ailing ship when she came upon the island of Juan Fernandez 400 miles west of Chile; and he lived there without human company for four and a half years before being rescued.

Perhaps the most convincing parallels between the two versions, which fuse in the mind's cinema screen, are the identical visual impressions of the fictional and real heroes at their moments of salvation. As described by his shocked rescuers, Selkirk's coat and cap of many goatskins, which had replaced his worn-out conventional clothes, surely provided the model for Crusoe's famous ragged image. And indeed, any uninformed visitor studying the handsome bronze statue of Selkirk above the door of the house in Lower Largo, Fife, that replaced his original family home, would immediately say: 'Crusoe!' It's an impression the town does nothing to discourage, keen as it is to attract tourists; so its biggest hostelry is called The Crusoe Hotel and local shops sell booklets with titles like *Crusoe's Village*.

The plate under the heroic Selkirk statue, created by Stuart Burnett of Edinburgh, reads:

> In memory of Alexander Selkirk, mariner, the original of Robinson Crusoe, who lived on the island of Juan Fernandez in complete solitude for four years and four months. He died 1723, leiutenant [sic] of HMS *Weymouth*, aged 47 years. This statue is erected by David Gillies, net manufacturer, on the site of the cottage in which Selkirk was born.

Holding a musket in his left hand, the bronze Selkirk has raised his right to shade his eyes while apparently searching for a ship on the far horizon. It is an impressive piece of work and a fine posthumous honour. Indeed, there was another that faded away with the demise of the famous sailor's last relatives to be resident in the town in the 1990s. The Jardine family gathered as many Selkirk-related artefacts as they could to create a little museum in the town – for which this writer was once asked to trace the sailor's gun. After a month on the telephone, a battered-looking claimant for the title – with the words 'Alexander Selkirk' burned into its butt – turned up in the attic of a private home in Ely, Cambridgeshire, and was duly bought and proudly returned to Scotland.

But the town was not always so proud of its famous son . . .

Born in 1676 the seventh son of local shoemaker John Selkirk, Alexander was often in trouble with the girls and the Church and, after a particularly unruly episode, was summoned to give an account of his behaviour to the Kirk Session in 1695 – but made his getaway to sea before the case came up.

He was to have a very different impact on the Kirk when he returned some seventeen years later after making his fortune.

But first, he had to endure a few episodes of less good fortune. Having taken to mathematics at school, he became an accomplished navigator and made several relatively uneventful journeys before joining the sixteen-gun *Cinque Ports* galley in 1703 as sailing master on a privateering venture to attack Spanish shipping and possessions in the New World. Commanded by William Dampier, the famous buccaneer, navigator and man of science sailing in the *St George*, the expedition had more than its share of bad luck as opportunities for taking plunder were missed or bungled and crew members fell out.

When the *Cinque Ports* parted company from the *St George* off Panama in 1704, Selkirk, now second-in-command of the former, was not seeing eye-to-eye with her new captain, Thomas Stradling, particularly about the condition of the worm-eaten ship with its ragged sails. Frustrated by the captain's lack of action on these points, the Scot opted to be abandoned on Juan Fernandez rather than stay on a ship he considered too rotten to float much longer.

Despite that, watching her depart he had severe second thoughts as he sat on the beach among his few possessions – a sea chest with clothing and bedding, a gun, a pound of gunpowder, ammunition, a flint and steel, a few pounds of tobacco, a hatchet, a knife, a kettle, a Bible, navigation books and mathematical instruments. Suddenly, he ran into the sea, calling after her, but she sailed on, ignoring him. And just as well, for the *Cinque Ports* did sink, just off Peru, with loss of most of her crew, although Stradling and seven others survived to be jailed in Lima for seven years – so no word got out that Selkirk was on the island.

He had been left there with enough food for two meals, and while that was initially alarming, he was relieved to find that the seventeen-mile-long, seven-mile-wide island was inhabited by goats and cats left by some previous (probably Spanish) visitors. He befriended both – and even danced with the easily tamed goat kids – though he sometimes had trouble catching the larger goats, which would supply him with the occasional stew.

There were also hundreds of rats to contend with, which added to his sense of challenge as he kept a fire burning on a high hill in the hope of being spotted by a passing ship. For the first eight months he had to bear up against a gnawing melancholy, and fear of being alone in such a desolate place. He built two huts with pimento trees, covered them with long grass, lined them with goatskins, and gradually began to feel at home. Juan Fernandez certainly had its compensations. The climate was fine, there was plenty of fresh water, fruit, cabbages, herbs, crayfish, goat meat and milk; and as he began to accept that he was not going to be rescued quickly, he resigned himself to appreciating the quality of his life and surroundings.

He acquired another piece of real estate – a cave in a nearby hillside – and his constant traversing of the island maintaining his 'properties' and searching for sustenance and sails on the horizon certainly kept him fit. And just as he began to enjoy his good health and his solitude, he saw sails – Spanish ones – twice. But he found himself running away from them, on one occasion even hiding up a tree. He did not want to reveal himself as he had heard of the inquisition methods of the Spanish. And he was not even sure if he could speak English now, far less Spanish. Indeed, when he was eventually rescued in February 1709, his lack of speaking ability was only one of the impressions that shocked his saviours.

Selkirk was taken on board by two Bristol privateers, the *Duke* and *Duchess*, under the command of Captain Woodes Rogers, who later wrote about the rescue in *A Cruising Voyage Round the World* (1712):

> Immediately our Pinnace return'd from the shore, and brought abundance of Craw-fish, with a Man cloth'd in Goat-Skins, who look'd wilder than the first Owners of them. He had been on the Island four Years and four Months, being left there by Capt. Stradling in the *Cinque-Ports*; his Name was Alexander Selkirk a Scotch Man, who had been Master of the *Cinque-Ports*, a Ship that came here last with Capt. Dampier, who told me that this was the best Man in her; so I immediately agreed with him to be a Mate on board our Ship.

Being taken on as a mate – and later put in command of one of Woodes Rogers' captured vessels – was a fortunate turn of events for Selkirk, who had to thank his lucky stars for the coincidence that Captain Dampier had recognised him through his weird and wonderful outfit – about which Woodes Rogers wrote:

> When his clothes were worn out he made himself a coat and a cap of goat skins, which he stitched together with little thongs of the same, that he cut with his knife. He had no other needle but a nail; and when his knife was worn to the back he made others, as well as he could, of some iron hoops that were left ashore, which he beat thin and ground upon stones. Having some linen cloth by him, he sewed him some shirts with a nail, and stitched them with the worsted of his old stockings, which he pulled out on purpose. He had his last shirt on when we found him on the island.

Such clothes were in stark contrast to the finery that he wore on a visit to Lower Largo after he returned to Britain a rich man in 1711. The Woodes Rogers expedition had been a great success and his share of the booty was £800 (about $100,000 today). It is said that he arrived in the town while the kirk service was in progress on a Sunday morning. He threw open its doors and heads turned and gasped to see the richly dressed prodigal standing in the aisle. As his parents and the rest of the congregation rushed up to greet him, the minister had to abandon the service.

It would be nice to end the story there, but its real conclusion is less happy. The truth was, Selkirk missed Juan Fernandez (now renamed Robinson Crusoe Island) and in Largo, he took to finding spots above the town where, overlooking the River Forth, he could sit and remind himself of life on his island. His love life became messy, too, as he ran off to London – and the Navy – with local girl Sofia Bruce in tow. Whether or not he married her was unknown and became a moot point after he definitely married another, English woman, Frances Candish, and made out a will in her favour.

For his first voyage as mate on HMS *Weymouth* was his last. Along with many other crew members, he died of yellow fever while sailing off the Gold Coast in December, 1721.

Sofia, the modest girl from his home town, lost the bitter battle over his considerable estate.

William Cullen (1710–90)

Creator of cold comfort

Scots are not normally shy about trumpeting their inventive achievements – 'Wha's like us?' is their not-so-tongue-in-cheek war cry – and while this might not always be an attractive trait, they can often reclaim a listener's affection by being self-deprecating about their lack of aptitude in other fields. This is historically evident in the way they can make significant breakthroughs then see the amusing side of not knowing quite what to do with them. Which is why they have often had to bow to America's conspicuous flair for taking an idea and running with it – developing a product so that it becomes not just marketable but an object of desire for consumers all over the world.

One such case in point is the refrigerator. Necessity being the mother of invention (most of the time), it would always have been hard to imagine that, in a small northern country as cold as Scotland, there would be much demand for the cooling of food and drink.

In hot countries, before the invention of refrigeration, the idea of artificial intervention to keep perishable food relatively fresh – and drinkable liquid more refreshing – had been around for millennia, despite absence of the ideal technology required to achieve best results. Various methods of drying, smoking, salting, pickling, heating, and icing were employed to preserve edibility, and the chill factor first found its place in caves before gradually moving, along with human ingenuity, from the cold depths of rivers, lakes, streams, or wells to cellars, snow holes, specially dug pits, outdoor window boxes, underground store-rooms lined with wood or straw and packed with snow and ice.

As far back as 1000 BC, the value of coldness in preserving food was recognised by the Chinese, who knew how to cut and store ice, while ancient Egyptians stayed cool by putting earthen jars full of boiled water out in the cold open air overnight. The more privileged people of Cairo also used their camel postal system to transport snow all the way from the Lebanese Mountains.

By similarly gathering ice or snow from their own mountains, first-century Romans cooled their drinks much as we do today; and in more recent times, the empire-building British would send tons of Norwegian ice 8,000 miles around the Cape of Good Hope to India and other UK charges, while the shipping of ice from America to tropical climes was undertaken by America's 'ice king', New Englander Frederick Tudor.

The obvious disadvantage with all these exercises was the fact that, due to melting or evaporation, the receivers always ended up with a good deal less than the dispatchers started with. While Tudor managed, through experiments with insulating materials, to build ice-houses that reduced in-storage melting from 66 per cent to less than 8 per cent, it might have been reasonable to expect a cool solution from a hot country.

It has to be something of an irony, therefore, that the first artificial refrigeration (cooling air by the evaporation of liquids in a vacuum) was invented by a shivering Scot as long ago as 1748. William Cullen got successful results at the University of Glasgow by letting ethyl ether boil into a partial vacuum, but – given the geographic factor – it was almost forgivable that in this case he did not develop the result into any practical purpose.

Indeed, while today's internet references (generally sourced from other countries) invariably credit him with the invention of refrigeration, Glasgow's own Mitchell Library can find little or nothing in terms of book references that place their man emphatically in that context.

Be that as it may, after Cullen's invention, it was left to a succession of clever people from various nations to apply the principle to commercial and domestic use. While the English physicist Michael Faraday liquefied ammonia to cause cooling in 1823 – leading to the development of compressors, changing gas to liquid – and the American inventor Oliver Evans designed the first refrigeration machine that used vapour instead of liquid in 1805, it was another Scot who, more than a century after Cullen's breakthrough, introduced vapour-compression refrigeration to the brewing and meat-packing industries.

Soon after moving from Glasgow to Australia in 1837, an overheated journalist called James Harrison felt compelled to set about designing his own refrigeration machine, and by 1855 he had succeeded in creating and patenting an ether liquid-vapour compression fridge.

To be fair, he was not being particularly indulgent or prescient about the current Oz enthusiasm for cold beer (and food) but he did have that country's long-term interests at heart: he realised that the export-marketing of her abundant livestock to, say, Europe would be practically impossible without large-scale shipboard refrigeration to survive the boiling equator. Unfortunately, he bankrupted himself trying to prove it, after setting up a shipment to London that was ruined because of a leak from the cooling chemical tanks. His bold move was not in vain, however. As other successful exporting voyages followed, it could be said that Harrison won the consolation prize of credit for opening the door to Australia's economic salvation.

In the meantime, icy developments had been going on apace elsewhere. In 1834, the first cumbersome refrigerating machine, using ether in a vapour compression cycle, was built by American inventor Jacob Perkins. In 1844, American physician John Gorrie built a refrigerator based on Oliver Evans' design to make ice to cool the air for his yellow fever patients. In 1876, German engineer Carl von Linden patented not a refrigerator but the process of liquefying gas that is part of basic refrigeration technology. And in 1879 and 1891 improved refrigeration designs were patented by the African-American inventors Thomas Elkins and John Standard.

It was about this time that nature stepped in with a timely push. Shortages of natural ice – which would normally be used in people's basic iceboxes that depended on simple insulation – were created by super-warm American winters in 1889 and 1890. And it wasn't just a domestic problem. Food shops and industries that were not equipped with large, albeit primitive, refrigerators to freeze and store fish, dairy products and meat just had to stand and watch their produce go bad. The imperative to develop and market the domestic refrigerator was now as clear as day, and by the early 1900s they had started to appear: basic wooden cabinets with water-cooled compressors.

Two American corporate giants took the lead. General Electric and General Motors were the early innovators, the first releasing a home refrigerator designed by a French monk in 1911, the second introducing in 1915 the first Guardian refrigerator, which was a predecessor of the famous Frigidaire.

In 1923, Frigidaire introduced the first self-contained units. Britain got its first batch of these in 1924, and the march of the fridge was halted only briefly by the consequences of their having used the toxic gases ammonia, methyl chloride and sulphur dioxide, the leaks of which caused several accidental deaths up to 1929. Thereafter, compressor fridges generally used Freon – a trade name describing a whole class of chemicals known as chlorofluorocarbons – with relatively minimal health risks. Soon, the production line was rolling again, and Frigidaire, GM's brand, went on to sell 50 million units by 1965. Nowadays the fridge is one of the world's most common domestic appliances – to be found in 99 per cent of North American and European homes.

If by some miracle William Cullen were to make his way back to today's world for an iced tea, would he be happy to take the credit for this? Probably not. He was a charming man by all accounts, and not a seeker of fame.

Yet even he would have to admit that, while he had never come closer to America than a couple of trips to the West Indies as a ship's surgeon, he had some influence on it, and not only through refrigeration.

William Cullen was essentially a medical man, though he developed a keen interest in chemistry. Born in Hamilton, Lanarkshire, in 1710, he went from the local grammar school to the University of Glasgow – where he was later to make his name in the world of science. His early medical training and experience included apprenticeship in Glasgow, service as a ship's surgeon, a period as assistant to an apothecary in London, and general medical practice in Scotland.

In 1744, after marrying minister's daughter Anna Johnstone, with whom he was to have seven sons and four daughters, he moved to Edinburgh University. Everywhere he went, his verbal skills were admired. His contributions to medicine and his widely used textbooks earned him an international reputation. He was elected a Fellow of the Royal Society of London in 1777.

His single published paper relating to chemistry was 'Of the Cold produced by Evaporating Fluids, and of Some Other Means of Producing Cold', which prompted Alexander Fleck, a former director of ICI, to say: 'His contributions do not seem to have been effective in causing improvements in practice.'

But Cullen's lively personality, rich imagination and compelling delivery as a teacher were legendary, attracting great attention and attendances from the student body. Advertised enthusiastically by word of mouth, his classes in Edinburgh grew rapidly from 17 students to 145. And the word even crossed the Atlantic. During his eleven years as professor of chemistry, the charismatic and articulate

William Cullen had forty American students, many of whom in turn sent their own promising students to Edinburgh in later years. Warm and welcoming to them all, he became something of an idol among two generations.

Could that be why, despite Scotland being unusually shy to make claims for a son of some achievement, he is generously given credit for inventing the cooling system that makes a Coca Cola taste so good on a hot summer's day?

In any case, he died on 5 February 1790 at his country home at Kirknewton in Midlothian, probably quite unsuspecting of the fact that his casual little experiment in 1748 would one day help to change the world and the operation of its food and drink supply lines.

James Small (1740–93)

Inventor of the swing plough

In today's world, so diverted as it is with personal advantage and profit, it is hard to imagine such a truly altruistic man as James Small, carpenter and ploughwright of the Scottish Borders, who seems to have been limitlessly ingenious as an inventor yet happy to remain relatively unsung and largely unrewarded for the huge advance he brought to the world through his inspired development of the swing plough in 1765.

His unique design revolutionised the face of agriculture for ever, and not just within his own environment and community. Often feeling that he was too shy for the good of his own reputation, no member of the latter has ever been, to this day, similarly reticent about making one specific and gigantic claim for Small's invention on his behalf – that it enabled the great prairies of America and Canada to become 'the breadbaskets of the world'.

But we don't even know what the man looked like. Seeking out his image today, his most ardent admirer would fail to find one; for even in his own land there is no painting, statue or commemorative plaque – though there are illustrations aplenty of his brainchild, which was the result of much thought, application and perseverance.

How did he go about realising it? From his birthplace in Dalkeith, a small town just south of Edinburgh, Small went to England to study various plough designs that were finding favour – or not – and took careful note of his observations before returning to Scotland, to Blackadder Mount in Berwickshire, in readiness to make the first-ever attempt at the development of a plough on a scientific basis. After many days and nights of candle-burning at both ends, he was satisfied with his design for the iron swing (or wheelless) plough – intended to replace the old Scotch plough of James Anderson of Hermiston, which itself had been a huge improvement on Scotland's previous labour-intensive, cumbersome and mainly wooden model that required up to twelve oxen. That unlamented affair often broke down, and while needing several people to operate it – one guide, one to keep it from getting choked with roots and stones, and another to 'whip' on the team – failed even to turn neat furrows.

As bad as that machine was, Small felt he had developed something good to the same degree. When he was ready, in a moment of high excitement, he took his concept to the recently opened Carron Iron Works in Falkirk to be cast and transformed into reality. It was an anxious time for him. Would the resulting metal contraption perform its intended purpose or would its theory prove to have been more promising than its practical application? He need not have worried. After exhaustive testing in the field – literally – his two-horse plough was hailed an immediate success, a dramatic improvement on its predecessor. And soon the neighbourhood – and the entire country – got to know of its effectiveness, not least its ability to carve clean, clear furrows of turned earth with a fraction of the energy that had once been required.

By 1780 James Small found himself turning out 500 of his ploughs per year for his customers – and turning a blind eye to the increasing number of blacksmiths and foundries that had quickly started mass-producing and adapting with impunity his basic design to suit *their* customers' particular requirements.

Soon, emigrating farmers were taking the Small-style machines with them to America, or having them built on arrival, and all the while the inventor took – rather than monetary profit – a quiet, private satisfaction from seeing how his invention swept the prairies to the general benefit of the world.

Not only had it made life easier for the farmer, it had thereby helped to combat humankind's most ancient enemy, hunger. Consequently, he rejected any entreaties to patent his design. And thus overworked and underpaid, James Small died a poor man, at sixty-three, in 1793. It may be hard to understand today, but it is also said that he died a happy man.

John McAdam (1756–1836)

Roadbuilder extraordinary

He was neither a dirty-fingernailed builder nor a grand engineer in the accepted sense, but John Louden McAdam was certainly a frequent coach passenger whose shoulders had been well and truly shaken. Such rough riding had presumably irritated him to the point of distraction before he got out his quill, his candles and his resolve to do something about it. The result was a significant contribution to making the world move more rapidly and smoothly than it had before he addressed the annoying impact of mud-puddled holes, stone bumps, wheel-breaking cracks, collapsing edges, unpredictable cambers and all the other drawbacks of tracks and carriageways that had grown organically over the years.

Borrowing some ideas from the ancient Romans, he came up with a new process for road-building, with three graded layers of broken and crushed rock and gravel which would, with the passage of time and traffic, firm into a smooth, hard surface considerably more durable and less hazardous than the usual composite of stones with compressed dirt and mud. Slightly convex surfaces saw that rainwater would effectively drain away, making his roads dryer and less rutted than those they replaced. It was a commonsense solution that proved to be a welcome and remarkably enduring one.

Indeed, McAdam's principles of road-making are still used on many of the world's highways today, and the system's success has elevated the Scot's name to the point that the highly adventurous word 'macadamization' has entered the (American) English language without apology.

John McAdam was born in Ayr, south-west Scotland, in 1756 and emigrated to America as a young man in 1770 after his father died, immediately entering the financial world of New York in the counting house of a merchant uncle. The plan was that he would stay and prosper as a merchant too but, while he initially managed to do the latter to an impressive degree, his failure to support the Revolution put the seal on the eager Tory's budding American career. After the war he was no longer welcome in the now-United States and he returned to Scotland in 1783, with his American wife Gloriana and their two children.

Having been metaphorically shown the road from that side of the Atlantic, John McAdam was not to know then that there would be a rich irony in the manner of his making his presence felt for the second time in the United States – the showing of his road-making system before its adoption by the people who had happily seen the back of him.

Despite much of his property and assets having been confiscated by the new American government, the still-young McAdam had sailed back to Ayrshire with a considerable fortune after little more than a dozen lucrative years away, and he soon purchased a fine estate near Maybole. It was there and then that his interest in road-making was truly sparked, for the estate's roads were rather less fine, as were its adjoining and nearby public roads.

Though wealthy enough to feel unobliged to bother with such apparently mundane matters, he determined to do something about them. He became a local road trustee, then – not content simply to register that the district's road network was in poor condition – applied his own agile brainpower to them. Then he put his hand in his purse to set up a series of road-making experiments at his own expense; not least among these being the first 'macadamized' road – on his Sauchie estate – which is still in use today.

Having thus learned a few things about effective road-surfacing techniques – and feeling his experiments were promising success – he became more ambitious and began looking to spread his ideas to improve the notoriously bad roads of the entire British Isles. His first step was a move to Falmouth in the southernmost county of Cornwall, where he continued his experiments as a government appointee. Then in 1806, with his subsequent appointment as paving commissioner in the western port of Bristol, he had a chance to really put his theories into practice, appalled as he was by the condition of the roads he oversaw.

He developed an inexpensive technique for implementing the new surfacing system and wrote two treatises documenting his work, *Remarks on the Present System of Road-Making* (1816) and *Practical Essay on the Scientific Repair and Preservation of Roads* (1819). Also responsible for reforms in road administration and adviser to many turnpike trusts, he ensured that public roads became the government's responsibility, financed out of taxes. His impressive efforts did not go unappreciated. In 1820 parliament awarded him £2,000, and in further recognition of his work, he was put in charge of all British highways as Surveyor-General of Metropolitan Roads in 1827. The consequent 'macadamization' of the country's roads did a great deal to improve travel and communication, and soon his road-paving methods were not only ubiquitous throughout his own land, they were adopted by almost all the major European countries – where coverage was almost 90 per cent – and by the USA.

America's first McAdam surface appeared on the Boonsborough Turnpike Road between Hagerstown and Boonsboro, Maryland, in the early 1820s; the second was laid in 1830 on the seventy-three-mile National Pike (or Cumberland Road); and soon 'tarmacadam roads' became standard, used on a massive mileage of highways and lesser roads all across the land.

So his system had well and truly taken root in America by the time John McAdam was struck down by a heart attack in 1836 on a visit to his Scottish boyhood haunts at Moffat in Dumfriesshire. He was eighty years old and, having put so much into his mission, he had worn out his health and his wealth. Though he died a poor man – but 'at least an honest one', he said shortly before his death – he was unquestionably rich in achievements acknowledged the world over.

And although 'macadamization' was replaced by more modern techniques in the early 1900s, his name lives on – mainly in the affectionate form of 'tarmacadam', shortened to 'tarmac'.

Robert Burns (1759–96)

The immortal poetic memory

When you consider how his name and work have travelled and grown in global celebration over the centuries, it fairly makes a Scot's fingers tingle to touch the tiny recessed bed in which Robert Burns was born in a modest thatched cottage – to a 'blast o' Janwar win'' – on the twenty-fifth of that first month of the year 1759.

How could his humble parents, William and Agnes Burnes, ever have expected that, nearly two and a half centuries after it, the birth of their first son in the rural hamlet of Alloway in Ayrshire would be annually hailed all over the world; that in a creative span of twenty-two years he would have composed 28,000 lines of verse and restored a huge body of Scotland's dying folk-song heritage; and that, by his death thirty-seven years later, he would have become Scotland's best-loved, most respected poet ever – apparently to remain so in perpetuity?

For some, it can be puzzling that Burns' poetry, which works best euphonically in the rhythmic roughage of an archaic country dialect that even Scots can strive to grasp today, has been such a successful export. So much so that countries like Russia and Romania have produced postage stamps in his honour; that the new year is greeted in scores of lands by the singing of his 'Auld Lang Syne' lyrics; that his 'immortal memory' is toasted not just at annual Burns suppers wherever Scots blood flows, but also by non-Scots in hugely important arenas – such as the United Nations. There, in 2003, 300 international guests heard Secretary-General Kofi Annan deliver the inaugural Robert Burns Memorial Lecture on the theme of the brotherhood of man. Speaking movingly of anti-Semitism, lslamophobia and racism in general, he quoted the key lines from the poet's 'A Man's a Man for a' That' as the touchstone of his address: 'That man to man the world o'er, shall brothers be for a' that.'

Such fame! And so deserved – for such soaring thoughts so well expressed despite their vehicle being the poet's local tongue; or perhaps because of. Is it this very closeness to his humble roots that seems to speak to people so eloquently? In any event, and perhaps in any tongue, his craftsman's lyrical skill would surely make his work an emotional delight.

His spontaneous surrender to a picture, a thought or a moment was also uniquely appealing. An inspired Burns would write wherever he found himself – at candle-lit desks, of course, but also on horseback, on country walks, or in inns where he was known to scratch his tumbling words on walls or windows. One such etched glass pane, from the Cross Keys Inn in the central town of Falkirk, is now preserved in the Victorian museum that sits beside his birth cottage. It begins: 'Sound be his sleep and blythe his morn / That never did a lassie wrang.'

Also among the museum's many fascinating exhibits relevant to the poet's work and life (including some original manuscripts) is a tiny leather 'travelling companion', holding a set of quill nibs, a knife and an ink bottle, which he presumably carried at all times. So why he did he have to scratch on glass? Was it writing surfaces he lacked when his inspirations came?

And of inspirations he was never short. He could be as angry as he could be sensuously gentle. When not puncturing lordly pomposity, he would be responding to the joys and tribulations of life and nature, from animal and human foibles through the 'fresh and fair' blooming of a riverbank, to the 'fond kiss' of a lover.

And neither was he short of lovers among the ranks of what he called 'rapture-giving Woman'. The handsome Burns could see the funny side of sex, as expressed in this mock epitaph to a wild friend in the town of Mauchline . . .

> Lament him, Mauchline husbands a'
> He often did assist ye;
> For had ye staid awa',
> Your wives they ne'er had missed ye!
>
> Ye Mauchline bairns, as on ye pass
> To school in bands thegither,
> O, tread ye lightly on his grass
> Perhaps he was your father!

But pursuit of females was a most serious enthusiasm for him – the father of eight illegitimate children – and love found him in a wide variety of ways, according to whims of his objects of desire. Apart from his loyal wife Jean Armour, the 'jewel' of 'The Belles of Mauchline' with whom he had four offspring, his many amorous adventures included, to list only the most notable: Nelly Kilpatrick, his harvest-field co-worker who first moved him to verse; the mystery of 'E'; Peggy Chalmers, who cast him aside; Clarinda, who never succumbed to him despite their intense love-letter romance; Maria Riddell, whose charms included intellectual challenge; and . . .

Perhaps the most piquant of his extramarital loves was Mary Campbell, with whom he fell in love in 1786, just before his career as a poet took off. With her, his life could have taken a completely different course and the world might have been deprived of his fabulous contribution. That year, pursued by creditors and the angry family of the pregnant Jean, he had accepted a position as a bookkeeper in Jamaica and 'Highland Mary', having agreed to go with him, went to the port of Greenock to await him while he set about raising the nine-guinea fare.

But she was to wait in vain, for his desperate attempt to do that – through publishing some of his stocked-up young man's poetry – was stunningly successful. The Kilmarnock Edition of his *Poems, chiefly in the Scottish Dialect* was an instant success, receiving reviews like this from the *New London Magazine*: 'We do not recollect to have ever met with a more signal instance of true and uncultivated genius.'

No one was more surprised than Burns himself. The praise echoed throughout the country and especially in Scotland's refined capital, where the name of the 'ploughman poet' was soon spoken with awe. Never had there been such a dramatic transformation of a penniless, reviled womaniser into a celebrated son of a diminished, post-Union Scotland that had been longing for an unapologetic champion of its identity and language. The young farmer with little formal education but a poetic gift of passion, wit and power was fêted and called by popular request to Edinburgh.

On arrival, he was greatly in demand to be the focus of fashionable parties and – though he sometimes feigned resentment of this, comparing himself to the 'intelligent pig' in a popular sideshow – he generally enjoyed the attention. And at one such party, another young man destined to be a companion of his in the Scottish hall of literary fame was there to see him relish it. Walter Scott, who was sixteen when he saw Burns at Dr Adam Ferguson's house, later recalled the buckskinned hero's impact thus:

I think his countenance was more massive than it looks in any of the portraits. I would have taken the poet, had I not known what he was, for a very sagacious country farmer of the old Scotch school; that is, none of your modern agriculturalists who keep labourers for their drudgery, but the *douce guidman* who held his own plough. There was a strong expression of sense and shrewdness in all his lineaments: the eye alone, I think, indicated the poetical character and temperament. It was large, and of a cast which glowed (I say literally *glowed*). I never saw such another eye in a human being, though I have seen the most distinguished men of my time. His conversation expressed perfect self-confidence, but without the least intrusive forwardness; and when he differed in opinion, he did not hesitate to express it firmly, yet at the same time with modesty.

To Highland Mary's misfortune, Burns was quite overwhelmed not just by the acclaim and celebrity prompted by his book but also by the fact that Jean Armour had now given birth to twins, with whom he was delighted. His head spinning with such distractions, he repeatedly postponed his departure for Jamaica and in October of the same eventful year in which he had met her, Mary died of a fever (or, some say, of pregnancy complications) while still waiting at Greenock. It would be several years before the poet could bring himself to express the pain he felt at her loss.

Yet another diversion was an intense and surprisingly enduring love-letter relationship begun in Edinburgh with the married Nancy Maclehose – whose pen name was Clarinda, while she called him Sylvander – which was never to be physically fulfilled, despite its on-paper passion.

In the meantime, Burns published new editions of his poetry, toured Scotland and began working on one of his most important projects, collecting and restoring traditional Scots songs for *The Scots Musical Museum*. Through his rewriting, repairing and completing scores of old, half-remembered folk songs, he did Scotland an immeasurable (and unpaid) service, generating interest in the country's culture across Europe and the world.

Generally speaking, though he felt he had finally found his calling after trying his hand unsuccessfully at flax dressing and farming in his now-late father's footsteps, he was aware of the fickle nature of his new-found 'friends' and fame and felt the need to secure an 'honest' living. Also being honest to her, he finally married Jean Armour and moved with her to a farm at Ellisland near Dumfries; but when the town seemed to hold more attractions than the too-familiar strain of farming, the family moved on to Dumfries itself, taking a house in Bank Street in 1791. While also working actively as an exciseman, in which job his uncanny ability to get fines from wealthier defaulters secured him promotion, Burns' pen became increasingly prolific. Here, he wrote some of his best-known works such as 'Scots Wha Hae', 'Is There for Honest Poverty', 'Ae Fond Kiss' and the acclaimed classic comic poem 'Tam o' Shanter'.

But hard work would be his downfall. As the new century approached, his health began to decline and he was plagued by recurring bouts of rheumatic fever. The tragedy came as his family expected. Far too young and with so much yet to offer, he died on 21 July 1796, probably from endocarditis contracted while toiling in the fields as a boy.

Thousands attended his funeral. But he was never to be forgotten. In 1801, on the fifth anniversary of his death, the first-ever Burns Supper was held by a small group of friends in his simple little birth cottage in Alloway, which is now open to the public – unlike its replica in Atlanta, Georgia – and within a few years Burns clubs were springing up all over Scotland and eventually (as we know) well beyond.

But from where had this great talent sprung up? William Burnes was a gardener from the north-east of Scotland, who moved south for self-improvement and built the Alloway cottage to support not only his market garden, but the family he and his local wife Agnes began in 1759 with Robert (who would remove the 'e' from his surname). By bringing together other parents to pay for a school-teacher for their children, William put a big effort into making sure Robert and his younger brother, Gilbert, got a good schooling – and the teacher, John Murdoch, would later report how well they could memorise whole passages of text.

It was in Alloway, too, that Robert's creative imagination was stimulated – by his mother's frequent singing of traditional songs and distant cousin Betty Davidson's telling tales of ghosts and witches. He was also inspired by animals and plants in the countryside around the farms the family later tried in vain to work successfully as tenants – Mount Oliphant, Lochlea and Mossgiel. It was seeing his father struggle that made Robert turn his hand assiduously to the plough; but it also embittered him about landowners' exploitation.

And sadly, William never lived to see his elder son's success that owed much to the parental gift of a thorough education and its basic acknowledgment of received standard English. And just to show he could use it if he felt inclined, Robert would occasionally write in that mode, as in his 'Ode For General Washington's Birthday' . . .

> See gathering thousands, while I sing,
> A broken chain exulting bring,
> And dash it in a tyrant's face,
> And dare him to his very beard,
> And tell him he no more is feared –
> No more the despot of Columbia's race!
> A tyrant's proudest insults brav'd,
> They shout – a People freed!
> They hail an Empire saved.

But fine as it was for the occasional stanza, he must have known there was some magic missing. Nothing could compare with his poetic command of the vernacular, as shown in his gloriously simple, Scottish and evocative 'Ye Banks and Braes o' Bonnie Doon':

> Aft hae I rov'd by bonnie Doon
> To see the rose and woodbine twine
> And ilk bird sang o' its luve
> And fondly sae did I o' mine

Charles Macintosh (1765–1843)

The long reign of his raincoat

There is something indefinably dramatic about a raincoat. Sometimes it's sinister, worn by shadowy, cigarette-smoking movie spies lurking behind its high-winged collars; sometimes it adds a certain dark glamour to the good guys – detectives, say, like Marlowe or Columbo or even Inspector Clouseau. But mostly that romantic Third Man image, combined with its sheer practicality, has made it an enduringly loved garment for ordinary Americans, especially when they visit the cold and wet far northern shores of Europe. For ordinary Scots, however, there is something ironic about how they recognise their transatlantic cousins principally by that dress code. For while refusing to share American appreciation of it and choosing to shun such a reliable protector themselves as something rather 'wet', they can't escape the widely acknowledged fact that, whether you call it a trench coat or a mac, the wonderfully waterproof creation that has survived a thousand lesser fashion trends was invented in Scotland.

It might seem odd to say that a coat is 'invented', but the word seemed apt when this species emerged, as it hinged on the development of the material with which it was created. Had he been alive today, the Scottish chemist who made the breakthrough, Glasgow-born Charles Macintosh, would have been gratified to see his brainchild's remarkable longevity 'across the pond' – where it is affectionately known by a misspelled version of his own name – but bemused by his own countrymen's less-than-enthusiastic feeling for what should have long been regarded as a godsend in the damp Caledonian climate.

It was no doubt such weather conditions that inspired him in the first place, when in 1823, at the age of fifty-eight, while working in the family fabric plant, he set about the challenge of creating the waterproof material that promised to minimise the discomfort of a hard Scottish winter.

In the context of a long quest to find uses for waste gasworks products, he began experimenting with India rubber – an exciting new substance – to see how its qualities might provide a waterproof element when applied, somehow, to a normal woollen cloth. Noting that coal-tar naphtha dissolved the rubber, he applied the resulting preparation to one side of the cloth then placed another layer of wool cloth on top. It worked! With important input and help from James Syme, an Edinburgh University medical student (and later eminent surgeon), his system was refined enough to produce a truly waterproof material that he was able to patent that same year – though, by adding a 'k' to make his name 'Mackintosh', the patent office made a historic error which has stuck to the resulting product to this day, when belted raincoats made from refined versions of the Scot's material are still known affectionately as mackintoshes, or macs, mainly in America though also to a lesser degree in Britain.

Introduction of the early products to the market was not so easy, however. While Macintosh did not attempt – initially – to get into tailoring himself, he supplied the waterproof material to tailors to make up. And while there were some notable successes (such as the outfitting of Sir John Franklin's Arctic expedition in 1824) it began to seem almost impossible to successfully tailor such an inflexible fabric. For soon after the manufacture of coats and other garments with his new material began – advertised as 'life preservers' for anyone who had to go out in the rain – some major problems became apparent, not least the frequent puncturing of the garments' fabric by tailors engaged in seaming them. The resulting penetration of rain into the cloth's natural oil caused the rubber cement to deteriorate too quickly. Another significant problem to beset early Macs was the fact that they reacted oddly to weather extremes – becoming stiff in winter, while in hot weather, they had a tendency to melt, sometimes causing two people wearing them to become literally inseparable.

Nonetheless, in 1830 Macintosh finally took on a partner – the Manchester firm of Thomas Hancock – to move into the ready-to-wear business . . . and on to more challenges. Their 'macs' were voluminous, neck-to-ankle garments, designed to keep the wearer completely dry in the era of the stagecoach; but soon, the enclosed comforts of the railway carriage were to render that style almost redundant. The aforementioned problems persisted too, and there was also the small matter of smell: wearers and their companions complained about the peculiar rubbery odour that was given out by the garments.

Yet it looked as if rubber and its various applications were here to stay. In a few years, the Amazon would be booming as the stuff began to feature in much more than rainwear. And in America, the cavalry was getting ready to ride to Macintosh's rescue . . .

Working in his garage to get away from his nagging wife, the innovative Charles Goodyear discovered in 1839 how to vulcanise rubber to produce resistance to temperature fluctuations, making it much more elastic and non-sticky in heat and less brittle in cold. And about ten years later, Joseph Mandleburg of Lancashire, England, successfully got to grips with the rubber smell in woollen waterproof garments, and then launched the first odour-free waterproof coat.

The invaluable input of these two men – plus the fact that the still-prominent waterproof-wear company Hodgman in Framingham, Massachusetts, had begun to import and sell Macs to set down the roots of their remarkable popularity in the United States – meant that Charles Macintosh's original dream was to prevail and indeed triumph after all. And that in the process the Scotsman's name was to be immortalised among all those for whom his waterproof material still reigns supreme.

The son of a well-established Glasgow dyer, Macintosh recorded several other scientific achievements for which he is not particularly remembered – notably a conversion process which used carbon gases to convert iron to steel much more quickly than any other method of the time – and was elected a Fellow of the Royal Society in 1823. He died twenty years later.

Walter Scott (1770–1832)

Scotland's romantic literary hero

Unlike his ploughman companion in Scotland's hall of literary fame, Walter Scott did not have to make any kind of class-crossing journey to be the toast of Edinburgh's polite society (and eventually far beyond). He was born into it as the son of a lawyer and a professor of medicine's daughter, and was quite at ease in it. Indeed, after a good Scots education, he followed his father's footsteps to also become a distinguished lawyer, counting among his professional achievements his posting as Sheriff-Depute of Selkirkshire. But other conspicuous talents tugged at his heart and at a certain moment he knew he was fated to live a life of two strands, exercising his brain, like a nineteenth-century John Grisham, not just on dusty old law books but on the creation of romantic adventure books, for which he became famous as 'the father of the regional and historical novel'.

But what was that certain moment? Scott was only sixteen when he met Robert Burns on *his* epic class-crossing journey in 1786, as the poet stepped on to the fine Edinburgh carpets of the Scotts' family friend, Dr Adam Ferguson. The boy never forgot the impact of their meeting, later recording it breathlessly in a keenly observed, and now precious, description of 'Caledonia's bard' (see pages 136–7).

As he was never shy of attention himself and indeed veered a touch towards flamboyancy, there can be little doubt that young Walter Scott was well impressed by old Edina's celebration of Ayrshire's champion versifier – and suitably inspired by it to find a similar kind of celebrity for himself. He did not fail.

Childhood polio had left him lame in the right leg, but Scott grew to be handsome and tall – over six foot – and managed to minimise his disability with the confidence and encouragement he found on frequent visits to his paternal grandparents' home in the Scottish Borders. And it was there, listening to his grandmother talk, that his fascination with the old tales and ballads of the area was awakened.

He had already started to collect such ballads as a teenager but –

after graduating from Edinburgh University in 1783 and qualifying as an advocate in 1792 – he did not begin to find his publishing feet until an avenue opened in the context of his interest in German works; so his first efforts to see the light were translations of ballads by Gottfried Augustus Burger (1796) and of Goethe's *Götz von Berlichingen* (1799). Overly academic for some, perhaps; but they gave Walter Scott a taste for publishing that he would thoroughly indulge and never lose in his lifetime, and his quill soon became a very prolific scratcher indeed.

His first major work, an impressive collection of old ballads with introductions and notes entitled *Minstrelsy of the Scottish Border,* appeared in 1802. He went on to write poetry for several years with the hugely successful *The Lay of the Last Minstrel* (1805), about an old Borders legend. That was followed in 1808 by *Marmion,* a historical romance concerning the attempts of a lord to marry a rich lady; then came *The Lady of the Lake* (1810) and *Rokeby* (1813) before his last poem, *The Lord of the Isles* (1815).

Some say Scott gave up poetry to sidestep comparison with Lord Byron, but he turned to fiction with astounding success, whatever his motives. One was surely to raise money to pay for the building of his own personal Gothic castle – Abbotsford, near Galashiels – which his flamboyance had driven him to begin in 1811. Another was a crisis in the business affairs of his printer-publisher associate James Ballantyne, to which he had contributed not just money but hack editorial work. When the final crash came, he accepted all Ballantyne's £130,000 debts and decided to literally 'write' them off. 'I am become a sort of writing automaton,' he wrote in his diary, 'and truly the joints of my knees, especially the left, are so stiff and painful in rising and sitting down, that I can hardly help screaming – I that was so robust and active.'

And he told Lord Henry Thomas Cockburn, with whom he had founded the Edinburgh Academy boys' school, that 'my right hand shall work it all off'. So in his later years there could be no respite in the prodigious output he had maintained while also practising as an advocate.

So busy was he that, to keep several projects going at the same time, he used two massive desktops. He began to write his way out of financial trouble with his first novel, *Waverley* (1814), which was essentially a historical fiction vehicle designed to retell swashbuckling tales of the '45 Jacobite rebellion while ostensibly following young

Edward Waverley's coming of age. It defined a new literary genre and was followed by a stream of similar successes, such as *The Tale of Old Mortality* (1816), *Rob Roy* (1817) and the widely loved *Ivanhoe* (1819) – depicting the rivalry between King Richard I and his evil brother John – which was made into a memorable film starring Robert Taylor and Elizabeth Taylor in 1952.

In all, Scott's passion for the printed word was expressed in no fewer than twenty-seven historical novels, and his last few years' work included *Woodstock* (1826), *A Life of Napoleon* (1827), *Chronicles of the Canongate* (1827), *The Fair Maid of Perth* (1828), *Anne of Geierstein* (1829) and *Count Robert of Paris* and *Castle Dangerous* (1831). His novels made him one of Europe's most famous literary figures, and he was created a baronet in 1818, making him a 'sir' and prompting George IV to remark: 'I shall always reflect with pleasure on Sir Walter Scott's having been the first creation of my reign.'

Scott's talent was also acknowledged in the respect and admiration of fellow scribes such as Hogg, Goethe and Wordsworth; of portrait painters like William Allan and Henry Raeburn; and of admiring 'Edinburghers' who saw to it that the city's soaring Scott Monument (built in 1844) and the nearby Waverley Station represented enduring tributes to the author's elevated status in the Victorian world.

While some critics have accused him of going too far in over-colourfully portraying wild Jacobite clansmen, credit is largely due to Scott for rehabilitating Scotland's image in the 1800s, reviving an interest in tartan, and even persuading King George IV to wear a kilt during his visit to Edinburgh in 1822.

And still the writer, poet and born storyteller had time to bring up the five children he had with Margaret Charlotte Charpentier, whom he married in 1797. And still he had time to become clerk to the Court of Session in Edinburgh.

But all his efforts would inevitably take their toll, and after a trip to Italy and a short illness, he died at his beloved Abbotsford in 1832, at the relatively young age of sixty-one. He was buried beside his ancestors in Dryburgh Abbey and all his debts were ultimately paid off from the profits from his books.

American Note. The march traditionally played to honour the US President, which includes the line 'Hail to the Chief who in triumph advances!', is based on verses from Sir Walter's *The Lady of the Lake,* put to music by James Sanderson (1769–1841).

Johnnie Walker (1800–59)

The man behind the drink

In this age of clever marketing ploys, when a new ice cream is given an old-sounding foreign name to imbue it with a sense of long establishment, you would not be surprised to learn that the famous red-coated figure of Johnnie Walker – whose ageless dynamic image so helps the world-beating sales of his eponymous whisky – was just an invention. But how surprised would you be to learn that he was real?

Of course, the original Johnnie Walker did not stride briskly around Kilmarnock in monocle, top hat and breeches like the figure on the whisky bottle; he was just an average Ayrshire lad who, after his farmer father's death, left his family's home at the age of fifteen to set up a grocery business in that town in 1820.

Well, not quite average. He turned out to be something more than a regular shopkeeper. Gradually, his shop began to find favour not so much for its groceries and dry goods as for its wines and spirits, particularly its own brand of whisky. It seemed John had a keen nose for blending tea, and as he began to apply the same principles to the qualities of Scotland's water of life, his talent found expression in Walker's Kilmarnock Whisky, which he sold to many a grateful customer.

Up to that point in the west of Scotland, malt whiskies and grain whiskies had been bottled singly, and there was little appetite – and even less of a market – for the oily stuff outside its native land. How that emphatically changed in the latter half of the nineteenth century owed much to the art of whisky blending refined by several pioneers, among whom the dedicated John Walker was an important player. With the invaluable help of a selection of his favourite Islay malts, he created a consistent taste and quality and, in so doing, managed to capture a certain depth of flavour that the 'single' could not match.

And appreciation of it did not just happen locally. When John's son Alexander joined him in 1856, the younger man spread its fame further and wider as he continued this tradition of creating harmonious blends 'to make our whisky' – in his own words – 'of such quality that nothing in the market shall come before it'.

By the time John died, in 1859, the single-minded Alexander had brought his own talents to bear on the business, not just revealing an inherited flair for blending, but also an aptitude for product promotion. This he did initially by getting over his message (with the aid of a few complementary drams, no doubt) to the many travelling salesmen who visited Kilmarnock as a centre for carpets and textiles. But he was soon pushing the Walker brand of whisky all over the world. His big helpers in that respect were ships' captains who, under the merchant venturers' system, would, wherever they landed, sell bottles on commission at the best price they could.

And as the British Empire expanded, Alexander made sure his product, now called Old Highland Whisky, went with it. Offices and representation were found in England (1880), Australia (1890) and South Africa (1897); and as he enhanced his whisky's reputation by winning the first special award for blended whisky at the Sydney International Exhibition and introducing the square bottle design with black-and-gold slanting label, he planned the conversion of John Walker & Sons to a limited liability business. That happened in 1886.

But it was not until 1906, nearly twenty years after Alexander's death, that the family's famed whisky took on the memorable brand name 'Johnnie Walker', which has since become known all over the globe. Alexander left the burgeoning business in the hands of two of his sons, Alexander Walker II and George Paterson Walker. And it was George who, having inherited his father's flair for marketing, masterminded the image of the much-loved 'Striding Man' in 1908 to give life and identity to the Johnnie Walker name and support the recent launch of Red Label and Black Label (which have since become respectively the world's largest-selling Scotch and its best-selling de luxe whisky).

It happened over a planned briefing lunch with Tom Browne, a well-known cartoonist of the time, when – we can assume – no reference was made to the original John Walker's facial features; for the exercise was all about capturing his pioneering spirit to give the product a compelling advertising device. Stirred by George's enthusiasm, the artist instantly picked up the challenge and quickly sketched a top-hatted, caped figure on the back of a menu. He presented it with a smile and a look of triumph. He had given birth to the Striding Man.

Thus Johnnie Walker the logo went on to stride across the world. And although his appearance and outfits regularly changed over the years as he was subtly updated by several other leading artists, few would deny that his original creation was something of a marketing masterstroke; on a par, perhaps, with Coca-Cola's famous fat italics.

Within twenty years the Johnnie Walker image was universally associated with the first truly global brand, sold in over 120 countries around the world, and especially America. The product also won another prestigious stamp – for among the devoted following it built up at home in Britain was none other than King George V himself. He liked Johnnie Walker whisky so much that in 1933 he granted a Royal Warrant to the company, which has remained an official purveyor of whisky to the Royal Household to the present day.

It was, in fact, Alexander Walker II who brought about most of these big follow-up business successes. After stepping into the blending role, as a highly astute businessman he took up responsibility for further development of the company and was eventually regarded as a colossus of the whisky industry and a forceful spokesman on its behalf. He was knighted for his efforts in 1920.

Sir Alexander retired in 1940, but his office still stands in John Finnie Street, Kilmarnock, which remains the centre for the blending and bottling of Johnnie Walker; a leading global name by any measure. Now produced by Diageo plc, the giant food and drinks multinational, it was – at time of writing – running neck-and-neck with Dewar's for the title of top-selling Scotch whisky brand in the United States.

Wherever he is now, the original John Walker is no doubt quite pleased that he decided to put a little nip – like a bright red hunting jacket – into the grey business of general provisions.

Alexander Bain (1811–77)

The man who gave us the fax

Ticker-tape parades through the streets of New York – fêting conquering heroes, VIPs or celebrities with a snowstorm of paper tape from every available window – have long represented a uniquely American expression of released euphoria, bringing out all the New World's glamour and confidence. These days, of course, while hi-tech communication has overtaken the stock market's old paper culture, the effect is preserved by jettisoning large amounts of regular shredded waste paper onto the parade route.

But who would ever guess that the original ticker-stuff itself, although part of a technology developed by others, originated in the brain of a humble crofter's son called Alexander Bain, born in 1811 on the remote northern edge of Scotland?

One of six brothers and six sisters packed into one of the occasional stone cottages that dot the peaty countryside around Watten, Caithness, a few miles north of Wick, he was not a conventionally clever lad. Indeed, when he walked a few miles to school at Backlass he did so only to sit and dream, and his academic slate recorded that apparently bleak fact. What it did not register was that the boy's apparent absence from the mainstream consciousness of schooling was, paradoxically, a sign that his was an extremely fertile mind, which, in later life, was to bombard the modern world with an impressive series of innovative ideas.

One of these was ticker tape – the system that speeded up telegraphic message-sending with an unimaginable leap. Another, which had a huge impact on the business life of the world in general, and of America in particular, was the facsimile – or fax – machine.

Most people assume this was a relatively recent development, certainly a device of the twentieth century, and in its modern guise as a smoothly designed telephonic device generally available to business and private purchasers, that is certainly true. But the fax machine as conceived by Bain, is a nineteenth-century idea that actually pre-dates fellow-Scot Alexander Graham Bell's telephone by thirty-three years. Bain was the first to describe the principle of scanning a picture or text line by line, and to develop a way of receiving the image by means of a 'chemical telegraph'. Despite his unhappy experience with formal schooling, he followed his vocational feelings with real success – 'instinct is untaught ability', he once said – and received a patent for his early fax concept in 1843, when he was thirty-two and styling himself, in what was then a newfangled term 'electrical engineer'.

For it was the then-new discovery of the powers of electricity that had, aptly, sparked his imagination. Having proved a lacklustre scholar and an even less capable shepherd – when he tried his hand at that job in the summer months – he was drawn instinctively to news of a penny lecture on 'Light, heat and the electric fluid' taking place in neighbouring Thurso in 1830. He walked twenty-one miles through the snow from Wick to hear it and, when he emerged, he was hooked. 'It set me thinking,' he said.

Because he had also shown interest in the craft of clockmaking – as a child he once made a model clock using heather for cogwheels and spring – his father had helped him become apprenticed to a clockmaker in Wick and, from there, he went to London and then Edinburgh to practise the trade. The workshop he had in Edinburgh's Hanover Street, between 1844 and 1847, now bears a plaque marking not only his incumbency but also the centenary (in 1940) of his development and patenting of the invention that combined both his intense interests: the original electric clock.

He also invented an earth battery, a mode of measuring ships' speed by vanes revolving in the water, various types of automatic telegraph, insulation for electric cables, an electric fire alarm, and a system of synchronising clocks between Glasgow and Edinburgh rail stations.

He greatly improved the speed of telegraph transmission by using punched paper tape to send messages: from 40 words a minute to about 300. The perforated tape is nicknamed 'ticker tape' because of the ticking sound the telegraph made when dealing with it.

Positively revelling in electricity's multitude of possibilities, in 1852 Alexander Bain expressed his enthusiasm for it thus:

> For many years I have devoted myself to rendering electricity practically useful, and have been extensively engaged, not only in this country,

but in America and on the Continent, in the construction and working
of the Electric Telegraph; while at the same time the employment
of electricity in the measurement of time has also engaged my
attention.

But it was his 'electrochemical telegraph', which we would call the fax
machine, that was destined (eventually) to create the biggest impact
of all his brainwaves.

How did it work? The principle was simple. At each end of a
telegraph wire was a sending and receiving machine. The sender
used a detector to scan an image or text line by line, point by point
and, as it swept over the page left to right, the transmitting needle
picked up impulses where there was text, but no impulse where there
was a gap. The two signals travelled over a telegraph wire to the
receiver, which applied them to chemically treated paper which made
marks corresponding to the signals from the sending needle – so
reproducing the transmitted text or image.

Though he never actually transmitted anything himself in this
fashion and the idea took an inordinately long time to reach the shops,
Bain is widely acknowledged as the father of the facsimile – even by
most of the many clever developers who came along behind him to
refine the concept. His invention was improved in turn by Frederick
Collier Blakewell (1847), Giovani Caselli (1865), G. Little (1867),
Senlecq de Ardres (1877), Shelford Bidwell (1881), N.S. Amstutz
(1892), Buss (1902), Arthur Korn (1904), Edouard Belin (1907),
Diekmann (1917), Western Union (1924), American Telephone &
Telegram Company (1924/1925), NEC (1927), Wise (1938), the
Xerox Corporation (& RCA) (1950/1961), the firm of Rudolf Hell
(1965), Magnafax-Xerox (1966) and Ricoh (1970). In 1971 the
first prototype of the laserfax appeared and, during the 1980s, the
modern facsimile, or fax, spread worldwide.

The general idea was put to commercial work long before that,
however. In 1865 the first commercial service began between Lyons
and Paris, and in 1895 America made such a system meaningful
in media communication with the advent of the Telediagraph,
developed by another clockmaker, Ernest A. Hummel, of St Paul,
Minnesota. The first of his machines was installed in the *New York
Herald* office in 1898, and by the following year there were versions
in the offices of the *Boston Herald*, *Chicago Times Herald*, *Philadelphia
Inquirer* and *St Louis Republic*.

At first it was all about words; but pictures had to come. An important factor was the reproducability of images thus sent, and by the 1920s the quality of facsimile transmission was beginning to allow that – although the time taken to transmit a photograph could run to several hours. The nut was clearly cracked, however, and refinement to high levels of efficiency, quality and sophistication was only a matter of time. Eventually, newspapers would be sending whole pages off to other lands for editionalised printing.

But for Alexander Bain, it was all too late. Unfortunately, his grasp of business advantage had not matched his hands-on flair for electro-technology. He won few financial rewards for his troubles and died a disappointed man in the Home for Incurables at Kirkintilloch, near Glasgow, in 1877.

James Dewar (1842–1923)

Man with a cool idea

What would a picnic or a long car trip or a walk in the hills be without James Dewar's cool invention? He it was, an industrial chemist from Scotland's central belt, who brought us the marvel of the vacuum flask that keeps our drinks warm or cold for impressively – and conveniently – long periods of time.

But this breakthrough, which has proved such a boon to the home, the campsite and even the armed forces, was almost accidental; for Dewar – who experimented on the liquefaction of gases like hydrogen, nitrogen and oxygen – had initially designed the vacuum flask to store his gases at temperatures low enough to keep them liquid.

This was 1892, and he was not thinking about the idea's domestic application until one of his assistants, a glass-blower called Reinhold Burger, noticed that it kept liquids warm as well as cold. Not surprisingly, the commercial possibilities of this were soon apparent and it wasn't long before two fellow-German glass blowers had formed a company to manufacture and market the first vacuum flasks for domestic use – in 1904. They held a contest to name the product and a Munich resident submitted 'thermos' (from the Greek word 'therme' meaning 'heat') so giving that widely familiar name to the producing company as well . . . Thermos GmbH.

Although the Germans had taken the initiative, they proved not over-jealous of their rights, and by 1907 had sold the Thermos trademark to companies in three countries – the American Thermos Bottle Company of Brooklyn, New York; the Thermos Bottle Co. Ltd of Montreal, Canada; and Thermos Ltd of Tottenham, England.

So the idea had come home again, to the quiet satisfaction (one assumes) of James Dewar who had by now been knighted for his achievements, which also included helping to invent the smokeless explosive cordite and liquefying and solidifying hydrogen.

His innovative product found fame not just in the home but in the most daring of highly publicised famous expeditions, including

Shackleton's to the South Pole and Peary's to the Arctic. It even became airborne with the Wright Brothers and Count Zeppelin.

And when the Second World War broke out in 1939, the American Thermos Bottle Company played an important role, with over 98 per cent of its output being allocated for military use in the field. After this enforced deprivation, the war ended with Thermos products being more in demand than ever with the people.

But how does the ever-popular invention work? It consists of two flasks, one inside the other, separated by a vacuum that reduces the transfer of heat, preventing a temperature change. The walls are of glass because it is a poor conductor of heat; its surfaces are usually lined with a reflective, silvery metal to reduce the transfer of heat by radiation. All of this rests on a shock-absorbing spring within a metal or plastic container, and the air between the flask and the container provides further insulation.

Born in Kincardine-on-Forth, halfway between Glasgow and Edinburgh, in 1842, Dewar was a student and lecturer at Edinburgh University before moving south to England to develop his work with low-temperature phenomena at the University of Cambridge. He later became professor of chemistry at the Royal Institution in London.

He died in 1923 after a career of great distinction and esoteric achievement much admired by his peers in the world of chemistry; but it is by the great mass of the public that he will long be even more appreciated for inventing the humble vessel that has made domestic life all over the world considerably easier.

Robert Louis Stevenson (1850–94)

The travelling storyteller

Robert Louis Stevenson disguised his greatness well. Anyone looking at him superficially would see a long, gangly, rather uncared-for bohemian figure haunted by the looming terminator that was his lifelong 'consumptive' illness. They would do well not to write him off, however, for this near-invisibility made him a keen observer of people – when, for instance, he colourfully described his fellow-passengers on his grim steerage voyage across the Atlantic. And there were always signs that betrayed the intellectual value of the man who would become the greatest of storytellers. The cultured Scots voice, for instance, commanded an impressive vocabulary, and from their dark, unwell sockets his sharp brown eyes shone with vivid intelligence.

It seems odd to record today, when he is held in such high esteem for his gigantic literary impact, that he was forever disappointing people who wanted him to be 'respectable'. From an early age, when growing up as a sickly only child in his well-off family's Georgian house, which still stands in Edinburgh's Howard Place, he was groomed to follow his father Thomas into lighthouse design and engineering. Though he tried, he found the calling of little interest and could only offer the saddened Thomas the half-hearted pursuit of a law degree at Edinburgh University. A formal photograph taken of Robert Louis Stevenson in wig and gown after admission to the bar in 1875 must have been of some consolation to his father and mother Maggie – but that was where the pursuit ended.

He was determined to become a writer, and knew he would need experiences in many parts as essential grist to his literary mill. Some 'respectable friends' he left behind would see him as a velvet-clad dandy and an impulsive, aimless vagabond; but there was a kinder way to look at it: that he was driven to be peripatetic by three understandable and irresistible forces – his writer's curiosity; his need to find better climes for his delicate health; and his burning desire to be with the one he loved.

Although he never lost his deep affection for Edinburgh and its 'windy parallelograms' and made much reference to Scotland in his work wherever he found himself writing, he lodged at various stages in his life in England, France, Switzerland, America, Australia and the South Pacific. Naturally enough, then, it was with travelogues that his publishing career began, in 1878 when he was twenty-eight. As a schoolboy, he had grown to love purposeless rambling tours in Europe, and one such post-graduation trip down the French River Oisé inspired his first full-length book, *An Inland Voyage*. The critics liked it, and his next effort was even more warmly received: the melancholic *Travels with a Donkey* (1879), based on the emotional diversion of a walking tour undertaken after he had fallen in love with the most inconvenient of people: Fanny Vandegrift Osbourne, a married American woman ten years his senior, whom he had met in the artists' village colony of Grez-sur-Loing before she returned to the USA.

The attraction seemed too unlikely to be mutual, so did she wish to encourage him or otherwise? Whatever it said, a cablegram she sent from California in August 1879 had an electrifying effect on him. Within days, he was a steerage passenger aboard a steamer of dubious seaworthiness setting off from the Scottish port of Greenock bound for America: a turbulent experience that informed his book, *The Amateur Emigrant,* in which he offered such evocative observations of fellow-passengers:

> The more you saw of Alick, the more, it must be owned, you learned to despise him. His natural talents were of no use either to himself or others; for his character had degenerated like his face, and become pulpy and pretentious. Even his power of persuasion, which was certainly very surprising, stood in some danger of being lost or neutralised by over-confidence. He lied in an aggressive, brazen manner, like a pert criminal in the dock; and he was so vain of his own cleverness that he could not refrain from boasting, ten minutes after, of the very trick by which he had deceived you.

Eleven days later, a sick and near-penniless Stevenson landed in New York. From there he set off on a cheap and anything-but-cheerful 3,000-mile train trip to California, whose two miserable weeks prompted the second part of his 'emigrant' book, *Across the Plains*; but when he arrived in what was then the fast-rising frontier town of San Francisco, it was love at first sight. He felt moved to capture the American spirit in verse:

See the great new nation
New spirit and new scope
Rise there from the sea's round shoulder
A splendid sun of hope

His love for Fanny Osbourne was of much more immediate import, however, and how the emaciated, apparently impoverished writer persuaded this well-rounded assertive woman to leave a properly employed, if flighty, husband is as big a mystery as the telegram message that sent Robert Louis Stevenson dashing across the ocean in the first place. She may well have had serious doubts, but he was greeted with delight, laughter and tears – also by her eleven-year-old son Lloyd – and she wrote to her lawyer friend Edward Rearden: 'It is almost more than amusing to meet again the only person in the world who really cares anything for me.'

In leaving Scotland so suddenly, Stevenson had certainly shocked his parents, but the estrangement proved temporary. When they heard of his dire circumstances they cabled him some life-saving money, and things looked up again for Robert Louis Stevenson when Fanny finally obtained her divorce and married him on 19 May 1880 in San Francisco. His parents had also been concerned about his interest in a married woman. But there was a surprising end-twist to that when, after a honeymoon at an abandoned silver mine site in the Napa Valley – which yielded his work *The Silverado Squatters* – the newlyweds set sail for Britain, where Fanny was introduced to the Stevensons at their later Edinburgh home in Heriot Row. She set about winning them as she had Robert Louis Stevenson, and was soon well liked by both mother and father.

Thomas Stevenson's death in 1887 seemed to end a super-productive seven-year period for his son, in which he wrote – while travelling a lot for his health's sake – some of his best-known work, including *A Child's Garden of Verses* (1886), *Kidnapped* (1886), *The Strange Case of Dr Jekyll and Mr Hyde* (1886) and the still-much-loved classic *Treasure Island* (1883), which was conceived at Braemar in his home country after he drew a map to amuse his stepson Lloyd. The evocation of a pirate adventure tale to go with the sketch seemed a natural next step, and soon the resulting ripping yarn was being serialised in the boys' magazine *Young Folks*, before becoming one of the most popular books of the time among all age groups. Even Prime Minister William Gladstone was said to have read it avidly, of which revelation Robert Louis Stevenson commented: 'He would do better to attend to the imperial affairs of England.'

Still shocked by his father's death and in search of the ideal climate to promote his health, in the summer of 1888 the author decided to 'play big', as he told a friend: 'I have found a yacht, and we are going the full pitch for seven months. If I cannot get my health back . . . 'tis madness; but of course, there is the hope . . .' And so the Stevenson 'clan' – including his wife, stepson and widowed mother – set off for the Pacific islands on the chartered yacht *Casco*, sailing south-west from San Francisco. He would never see Europe again. In Honolulu, he finished *The Master of Ballantrae* (1889) and, after three cruises in these gentler climes, which seemed to promise him better health, the Stevenson party decided to settle in Western Samoa.

It was to a very handsome home, called Vailima, that he and Fanny chose to retreat, where he became known as Tusitala – 'the teller of tales' – by the natives, who saw him as a good friend as he helped them fight against the injustices of some of the British governors. Ironically, while feeling more robust than he had for years, it was here that Robert Louis Stevenson died – in front of his shaving mirror – only four years after his arrival. It was the end of his long, draining battle with tuberculosis. He was only forty-four, and lying unfinished on his desk were two novels – *St Ives* and *Weir of Hermiston*, which, although a fragment, is generally acknowledged to be a masterpiece of passion and justice set a world away, in the beloved, cold, northern city of his birth.

In his very full life of travels and travails, Robert Louis Stevenson often thought of his own impending end, so it is not surprising that he found the time to pen his own epitaph, which is now engraved on a tablet at his grave on Mount Vaea in Samoa:

> Under the wide and starry sky,
> Dig the grave and let me lie.
> Glad did I live and gladly die,
> And I laid me down with a will.
>
> This be the verse you grave for me:
> Here he lies where he longed to be;
> Home is the sailor, home from sea,
> And the hunter home from the hill.

Arthur Conan Doyle (1859–1930)

Creator of Sherlock Holmes

> The chief piece in Beeton's Christmas Annual is a detective story by
> Mr A. Conan Doyle, A Study in Scarlet. This is as entrancing a tale of
> ingenuity in tracing out crime as has been written since the time of
> Edgar Allan Poe. The author shows genius. He has not trodden in the
> well-worn paths of literature, but has shown how the true detective
> should work by observation and deduction. His book is bound to have
> many readers.

Thus *The Scotsman*'s book review section introduced its readers on
19 December 1887, not just to the literary genius of doctor-writer
Arthur Conan Doyle but to his 'true detective', by whom all other
detectives were henceforth to be judged – the cultivated sleuth in the
deerstalker hat who was as clever, coolly calculating and uncannily
infallible as he was thoroughly English.

But Conan Doyle was born in Scotland – in Edinburgh's Picardy
Place, to be precise, in 1859 – and so also, by extension, was at least
the idea behind the character of Sherlock Holmes. But which of
them is perceived to be the more important Scot in the great scheme
of things?

As it is possible to argue convincingly that in global terms the
fictional pipe-smoking consulting detective, chemist, violin player,
boxer and swordsman has become bigger and better known than his
creator, it is understandable (if not too pleasing to a Scot) to suspect
that there are more fans of the detective than of his creator – and the
number of visitors who still seek out the Holmes' non-existent 'home'
at 221b Baker Street, London, provides some support for that idea.

But surely the author gets the main recognition in his home city?
Not as clearly as you might expect. It comes as a surprise to find
that the handsome if literal statue erected outside Conan Doyle's
birth house – now ambushed by one of the Scottish capital's busiest
intersections – depicts the invented detective rather than the real-
life writer.

Wherever Conan Doyle is now, however, it may be of some consolation to him to know that the statue is at least dedicated to him, as can be deduced by simply observing (as Holmes might put it) the inscription written upon it . . .

In memory of
SIR ARTHUR CONAN DOYLE
Born on 22 May 1859 close to this spot.

Donated to the City of Edinburgh by Edinburgh and Lothians branch of the Federation of Master Builders on the Federation's 150th anniversary.

Unveiled on 24 June, 1991, by Professor D. Chisholm, President, The Royal College of Surgeons, Edinburgh.

The author's spirit might also be consoled by the conspicuous name of the nearby pub across the flow of traffic from which the statue's gaze seems to be turned – it is the Arthur Conan Doyle. And he might also be pleased to know that – after being threatened with demolition in favour of an American fast-food outlet – Liberton Bank House, where he grew up in later childhood on the south side of the city, was at time of writing earmarked for preservation by being transformed into a special school.

The city is, in fact, rich in landmarks relevant to the life of the author – from 23 George Square, where he lived as a university student, through Lauriston Gardens, where a murder takes place in *A Study in Scarlet*, to the adjoining Lonsdale Terrace, where No. 15 was his last Edinburgh residence.

While technically Scottish, as one of ten children in a financially stretched family with Irish Catholic roots, he was a man of many parts – sustained through his youth not so much by his alcoholic civil servant father as by his long-suffering, hard-working mother and a couple of wealthy uncles who paid for a Catholic boarding-school education south of the Border.

He also spent a year on the Continent before returning to Scotland to enter Edinburgh University in 1876 for the 'long, weary grind' of a medical student. In view of his later literary success, you have to wonder if he was cut out for what he called 'the art of curing'. The creative urge in him – inherited perhaps from his political-cartoonist grandfather and even his amateur-painter father – constantly pulled at his sleeve. He had always had a love of books, which fed his desire to write; and several of the characters he would meet at Edinburgh's famed School of Medicine were more diligently studied than the course work itself, and mentally absorbed for future reference.

The character of Sherlock Holmes is believed to have been based on that of Dr Joseph Bell, one of the medical school teachers who was thirty-nine when a seventeen-year-old Doyle first met him and was deeply impressed by him. In describing him later, the author almost seemed to be describing Holmes: 'He was a thin, wiry, dark man, with a high-nosed acute face, penetrating grey eyes, angular shoulders.' Dr Bell 'would sit in his receiving room with a face like a Red Indian, and diagnose the people as they came in, before they even opened their mouths. He would tell them details of their past life; and hardly would he ever make a mistake.'

And an 'elementary' deduction is often made that Holmes' faithful foil, Dr Watson, was based on Dr Patrick Heron Watson, who was made President of the Royal College of Surgeons some ten years before the publication of *A Study in Scarlet.*

But Conan Doyle was a doer as well as a dreamer and successfully graduated to be a (rather unconventional) doctor who, in typically adventurous fashion, started practising aboard a whaler and an African cargo steamer. It was when he settled down to practise in London and Southsea that he began to push his other talents into the public consciousness. In Southsea in early March 1886, he began work on *A Study in Scarlet,* his first story featuring Sherlock Holmes, which was finished by late April.

Though it was twice rejected by unenlightened publishers that summer, he did not have to suffer the endless humiliations that are traditionally heaped on new authors; for by October it was accepted by Ward Lock – with a payment of £25 for the complete copyright – to be the main feature in the following year's *Beeton's Christmas Annual.*

That might have been that, for such an item would normally enjoy only a single print run in the 'annual' context before being quietly forgotten. But – encouraged no doubt by the favourable reviews the piece received – the publisher decided to issue it as a separate book the following year. It was this inspired decision that would bring to the world its most-loved detective.

In the wake of more good reviews, American interest was stirred – first with the syndicator and publisher S.S. McClure, and then with Joseph M. Stoddart, who commissioned works by him (and Oscar Wilde) for *Lippincott's Magazine,* which proved such a success that

Sherlock Holmes was now assured of a continuing future. There were to be more and more stories, from 'A Scandal in Bohemia' and 'The Crooked Man' to 'The Adventure of the Blue Carbuncle' and the memorable *Hound of the Baskervilles.*

Indeed, while the moustached, gentlemanly Doyle was to write other works of real note, such as *The Lost World* and *The White Company,* the series of short stories that he began for *Strand Magazine* in 1891 spawned something of a one-man Holmes industry that featured the famous detective in no fewer than fifty-six such shorter stories and two more long ones.

How he managed to accommodate all of these in his incredibly busy life was another question. For the good twice-married doctor was also a big traveller, lecturer and sportsman (into football, cricket, golf and skiing) as well as would-be politician (who twice failed to win an MP's seat in Scotland) and champion of unusual causes (such as a campaign to repeal a 200-year-old witchcraft act being used to persecute spiritualist mediums). He even found time to establish and run a field hospital in the Boer War at the turn of the twentieth century, for which admirable initiative he was knighted in 1902.

Conan Doyle's own Holmes industry went on until three years before he died in 1930 after a heart attack. But as we all know, the great detective did not die with his creator but went on to live a burgeoning life of his own . . . celebrated in (often new) words and pictures wherever in the world thinking people were intrigued by a cerebral challenge.

Were? We should say 'are'. For it is a logical conclusion, bearing in mind all the available evidence, as Holmes might say, that the incomparable Victorian detective is likely to be with us for a very long time to come.

James Matthew Barrie (1860–1937)

Magician with words

To stand in the old wash-house in the garden of J.M. Barrie's modest, small-windowed birth house is to sense the happy, creative forces that were ignited there along with the coals of the brick-rimmed iron clothes boiler. It's a tiny, cosy, hedge-fringed place a few steps from the house, and you can imagine, on a cold Scottish day, the tepid warmth lingering within the pores of its (now) prettily whitewashed stone walls.

There are, and presumably were, a few baskets and stools to sit on, so it was the ideal place for childhood friends to keep warm and entertain each other. And that is just what the young James Barrie used it for . . . putting on little plays from the age of seven, and charging admission fees of marbles or spinning tops to his already-growing fan base who relished his flights of fantasy, which often ended up with a dramatic struggle between actors trying to push each other into the boiler.

In his childhood days, of course, the Barries' friends and neighbours in Kirriemuir, the 'little red town' nestling in the agricultural hinterland of the coastal county of Angus, would not have seen the plain, foursquare house at 9 Brechin Road as modest. It was, in fact, larger than average, with its two storeys and resident human engine-room of James' two strong parents, successful handloom weaver David and his wife Margaret Ogilvy, who inspired the boy with her love of literature.

Compared to the gigantic international name that he became, however, J.M. Barrie's origins were indeed humble. The shy, often-lonely writer may never have driven into America on a golden chariot, but the impact of his work on that land, and specifically on Hollywood – and so the world – has been massive. At time of writing, for instance, Johnny Depp was starring as Barrie in the movie *Finding Neverland*, about the shy author's life and times. But films spawned from his *Peter Pan* and Neverland have emanated regularly from the

US studios ever since the play about the boy who never grew up had its premiere in the Duke of York Theatre in London over a century ago. It was a hit from the very start. So much so that the hansom cab drivers who queued outside expecting to pick up theatre-goers at the usual time of around 11.30 p.m. could not understand why they were kept waiting for so long. They learned later that it was all about standing ovations and curtain calls.

But while its instant success may have taken the then 44-year-old Barrie somewhat by surprise, it was no fluke. James Matthew Barrie was supremely well equipped to be an author and playwright. And that was not all down to the childish fun in the wash-house – his inspiration for the Wendy House in Peter Pan – which is only one of several Barrie-connected houses in Kirriemuir that give rise to some confusion among visitors.

There is also a picturesque cottage with a small but eye-catching window, which calls itself 'A Window in Thrums', after one of his works of fiction. Many people think of it as Barrie's birthplace, though he was never known to even step inside it. Neither did it even feature in the book. It is pretty, however, and worth noting if only for its dubious and mysteriously rooted claims.

More likely to have been the 'real' window in Thrums – where the work was penned – is 'Strathview', his other Kirriemuir residence at 1 Forfar Road. This deceptively large end-terrace house was where he moved to at the age of twelve – when a clerical job lured his father back to the town after a short spell in nearby Forfar – and where he decided to become an author. Born in 1860, the Barries' seventh surviving child out of ten may have lived there as part of the family for only a year before joining his brother Alexander in Dumfries, but the three-bedroom house was a place to which he would often return to for peace and inspiration, even when he was a famous figure in London.

Duncan and Sheila Philip, relatively recent owners of Strathview, were convinced that that the Thrums idea came from its upstairs window. 'I can just imagine Barrie rounding the top of Bellies Brae and catching a glimpse of his mother by the drawing room window, watching the local characters walk by,' Duncan said.

And Sheila added: 'There is definitely a warm, peaceful atmosphere throughout the house, and, of all the rooms, that feeling is strongest in the garret where Barrie worked as an author and wrote at least two novels.'

Not many people can say their mother was educated at the same school as the author of *Peter Pan*; but mine was – albeit a good couple of generations later! That was Forfar Academy, and a fine school it must have been, too, if I may judge by her enquiring mind. Barrie had that, plus his time at Glasgow Academy and Dumfries Academy, which also delivered the same kind of good old Scots education incomparably endorsed by fellow-pupil and brother Alexander becoming nothing less than Chief Inspector of Schools for Scotland.

But James was well equipped to become an author and playwright not only by virtue of this fine education, crowned by an MA degree taken at the University of Edinburgh, but also by his journalistic training – he first worked for the *Nottingham Journal* before moving to London as a freelance writer – and his own fertile imagination and intensely focused motivation. From a very early age, he had no doubts about what he wanted to do. When his adventure magazines failed to arrive on time, he would make up the following episodes himself and read them to his much-loved mother. 'From the day on which I first tasted blood in the garret my mind was made up,' he wrote. 'There could be no hum-dreadful-drum profession for me: literature was my game.'

There was another vital factor, at least with regard to the genesis of *Peter Pan*. When James was only six, his brother David, his mother's favourite, died, at the age of thirteen. And while James tried in vain to become his replacement for her, he also realised that 'I had not made her forget . . . when I became a man, he was still a boy of 13.'

The brother who never grew up was surely one of the seeds of his most famous story. But it also owed something to Barrie's befriending in London of the five boys of neighbours Arthur and Sylvia Llewelyn-Davies for whom he spun fantastic Pan-style tales, while the children themselves were the inspiration for *The Lost Boys*.

The final piece of the jigsaw was, of course, Barrie's own way of looking at life. It seems *Peter Pan* was largely autobiographical, as he himself never really wanted to grow up. 'The horror of my boyhood was that I knew a time would come when I must give up the games, and how it was to be done I saw not,' he once wrote, 'I felt I must continue playing in secret.'

Though the theatre was to become his adult playground, and his success in the medium was record-breaking – with no fewer than five London stagings, including *The Admirable Crichton* and *Quality Street* in 1902–03 – adulthood and its requirements certainly revealed his shortcomings. Not long after his first full-length play *Walker London* was staged in London in the early 1890s, he had met and married the beautiful young actress Mary Ansell. But for all his love of children, the couple had none and divorced in 1909 at the height of his fame and productivity. This has inevitably led to speculation about his sexuality and his relationships with The Boys. But one of them said later: 'I don't think Uncle Jim ever experienced what one might call a stirring in the undergrowth for anyone – man, woman or child.'

J.M. Barrie's literary output was mountainous. He wrote not only memorable novels such as *The Little Minister* (1891), *A Window in Thrums* (1889) and *Sentimental Tommy* (1896), but most of his work was as a playwright, and well remembered among his stage productions are *Quality Street* (1901), *The Admirable Crichton* (1902), *What Every Woman Knows* (1908), *Dear Brutus* (1917), *Mary Rose* (1920) and *The Boy David* (1936). But his *Peter Pan, or The Boy who Would Not Grow Up* (1904) has always been the epicentre of his celebrity.

This perceptive, complex and magical childhood fantasy caught the imagination like no other production before or since. And while the talent, time and attention he gave to it – and his entire prodigious literary output – may have inhibited his growth as a human being, they certainly won rewards for him in many other ways.

As he came to the end of his life, the quiet handloom weaver's son was loaded with honours – including a baronetcy (in 1913), the Order of Merit, the Chancellorship of Edinburgh University, and the Rectorship of St Andrews University, where he delivered a moving address on 'courage' in 1922. 'You come of a race of men the very wind of whose name has swept to the ultimate seas,' he told the students, and the sound of it was poetry.

This exciting mastery of words was silenced when Sir James Matthew Barrie died in 1937 at seventy-seven. But just like his famous immortal hero, he seems destined to live forever, at least in our collective memory.

Harry Lauder (1870–1950)

Darling of the diaspora

A curious thing about those Scots who can't wait to leave Scotland is that, once away, they can think of little else, with a tear in their eye, but their native land. It was this phenomenon that made the legendary entertainer Harry Lauder so celebrated all over the world, or at least all over the Scottish diaspora – from Australia and Canada through Indonesia and China to Malaysia and the Philippines – in the early years of last century.

In global terms he was Big with a capital B, especially in America, which he toured no fewer than twenty-two times from 1908; and wherever he went he was greeted, if not mobbed, by welcoming crowds. But in human terms he was small – a dynamic, kilted, five-foot-three-inch package of cheeky Caledonian pride who, although he died over half a century ago, still figures large in Scotland's folk memory, thanks to his magical talent for playing on patriotic heartstrings at home or abroad.

This he did through the feisty, affectionate performance of sentimental Scottish songs, woven through with perfectly timed, self-deprecating banter; and although he was a big winner who became very rich, it has to be said that some fellow-countrymen did not appreciate this non-drinker's portrayal of the drunken, penny-pinching Scot contained in his bonneted, kilted caricature with its famous crooked walking stick. They felt it thrust Scotland's emerging image as a modern, civilised place back to somewhere it was urgently trying to leave. And as for penny-pinching, few can match Scots for generosity – so why did he peddle such an odd view of his own culture that has persisted to this day?

Perhaps the answer lay in his background. Born in 1870 in Edinburgh's sandy suburb of Portobello, Henry MacLennan Lauder was one of eight children who, after the death of his father – a master potter – worked as a pit boy in a coalmine near Hamilton. Though not exactly poor, he grew up in a lifestyle where pennies had to be watched in order to survive, but were occasionally squandered by the less strong on payday. So, misguided or not, his view of the typical Scot was largely subjective and, as such, perhaps forgivable. And no matter how rich he became – as the world's highest-paid stage performer, commanding $1,000 a night plus expenses – he could not forget his early pit-boy days, when he cheered himself up with a song to soften the hard edges of the dark life underground.

He cheered up his co-workers too, and soon they were making requests for 'another wee sang, Harry!' Encouraged by them to enter local talent contests, he did amateur singing on the weekends, and won prize money doing it. He eventually came second in a contest that gave him the chance to sing in small music halls. And so he was on his way – first with a concert party to Belfast, then on to international fame. But not before finding time to marry his sweetheart Nancy, daughter of the local colliery manager, who inspired him to write 'Roamin' in the Gloamin'' and 'I Love a Lassie'.

At first, his music-hall routine had been based on the simple performance of comic songs, but he soon developed a distinctive act as amusing introducer, composer and performer of his own such Scottish songs. Few of his footlight fans seemed to worry about his cartoon Scot, and as his shows became more and more talked-about at home, his fame spread first across the British Isles and then all across the Empire. His tunes were so popular that everyone seemed to know at least their choruses. He recorded hundreds of selections for many labels, and as the first British recording artist ever to sell a million records, he became (and remains) the highest-selling Scottish recording artist ever . . . still celebrated today through the singing of many of his songs.

But in the days before everyone had record players and access to easy air travel, he put tremendous energy into bringing his live performances to the people at home or abroad. Often his tours would keep him away from Britain for over two years.

The writer H.V. Morton met him on a rare moment back in Scotland in 1928 and described him as 'small, sturdy and smooth of face', adding:

> He wore hexagonal glasses and smoked a six-inch briar pipe. His Glengarry was worn at a jaunty angle and, as he walked, the almost ankle-length Inverness cape which he wore exposed a bit of a MacLeod kilt. The superior person will perhaps sniff if I suggest that no man

since Sir Walter Scott has warmed the world's heart to Scotland more surely that Sir Harry Lauder. His genius is a thing apart.

He was certainly a master of the pithy phrase that not only made you smile but made you think. 'Happiness,' he once said, ' is one of the few things in this world that doubles every time you share it with someone else.'

In thus entertaining the world, he did several tours of Australia, where he liked to visit a brother who had emigrated there. Indeed, he and his wife were there with their son John when the Empire mobilised for the First World War. John was the Lauders' only child, born in 1891 and planning a career in law after being educated at the City of London School and Cambridge University. However, as he sat with his parents at lunch in a Melbourne hotel in August 1914, he was called up to fight for his country through a telegram handed to him by a hall porter. It read: 'Mobilise. Return.'

'You know your duty, son,' said the 44-year-old father in answer to the enquiring eyes of his 23-year-old son; but there was to be good reason for the sad trepidation in his voice. A year and a half later, it was another telegram – delivered on the first day of January 1917 to his hotel room in London, where he was playing the Shaftesbury Theatre – that told Harry some dreadful news just as he was expecting his son home:

> Capt. John Lauder killed in action, December 28.
> Official. War Office.

Captain John Lauder of the 8th Argyll and Sutherland Highland Regiment was killed at Poiziers in France in late December 1916, the victim of a sniper's bullet. His distraught father wrote later: 'I felt that for me everything had come to an end with the reading of that dire message. It seemed to me that for me the board of life was black and blank. For me there was no past and there could be no future. Everything had been swept away, erased, by one sweep of the hand of a cruel fate.'

But the show had to go on. As he said, 'Carry on! were the last words of my boy to his men, but he would mean them for me too.' To the rapturous applause of an openly weeping audience – the like of which he had never seen before – Lauder returned from Scotland to the London stage three nights later with an act that featured a truly painful item for him: a song about the boys coming home.

Despite – or perhaps because of – this heartbreaking personal tragedy, he resolved to get more deeply involved in war work. Unable to serve as a soldier because of his age, he sought a green light to entertain Allied soldiers in Europe, and got it. 'It's the least I can do for memory of John,' he said, as he became the first performer ever to entertain frontline troops (British and American) among the bullets of the battlefield. Travelling with a small, specially built piano tied to a military vehicle, he sang and joked his way across war-ravaged France – ending each of his shows with his theme tune, written in honour of John, 'Keep Right On to the End of the Road' – to the rare delight of his conflict-weary audiences.

But that was by no means his only contribution to the war effort. It was said that the patriotic Lauder was worth a battalion to that cause as he worked tirelessly to recruit soldiers – pulling in more than 12,000 during the remainder of the war – and to raise huge sums for war charities, including the Harry Lauder Million Pound Fund for war wounded. He even created a pipe band to stir the blood of the young and encourage them to join up. And when in the USA, he used his celebrity to urge his American fans to lobby their president and politicians to enter the conflict. Did he affect the ultimate course of events? We shall never know, but . . .

For all of this – even before his repeat performance in the Second World War at the request of his admirer Winston Churchill, who called him 'Scotland's greatest ever ambassador' – Harry Lauder was made the 'first knight of the music hall' in 1919 under the ceremonial sword of King George V.

Among his many other honours were the Freedom of the City of Edinburgh in 1927 (the year his wife died) and – posthumously – the naming of a modern bypass near his birthplace of Portobello as Sir Harry Lauder Road. His other achievements included the writing of several books, among them four volumes of memoirs, and his appearance in numerous movies.

The curtain came down on Sir Harry Lauder's last performance in Glasgow's Gorbals in 1947, and three years later he died in Lanarkshire at the age of seventy-nine. He was buried after the most memorable funeral ever to be seen in closed-for-the-day Hamilton – where Pathé, the cinema news service, reported that among the grieving, street-lining crowds were wreaths not only from Mr & Mrs Winston Churchill, but also from the Queen.

The end of Sir Harry's road was a long way from a 'wee sang' in a coalmine.

Alexander Fleming (1881–1955)

The 'accidental' lifesaver

There was something of the absent-minded boffin about the shy, short, bow-tied Alexander Fleming. The 47-year-old Scottish professor of bacteriology was not the most organised of people and, being happy to live with some faith in serendipity – 'one sometimes finds what one is not looking for' – he was not overly surprised when he returned to his laboratory at London's St Mary's Hospital after a two-week vacation in September, 1928, to find some mould had colonised his working equipment. But he was intrigued when he noticed something unusual about its behaviour.

He had left a culture dish smeared with staphylococcus bacteria (which turns wounds septic) exposed in a dark corner of his workbench. Spores had drifted in through the window and taken root on the dish, and around the resulting mould there was a clear absence of staphylococcal colonies. The realisation that these had been killed or at least inhibited by the mould was Fleming's 'eureka' moment – and a catalytic point in the treatment of bacterial infections. Surely the first antibiotic had been discovered? Surely the principle could now be developed to benefit all humankind?

Fleming immediately saw such possibilities for his discovery, which he called penicillin because the substance had been produced by the fungal mould *Penicillium notatum*. But his excitement was to be short-lived, for when he presented his findings to the Medical Research Club in 1929 its members could raise little or no interest. A similar response greeted his report on penicillin and its potential uses in the *British Journal of Experimental Pathology*. Other scientists tried in vain to replicate Fleming's result, not realising that an accidental conjunction of temperatures, helped by the open window, had been the key – so much so that when in later years he found himself in a modern, air-conditioned lab in America, he remarked that 'I would never have made my discovery in these conditions'.

In any case, paradoxically, interest in penicillin began to fade in the years immediately after its discovery – as it was ineffective on animals when given by mouth, and proved apparently impossible to produce in volume. Growing and refining it was clearly a complex challenge, which would be better suited to chemists or scientists, and their help would not be forthcoming until the imperatives of the Second World War revitalised interest – on a massive scale, particularly in America – as such a new anti-bacterial would surely prove vital to the successful treatment of wounded soldiers.

Known as 'Alec' to his seven siblings, Alexander Fleming was born into a family working an 800-acre sheep farm near Dalry in Ayrshire, south-west Scotland, in 1881. He was a bright pupil at Kilmarnock High School and in his spare time loved to roam the glens, rivers and woods of the countryside – 'where we unconsciously learned a great deal from nature' – with his brothers and sisters. After his father died and his eldest brother took over the farm, the fourteen-year-old Alec joined three Fleming brothers (one a medical student) and one sister living together in London. He went to the Polytechnic School in Regent Street, and started his working life in a shipping firm. Not being enthralled by the prospect of a career in that field, he decided to study medicine and eventually entered St Mary's Hospital in London, where he proceeded to live out his expected quiet life as a respectable, anonymous bacteriologist. Until penicillin crashed into his life.

Which is not to say he had not been enterprising up to then. He had pioneered the introduction to Britain of Salvarsan, a killer of the micro-organism that causes syphilis, and while serving in the Royal Army Medical Corps in the First World War, began work that would to lead to his discovery in 1922 of lysozyme – a bacteria-killing protein found in tears. But penicillin was the Big One, and in 1929 he got a hint of its effectiveness in humans when his assistant's infection was relieved through washing out the sinus with a penicillin broth.

Fleming was no chemist who could properly isolate the substance, however, and he must have been pleased when, prompted by the war requirement about a decade later, a few Oxford University scientists began intensive research based on his original report – and were encouraged in May 1940, after injecting eight mice with a lethal dose of streptococci, and four of them also with penicillin. The latter four survived.

Thus emboldened, they began to scale up production – using bed-pans, milk churns and bathtubs – with a view to experimenting with penicillin on humans. Their first patient, a 43-year-old policeman, died from staphylococcal infection, which he had at first appeared to be defeating under a four-day penicillin course; but a fifteen-year-old boy suffering from streptococcal septicaemia made a full recovery.

So the era of antibiotics had begun in earnest . . . in February 1941. But although they could thus show penicillin's ability to kill infectious bacteria, the Oxford scientists could not produce the quantities needed for large-scale clinical trials on humans. They looked across the Atlantic for help, and on 9 July 1941, two of them, Dr Howard Florey and Norman Heatley, set out for the USA with a small package of penicillin that would be the seed of a new miracle.

So, with the help of Heatley and a mouldy cantaloupe, it fell to America's scientists and pharmaceutical industry to meet the challenge of large-scale production. And by November of that year Dr Andrew J. Moyer, at his lab in Peoria, Arizona, to which the British team had been sent – as its scientists were already working on fermentation methods to accelerate fungal culture growth rates – had succeeded in increasing the yields of penicillin tenfold.

Its first tests for military use took place in the spring of 1943, with studies on American soldiers with chronic bacterial infections, and by autumn it was being used in combat zones, where it was limited to US and Allied military and to patients with life-threatening infections. Flight crews of the Eighth Air Force stationed in Britain were the first to benefit from it directly and, although there was strict rationing during the war, the armed forces received 85 per cent of America's production – 231 billion units in 1943 and, as production systems improved, 1,633 billion in 1944 and 7,952 billion in 1945. Finally mass-produced by the American drugs industry and given to all soldiers before active service, penicillin became the war's 'wonder drug' and saved the lives of thousands of wounded men.

Fleming was knighted for his work in 1944. The following year he shared with Florey and Ernst Chain – a chemist who had worked on medicinal properties of penicillin – the Nobel Prize for medicine 'for the discovery of penicillin and its curative effect in various infectious diseases'. And in 1990, Oxford University gave an unprecedented honorary doctorate to Norman Heatley for his work on the drug. Dr Moyer from the Peoria Lab was inducted into the Inventors' Hall of Fame and both the British and Peoria laboratories were designated as International Historic Chemical Landmarks.

Of his honour, Heatley, ninety-two and still living in Oxford at time of writing, said: 'This is an enormous privilege since I am not medically qualified . . . I was a third-rate scientist whose only merit was to be in the right place at the right time.'

Despite being the only member of the Oxford team still alive, he was certainly not about to upstage the equally diffident Scot whose 'accidental' achievement created the world's most effective life-saving drug that would conquer some of mankind's most ancient scourges. Sir Alexander Fleming died in 1955 and was buried in St Paul's Cathedral, London.

John Logie Baird (1888–1946)

The original man of vision

Margaret Baird glowed with pride when she talked about her famous husband, but her disappointment with mysterious powers-that-be was equally plain to see. She could not understand why, in an age that scattered honours on people of relatively minor achievement, there had been no acknowledgement of the globally significant pioneering television work of John Logie Baird. 'I feel terribly sad that Logie wasn't properly honoured by his country,' she said, a decade before she died in 1996 at eighty-nine.

She had lived half a century beyond her husband and had come to see many of the changes in society he had foretold – not least the idea that every sitting room would one day have a TV set: a prediction so alarming to a 1920s reporter that he fled from Baird's presence thinking he was a dangerous lunatic.

But in a world that was now taking TV for granted, Mrs Baird clearly had fun making people gasp by saying, just by the way: 'Television? Oh, yes, my husband invented it.'

John Logie Baird always thought about sixty years ahead of his time, she explained to Dorothy-Grace Elder, who interviewed her for the *Scotsman Magazine.* 'Britain could have had colour TV in the Thirties if people had listened to him. And he went into video in 1928, recording moving images on wax discs.'

The pioneering genius was born in Helensburgh, a son of the manse – which is now a private house bearing a plaque that reads: 'John Logie Baird, inventor of Television, was born in this house on August 13, 1888'. There is also a monument to him tucked away in a local park.

It was in England, though, that he did most of his important work, having moved there after studying electrical engineering at Glasgow University and trying his hand at being a sales representative. Specifically, it was in his attic workshop in London's Frith Street that he made the first television transmission of a moving image on 30 October 1925 – a hugely exciting advance on his earlier transmission of the static shadow of a Maltese Cross across ten feet in his laboratory in Hastings.

When Baird received a screen image of a doll's head on that October night – 'not as a mere smudge of black and white but as a real image with detail' – he ran across the street to hire an office boy as a live model to front the camera.

'I placed him before the transmitter and went into the next room to see what the screen would show,' he recalled in an interview in the USA six years later.

> It was entirely blank and no effort of tuning would produce any results. Puzzled and disappointed, I went back to the transmitter and there the cause of the failure became at once evident. The boy, scared by the intense white light, had backed away from the transmitter.
>
> In the excitement of the moment I gave him half a crown and this time he kept his head in the right position. Going again into the next room, this time I saw his head quite clearly. It is curious that the first person in the world to have been seen by television should have required a bribe to accept that distinction.

Three months later, Baird gave two demonstrations of 'true television' – to the press and to members of the Royal Institution. 'We saw the transmission by television of living human faces, the proper gradation of light and shade and all movements of the head, of the lips and mouth and of a cigarette and its smoke were faithfully portrayed on a screen in the theatre,' wrote Dr Alexander Russell of Faraday House later. 'Naturally, the results are far from perfect. The image cannot be compared with that of a good kinematograph film. The likeness, however, was unmistakable and all the motions are reproduced with absolute fidelity. This is the first time that we have seen real television and Mr Baird is the first to have accomplished this marvellous feat.'

Despite the system's development eventually parting company from him, it can't be denied that this first heady breakthrough belonged to Baird. His mechanical set-up was pitched against the formidable resources of the giant Marconi company and, despite working in an attic on a shoestring, begging £10 batteries from friends, 'he won' – his widow claimed quite categorically – 'he was the first. And he was determined to get that first for Britain and for Scotland.'

But while Baird continued experimenting with his mechanical system, his rivals were looking into electronic systems, and he was devastated when, after working on ideas and trial programmes with the BBC 'for ages', the corporation – under fellow-Scot but old adversary Lord Reith – chose Marconi to take its TV plans forward. 'My husband was appalled,' said Mrs Baird, a South African-born concert pianist who had two children with John Logie Baird. 'But with typical courage, he plunged deeper into colour TV work.'

Meanwhile, news of his achievement had crossed the Atlantic and he began to pin his hopes on the more entrepreneurial spirit of America. Taking a business trip to assess possibilities, he was amazed to receive a hero's welcome – complete with pipe band – when he arrived in New York in 1931. He felt there was more chance of his developing television in the USA, and said so in a radio broadcast:

> The whole atmosphere of New York is very different from that of Europe. It is an atmosphere of 'go ahead' vigour, welcoming of novelty and enterprise. The people here are, to use a New York expression, 'all out for progress', whereas in Europe we are inclined to look with distrust and suspicion on anything new . . .
>
> Throughout the world the highest scientific thought is being devoted to television. Vast strides have been made and will be made in this new art. I myself look forward to seeing at no distant day, television theatres supersede the talkies, and the home television become as common as the home radio is today.

But after he returned to Britain a promising deal he had concluded for a jointly operated television station with Donald Flamm – owner of New York's WMCA radio station – was barred by the Federal Radio Commission in Washington on several spurious grounds, one of which was that Baird's company was foreign and, as such, should have no part in American broadcasting.

It could all have been so different if the commission had been more magnanimous. Baird, whose heart and health would have certainly appreciated a move to sunny California or Florida, could have followed in the footsteps of telephone inventor Alexander Graham Bell (see page 80), whose Scottish ingenuity was welcomed even before he became one of America's developmental heroes. As it was, Britain's cold, damp, wartime climate – in more ways than one – so weakened the television inventor that he died in 1946 at the cruelly early age of fifty-seven.

A genius, a world-beater, and a true prophet without honour in his own land.

Robert Watson-Watt (1892–1973)

Opener of the eye in the sky

Of all the defence mechanisms, brainwaves and acts of defiance that kept Britain free of Nazi occupation during the Second World War, the most important had to be Radio Detection and Ranging – or radar for short. Along with Winston Churchill, it arrived just in time to save the country in its darkest hour. But unlike Churchill, its brilliant inventor never seemed to get full credit for his amazing achievement, whose peacetime application remains vitally important today – keeping, as it does, aviation and shipping running like clockwork.

Bespectacled and ruddy-cheeked, the studious-looking Scot was not everyone's picture of a war hero. But his lack of fame then, and even now, was and is more to do with the culture of secrecy that surrounded breakthroughs like his at times of international tension. And Robert Watson-Watt's achievement did not go entirely unacknowledged, as he was quietly knighted during the war to which he contributed so effectively.

A direct descendant of James Watt, the famous steam pioneer, Watson-Watt was born in 1892 in the cathedral 'city' of Brechin – actually a small town eight miles inland from Scotland's north-east coast – and studied engineering, before teaching physics, at Dundee's University College, which was part of St Andrews University at the time.

When he found his next challenge down in England he approached it rather warily, as studying the weather in the Meteorological Office of the new Royal Aircraft Establishment at Farnborough in Kent was a far cry from the heavy engineering he was mentally geared up to. But he found himself becoming intrigued by the possibilities of applying radio to predict the approach of bad weather, which airmen could then be warned about.

His interest in the reflection of radio waves quickly grew, and when only twenty-eight, he took out a patent concerning radio location by means of short-wave radio. He worked on improvements to relevant systems throughout the 1920s and, as his endeavours came to the notice of the British government, he was asked in 1935 if, based on such a principle, he could give some thought to developing a 'death ray' capable of taking out enemy aircraft. His answer was an emphatic 'No', but he offered a considerable consolation: the suggestion that such a 'ray' idea could perhaps be applied to the problem of locating approaching enemy aircraft.

As radio waves always travel at the speed of light, he explained, the position of any large object from which they bounced could be easily worked out. Not surprisingly, great interest was expressed in such a proposition and, before the year was out, Watson-Watt was perfecting a system that could follow an aircraft – as a blip on a screen – by the radio-wave reflection it sent back.

This was the birth of radar, right on time to catch the war clouds gathering over Europe, and as its military significance was immediately appreciated, further research and development had to go underground. Successful trials of the new system were carried out in total secrecy on a remote Suffolk airfield and, as Watson-Watt's team worked on under his guidance, five radio location stations were set up along the south coast of England. And soon, with war becoming a distinct possibility and radar now having an effective range of seventy-five miles, the government made plans for another twenty stations to act as an insurance policy against enemy invasion from across the English Channel

Watson-Watt's work was thus Britain's stunning trump card when the conflict did begin . . . and Luftwaffe planes finally did drone over the horizon in frightening waves. Radar came into its own particularly during the Battle of Britain, by alerting defending RAF fighters to the position of attacking enemy planes in all weathers and as easily by night as by day. So with 'the few' numerically disadvantaged British pilots showing memorably selfless courage that maximised their remarkable technical advantage, the apparently unequal battle turned – much to the Germans' surprise – in Britain's favour. Radar also helped to knock out scores of German aircraft when a badly stung Hitler switched his tactics to night bombing.

The ingenious inventor of radar must have felt very sorry, however, that the United States had not managed to similarly benefit from such a system when waves of Japanese planes attacked Pearl Harbor in 1941. Although he had visited America to help its technical teams complete its radar system, and although that was in place in time – and showed the enemy planes approaching – its warning was tragically ignored through a misreading of the big blip on the screen as a flight of American B-17s due in from the mainland.

Nevertheless, Sir Robert Watson-Watt must have been more than reasonably satisfied with his world-changing achievement when he died in 1973 in Inverness, the northern Scottish town to which he had retired. Quietly . . .

Sean Connery (1930–   )

Bottom drawer to superstar

Writing on the British side of the Atlantic, it is not always easy to judge the degree of impact that this or that important Scot has had on America. On occasion, therefore, a San Francisco-born-and-resident contact has been called in to make a judgement out of ten. Thus we know that Sir Sean Connery couldn't have made bigger waves in the USA, for – after our contact's circle of friends had been sounded – the figure that came back was ten-out-of-ten.

Something for native Scots to bask in the reflection of? Well, perhaps surprisingly, yes.

There are few people of his generation living in Sir Sean's Edinburgh today who won't claim to have some memory of, or connection with, 'Big Tam' – as the over-familiar call him, affecting to have known him before he chose to use his middle name – and some might even be telling the truth. The fact is that Scotland in general, and Edinburgh in particular, is uncharacteristically proud of its super-famous film-star son. Why uncharacteristically? Because it has long been a dour, inexplicable Scottish trait to pour scorn on the Scots who have done well beyond the country's borders. So why, having done miles better than most, is Sir Sean still so favoured at home? He is admired by politicians who seek his endorsement; by bank clerks who see in him the man they'd love to be; and of course by women, among whom you can number hotel chamber maids who compete with each other just to enter his room and breathe his (shaken, not stirred) after-shave.

What's his secret? I believe that, as a mature role-player, he is unusually comfortable being a two-in-one person – a passionate Rangers-supporting Scot and a world movie icon – and sees no conflict between the parts. If some Scots' traditional resentment of such figures is largely born of a fear that they and the old country's culture will be abandoned by the Talented One as he or she flies over the horizon, Connery has never done that. Despite all his years and layers of global success, he has always returned to express a burning love for his homeland. This may have led him down some tricky alleyways (such as support for the Scottish Nationalist Party, an allegiance said to have delayed his knighthood) but its obvious sincerity has been appreciated. And when he finally arose to accept the honour from the Queen in 2000, he looked like the King of Scotland: no one can wear a kilt with such presence and aplomb.

Some, of course, are not satisfied with that and argue that, if he feels so much for Caledonia, why doesn't he live there? Americans might equally argue that, if he thrives on the largesse of Hollywood, why doesn't he make his home in America? These are obviously taxing questions, in more ways than one, for a man who has lived in Spain and was latterly resident in the Bahamas, though he has run an office in Culver City, California, for his erstwhile film production company, sentimentally named Fountainbridge Films.

Fountainbridge is, of course, the name of the street in west Edinburgh where, at No. 176, he grew up as one of two brothers born of working-class (but conspicuously handsome) parents. His father, Joseph, was a truck driver and his mother, Euphemia, a charwoman. Their crowded family apartment had only two rooms and no interior toilet, and the baby Sean slept in the bottom drawer of his parents' wardrobe. Their home has long been demolished but, perhaps a hundred steps from where it used to be, there is a plaque on a high garden wall in his honour. Sir Sean is reported to have said, on seeing it, that 'they might have waited till I was dead'. But it is hardly a fitting marker for so big a presence on the world stage. One can imagine that if the Scottish capital were an American city, it would be comprehensively promoted with signs and posters as 'Connery's Town'. This one-foot-square colour-tinted plate sits on the wall opposite the entrance to the old Fountain Brewery and is almost too high – at something like nine feet – to read. 'You would have to be ten foot tall to see it,' he has said. Certainly, the camera-festooned Chicago couple at the spot when this writer went to check it out were having a hard stretch to register the words:

> Commemorating the Century of Cinema 1996
> SEAN CONNERY
> Born Fountainbridge
> 25th August 1930
> Oscar-winning actor
> International Film Star
> The Scottish Film Council

A more fitting tribute by far would be the proposed Connery Filmhouse, possible new home of the Edinburgh International Film Festival. Sir Sean was on hand to see the model of architect Richard Murphy's £20 million vision unveiled in the city in September 2004, and he obviously approved – with one reservation, expressed to Tim Cornwell of *The Scotsman*: 'It's very flattering, but there's one thing wrong. I think if it's using Connery, it's better with the whole name.'

While this impressive flight of modern fancy was only at the design stage, it bore not just Connery's name but his picture – in the form of a miniature from *The Name of the Rose*, one of his most remembered films, released in 1986.

Neither can it ever be forgotten, of course, that Connery skyrocketed to international fame in the 1960s as the suave, confident secret agent 007 in six movies of Ian Fleming's Bond stories. Portraying such an English hero could never have been an easy matter for a simple lad with an Edinburgh accent, but he – and his amazingly expressive eyebrows – rose to the challenge to the satisfaction not just of the public who said a big yes to *Dr No* (1962), but of the producers. So over the next decade, more Bonds came thick and fast: *From Russia, With Love* (1963), *Goldfinger* (1964),*Thunderball* (1965), *You Only Live Twice* (1967) and *Diamonds are Forever* (1971). Eventually feeling in danger of being typecast, however, he branched out with an Agatha Christie whodunnit, *Murder on the Orient Express* (1974), John Huston's adaptation of Rudyard Kipling's *The Man Who Would Be King* (1975), the medieval romance *Robin and Marian* (1976) and Peter Hyams' sci-fi film, *Outland* (1981). He resurfaced as a noticeably older Bond in the 1983 adventure, *Never Say Never Again*.

The maturing Connery's 1990s featured such great films as *The Hunt for Red October* (1990, as a Russian submarine commander); and 1993's *Rising Sun* (as an expert in all things Japanese); *Dragonheart* (1996); and the successful contemporary action dramas *Just Cause* (1995) and *The Rock* (1996). In 1999, he starred in and produced *Entrapment*, a love story-thriller, co-starring Catherine Zeta-Jones. The year 2000 brought what many have said to be one of his best films, *Finding Forrester*, and in 2003 he made the acclaimed *League of Extraordinary Gentlemen*, while 2004 saw the making of *Josiah's Canon*, in which he played a Holocaust survivor planning a bank heist in Switzerland. But it was as a representative of the other side of the law – an Irish cop – that he gave his most memorable, Oscar-winning performance in *The Untouchables* (1987).

In all, he has made around seventy films in a non-stop tour de force of a career that the poor boy from Fountainbridge can be more than satisfied with, as he looks back at his magical life from his Bahamian poolside. He has been twice married, to remarkable women: to actress Diane Cilento (with whom he has an actor son, Jason) from 1962 to 1973, and latterly, for almost thirty years, to artist Micheline Roquebrune. It could have turned out a lot differently . . .

Life did not look too promising for lads like him who left school at fourteen in the 1940s. There were jobs, nevertheless, and the young Sean tried his hand at many of them. It is almost the stuff of legend that he began his working life as a milkman, and those who witnessed his deliveries can still dine out on the memories. But the wide world beckoned and at sixteen he enlisted in the Royal Navy. Like many young men in that service, he opted for a tattoo but unusually, he did not live to regret it, as his tattoos reflect two of his big lifelong loves – Scotland and his family. One reads 'Mum and Dad', the other 'Scotland Forever'.

His naval career was abruptly cut short, after three years, by a stomach ulcer. When he came back to Edinburgh he went like a dose of salts through one job after another: bricklayer, lifeguard and French polisher (in which role he is reputed to have held no fewer than five appointments with cabinet-making firms). He was a steel worker for eight weeks, and a male model at Edinburgh College of Art. He sampled cement mixing, he cleaned the printing machines for the *Edinburgh Evening News*, and he was a lifeguard at the now-defunct open-air Portobello swimming pool – where his looks and physique were much admired by the girls from the nearby Duncan's chocolate factory.

No matter what you worked at in Edinburgh in those days, you were almost bound to have bumped into 'Big Tam', or at least someone who knew him. 'I used to watch him and his super-fit colleagues doing their press-ups at the pool,' recalls an old contemporary, 'and one day much later I recognised him retrospectively, as it were, when he appeared in a television production, and I thought: "I've seen you before".'

Indeed, Sean spent much of his free time bodybuilding, and it was to that pastime that he owed the eventual breakthrough into acting. The hobby brought him into a bid for the 1952 Mr Universe title in London. He took third place and was duly noticed.

But Sean Connery was no overnight success. Like many a hopeful Scot before him, he did not find the streets of London paved with gold. 'I spent a lot of time alone,' he told an interviewer. 'I was living in a basement eating minestrone, which would last me three days. In the winter I would cycle up to Chelsea library – because it was warm there – and read and read.' He did some modelling before getting his chorus part in the London stage production of *South Pacific*. He played some bit parts and, as his hard work began to pay off, won some praise for his performance in the TV play *Requiem for a Heavyweight*. And from those modest beginnings, he was to start building the track that would take him all the way to becoming an international film icon.

There followed a series of films – *Hell Drivers* with Sid James and *Time Lock*, but, before these were released in late 1957, Sean would sign a long-term deal with 20th Century Fox, worth £120 a week. It produced little work, however – his accent was seen as a problem – and he had to make do with a small part as a sailor in Terence Young's *Action Of The Tiger*.

Unable to offer him anything more, Fox now loaned Connery out for *Another Time, Another Place*, with a fading Lana Turner playing a newspaperwoman seduced by Sean's war correspondent in London during the Blitz. Sadly, the movie was a failure, but Terence Young had not forgotten the Scot's screen presence, and neither had another very important person who met him during the making of the movie – Cubby Broccoli.

Four years later, Connery's name kept coming up when Broccoli and Harry Salzman were preparing to bring Ian Fleming's Bond novels to the screen, with Young as director. Rex Harrison, David Niven and Cary Grant had all said 'No' to the part and Connery should have had a clear field; but reservations kept being expressed about his accent and rough edges. It couldn't be denied that Harrison, Niven and Grant were more in the posh, private school image that Fleming had presumably meant for his hero – also a Scot, but educated under the tall tower of very expensive Fettes, Alma Mater of Tony Blair. Connery had only ever delivered milk to that school.

Nevertheless, the self-made Broccoli – said to be from the Italian family who developed the vegetable of that name by crossing a cauliflower and a pea – was not unsympathetic to simple roots. And he had a brainwave that would settle all doubts. Among the Scot's more recent films had been a silly Disney fantasy about leprechauns called *Darby O'Gill and the Little People* in which he played a burly farmhand who won a fist fight with a village bully.

Aware that he was no judge of masculine appeal, Broccoli obtained a copy of that film and called his wife Dana, who later recalled the catalytic moment that was to be the making of Sean Connery: 'One day Cubby called me and said: "Could you come down and look at this film at the Goldwyn Studios? I think I've found the guy but I don't know if he has sex appeal." I went and watched the film. I saw that face and the way he moved and talked, and I said: "Cubby, he's fabulous!" He was just perfect. He had star material right there.'

Despite United Artists sending a telegram that read 'See if you can do better', Connery was offered the part and accepted. So in November 1961, he signed up as James Bond in a deal that would hold him for six years. And not even author Ian Fleming demurred. 'When I first met Fleming, there was no dissension between us on how to see Bond,' the actor told interviewer Sheldon Lane in 1965. 'I saw him as a complete sensualist – senses highly tuned, awake to everything, quite amoral. I particularly like him because he thrives on conflict.'

There was acknowledgement that some smoothing-out would have to be done, and *Dr No* director Young – a quintessential Englishmen with many Bond-like qualities himself – took Connery under his tutoring wing, teaching him how to walk, talk and even how to eat and dress. Connery knew he was ready to become Bond when Young took him to his own tailor to have a suit made in London's Savile Row. Thus transformed into a Young-style gentleman, it was a new man with new confidence who went out on his first outing as James Bond, for which he received an upfront fee of £5,000. And the rest, as they say, is history. As it happened, he did not lose all his Scottish edges on screen – and proved that they could be compelling to the point of winning him *People* magazine's title of 'sexiest man alive' while incidentally propelling him towards being one of the world's most adored and bankable stars, commanding millions per movie.

In the spring of 2006, he finally called it a day, vowing to make no more films. But now, in his mid seventies, he could reflect with some satisfaction that it hadn't been a bad career for the baby from the bottom drawer in Fountainbridge.

Jim Clark (1936–68)

Conqueror of the Brickyard

In any overview of the life and times of Jim Clark, racing driver extraordinary, we are told he was a man who could hold his fame like some fellow-Scots can hold their whisky; a man of world-scale achievement, which could only be matched by the depth of his niceness and modesty. He certainly had smiling eyes and a shy, likeable face, which in many ways belied the macho world of speed in which he lived (and prematurely died). This picture of a gifted gentleman is confirmed by quotes from many contemporaries, not least his friend and equally famous Scottish rival, Sir Jackie Stewart, who said of him (in an interview with David Frost): 'He was the best racing driver I ever raced against . . . he was smooth, he was clean, he was honest, he was courteous, he was dignified, on and off the track . . . a master.'

This writer also had reason to be impressed by Jim Clark. Having dealings in different offices in the same building in London's Fleet Street, we once passed on the stairs as he dashed down to the street. As a fan, I felt I knew him and said spontaneously, 'Hi, Jim' – to which he smilingly replied, not knowing me at all: 'Hi there, how are you?' Despite having interviewed a number of well-known people in-depth over the decades, I treasure that small, superficial moment as a piquant brush with the life of an immortal great.

But America also had reason to be impressed by this polite young racer, who numbered among his many achievements two Formula I world championship titles. For in 1965, only a few years into his track career, he set the US motor-racing world back on its heels by registering a stunning triumph in the Indianapolis 500, jewel in the crown of the once all-American race calendar. Not only did US drivers have a wake-up call; the rear-engined design of Clark's winning Lotus began to change the style of their race-cars from that moment on.

So who was this little Scottish upstart who so upset the Brickyard?

Jim Clark was born into a farming family at Kilmany near Cupar in Fife – north of the Scottish capital of Edinburgh – in 1936. He was the only son among five children, and his early enthusiasm for sheep rearing allowed his parents the hope that he would follow his father into a farm career; but when he caught the speed bug, it was not to be. After a family move to the Borders – where the town of Duns now has a museum room devoted to him – he became intrigued by sports car racing there and, on joining the Borders Reivers team, chalked up some impressive local victories in a Jaguar. Thus encouraged, he was soon off to the Brands Hatch track in England where, in late 1958, he raced a Lotus Elite so well that he made a big impression on Colin Chapman, who just beat him to the flag. Chapman was, of course, the prime mover at the Lotus racing operation and wasted no time in inviting Clark to test a Lotus Formula II car.

The lad did not disappoint, and so his short but potent career was exclusively with the Lotus team, for which he drove from the Dutch Grand Prix in 1960 until his untimely death in 1968. In all, he won 33 Grand Prix pole positions and 25 victories in just 77 starts. He was only three years into his driving career when he won seven out of the ten races in 1963 – to gain his first world championship title. And he repeated that world-beating performance in 1965, when he again won the championship. That was the year he also won the Indianapolis 500, much to the chagrin of his rivals.

His appearances in the Indy races of 1963 (when he came second) and 1964 (led, but retired) had put the cat among the racing pigeons. The drivers of the big front-engined roadsters initially laughed at the 'funny' European rear-engined Lotuses, but by the start of the 1964 race as many as twenty-one of the sixty-one entered cars were rear-engined.

In the event, Clark became the first driver to top 160 m.p.h. at the Brickyard and won the 1965 Indy 500 after leading for no fewer than 190 out of the 200 laps. America in general, and intense rivals like Parnelli Jones in particular, gasped with surprise – and admiration – for a world champion driver who was apparently without equal.

Meanwhile, however, a second Scots star was rising fast. Jackie Stewart had already served notice in Europe that he was about to challenge all the established great drivers of the day, and when he and his famous English team-mate Graham Hill got moving at the following year's chaotic Indy 500, Jim Clark did not have it all his own way. Described by one newspaper as 'the most fantastic, confused and incredible 500', the race's result is still a matter of controversy today among motor-racing aficionados. The complexities that arose after a sixteen-car tangle that stopped the race for over an hour resulted in Hill being declared the surprise winner – though Clark thought he had won, and Stewart probably would have won if his engine had not blown up.

Just before that point, he had taken the lead from Clark, who had spun twice, and it looked – in his own words – 'as if we were about to give them a double Scotch'. But it was not to be even a single Scotch. While Clark's crew continued to flash the P-1 sign to him, the race ended with Hill being declared winner and – despite protests that he had been incorrectly scored with an extra lap – he went home to England with the winner's cheque for $156,297.

Just how much Stewart received for his official sixth place, I don't know, but on his return to Scotland, I had occasion to be sitting with him (and his editor for a magazine column) in Glasgow's Lorne Hotel, when a waiter came up to congratulate him on his exciting performance. He smiled and said: 'At least my bank manager's happy with me at last!'

Soon, of course, the 'double Scotch' effect became apparent to all, as – the Lotus having become temporarily uncompetitive after an engine rule change – Clark's career fortunes began to level out while Stewart's rose. Ironically, it was just after a South African Grand Prix win had marked a brighter start to his 1968 season that Jim Clark tragically lost his life when his Lotus left the track and crashed into trees in a Formula II race at Hockenheim. He was thirty-two.

Many people still say his natural talent was such that, had he lived, he would have broken every record in the book. But that ignores the fact that he would have had to contend with Stewart, who quickly took on his friend's mantle and went on to do what he might have done. The new Scot on the scene, a garage-owner's son from Dumbarton, won his first of three world titles in 1969 and the other two in 1971 and 1973. And in all, he won 27 of the 101 races he competed in.

But Clark and Stewart are not the only two Scots to have had an impact on the motor-racing life of America . . .

Dario Franchitti may have an Italian-sounding name, but he comes from the little town of Bathgate, in the Scottish central belt between Glasgow and Edinburgh, and cites many Scottish cultural references in his published biographies – he admires fellow-Scot Sean Connery; rates Edinburgh and Glasgow respectively as first and second before

San Francisco in his choice of top cities; keeps a house in Dalgety Bay, Scotland; and was married – to film star Ashley Judd – at the old home of Andrew Carnegie, Skibo Castle near Dornoch, Sutherland, in 2001.

Franchitti began his career in karting, becoming the Scottish Junior Champion at the age of eleven. By 1994, he was having significant success in Formula III racing. He moved to the USA to become involved in the Championship Auto Racing Teams (CART) competitions, and almost clinched the championship in 1999. His transition to the Indy Racing League (IRL) IndyCar Series in 2003 was one of the most highly anticipated in the league and only spoiled by a back injury sustained in a motorcycle accident. He was literally back on track in 2004 and 2005 with the successful Andretti Green Racing team, and at time of writing it seemed only a matter of time before the 31-year-old took the Indy 500 chequered flag.

Now based in Nashville, Tennessee, Dario is frequently put forward in Europe as a potential Formula I driver, and he calls Jackie Stewart the person to have most influenced his life, after only his father George and mother Marina. Watch this space . . .

Tom Farmer (1940–   )

Kwik way to a billion

Anyone who can get an American corporate giant to deposit more than one and a half billion dollars into his bank account has to be a serious player on the world's business stage. But the recipient in this case – the Scots entrepreneur Sir Tom Farmer – owed much of it, metaphorically at least, back to the United States. For he admits gracefully and gratefully that he got the inspiration for his world-famous Kwik-Fit enterprise from the time he lived in California; and, in the end, after it grew to be the biggest automotive repair chain in the world, the learning feeling was entirely mutual and reciprocal.

It was no surprise to Scots watching its rapid growth from home that Sir Tom's huge company eventually attracted the attention of a diversifying Ford around the turn of the millennium. The surprise was that, up to then, there had never been a direct involvement from that side of the Atlantic in its thirty-year history. The whole culture of his company, not least the happy-zappy name – which became a household word throughout Europe and much of the world – was a Scottish tribute to the American way of doing things, and as such a supreme example of cultural cross-pollenisation in business.

How did it happen? The youngest of a brood of seven children, Tom Farmer was born in Leith – the Scottish capital's port area – in 1940, and, like his shipbuilder father, was interested in ships; but when a medical test proved him colour-blind, he failed in his first ambition to become a merchant seaman. Keen to get going in life, however, he left Holy Cross School at fourteen to become a store boy with a tyre company – where, while sweeping the floor, his entrepreneurial instincts saw him studying out of the corner of his eye just how such a business worked. For he already knew he wanted to do something like that for himself. And today, as he sits in the smart surroundings of his clean-lined modern office which fills a handsome old Edinburgh house, the maturing Sir Tom, now engaged in yet another ambitious car-oriented scheme, recalls being quite a dynamic youth who dabbled in ventures such as cooker cleaning, a service which he advertised with the eye-catching spelling 'Kookers Kleaned'. It was to come back and help him . . .

Hanging on the office wall behind him is a painting of a modest corner premises in the city's Buccleuch Street near the university. This was the former grocer's shop where, when he was in his early twenties in the mid-1960s, he started his first serious business, Tyre and Accessory Supplies. Drawing on that early tyre-firm experience, he bought tyres at a discount and offered the refreshingly new service of fitting them for customers outside the relatively quiet shop he rented for what sounds today like an absurd figure: £5 a week.

He was still only twenty-eight when, six years after opening it, he sold that company to the English-owned Albany Tyre Service. And when he then suggested to his young wife Anne that they take their two little children to California 'to retire' on the considerable fortune the sale had yielded, 'she just said, "fine"'.

They went to live in Orinda, in Marin County, outside San Francisco, where Tom had a sister, but the couple of years they spent there felt like a vacation, as they went out of their way to see and savour all the local sights and experiences. It turned out, however, that what Tom was savouring most of all was the American way of doing business. And when he had been there, done that as a tourist, 'my inactivity became a real problem . . . it didn't suit me . . . and I started to look around for interesting ideas'.

It did not take him long to see several. 'This was around the time when the idea of specialisation was beginning to spawn a number of uniquely dedicated companies in the US,' he recalls.

> Becoming more and more popular were establishments that – unlike conventional garages that dealt with the total automotive repair repertoire – did just transmissions, or just exhausts, or just engines, or a small group of products like tyres and batteries. There were even firms that resprayed – and dried – the body of your car in one working day.
>
> This was all fascinating to me. Rather like the drive-in-and-out convenience of the fast-food chains like McDonald's and Kentucky Fried Chicken, what they had was speed, instant reactions and value for money. I sensed something important was happening and I went to visit as many of them as I could, to look around, make friends and ask questions.
>
> I was attracted by the whole idea of specialisation, as I had previously been touching on that with tyres and car accessories,

so to some extent I was topping up what I already knew. But there were other factors that impressed me, such as the Americans' level of customer service – something the British were not too good at in the Seventies – and the respect they expressed for good employees through good remuneration. All in all, I was intrigued by the thought of bringing all that back to Scotland.

Sir Tom is a tidy man in his sixties, with neat, well-balanced features, a friendly smile, thinning brown hair, and a liking for dark business suits. He drives a top-of-the-range Mercedes and his office is always pristine. But for the rest, he has few pretensions, still speaking with a gentle Scottish accent and being happy to deal personally with customers – often to their surprise, for he is something of a legend in Scotland. One night, when he was working late and the staff had gone home, a difficult client telephoned his previous HQ and demanded to speak to the manager.

'This is Tom Farmer,' came the reply.

'Aye,' said the disbelieving caller, 'and I'm Sean Connery.'

Sir Tom's considerable achievements may have been recognised by the Queen with the bestowal of a knighthood in 1997, but the one-time store boy has developed few social or intellectual pretensions. 'We all have different qualities to offer society,' he says. 'When we were born God gave some people high intellect. He gave some high energy, and He gave some a good dose of common sense.'

Where would he put himself? 'High energy and common sense,' he responds without hesitation. 'What these two qualities give you is the ability – when you see an opportunity – to reach out and do something about it immediately.'

If that means he is denying himself intellectual talents, Sir Tom can nevertheless be quite philosophical and back that up with strong evidence of late-night reading. Explaining his decision to return to Scotland from the USA after a couple of years, for instance, he quotes Alfred Lord Tennyson from 'Hands All Round': 'That man's the best cosmopolite who loves his country best'.

And so, like the good cosmopolite and incurable entrepreneur that he is, Tom Farmer took not just his family back to Scotland in the early 1970s but also a lot of America's spirit, in the form of many new and exciting ideas.

Indeed, he had three favourite ones, all based on the specialisation principle, and he was determined to try them all. There was the super-quick paint-spraying venture ('a straight copy of the American idea') that got so busy that the supply of skilled painters could not keep up with the forty-cars-a-day demand. There was World of Sound, focusing on car radios and stereos. And there was that other little idea specialising in high-speed, while-you-wait fitting of exhaust pipes, brakes and tyres. He was sure it had great promise but what it really needed was a slick, easy-to-remember name.

That was when his Kooker Kleaning past came back to him. 'I was not too well at the time,' he recalls. 'Just lying in bed with 'flu, thinking and thinking . . . then, as I remembered the cooker idea, it came to me in an Archimedes moment – Eureka! Kwik-Fit was born. It was just the perfect name. It explained so clearly what we would be trying to do.'

Soon, he had called together many of his old gang of fitters from Buccleuch Street and the rest is history. Starting with one local station in Edinburgh in 1971, the chain just 'growed and growed like Topsy' at a speed he himself had not anticipated. At a time when you often had to make appointments a week ahead with conventional garages, the while-you-wait-and-watch convenience and American-inspired cheerful customer service caught on quickly. While people all over Britain, from schoolchildren to grandmothers, knew the company's catchy televised slogan 'You can't get better than a Kwik-Fit fitter', the company's station-count had topped the 400 mark within 17 years – not just planting Farmer flags in Scotland and England but also on mainland Europe, in Holland and Belgium, where there were no fewer than 50.

A cosmopolite he may have been, but the port-raised Farmer was anything but insular: a charge that is often set against British business people. Despite his fast-rising wings and growing fame, the dapper entrepreneur kept his smart black shoes tied firmly on the ground over all the years in which his company grew out further and further, to France and North Africa; then on to Thailand and even the Pacific Islands. 'Why did I do it?' he asks himself. 'Well, on my travels to Amsterdam or Paris or further afield, I couldn't help noticing that there were an awful lot of cars in the streets of these cities, and to me these represented business, of course.'

When Kwik-Fit had finished expanding, it had over 2,500 outlets and 11,000 employees across the world. So phenomenal was its growth that £100 invested at its birth in the early 1970s would have been worth £23,000 at the time of its sale to Ford.

That time was 1999, and there were many reasons for Ford's bold buying strategy (which kept on Sir Tom as Kwik-Fit chairman for the transition period). The idea was not just about taking over a now-famous brand name and growing it to be even bigger in the States. 'Ford wanted to cement its position in Europe in the light automotive repair industry,' says Sir Tom, 'and ours was the biggest organisation of that type in the world.'

In Kwik-Fit the American giant saw development potential for its embryonic policy in the 'after-market' business – which meant building strong permanent bonds between itself and its car customers: an after-care programme in which a Ford purchaser would have his or her car, and its parts requirements, looked after through the organisation for life, and so would – presumably – always came back to Ford for the next purchase.

As Kwik-Fit had already diversified into parts, mobile fitting and insurance, its acquisition represented for Ford a ready-made basis on which to build. 'When Ford executives came to see me for the early discussions it was clear that they were most interested in developing the parts business,' says Sir Tom. 'It is, after all, extremely lucrative – when you consider that a £10,000 car is probably worth £25,000 when you break down and sell all its parts separately.'

Indeed, while the gigantic $1.6 billion price paid made many people gasp, Ford's muscle and positive after-market business plan behind the final stage of Kwik-Fit's global spread seemed to make sense to most business commentators; so it was with some surprise that, only a couple of years later, they learned that reverse gear was suddenly being engaged with a back-to-basics philosophy, and that the project was to be stopped in its tracks.

'Profit margins had been squeezed at Ford over that period,' explains Sir Tom, 'and there had been top management changes: people coming in with different ideas.'

So in mid-2002, Ford announced that, despite having originally hoped to raise about £800 million from divesting itself of the Scottish car-repair empire, it had agreed to sell it for £330 million – about a quarter of the 1999 purchase price – to the European private equity group CVC Capital Partners. The car giant retained a 19 per cent stake in Kwik-Fit, allowing it to benefit from future growth.

As the beneficiary of all these corporate machinations in what was clearly a massive personal coup, Sir Tom ironically found himself explaining on Ford's behalf that, while it had bought Kwik-Fit in more buoyant times and had had 'grand plans' for the chain, 'circumstances have changed throughout the world and it has decided it wants to concentrate on its core business'.

In view of this awesome financial success and his company's general track record of super-fast growth, some people (and not a few Scots) have called Sir Tom lucky. And he might agree, although he remembers how 'we worked like Trojans' and how young employees were selected for their high energy and communicating personalities which complemented their bosses' sense of mission and also pleased the customer.

Yet Sir Tom does not think of himself as driven, especially not these days, when he is 'taking time to smell the flowers'. He denies being a 'workaholic' and likes to add that 'people should work to live, not live to work'.

Though he can still skip up the stairs of his smart new office, urgency is no longer a big consideration, a fact perhaps reflected in the less-than-kwik title of his new co-ownership enterprise – Tyres 'n' Wheels Farmer Autocare – which he runs alongside several vast property projects. You sense that he wouldn't worry too much if Autocare's growth pace turned out to be considerably slower than Kwik-Fit's.

For Sir Tom, working to live means sheer enjoyment of his daily endeavours. And he has never found them tiresome or boring or (excuse the expression) exhausting. 'It's been wonderful,' he says, with genuine surprise.

> What happened with me was quite exceptional. Sometimes I have found myself wondering if it's all a dream. But I wouldn't want to be pointed at as some kind of template for success. I would hate people to be saying to each other: 'There's Tom Farmer – you haven't done well with your life if it doesn't measure up to his.'
>
> Success is relative. I was reminded of that by my son John when I complained about some Joe Bloggs having reached his 'comfort level'. John said: 'Why shouldn't he enjoy his life?' And he was right. Not everybody needs to be a Tom Farmer – and if they were, there would be no one to work for me!

The Farmer formula for success, however, would be a hard one to beat. 'There's a great benefit in being second first, or maybe I mean first second,' he says.

> In being able to look at how other people do things, and take what they're doing and adapt it and change it for your own market. The

pioneers of this world are not necessarily always the most successful. I was able to see a lot of things that were happening and I always had quite an inquisitive mind. I remember a tour of America with my son in which we just talked to people in big retailers like Sears, Roebuck & Co. We'd always pick up something and come back to Scotland and adapt it accordingly.

What then happened turned the tables a bit. We set up a number of training schools in a programme called, very simply, the Kwik-Fit Way. Then we found American companies starting to make visits to Edinburgh to spend time with us, to see how we were doing it, as did other companies from all over the world. What were we doing that was new? Why were we so successful? What was the secret sauce we had? It was actually very simple. We were just doing what many good US firms were doing . . . only changing it a little to try to do better.

The US widened my whole thinking . . . I built tremendous relationships with tyre companies like the Big O and Discount Tires . . . I made more friends in America than anywhere else in the business.

Sir Tom likes to feel that, despite Ford's change of heart, his remarkable company had a big impact on US corporate life – without ever having been there.

It would just be returning the compliment to America, he feels.

Tony Blair (1953–   )

The presidents' vital friend

From the top of the little front lawn of 5 Paisley Terrace you get a spectacular view across the glittering River Forth estuary and its islands into the Kingdom of Fife beyond. Tony Blair may have been only nineteen months old when he left this modest 1930s bungalow in Edinburgh's elevated Willowbrae district, but even then, playing in the garden or gazing out the front window, he must have had a sweeping sense of space and the limitless possibilities that lay before him.

Grand thoughts perhaps, and it has to be said that the underwhelming impact of the house itself seems hardly worthy of them, with even its owners admitting its need for 'love and attention' when it was offered for sale with a starting price of £155,000 in late 2004.

But it was in this unremarkable two-bedroom semi-detached house, similar to all the others in the neighbourhood, that his parents, Leo and Hazel, lived when Anthony Charles Lynton Blair was born on 6 May 1953, at Edinburgh's Queen Mary Maternity Home. At the end of the following year the family left for Australia, where Leo – a Conservative tax inspector who studied hard to become a lawyer – had been offered a lecturing job. It lasted five years, after which they returned to the UK to live in the English cathedral city of Durham, though Tony picked up his Scottish roots again when he spent 1966 to 1971 at one of the capital's most prestigious private schools, the Disney-towered Fettes College.

Having followed the professional (if not political) example of his father and gone on to study law at Oxford University, he became a practising trial lawyer after graduation in 1975, and simultaneously developed an interest in national politics – an interest abruptly heightened when he was elected Labour MP for Sedgefield, near Durham, three years after marrying fellow trial lawyer Cherie Booth in 1980. They had four children together, the latest christened Leo after the PM's father.

Blair served as Labour's trade and industry spokesman before being made Shadow Secretary of State for Energy. In 1989 he moved to the employment brief, and when his leader and mentor, fellow-Scot John Smith, died unexpectedly in 1994, Blair's fresh face seemed to promise considerable consolation as he took over the mantle.

It was to be an interesting journey. Though he had thought long and hard before choosing left-wing philosophy over the mores of his own relatively privileged background, he decided to draw on the latter to play the power game differently from his predecessors. He was the first Labour leader to see that, if it wanted to win its first taste of government since 1979, his party would have to shed much of its traditional socialist baggage and embrace a degree of free enterprise, while still keeping the old guard on-side.

It was a difficult balancing act, but he pulled it off. 'Ours is a philosophy, not of the past, not some relic of a museum, but of the future,' he told applauding supporters at a local Labour club at the end of his first campaign. And having espoused a refreshing political centralism and coined the seductive slogan 'New Labour, New Britain', he was on his way to real power.

It seemed people from every walk of life liked his boundless energy and easy, articulate command of argument. By the end of his first year as leader, the party had gained a strong lead in the opinion polls and its membership had risen by 150,000. So no one was surprised when, with its emphatic election in 1997, Blair became, at forty-three, the youngest British prime minister in 185 years. Nor was there much surprise when, in May 2001, he again swept to victory in the general election with a stunning 167-seat advantage in the House of Commons, the largest second-term majority in British history.

So Blair's administration had not only the numerical muscle but also the public mandate to carry out some pretty radical changes. It was a huge bank of political goodwill that seemed impossible to spend, as his government charged through an impressive agenda that included . . .

Granting the Bank of England the right to set interest rates without government consultation; signing the EU's Social Chapter, aimed at harmonising European social policies; setting up an elected post of Mayor of London at the head of a new capital-wide authority; reforming the House of Lords, upper chamber of Parliament; implementing a £42 billion investment programme in health and education; orchestrating the 1998 Good Friday peace accord between

Northern Ireland's Republicans and Unionists; devolving local legislative and executive power to assemblies in Wales and Scotland; and on the foreign policy front generally aligning with the USA rather than Europe.

In short, it did many good things that won much approval. But the last two points were rather more sensitive and controversial. Indeed, Blair's enthusiasm for both Scots and Americans was to see him spending much of his political capital.

On the Scottish front, not only did he turn something of a blind eye to the rapidly escalating cost of the brand new parliament building in Edinburgh, but at any given time his UK political appointees included an inordinate number of high-profile Scots – Gordon Brown as Chancellor, George Robertson as Defence Secretary, Robin Cook as Foreign Secretary, Alistair Darling as Transport Minister, John Reid as Health Minister. Even the UK Parliament's Speaker, Michael Martin, was from Glasgow – not to mention Labour Party Chairman Ian McCartney – and as his long honeymoon period began at last to fade, one could sense a growing English resentment at so many Scots (now with their own parliament, after all) having such big bites of the UK cherry.

Added to which, some senior cabinet Scots proved less than faithful as Blair's enthusiastic development of the 'special relationship' with the USA (first mooted by Churchill to keep the post-war Soviets at bay) brought real troubles down on his head. The turn of international events made him look increasingly embattled.

At first, it had all looked pretty positive. From the moment President Bill Clinton first visited the newly elected Blair at Downing Street in May 1997, there was an extra-special personal quality about the relationship between two men with so much power and so much ambition that would benefit from mutual help – the president in his second term seeking his place in history, the premier beginning his first term and determined to win a second. Together they would tackle the Northern Ireland problem, Iraq, Kosovo and . . . what Blair did not expect to have to deal with just after his first landslide victory was Clinton's sexual indiscretions, when his improper relationship with White House intern Monica Lewinsky threatened to bring him down through an impeachment process.

A good deal of Blair's credibility was spent on that when, at a Washington press conference ostensibly about Iraq weapons inspections, he found himself defending Clinton's 'pretty impressive record' and urging everyone 'to focus upon the issues we were elected to focus upon'.

It was almost a relief when, at the end of that year, 1998, the two countries got down to the serious business of launching joint air strikes aimed at degrading Iraq's ability to produce weapons of mass destruction, and employing military strategies during the 1999 Kosovo crisis to force then-Serbian president Slobodan Milošević's troops to withdraw.

But the president's second term expired at the end of 2000, and no sooner had the two natural bedfellows bid each other a fond farewell than a new American challenge came Blair's way, with the highly disputed election of George W. Bush. Though they came from opposite sides of the political spectrum, it was seen as important by each that the Blair–Bush alliance should be just as strong as the Blair–Clinton one. And if there were any doubts about that, they were blown away by the explosive force of Osama Bin Laden's attack on New York's twin towers on September 11, 2001.

In the subsequent 'war against terrorism' British troops joined US and other allied forces in a war that failed to find Bin Laden but overthrew the Taliban regime of Afghanistan. And in a move thought by many to be a step too far, Blair further cemented Britain's position as America's closest European ally, with his unswerving support of a war against Iraq in the spring of 2003. Both leaders having accused Iraqi President Saddam Hussein of developing chemical and biological weapons in violation of UN Security Council resolutions, they embarked on a risky strategy of convincing their respective peoples that, as weapons inspections had failed, military action was justified.

The Security Council refused to sanction force, but Bush and Blair pushed on regardless of that – and fierce opposition from disillusioned supporters, shocked political colleagues and record numbers of anti-war protestors, including over a million in London. American and British forces began attacking Iraq in March 2003, flattening much of Baghdad, ousting Saddam's regime within a few weeks, and eventually capturing the tyrant himself, who had exchanged his many golden palaces for a hole in the ground. But the challenge of stabilising and rebuilding the country had been clearly underestimated, as unyielding insurgent activity repeatedly blew apart any attempt to calm things down, particularly the aborted election plan of January 2005.

Even left-wingers could have forgiven Blair his political allegiance and personal warmth towards Bush, the repeated displays of buddy-style hospitality as each hosted the other at his office or home on the range, as it were. Even the exaggerated suspicion of Iraqi WMD justifying the war could be forgotten by others. But what could never be forgiven by most voters was the flouting of the Security Council. This, they argued, made the war illegal, and while Bush sailed through into a second term at the end of 2004, the once-'Teflon' Tony never really recovered from the charge.

Though he broke Clement Attlee's record as the UK's longest continuously serving Labour prime minister in August 2003, Blair's popularity slumped amid allegations that he had misled the public about the Iraqi weapons threat, and there was little surprise that, when he was elected for the third time in May 2005, it was with a paper-thin majority.

Sooner rather than later, it seemed, the Blair family would be leaving 10 Downing Street and moving into the elegant £3.6 million home in London's Connaught Square purchased during the busy years in anticipation of less-busy times.

An unhappy end to a remarkable journey. But all things considered, still a far cry from 5 Paisley Terrace.

BIRLINN LTD (incorporating John Donald and Polygon) is one of Scotland's leading publishers with over four hundred titles in print. Should you wish to be put on our catalogue mailing list **contact**:

Catalogue Request
Birlinn Ltd
West Newington House
10 Newington Road
Edinburgh EH9 1QS
Scotland, UK

Tel: + 44 (0) 131 668 4371
Fax: + 44 (0) 131 668 4466
e-mail: info@birlinn.co.uk

Postage and packing is free within the UK. For overseas orders, postage and packing (airmail) will be charged at 30% of the total order value.

For more information, or to order online, visit our website at **www.birlinn.co.uk**

Birlinn *Limited*
IMPRINTS: JOHN DONALD · POLYGON

MURDER OF A LADY

A Scottish Mystery

ANTHONY WYNNE

WITH AN INTRODUCTION BY
MARTIN EDWARDS

This edition published in 2015 by
The British Library
96 Euston Road
London NW1 2DB

Originally published in London in 1931 by Hutchinson

Cataloguing in Publication Data
A catalogue record for this book is
available from the British Library

ISBN 978 0 7123 5623 7

Typeset by Tetragon, London
Printed and bound by CPI Group
(UK) Ltd, Croydon CR0 4YY

CONTENTS

	INTRODUCTION	7
I.	MURDER AT DUCHLAN	11
II.	A FISH'S SCALE	13
III.	BROTHER AND SISTER	19
IV.	INSPECTOR DUNDAS	29
V.	THE SOUND OF A SPLASH	34
VI.	OONAGH GREGOR	41
VII.	A WOMAN WHO SEES A GHOST	48
VIII.	HUSBAND AND WIFE	53
IX.	A HEAT WAVE	56
X.	"DUCHLAN WILL BE HONOURED"	68
XI.	FAMILY MAGIC	77
XII.	THE SECOND MURDER	85
XIII.	"A CURSE ON THIS HOUSE"	99
XIV.	A QUEER OMISSION	102
XV.	THE REAL ENEMY	108
XVI.	INSPECTOR BARLEY	114
XVII.	"WHAT AN ACTRESS!"	121
XVIII.	SECRET MEETINGS	130
XIX.	ACCUSATION	136
XX.	EOGHAN EXPLAINS	142
XXI.	CHEATING THE GALLOWS	147
XXII.	TORTURE	156
XXIII.	FOOTPRINTS	165
XXIV.	BY THE WINDOW	173
XXV.	A PROCESS OF ELIMINATION	181

XXVI.	ONCE BITTEN	188
XXVII.	MAN TO MAN	194
XXVIII.	"READY?"	202
XXIX.	PAINFUL HEARING	205
XXX.	THE GLEAM OF A KNIFE	212
XXXI.	THE INVISIBLE SLAYER	215
XXXII.	MOTHER AND SON	221
XXXIII.	THE SWIMMER	233
XXXIV.	"SOMETHING WRONG"	239
XXXV.	THE CHILL OF DEATH	242
XXXVI.	THE MASK	249
XXXVII.	THE SWIMMER RETURNS	256
XXXVIII.	THE FACE IN THE WATER	258
XXXIX.	DR. HAILEY EXPLAINS	261
XL.	THE END	268

INTRODUCTION

Murder of a Lady, first published in 1931, is an excellent example of the "impossible crime" mystery, written by a long forgotten master of this ingenious form of detective puzzle. Set in the author's native Scotland, the story gets off to a cracking start, as the Procurator Fiscal calls on Colonel John MacCallien, and his guest Dr Eustace Hailey, late one evening. He brings news that Mary Gregor has been stabbed to death in nearby Duchlan Castle: "I have never seen so terrible a wound." The dead woman was found crouching by her bed, but there is no trace of a murder weapon. The door of her room was locked, and so were all the windows.

Another murder follows, and suspicion shifts around a small cast of suspects. One tantalizing question is: why were herring scales found at the crime scenes? (The book had at one time an alternative title, *The Silver Scale Mystery*.) Luckily, Dr Hailey happens to specialize in solving this kind of conundrum, although he opts to work independently of the police: "I'm an amateur, not a professional, and my studies of crime are undertaken only because they interest me... I follow a line of investigation often without knowing exactly why I'm following it – it would be intolerable to have to justify and explain every step... The detection of crime, I think, is an art more than a science, like the practice of medicine." Later, he adds: "Detective work is like looking at a puzzle. The solution is there before one's eyes, only one can't see it... because some detail, more aggressive than the others, leads one's eyes away from the essential detail."

Hailey is, in other words, the archetypal "Great Detective" of the type so popular during "the Golden Age of Murder" between the wars. Anthony Wynne, his creator, contributed an essay about him to a book called *Meet the Detectives*, published four years after *Murder of a Lady*, in which Hailey expresses the view that: "The really interesting crimes are those committed by people who, in ordinary circumstances, would have lived all their lives without apparent fault." Hailey "never blames the criminal so whole-heartedly as to be unable to see and feel his tragedy". He maintains that the psychology of the criminal is key: "more often I come to the truth indirectly by an understanding of the special stresses to which he was subjected immediately before the crime took place."

Hailey and his creator were admired in their day, and Dorothy L. Sayers was among the critics who reviewed him favourably: "Mr. Anthony Wynne excels in the solution of apparently insoluble problems." Hailey first appeared in the mid-Twenties, and his career lasted until 1950, but by then, readers' tastes were changing, and elaborately concocted whodunits were no longer fashionable – unless written by Agatha Christie. The late Robert Adey, author of the definitive study *Locked Room Murders*, lists no fewer than 33 books and stories written by Wynne which feature "impossible crime" elements. As he points out, Wynne "soon established himself as the champion of [a] form of impossible crime: death by invisible agent. Time after time he confronted his... detective with situations in which the victim was killed, quite on his own, in plain view of witnesses who were unable to explain how a close-quarters blow could have been struck."

There is, of course, a striking contrast between such elaborate game-playing plot material and the examination of criminal psychology, and Wynne's real focus was the former, rather than the latter. He did not lighten his books with as many macabre trappings or as much gleeful humour as did John Dickson Carr, the American novelist who is commonly regarded as the finest of all specialists in locked-room mysteries, and this may help to explain why his work has faded from view. But his best work remains attractive to readers who love a cunningly contrived puzzle.

Anthony Wynne was the pseudonym of Robert McNair Wilson (1882–1963), a Glasgow-born physician who developed a specialism in cardiology after working as assistant to Sir James Mackenzie, whose biography he wrote. McNair Wilson published on a range of scientific and medical subjects, as well as on historical topics, especially in connection with the French Revolution. He was also fascinated by politics (in the early Twenties, he twice stood unsuccessfully as a Parliamentary candidate for the Liberal Party) and by economics. His obituary in *The Times* noted that "he developed a deep interest in monetary problems; for a time they dominated his conversation, and he wrote several books challenging what he considered to be the unjustifiable power wielded by moneyed interests." These included *Promise to Pay: An Inquiry into the Principles and Practice of the Latter-day Magic Sometimes Called High Finance* (1934).

McNair Wilson was medical correspondent of *The Times* for almost thirty years, and was admired by Lord Northcliffe, whose biography he wrote; at one time he was also engaged to write chatty feature articles for another newspaper, the *Sunday Pictorial*. "His lively and inquiring mind could not be bound to any one subject for long, however great and however interesting," his obituarist said. "Writing and conversation were... his chief pleasures." He wrote little fiction in the last two decades of his life, but one likes to think that he would be gratified that a twenty-first-century revival of interest in Golden Age detective fiction has resulted in the re-emergence of Dr Hailey after many years in the shadows, and the republication of this intricate mystery as a British Library Crime Classic.

Martin Edwards
www.martinedwardsbooks.com

CHAPTER I

MURDER AT DUCHLAN

MR. LEOD MCLEOD, Procurator Fiscal of Mid-Argyll, was known throughout that county as "the Monarch of the Glen". He deserved the title, if only because of the shape and set of his head and the distinction of his features. A Highlander, full length, in oils, dignified as a mountain, touchy as a squall, inscrutable, comic in the Greek sense. When at ten o'clock at night he came striding in, past the butler, to the smoking-room at Darroch Mor, even Dr. Eustace Hailey gasped, giving, by that, joy to his host, Colonel John MacCallien.

"I must apologize, gentlemen, for disturbing you at this unseasonable hour."

Mr. McLeod bowed as he spoke, like a sapling in a hurricane.

"Won't you sit down?"

"Thank you. Yes. Yes, I will. Dear me, is it ten o'clock?"

John MacCallien signed to his butler, who moved a table, furnished with decanters and siphons, closer to his visitor. He invited him to help himself.

"That's too kind of you. Well, well..."

Mr. McLeod poured what seemed to Dr. Hailey a substantial quantity of whisky into a tumbler. He drank the whisky, undiluted, at a gulp. A sigh broke from his lips.

"Believe me, gentlemen," he said in solemn tones, "it is not lightly that I have troubled you. I heard that Dr. Hailey was staying here. It seemed to me that the gravity of the case and our remoteness from help gave me title to lay his skill under contribution."

He moved uneasily as he spoke. Dr. Hailey observed that his brow was damp.

"There's been murder," he said in low tones, "at Duchlan Castle. Miss Mary Gregor has been murdered."

"What!"

"Yes, Colonel MacCallien, it's too true. Murdered, poor lady, while sleeping in her bed last night." The Procurator Fiscal's hand was raised in a gesture which expressed condemnation as well as horror.

"But, it's impossible. Mary Gregor hadn't an enemy in the world." John MacCallien turned to Dr. Hailey. "Even tramps and tinkers turned to bless her as she passed them, and with good reason, for she was constantly helping them."

"I know, Colonel MacCallien, I know," Mr. McLeod said. "Who is there in Argyll who does not know? But I state the fact, there she lies, murdered." The man's voice fell again. "I have never seen so terrible a wound."

CHAPTER II

A FISH'S SCALE

MR. MCLEOD wiped his brow, for his habit was sudorific. His nostrils expanded.

"It was no ordinary knife which made that wound," he declared in hoarse tones. "The flesh has been torn." He turned and addressed himself to Dr. Hailey. "Miss Gregor was lying crouching beside her bed when they found her." He paused: the blood diminished in his face. "The door of that room was locked on the inside and the windows of that room were bolted."

"What, a locked room?" John MacCallien exclaimed.

"That's it, Colonel MacCallien. Nobody can have gone into that room and nobody can have come out from it. I have examined the windows myself, yes, and the door, too. You could not close these windows from the outside if you tried. And you could not unlock the door from the outside."

He shook his head, closing his eyes, meanwhile, as though he had entered into communion with higher powers. After a moment he turned to Dr. Hailey.

"The wound," he stated, "is in the left shoulder, near the neck. So far as I could judge it is three or four inches deep, a gash that looks as if it had been made with an axe. And yet, strange to say, there seems to have been little bleeding. Dr. McDonald of Ardmore, who examined the body, says that he thinks death was due to shock more than to the wound itself. Miss Gregor, it appears, has suffered for many years from a weak heart. There would not be much bleeding in that case, I suppose?"

"Possibly not."

"There's a little blood on the nightdress, but not much. Not much." Mr. McLeod gulped his whisky. "I telephoned to Police Headquarters in Glasgow," he stated, "but this being the Sabbath day I don't look to see Inspector Dundas, who is coming, until to-morrow morning. I said to myself, when I heard to-night that you were staying here: if Dr. Hailey will be so good as to examine the room and the body immediately, we shall have something to go upon in the morning." He rose as he spoke: "I have a car waiting at the door."

John MacCallien accompanied his guest to Duchlan.

They were greeted in the hall of the Castle by the dead woman's brother, Major Hamish Gregor, whom Mr. McLeod called "Duchlan". Duchlan looked like an old eagle. He shook Dr. Hailey's hand with sudden and surprising vigour but did not speak a word. Then he conducted John MacCallien to a room adjoining the hall, leaving Mr. McLeod to take the doctor upstairs.

"Who knows, this blow may be mortal," the Procurator Fiscal confided to his companion in a loud whisper as they ascended the oak staircase. "Duchlan and his sister were all things to each other."

The stair ended in a gallery; from this several passages radiated. They passed along one of these and came to a door from which the lock had been cut away. Mr. McLeod paused and turned to the doctor.

"This is the room; nothing but the lock of the door has been disturbed. I had a great shock myself when I entered and I would therefore prepare your mind."

Dr. Hailey inclined his head, responding to the Highlander's gravity with a reserve which gave nothing away. The door moved noiselessly open. He saw a woman in a white nightdress kneeling beside a bed. The room was lit by a paraffin lamp which stood on the dressing-table; the blinds were drawn. The kneeling figure at the bed had white hair which shone in the lamplight. She looked as if she was praying.

He glanced about him. There were framed samplers and pieces of fine needlework on the walls, and many pictures. The furniture was old and heavy; a huge four-poster bed in mahogany with a canopy, a wash-stand that looked as if it had been designed to accommodate a giant, a wardrobe, built like a feudal castle, and, scattered about among these great beasts, the small deer of tables and chairs, smothered, all of them, in faded and tarnished upholstery.

He walked across the room and stood looking down at the dead woman. Mr. McLeod had not exaggerated; the weapon had cut through her collar-bone. He bent and drew back the nightdress, exposing the whole extent of the wound. The look of pity on his face changed to surprise. He turned and signed to Mr. McLeod to approach. He pointed to a pale scar which ran down the breast from a point slightly above and to the inside of the end of the wound. The scar ended near the upper border of the heart.

"Look at that."

Mr. McLeod gazed for a moment and then shook his head.

"What does it mean?" he asked in a whisper.

"It's a healed scar. So far as I can see it means that she was wounded long ago nearly as severely as she was wounded last night."

"May it not have been an operation?"

"There are no marks of stitches. Stitch marks never disappear."

Mr. McLeod shook his head. "I never heard that Miss Gregor had been wounded," he declared.

He watched the doctor focus his eyeglass on the scar and move the glass up and down. Sweat broke anew on his brow. When an owl screeched past the window he started violently.

"This old wound," Dr. Hailey announced, "was inflicted with a sharp weapon. It has healed, as you see, with as little scarring as would have occurred had it been stitched. Look how narrow and clean that scar is. A blunt weapon would have torn the flesh and left a scar with ragged edges."

He pointed to the new wound. "There's an example of what I mean. This wound was inflicted with a blunt weapon. Offhand, I should say that, at some early period of her life, Miss Gregor was stabbed by somebody who meant to murder her. It's common experience that uninstructed people place the heart high up in the chest whereas, in fact, it's situated low down."

He had been bending; he now stood erect. His great head, which excellently matched his body, towered above that of his companion. Mr. McLeod looked up at him and was reminded of a picture of Goliath of Gath which had haunted his childhood.

"I never heard," he said, "that anybody ever tried to murder Miss Gregor."

"From what John MacCallien said I imagine that she was the last woman to attempt to take her own life."

"The last."

The doctor bent again over the scar.

"People who stab themselves," he said, "strike one direct blow and leave, as a rule, a short scar; whereas people who stab others, strike downwards and usually leave a longer scar. This scar, as you see, is long. And it broadens as it descends, exactly what happens when a wound is inflicted with a knife."

He moved his eyeglass to a new focus over the recent wound. "The blow which killed, on the contrary, was struck with very great violence by somebody using, I think, a weapon with a long handle. A blunt weapon. The murderer faced his victim. She died of shock, because, had her heart continued to beat, the wound would have bled enormously."

The screech owl passed the window again and again Mr. McLeod started.

"Only a madman can have struck such a blow," he declared in fervent tones.

"It may be so."

Dr. Hailey took a probe from his pocket and explored the wound. Then he lighted an electric lamp and turned its beam on the woman's face. He heard Mr. McLeod gasp. The face was streaked in a way which showed that Miss Gregor had wetted her fingers in her own blood before she died. He knelt and took her right hand, which was clenched so that he had to exert force to open it. The fingers were heavily stained. He looked puzzled.

"She clutched at the weapon," he declared; "that means that she did not die the moment she was struck."

He glanced at the fingers of her left hand; they were unstained. He rose and turned to his companion.

"Her left hand was helpless. She grasped the weapon with her right hand and then pressed that hand to her brow. Since there was little bleeding, the weapon that inflicted the wound must have remained buried in it until after death. Perhaps, before she collapsed, she was trying to pluck the weapon out of the wound. The murderer was a witness of this agony for he has taken his weapon away with him."

Mr. McLeod was holding the rail at the foot of the bed; it rattled in his grasp.

"No doubt. No doubt," he said. "But how did the murderer escape from the room? Look at that door." He pointed to the sawn part of the heavy mahogany. "It's impassable; and so are the windows."

Dr. Hailey nodded. He walked to the window nearest the bed and drew back the curtain which covered it. Then he opened the window. The warm freshness of the August night entered the room astride a flood of moonlight. He relit his lamp and examined the sill. Then he closed the window again and looked at its fastenings.

"It was bolted, you say?"

"Yes, it was. The other window is bolted too." Mr. McLeod wiped his brow again. He added: "This room is directly above Duchlan's study."

Dr. Hailey moved the bolt backwards and forwards. The spring which retained it in position was not strong and seemed to be the worse of wear.

"Did Miss Gregor sleep with her windows open?" he asked.

"I think she did in this weather. I've ascertained that the windows were open last night."

The doctor turned the beam of his lamp on to the floor below the window and immediately bent down. There were drops of blood on the floor.

"Look at these."

"Was she wounded on this spot, do you think?" Mr. McLeod asked in hushed tones.

"Possibly. If not she must have come here after she was wounded. Notice how small the quantity of blood is. Only a drop or two. The weapon was in the wound." He bent again and remained for a moment looking at the stains. "The odds, I think, are that she was wounded here. When a blade remains in a wound it takes a second or two for the blood to well up and escape. No doubt she rushed back to her bed and collapsed just when she reached it."

"The murderer didn't escape by the window," Mr. McLeod declared in positive tones. "There's no footmark on the border below, and the earth is soft enough to take the prints of a sparrow. If you'll look to-morrow you'll see that no human being could climb up or down those walls. They're as smooth as the back of your hand. You would need a scaffolding to reach the windows."

He had evidently considered all the possibilities and rejected them all. He wiped his brow again. Dr. Hailey walked to the fireplace where a fire was laid and scrutinized it as he had scrutinized the window.

"At least we can be sure that nobody entered by the chimney."

"We can be quite sure of that. I thought of that. The chimney-pot would not admit a human body. I've looked at it myself."

It remained to examine the place where the body was kneeling. There was a quantity of blood on the floor there but much less than must have been found had the wound not been kept closed until after death.

Dr. Hailey moved the beam of his lamp up and down the little, crouching figure, holding it stationary for an instant, here and there. He had nearly completed his search when a gleam of silver, like the flash of a dewdrop on grass, fixed his attention on the left shoulder, at the place where the neck of the nightdress crossed the wound. He bent and saw a small round object which adhered closely to the skin. He touched it; it was immediately dislodged. He recognized a fish's scale.

CHAPTER III

BROTHER AND SISTER

DR. HAILEY asked Mr. McLeod to confirm his opinion of the scale. The Procurator Fiscal did so without hesitation.

"Yes, it's a fish's scale, a herring's. There's no other scale of any fish that looks like that, as any man or woman on Loch Fyne-side will tell you."

"If that is so we shall have to look for a weapon with a use in the herring fishery."

He spoke with an undertone of excitement in his voice. Mr. McLeod agreed.

"It looks like it. It looks like it. The fishermen use an axe sometimes, I believe, though I've never had much to do with them. It's a wonder there's no more of these scales. You'll get hundreds of them on your fingers if you so much as handle a herring."

"Still, the blade had probably been cleaned."

"It's very difficult to clean away these scales. You're apt to miss them because they lie close to whatever they touch."

Mr. McLeod's agitation was increasing. The discovery of the herring-scale seemed to have shaken him almost as much as the discovery of the murder itself, possibly because so many people in Argyllshire earn their living directly or indirectly from the Loch Fyne herring fishery. Dr. Hailey opened a penknife and very gently and carefully lifted the scale on its blade. He carried the scale to the dressing-table where the lamp was burning.

"There will be no objection, I take it," he asked, "to my retaining possession of this? Happily, you saw it in position and can confirm the fact of its presence."

He laid the knife down as he spoke and took his watch from his waistcoat pocket. He opened his watch. He was about to place the scale in the lid when Mr. McLeod objected that so important a piece of evidence ought to be shown to Inspector Dundas.

"I think, Doctor," he protested, "that it will be well if you leave the scale in the room here, for Dundas to see. He's a pernickety body that doesn't thank you for giving him advice, and if we remove any piece of the evidence the chances are that he'll make himself disagreeable."

"Very well."

Dr. Hailey put the scale in one of the small drawers of the dressing-table. He closed the drawer.

"I should like," he said, "to open the window again before we go downstairs. I saw a boat moored near the house."

"The motor-launch. It belongs to Duchlan's son, Eoghan."

When the curtain was drawn the moonlight made the lamp seem feeble and garish. Dr. Hailey threw up the window and looked out over the quiet waters of Loch Fyne, across which a silver streak that moved and shimmered below him led into the mouth of a burn. He could hear the gurgling of this stream as it ran round the side of the castle. He leaned out of the window. A wide flower-bed illuminated now by the light from the study window below, separated the carriage-way from the walls. The carriage-way ended at the front door, to the left of the window. Further still to the left, a steep bank fell to the burn.

The boat was anchored off the burn's mouth; its white hull gleamed dully in the moonlight and made sharp contrast with the black bulk of a jetty built just within the little estuary.

"Put the lamp out, will you?" he asked his companion.

He turned, when McLeod had obeyed him, from the loveliness without to the fear within. Miss Gregor's white hair shone in the moonlight with an added lustre that made her nightdress seem dull. In the dark setting of her chamber she looked remote, ghostly, pathetic. Mr. McLeod took the lamp, opened the door and went out into the corridor. He relighted the lamp.

When Dr. Hailey joined him he was holding the lamp in both hands. The glass funnel shook, making a small, rattling sound.

"I can't bear to look at yon poor woman," he confessed. "Did you notice the moonlight on her hair? I believe she was praying in her last moments."

He glanced about him. The doctor feared that the lamp would slip from his shaking hands.

"There's an awful eerie feeling about this house. I did hear once that it was haunted."

He seemed reluctant to leave the scene of the murder, as if the horror he was experiencing gave him some macabre kind of enjoyment. The association in his mind of religious ideas and gross superstition was, perhaps, the explanation. After all, Dr. Hailey reflected, it has taken mankind all the centuries of its history to effect a separation between the spiritual and the demonic.

"I'm afraid," he said, "that Miss Gregor had but little time after she suffered that blow."

"Oh, sir, sir. 'In the middle of life we are in death.'"

Mr. McLeod spoke the familiar words lovingly, nodding his head to give them emphasis. He belonged, apparently, to that considerable company of elderly men who find security and strength in accustomed phrases. But his fears were too lively to be dispersed for any length of time.

"It's an awful thought," he exclaimed, "that the hand of death may be here, within these walls, at this moment."

He began to gibber. He glanced about him like a dog watching shadows. His lively imagination made disturbing play with his features.

"Aye," he repeated, "Mary Gregor was on her knees during that last awful moment. Her strength was ever in prayer."

His voice fell. It had come to his mind apparently, that the dead woman's plea had not been granted, for he added in tones that carried a heavy burden of fear:

"The Lord gave and the Lord hath taken away."

His head was shaking in the manner of a man possessed of information which he is in no mind to disclose. The lamp began to rattle again. Dr. Hailey took it from him.

They went downstairs to Duchlan's smoking-room. Dr. Hailey had a quick impression of an antique dealer's showroom. The place seemed to be full of stuffed animals and antlers and old oak. The old man rose to receive them and presented them to arm-chairs with a ceremonious wave of his hand. Either he was dazed by the calamity which had befallen him or he was so schooled in courtly manners as to be incapable of forgetting them.

"Well, Doctor?" he asked, in a clear, rather shrill voice.

"I'm afraid I can offer no enlightenment so far."

Dr. Hailey shook his head. He was observing the room and its owner with an attention of which the vacant expression in his eyes gave no indication. Between the bedroom upstairs and this over-crowded apartment there was, he recognized, an affinity that deserved consideration. Both rooms revealed confusion of mind; in both the determination to cling to everything which the occupants had ever possessed was apparent. Duchlan kept the pelts and horns of the beasts and birds he had killed; his sister kept her samplers and good works. Both brother and sister seemed to set value on ugliness and discomfort. The chair in which he was sitting hurt the doctor's back; those he had seen in Miss Gregor's room were equally ungenerous as they were equally unlovely. But generations of Gregors had sat in them. Duchlan Castle, it seemed, contained the cast-off clothing of generations.

"My dear sister," Duchlan said, "was without an enemy in this world. It is not conceivable that anyone can have borne a grudge against her." He smoothed his kilt on his knees with a gesture that caressed that garment. "Believe me, her days were days of service."

He spoke with the assurance of an officiating priest. His face was set in an expressionless mask. But a trickle of blood had come to his cheeks.

"Her ways were ways of blessedness," he added. "And her paths were peace."

Silence received this tribute. Dr. Hailey felt uncomfortable. No doubt the old man meant what he said but his pride of family was so unashamed that he gave the impression that in praising his sister he was also praising himself.

"Will you tell the doctor all that you know, Duchlan?" Mr. McLeod said.

"It isn't much, I fear. Our lives were not eventful." Duchlan turned to his visitor and, at the same time, advanced his hands to grasp the ends of the carved arms of his chair. His hands were thin and white; and he raised and lowered his fingers in a way that recalled the movements of a spider's legs. "My dear sister and I," he stated, "dined together as usual last night. I thought she looked rather tired, for she had been very busy all day."

He paused to adjust the silver ornament which was attached to his waistbelt and which, Dr. Hailey saw, bore a coat of arms. This act, too, was caressing, as if a deep satisfaction resided in the possession of chieftainship. "My sister," he went on, "told me that she had a headache. I suggested, before we went into dinner, that we might, for once, dispense with the services of our piper during the meal. But she rejected the idea. 'My dear Hamish,' she said, 'surely you remember that our father had the pipes played at dinner even on the night of his death.' Our Highland customs were dear to her both for themselves and by reason of their associations. I knew that she was suffering greatly, but she welcomed Angus, my piper, with perfect grace, and, when his playing finished, rose and handed him the loving cup. I'm sure he knew and appreciated her courage. That, Dr. Hailey, was my dear sister on the last night of her life, thoughtful and careful of others; true to the traditions and customs of our family."

Tears gleamed in Duchlan's eyes. He wiped them away.

"We were alone at the meal, she and I, because my daughter-in-law was feeling unwell—and my son had not yet returned. Believe me, I felt my mind carried back to the days when my father, the late Duchlan, used to occupy my place and when he seemed to his children a being of supernatural goodness. Mary's thoughts had been moving in unison with mine, for she told me that she believed our father was the noblest man who ever trod this earth. 'His house,' she said, 'is full of his goodness.' Then she spoke about my little grandson. How earnestly she hoped that he would prove worthy of the traditions of which he is heir. 'If only it can be impressed on him,' she said, 'that there is no privilege except that of serving.' The coming of the little lad to stay with us a year ago, while his father was stationed in Malta, was a supreme joy to her, since it gave her an opportunity of influencing him.

"Believe me, she had made the very most of that opportunity. It was her sincere conviction that the basis of character must always be religion. 'The fear of the Lord,' she used to say again and again, 'is the beginning of wisdom.' She laboured to inculcate that fear in the child's heart. It was given to her, as to few others, to be able to penetrate the childish mind. I think the perfect simplicity of her own character was the explanation. She could suggest a whole world of ideas with a gesture. Her spirit delighted in love and beauty; but her thoughts were never suffered to escape from the control of conscience. If she believed in mercy, she never shut her eyes to justice. A child, she used to urge, must be able to count upon the divine attributes as upon the light and the air. He must learn to know all the loving-kindness of which the human heart is capable, but he must learn at the same time to recognize that even love is conditioned by righteousness. The texts which were most frequently on her lips were those in which testimony is borne to the holiness that limits and purifies even the most gracious of our human feelings."

Duchlan's face became grave. He raised his hand in a gesture which was part benediction, part protest.

"I will not disguise from you," he continued, "that these views of my dear sister were not welcome to all who had the duty of caring for the child laid upon them. In these modern times there is, everywhere, a relaxing of discipline. Sentimental ideas, corrupt in their essence, have too often replaced the old ideas of justice and responsibility. Children to-day hear too much about forgiveness, about mercy, about love, about kindness; they hear too little about the consequences which must issue from every breach of the moral law, however trivial. We are moving far away from the austere virtues of our fathers. It was Mary's task, her sacred mission, to do what lay in her power to correct that error."

The gravity of his tones was unrelieved by any inflection so that what he said sounded like a recitation carefully committed to memory. So strong was this impression that Dr. Hailey ventured to suggest that modern ideas were not necessarily wrong because they were based on the good rather than on the evil which is in human nature. He watched the old man as he spoke and saw him recoil sharply.

"My dear sister had a boundless faith in the goodness of human nature." Duchlan retorted. "But that faith was based on her deep religious conviction that man is born in sin. She hated evil too fervently to make terms with it, or to pretend that it was mere error. 'I have no patience,' she often told me, 'with the namby-pamby sentimentalism that excuses every fault in the name of love.' When she said that she always quoted the text: 'Whom the Lord loveth, he chasteneth.'"

Duchlan's tones were passionate, as if the slight criticism he had encountered had awakened doubts in his own spirit that must, at all cost, be suppressed. He waved his skinny hand.

"Believe me," he added, "Mary's faith was a tower of strength. Again and again I found help and comfort there when my own faith wavered. Her character was built on the rock. She was steadfast, immovable. My own nature had never approached the degree of resistance to evil which was her outstanding merit. But she gave me strength."

The old man wiped his eyes again.

"You will forgive these small details," he apologized. "Since you have been so very kind as to help me in this calamity, I feel that I owe it to you, and to her memory, that you should know a little of my dear Mary's character and life." He bowed his head. "She went up to her room soon after dinner. Her maid, Christina, brought her a glass of milk about ten o'clock. She always drank a glass of milk just before going to sleep. Christina left her at a quarter past ten. She was then lying down and seemed, already, to have fallen asleep. Christina blew out the single candle with which the room was lighted."

"Was her maid the last person who saw Miss Gregor alive?" Dr. Hailey asked.

"The last." The old man raised himself in his chair. "I am glad that it was so, for they were old and dear friends. Christina closed my dear father's, the late Duchlan's, eyes. She has shared our joys and sorrows with us for more than thirty years."

Each time that he mentioned his father, Duchlan lowered his voice. That tribute was impressive; but Dr. Hailey could not forget what John MacCallien had told him about the late laird of Duchlan. The man had been a tyrant, strong-willed and stiff-necked, who had brooked no opposition to his will. He had been, in addition, especially in his later life, a very heavy drinker, and his carouses had brought both fear and shame on his family. Was it from these uneasy scenes that his son and daughter had drawn their reliance on one another? Doubtless they had had need of such comfort as they were able to get and bestow.

"Your sister did not use a paraffin lamp in her room?" he asked.

"No, sir." A faint smile appeared for an instant on the old man's lips. "Doubtless," he said, "you think that we live far behind these modern times, but it is a fact that Mary looked upon paraffin lamps with the anxiety which new inventions must always awaken in old minds. We were born and brought up in the age of candles, and that gentle form of illumination remained the most attractive to both of us. Our drawing-room was always lighted by candles and was always, I know, very much admired when so lighted, even by those who have grown accustomed to electricity. My son spoke recently of installing electric light in the castle; Mary begged that that innovation might be postponed until after her death."

This statement, like those which had preceded it, was made with a vehemence which detracted from its effect. Again the doctor had the impression that Duchlan was acting as a mere mouthpiece. Even from her death-bed his sister seemed to direct his thoughts and words.

The temptation was great to ask him what his own opinion about the upbringing of children and paraffin lamps and electricity might be.

"Did your sister," he inquired, "leave Duchlan much during the year?"

"Never. Her life was here, in this house. Long ago, she used to travel sometimes to Edinburgh, and at very rare intervals she went to London for a week or so during the season. But latterly these excursions were wholly abandoned." Duchlan leaned back in his chair and closed his eyes. "Every detail of the management of this house and its surroundings was in her hands. Nothing was left to chance; nothing was overlooked or neglected. She was a wonderful manager, a wonderful director, a wonderful housekeeper. All she did, too, was done without haste or bustle, and without waste. I assure you that but for her admirable skill and foresight it would, long ago, have been impossible for me to have remained in the Castle. I should have been compelled to let my shooting every year and perhaps to have gone into permanent residence in one of the smaller houses on the estate. Mary had a horror of such a step which never ceased to disturb her."

The doctor took a silver box from his waistcoat pocket and, after a moment of silent deliberation, opened it and took snuff. He performed this act with much grace, but the vacant expression of his face remained unchanged.

"How was her death discovered?" he asked.

"It was discovered when the housemaid, Flora, took up my sister's early morning tea. My sister had apparently locked the door of her bedroom, a thing she had never done before. Flora got no reply when she knocked on the door. She called Christina, and then Angus, but they, too, failed to get any response. Angus came for me." The old man broke off and bowed his head for a moment. "My son had come back over night," he resumed. "He has been in Ayrshire on military duty. I roused him. We sent for a carpenter, who cut the lock out of the door. We sent also for Dr. McDonald of Ardmore. He came before the door was opened."

Duchlan lay back in his chair. His face, the skin of which resembled parchment, was pinched like the face of a corpse. He seemed to breathe with difficulty.

"You are quite sure," Dr. Hailey asked, "that Miss Gregor was not in the habit of locking her bedroom door?"

"Absolutely sure."

Duchlan's black eyes flickered as he answered the question. The doctor shook his head.

"So that," he said, "last night she reversed the habits of a life-time?"

The old man did not reply. He moved uneasily in his chair while his fingers began to drum on its arms. Suddenly he leaned forward listening. They heard a car drive up to the front door.

CHAPTER IV

INSPECTOR DUNDAS

INSPECTOR ROBERT DUNDAS was a young man with a shrewd expression. His manner of entering the smoking-room at Duchlan announced that he came to conquer. The mixture of cordiality and aloofness in the way he greeted the old laird indicated that he proposed to allow no consideration to interfere with the discharge of his duty.

He was not very tall, but his slight build made lack of height unimportant. Dr. Hailey thought of the word "wiry", for there was a hard quality as well as a quality of suppleness. Dundas's brow and eyes were girlish, but his mouth seemed well fitted to administer a bite. It descended at the corners and was furnished with lips of a singular thinness. Mr. McLeod, who knew the young man, introduced him to John MacCallien and the doctor, and Dundas informed each of these in turn that he was pleased to meet him. He did not look pleased.

"I lost no time, as you see, Fiscal," he said to Mr. McLeod.

His manner was quiet, with the pained restraint of an undertaker at work. But his blue eyes searched the room. They chilled when he learned what Dr. Hailey had already done.

"Before I go upstairs myself," he stated, "I should like to know who are at present living in this house." He turned to Duchlan and whipped a thin notebook out of his pocket. "I want a complete list, if you please."

The last remark was made in the manner of a doctor taking stock of symptoms, the significance of which can be understood only by himself. Duchlan bowed stiffly.

"I had better begin with myself," he said. "Then there is my son Eoghan and his wife. I have only four indoor servants…"

Dundas raised a manicured hand.

"One moment, please. You are Major Hamish Gregor, late of the Argyll and Sutherland Highlanders, and laird of Duchlan in the county of Argyll?" He wrote quickly as he spoke. "How old are you, sir?"

"Seventy-four."

"Older or younger than your late sister?"

"Older."

"What about your son? He's an officer in the Army, isn't he?"

"Eoghan is a Captain in the Royal Regiment of Artillery."

"On leave?"

"No. My son returned from Malta a month ago He had been there rather less than a year. He is now carrying out special duties in Ayrshire."

"I see. So he's only here for a day or so?"

"He arrived last night. I am not aware when he must return."

"Age?"

"Thirty-two."

"Is he your only son?"

"My only child."

"You are a widower, I believe?"

"I am."

"How long have you been a widower?"

Duchlan frowned, but after a moment his brow cleared.

"Since my son was four years of age."

"Twenty-eight years."

"Quite so."

"Has your sister lived with you during the whole of that period?"

"She has."

"So that she brought up your son?"

"Yes."

The busy pencil appeared to have been outstripped for Dundas asked no more questions until he had written during several minutes. Then he raised his head sharply.

"How long has your son been married?" he demanded.

"Three years and a few months."

"Any children?"

"One boy of two years."

"His wife's name? Full maiden name?"

"Oonagh Greenore."

"Irish?"

A faint smile appeared on Duchlan's lips.

"I believe so," he said gravely.

"Did Mrs. Gregor accompany her husband to Malta?"

"No, she remained here because of her son."

"Did she go to Ayrshire with him?"

"No."

"How old is she?"

"Twenty-four."

"Was he..." Dundas's fair head gleamed in the lamplight as he raised it in the quick, uncomfortable way that was apparently habitual—"was she on terms of affection with your late sister?"

Dr. Hailey moved uneasily in his chair, but he watched closely the effect of this question on the old man. Duchlan's black eyes flashed.

"I suppose," he said, "that I can pardon such a question by recalling the fact that you had not the privilege of knowing my sister."

"No offence meant, sir."

"So I have presumed." Duchlan passed his hand over his long chin. "My daughter-in law," he declared, "felt for her aunt the same respect and love which all who knew her felt for her."

Dundas wrote. "Relations cordial," he quoted from his memorandum in tones that set Dr. Hailey's teeth on edge. "So much can't be said in every case," he remarked reassuringly. "Very good. Now we can come to the servants. That was your butler, I take it, who admitted me."

"My piper, Angus MacDonald."

"Acting in the capacity of butler."

"Forgive me, Mr. Dundas, but you appear to be but ill-informed about Highland custom. Angus is first and foremost my friend, the friend of my family. He was piper to my father, the late Duchlan, who held his friendship an honour; should I predecease him, I pray God that he may serve my son. Our pipers stand remote from the class of domestic servants; but in these difficult times we are compelled to ask from them an extended range of service."

"Isn't it six of one and half a dozen of the other, sir?" Dundas remarked coolly. "I mean, piper or no piper, the old man is in fact acting as butler?"

"No."

The policeman shrugged his shoulders. He had the air of a modern jerry builder visiting a Gothic cathedral; there was no recognition of beauty, but in some sort, respect for age and mass, to be expressed later in exaggeration of both. Dundas, Dr. Hailey felt sure, would boast about his visit to Duchlan and embellish boasting with spurious detail. It seemed that Duchlan was not unaware of this probability for his face expressed a degree of ferocious anger that is seen only in the faces of men and carnivorous birds.

"Have the goodness, sir," he exclaimed, "to leave that alone which you do not and cannot understand. Confine yourself to your business."

"Very well. How old is your piper?"

"Sixty-eight."

"Married or single?"

"Single."

"The other servants?"

Duchlan considered a moment. His eyes were still glowing with anger, but he had himself in control.

"I employ the services of a cook and a housemaid," he stated. "They are sisters named Campbell. In addition, there is my son's old nurse, Christina, whose position is not that of a servant."

He paused, challenging Dundas to utter any syllable of comment. The policeman gazed at the carpet.

"Christina is sixty. She's a widow. Her name is Graeme. She has acted latterly as maid to my sister, as well as nurse to my grandson."

"Are the Campbells local people?"

"They are."

"Their Christian names?"

"Mary and Flora. Mary, my cook, is twenty-eight. Her sister is twenty-five."

The old man gave these facts and figures in tones of contempt. He sneered at the policeman and his notebook, baring his long teeth like a dog. But the doctor thought that, behind this mask of scorn, there was relief that the task of dealing with the murder had been committed to so narrow an intelligence.

CHAPTER V

THE SOUND OF A SPLASH

An uneasy silence filled the room. Dundas broke it.

"There's one question," he remarked, "that I wish to ask before I go upstairs. It's this: Did you expect your son to return last night?"

"We expected him to return soon."

"Please answer my question."

"We did not know that he was coming last night."

"How did he come?"

"By motor-boat."

"What?"

Duchlan's eyes flashed again.

"He came by motor-boat."

"Is that the quickest way?"

"You must ask him that yourself."

Dr. Hailey accompanied Dundas to Miss Gregor's room. Before they entered the room the policeman told him that he proposed to conduct the investigation single-handed.

"I know very well, Doctor," he said, "how big your reputation is as an amateur detective. And I'm, of course, indebted to you for the preliminary work you've done here. I shall be honoured if you agree to stand by me during the examination of witnesses. But I mean to ride the horse myself. There must be no independent lines of inquiry."

He paused, having observed the flush which had risen to his companion's cheeks.

"Very well."

"Please don't be angry. Put yourself in my place. This is the chance of my life. I'll never get another if I fail. And I'm a solitary worker. Can't go in double harness. Can't concentrate if ideas are brought to me. My mind runs on its own scents, so to speak. So I say, 'Come with me, but don't confuse me.' And don't run on ahead of me. That's not being rude. It's being honest." The man's face was so earnest that the tactlessness of his address was discounted. The doctor smiled.

"I'm to have a seat on the bench, so to speak?" he asked in genial tones.

"Exactly. As a distinguished stranger."

"And if I decline that honour?"

"I'll be sorry. But not so sorry as if you had begun to work on the case independently of me."

Dr. Hailey nodded assent.

"I'm staying for another week at Darroch Mor," he said. "You may command my services at any time during that period."

"You won't come here at all?"

"No."

Dr. Hailey's habitual good-humour had reasserted itself. His large face expressed neither hostility nor contempt. It was not, perhaps, at any time an expressive face, but there was a gentleness in its aspect which conveyed its own message. The man compelled confidence and liking without moving a muscle.

"I do hope you'll make a great success," he said in quiet tones. "Nobody knows better than I do how much success in cases of this kind is conditioned by chance. It's like playing Bridge; a bad hand may discount the greatest ability."

"Oh, yes, one realizes that."

Dundas spoke in tones which suggested that his luck had not, so far, deserted him. But his manner had changed nevertheless. He opened a gun-metal cigarette-case and offered it with a smile that conveyed the suggestion of a wish to be friendly.

"I feel," he apologized, "that you may think I've been rude and ungrateful. It isn't that. Crime is your hobby; it's my business. If you fail, nobody's going to blame you; if I fail somebody else will be sent the next time." He paused. "And there's another point. If you work with me and we find our man, the credit will go to you, no matter how modest you may be. The public loves amateurs. Credit is the goodwill of my business. It's my only possession."

"I understand perfectly. Believe me, I didn't thrust myself in here." Dundas nodded.

"What do you think of the case?" he asked suddenly.

The doctor met this advance with a smile which conveyed a gentle rebuke.

"My dear sir, if I told you shouldn't I be prejudicing your judgement?" he asked.

He smiled again when the detective's face reddened.

"All the same," Dundas exclaimed, "I'd like to know your opinion, that is, if you've formed any opinion at all."

Dr. Hailey shook his head.

"I haven't formed any opinion. When you arrived I was listening to Duchlan talking about his sister. The only clear idea I obtained from that recital was that Miss Gregor ruled this house with a heavy hand. Her brother appears to have allowed her to do exactly what she liked; he had no ideas, I think, except her ideas. Now that she's dead, he seems to be clinging to her ideas and precepts like a disciple who has lost his master. He can't endure the slightest criticism of them."

Dundas raised his eyebrows. It was clear that he saw no help in these personal details.

"I'm afraid," he confessed, "that my concern must be with those who wanted Miss Gregor out of the way, not with those who find it difficult to live without her."

They parted. The doctor descended the staircase. It was the first time, he reflected, that he had been dismissed from a case. But he meant to abide by his decision. He told Duchlan and the others frankly how the matter stood.

"Dundas is like that," Mr. McLeod said in tones of regret. "He always wants to do everything himself. So far, I'll admit, he's had the luck on his side."

"Let us hope it won't desert him."

John MacCallien rose to go. He held out his hand to Duchlan.

"You know how distressed I feel," he said. "This policeman, I'm afraid, is an additional burden."

"Thank you, John." Duchlan turned to Dr. Hailey. "Believe me, my gratitude is very real. I'm sorry that you have not been able to continue your inquiry." He shook his head as he spoke. But in spite of the melancholy expression on his face the doctor had the same impression he had experienced when taking leave of Dundas. The laird of Duchlan, no less than the policeman from Glasgow, was glad to see him go. Duchlan rose and glanced at the clock. Then he took a thin gold watch from his pocket and looked at that, too.

"Shall I send for the car?" he asked John MacCallien.

"No, please don't."

"Then may I walk with you as far as the lodge? I feel that I need air."

"My dear Duchlan, it's very late. Do you think you ought to venture out?"

"Ah, what hurts me is sitting here, alone."

The moon had come westward, and was high above their heads as they emerged from the Castle. In this light the sham medievalism of the building was tolerable largely because one could no longer see it. There had happened at Duchlan what happened all over the Highlands when the lairds became rich in the middle of the nineteenth century, namely, an attempt to turn the old bare house of the chiefs of the clan into a feudal castle on the English model. Turrets, balustrades, and the rest of the paraphernalia of baronialism had been heaped about a dwelling formerly humble and beautiful, to the profit of the local builder and the loss of the community.

The old man walked slowly and the journey to the lodge took a long time. John MacCallien tried, once or twice, to talk but failed to awaken any response. Dr. Hailey noticed that each time Duchlan stopped, and he stopped frequently, he turned and looked out, across the loch. On these occasions he seemed to be listening. Once, when a seabird screeched, he dropped his walking-stick. The doctor began to observe him and soon made up his mind that this excursion was predetermined. But to what was he listening? The night was still and without voice.

"My sister delighted in this walk," he told his companions. "She had travelled widely but maintained that the view from the north lodge was the most beautiful she had seen. I like to think that she may be watching us now."

He addressed Dr. Hailey. "We Highland folk," he said in low tones, "partake of the spirit of our hills and lochs. That's the secret of what the Lowlanders, who will never understand us, call our pride. Yes, we have pride; but the pride of blood, of family; of our dear land. Highlanders are ready to die for their pride."

It was gently spoken, but in accents which thrilled. Duchlan, clearly, was assured of the reality of those ideas on which his life was based. He had marched all the way to fanaticism; but, your fanatic, the doctor reflected, is ever a sceptic at heart.

They reached the lodge. The old man struck a match and looked at his watch.

"It's two o'clock," he announced, "or so I make it. What do you say, Doctor?"

"I'm afraid my watch has stopped."

John MacCallien held his wrist up to the moon.

"Yes," he declared, "just two o'clock precisely."

"I bid you good morning, gentlemen."

Duchlan bowed ceremoniously and turned back. They watched him until his figure could no longer be distinguished from the shadows.

John MacCallien was about to pass through the lodge gates when the doctor put his hand on his arm.

"I should like to see Duchlan reach home," he said.

"Oh, he's on his own ground, you know."

"Listen, my dear fellow. You go back to Darroch Mor and leave the front door on the latch for me. I'll follow as soon as I've satisfied myself that everything's all right."

"I'll come with you."

The doctor shook his head.

"Forgive me, if I say that I would rather go alone. And allow me to postpone explanations."

"My dear Hailey."

"I have good reasons for what I'm doing."

John MacCallien belonged to that rare type which is content to leave other folk to conduct their affairs in their own way. He nodded, took out his pipe, and began to fill it.

"Very well."

Dr. Hailey left him and hurried along the avenue after Duchlan. As he had foreseen, the old man was capable of walking fast when occasion required. He did not come up with him. When he reached the castle, he assured himself that Duchlan had not returned home; the light was still burning in the window of the study and the room was empty. Very cautiously, he approached the lighted window without, however, crossing the flower-bed which separated it from the carriage-way.

Where had the old man gone? He walked along the front of the house, passing from the carriage-way to the steep bank which he had seen from Miss Gregor's window. He descended the bank, keeping a sharp look-out to right and left. But he reached the burn without seeing anybody.

The stream broadened out above the jetty. It was high tide and the water was deep. He had an excellent view of the motor-boat. He raised his eyeglass to determine if there was anyone aboard and concluded that there was nobody. He thought of walking down the jetty and then decided against a course which must make him conspicuous to anybody standing among the trees on the far side of the burn. Doubts of the process of reasoning which had brought him back to the castle began to assail him; but when he recalled that process he put them away. Duchlan had fussed with his watch both before leaving the castle and at the lodge gate. He had been at pains to impress on the minds of his companions that two o'clock had struck before he left them. The inference seemed justified that he was anxious that some event, timed to occur at two o'clock, should not be laid to his account.

A twig snapped amongst the trees on the opposite side of the burn. Dr. Hailey turned and stood listening. He heard a window being opened. He crouched down. Footsteps approached and passed. Then the moonlight showed him a woman descending towards the jetty.

She walked slowly, seeming to linger at every step. He could see that she was young. As she approached the end of the jetty she stood and turned. The moon gave him a view of her face and he observed the tense, strained poise of her head. Suddenly she raised her arms and stretched them out towards the castle. She remained in this attitude for several seconds. Then her arms fell to her side and she turned to the water which shone and glimmered round the pier at her feet. A sound, like a subdued cough, which seemed to come from close at hand, made him turn his head and gaze into the shadows across the burn. A splash recalled him. The woman had disappeared.

CHAPTER VI

OONAGH GREGOR

DR. HAILEY ran to the end of the jetty. The woman was struggling in the water a few feet away. He threw off his coat and jumped in.

She sank as he approached, but he dived and a moment later brought her to the surface. The moon gave him a glimpse of her face and he saw that she had fainted. He brought her to the bank. Then he laid her down and began artificial respiration.

He was not immediately successful and paused for a moment to breathe himself. He lit his lamp and glanced at the woman's face. She was beautiful, with jet black hair.

An exclamation broke from his lips. Two long bruises made semi-circles round her throat. He bent to examine them. The purple colour was deep and fixed. The bruises had been inflicted at least twelve hours before. No doubt could exist that somebody had attempted to strangle this girl.

The discovery shook his nerve, but he realized the necessity of immediate action. He extinguished the lamp and set to work again. At last she breathed naturally. When he stopped to allow the rhythm of breathing to establish itself, he thought he heard footsteps behind him. But his lamp failed to reveal anybody. Her breathing was fitful and seemed ready to cease at any moment. He continued his work and laboured for what seemed a very long time before her distressed sighing was disciplined to regularity. Her pulse had acquired a larger volume. He illuminated her face once more and raised one of her eyelids so that the strong stimulus of the light might reach her brain. She moved and closed her eyes firmly, resisting him. A moan broke from her lips. A moment later he caught the words—"your sake" and "failure".

He patted her cheek, calling to her. After a moment she opened her eyes. She gazed vacantly into the darkness.

"I was so frightened."

She raised her hand as though inviting help. He took it and rubbed it. He felt her fingers tighten.

"I was so frightened..."

"Don't worry. You're all right now."

The vacant look in her eyes changed to fear. She withdrew her hand sharply.

"Where am I?" she cried in tones of great distress.

"You're all right."

"Oh, no, no." She caught her breath and then, with a swift gesture, pushed his hand away so that the beam no longer shone on her face.

"I was drowning?"

"Yes."

"You shouldn't have rescued me."

She clutched at him with both her hands. "I feel terribly weak... dreadful."

He took his flask from his pocket and opened it.

"Drink a little of this," he urged.

"What is it?"

"Brandy."

She obeyed him and the spirit kindled her anxiety.

"Why did you rescue me?" she moaned, then, suddenly and with bitterness: "Who are you?"

He told her. When he had spoken she remained silent for a few minutes. Then she said:

"I'm Oonagh Gregor. Eoghan Gregor's wife."

"So I guessed."

She offered no further explanation. He heard her begin to shiver and made her drink again from his flask.

"Are you strong enough to walk to the castle?"

"No. No."

"You can't stay here."

A sob broke from her lips. "Please don't ask me to go back there. I... I can't go back there."

"Why not?"

Her teeth chattered and her breath came in short gasps. He recognized that she was making a great effort to control herself.

"Please don't ask me, Dr. Hailey. I can't go back."

"Very well then, you must come to Darroch Mor, at once."

"Oh, no."

"I insist."

He stood erect as he spoke and, for the first time, realized how exhausted he was and how stiff. His wet clothes clung to his body inhospitably. He held out his hands to her, but she refused them.

"Please leave me," she cried. "Please go back to Darroch Mor yourself." Her voice failed. Her posture expressed utter dejection.

"Listen to me," he urged in gentle tones. "Whatever your motive in jumping into the water may have been, that attempt has failed. Providence, if I may say so, has preserved your life. And surely for a purpose. You cannot repeat the attempt because, if need be, I shall remain with you till morning. And I'm stronger than you are. In the morning I shall hand you over to the police if I think there is the least likelihood of your repeating your attempt."

"You don't understand. My life isn't worth saving. I promise you that it isn't worth saving."

"There's your son."

She cried out:

"Don't remind me of him."

"I must remind you of him."

"He'll forget. He won't remember. He won't know..." She broke off, wringing her hands.

"Would you leave him to strangers?"

"Strangers. It's I who am the stranger."

Dr. Hailey remained silent a moment then he said:

"I saw those bruises on your neck."

Her hands went up to the collar of her dress. She drew it more tightly round her neck. She did not answer him.

"A doctor can see at a glance that you were attacked by someone within the last twenty-four hours."

Still she offered no explanation. After a little while he urged her to tell him what had happened.

"If you're frank with me, I think I may be able to help you," he said. "Believe me, it's folly not to be frank in such cases as this."

"I would rather not talk about it."

Suddenly she raised her face to him.

"In a sense your knowledge of those bruises is a professional secret?" she asked.

"Possibly."

"Promise me you won't tell anybody about them."

He considered for a moment.

"Very well," he said. He extended his arm. "I insist on your walking. You mustn't sit still. It's as much as your life's worth."

She rose and, after a moment's hesitation, took his arm. He thought that her weakness was passing; a moment later she reeled and would have fallen if he had not supported her.

"I don't think I can walk."

"You must try."

He gave her his flask again and made her drink from it. They stumbled laboriously along the shore of the loch towards a clump of trees through which the carriage-way passed. When they reached the first of these trees he stood to allow her to breathe herself.

"I think you would comfort yourself," he told her, "if you confessed why you tried to take your life."

"No."

"Duchlan knew that you were going to drown yourself."

She started away from him and then caught at the trunk of a tree. In the silence which fell between them, he heard the screech owl keeping its vigil beside the castle.

"How do you know that?"

"He came down here a little time ago."

"He told you?"

"No. Nothing."

She sighed, expressing her relief. She took his arm again.

"It's my business to guess what people do not tell me," he said, "and that has become my habit. If your father-in-law knew what you were going to do, he must have approved, since he did not prevent. That can only mean that he associates you in some way with the death of his sister."

He paused. He was aware that she had listened to him with breathless attention.

"Well?"

"I can't tell you anything."

"You don't deny the justice of my reasoning."

"I can't tell you anything."

He considered a moment, wondering whether or not to try further to probe the secret. At last he said:

"I may be wrong but Duchlan impressed me as a man who would sacrifice anybody to his family pride. I fancy he has persuaded himself that his position as head of his family is a responsibility which must at all costs be discharged. He was prepared to let you drown. Your life constituted, I conclude, a danger to his family."

"Please don't go on. I... I can't bear it. Not just now at any rate."

She pleaded rather than protested. She was leaning heavily on his arm.

"Forgive me."

They reached the carriage-way and turned left handed towards Darroch Mor. After a few paces she stopped to breathe.

"Will you not leave me here?"

"No."

"If you only understood."

"Perhaps I do understand."

She seemed to summon all her courage. She began to walk again and slowly and painfully they came to the lodge where Duchlan had turned back.

"I can't go to Darroch Mor."

He thought that she was about to try to escape from him, but realized a moment later, when she sank down on her knees, how greatly he had overestimated her strength. He bent and picked her up and carried her some way in his arms.

"Can you walk a little now?"

"Yes, I think so."

She made an attempt but failed. Again he carried her and again found himself overcome.

"We stayed too long on the shore."

She did not answer. She did not seem to care what happened or where he took her, so long as he didn't take her back to Duchlan. After what seemed a long time, they came to the gate of Darroch Mor. She drew back suddenly:

"I can't come in."

She stood facing him; he could see that she was panic-stricken like a hunted creature.

"How can you stay out here?"

She shook her head.

"You don't understand."

"I refuse to leave you. Very soon Colonel MacCallien will come to look for me."

She caught at his arm, and held it in tense fingers.

"Were you alone when you rescued me?"

"Yes."

"But Duchlan was watching?"

"He may have been."

"Did he see you rescue me?"

"I don't know."

She glanced at the moon.

"If he was watching he must have seen. He'll know that we've come here."

"Perhaps."

She shuddered.

"He'll send Eoghan."

Suddenly she grew still, listening. They heard footsteps approaching from the direction of Duchlan.

Dr. Hailey turned and saw a tall man striding toward them. He flashed the beam of his torch on the man's face. The girl uttered a cry of dismay.

CHAPTER VII

A WOMAN WHO SEES A GHOST

HER HUSBAND'S ARRIVAL exerted a singular effect on Oonagh. She seemed to gather her wits and discipline them in an instant. When Eoghan demanded in tones in which anxiety and anger were mingled why she had left Duchlan, she answered:

"Because I had something to say to Dr. Hailey."

The words were spoken with a degree of assurance which was the more remarkable from the brightness of the moon. It seemed to the doctor that Gregor must observe the condition of his wife's clothing. But apparently he was too agitated to observe anything.

"It's dreadfully inconsiderate of you," he cried, "especially at such a time. My father roused me to come to look for you. He's terribly distressed."

"He knows that I wished to talk to Dr. Hailey."

"But not at this hour, surely!"

"Did your father tell you where to find me?"

"He said you might be here."

"He knew where I was."

Eoghan remained silent, gazing at his wife. He faced the moon and Dr. Hailey saw that his features expressed a deep melancholy.

"I should like you to come back with me now."

"No, Eoghan."

"What?"

"I can't come back to Duchlan."

A look of bewilderment appeared on the young man's face.

"Why not?"

"I can't."

"You must come back."

She shook her head.

"Dr. Hailey is going to ask John MacCallien to put me up for the night."

"Oonagh—"

Eoghan tried to grasp his wife's arm. She shrank from him.

"Please don't."

"Surely, Doctor," he cried, "you can't approve of behaviour of this sort? We have sorrow enough at Duchlan…"

He broke off. Dr. Hailey considered a moment and then turned to him.

"I should like you both to come into the house with me," he said, "I have something to tell you." He glanced at Oonagh, whose face expressed a lively dissent. "I shall not try to persuade you against your will. All I want is to put you and your husband in possession of certain facts."

"I don't wish to hear them."

He realized that she feared the discovery of her attempted suicide and pitched about in his mind for some means of avoiding that discovery. There were none. He weighed the danger and took his decision.

"I have just rescued your wife from drowning," he told Eoghan in matter-of-fact tones.

"What!"

"It's as I say. The bank of the burn, under the castle, is very steep and it's easy, as you know, to slip on that steep bank. There's nothing to break the fall till the burn is reached and at high tide the water in the mouth of the burn is deep."

He spoke in challenging tones. He added: "Please don't ask any questions just now; I shall not answer them."

He watched the young man and saw his expression change from melancholy to fear. Eoghan's fists were clenched. Suddenly he caught his wife's arm, holding it in a strong grip. This time she did not shrink from him. They walked to the door of the house in silence. It was ajar. Dr. Hailey led the way into the smoking-room and switched up the light. An exclamation of dismay broke from Eoghan's lips when he saw his wife. He came to her and put his arm round her to help her to a chair. A fire was laid in the grate; he stooped and lit it. Oonagh's eyes followed every movement, but her face remained expressionless.

It was an interesting face in spite of its weakness. Even in her distress, the girl managed to convey a remarkable impression of vitality. Dr. Hailey glanced at Eoghan. There was vitality in his face too, but it was clouded by his melancholy. Oonagh, he thought, was one of those women who need to depend on a man's direction. Was this man capable of giving her the support without which her vitality must constitute a danger?

"As you know," he said, "I had an opportunity of inspecting Miss Gregor's body this evening. That inspection has convinced me that she was killed by someone possessed of great strength and using a weapon taken from a fishing-boat. That's the first fact that I wish to make known to you."

He sat down and put his eyeglass in his eye. Although his clothes clung to him rather dismally he had not lost his kindliness of manner.

"Why do you think the weapon was taken from a fishing boat?" Eoghan asked.

"Because I found the scale of a herring near the edge of the wound."

Oonagh raised her head sharply.

"That would mean that the scale had been on the blade of the weapon?"

"I think so. I don't see how it could have reached the place where I found it in any other way. There was only one scale, so I conclude that the weapon was wiped before being used."

The girl moved her chair nearer to the fire. He saw her knuckles whiten as she grasped its arms.

"Queerly enough," Eoghan said, "I bought some herring from a fishing boat on my way across the loch last night. They were pulling in the net when I passed them and I couldn't resist the temptation. The launch is full of herring scales."

He spoke calmly but his words exerted a strong effect on his wife, who bent closer to the fire as if to hide her uneasiness. A lambent flame revealed the tense expression on her face.

"Still, you didn't visit your aunt, did you?"

"Yes, I did."

"I understand, from what your father said, that he called you early this morning to help to break into Miss Gregor's room."

"Oh, yes. But I went to her room before I went to bed last night. Her door was locked."

Dr. Hailey waved his hand in a gesture which indicated that he would not at present concern himself with that aspect of the matter.

"The second fact I wish you to know," he said, "is that some time elapsed between the infliction of the wound and the death of Miss Gregor. During this time the murderer remained in the room. That is certain, because, had the weapon been withdrawn from the wound before death, a very much larger quantity of blood must have been spilt."

"Have you any idea," Eoghan asked, "how the room was entered?"

"Possibly by the door. The door was locked in the morning but..."

"It was locked when I tried it at eleven o'clock last night."

"Even so, you don't know when, exactly, the key was turned, do you?"

"I know," Oonagh said in quiet tones.

"What?"

She faced Dr. Hailey. He saw that excitement had returned to her eyes.

"I went to Aunt Mary's room just after ten o'clock," she said. "I knocked and then opened the door. Christina was just going to leave the room. I took her candle from her and went towards the bed where Aunt Mary was lying. When Aunt Mary saw me she sat up and began to gasp. I was frightened and went out and shut the door. I heard her get out of bed and run to the door. She locked the door. Christina had gone away."

Oonagh's voice had become louder but was still subdued. There was an assurance in her tones that carried conviction.

"How do you know Miss Gregor locked the door?" Dr. Hailey asked.

"Because I tried the handle. I thought that perhaps she was ill and that I ought to go into the room again."

"You are quite sure of that?"

"Absolutely sure. I tried the handle several times."

"Did you call to Miss Gregor while you were trying the handle?"

"Yes. She didn't answer me."

Dr. Hailey turned to Eoghan.

"Did you call to her when you tried the handle?"

"I did, yes. I got no answer. I thought she had fallen asleep."

"Aunt Mary seemed to be terrified of me," Oonagh stated. "I have never seen anyone look so terrified in my life."

"She wasn't easily frightened, was she?"

A smile flickered on the girl's lips.

"Oh, no." She added: "Until that moment I had been frightened of her."

"Do you think she was calling for help?"

"No, that's the strange thing. I think she was just dreadfully afraid. Panic-stricken. Like a woman who sees a ghost. She didn't try to call Christina back."

Dr. Hailey leaned forward.

"How were you dressed?" he asked.

"I was in my night-dress. I was wearing a blue silk dressing-gown."

CHAPTER VIII

HUSBAND AND WIFE

THE ROOM GREW SILENT. Oonagh pushed aside her heavy fringe, and revealed a high brow.

"Why did you go to Miss Gregor's room?" Dr. Hailey asked her.

The girl glanced at her husband before she replied.

"Aunt Mary and I had quarrelled before dinner. I wanted to talk to her."

"To make up your quarrel?"

"Yes."

The monosyllable came firmly.

Dr. Hailey nodded.

"Duchlan told me," he said, "that you had gone to bed before dinner because you weren't feeling well."

"I wasn't feeling well. But that was the result of my quarrel with Aunt Mary."

The doctor rose and took out his snuff-box.

"My position," he said, "is a little difficult. I told Inspector Dundas that I wouldn't try to double his work on the case. If I ask any more questions I'm afraid I shall be breaking that promise. My object in bringing you here, as you know, wasn't to get information but to give it. I wanted you both to realize that this case presents very great difficulties which will certainly tax the resources of the police to the utmost."

He took a pinch of snuff. Eoghan asked.

"Why did you want us to realize that?"

"So that your wife might feel able to return with you to Duchlan."

"I confess I don't follow."

Dr. Hailey glanced at Oonagh. She shook her head. He took more snuff to avoid making an immediate reply, and then said:

"I fancy it is better to tell the truth. Your wife was trying to drown herself when I rescued her."

Eoghan jumped up.

"What!" The blood ebbed out of his cheeks. "Is this true?" he demanded of Oonagh.

"Yes."

"That you tried to—to drown yourself?"

"Yes."

He turned fearful eyes to Dr. Hailey.

"I insist on knowing the whole truth. Why is my wife with you at this hour? How does my father know that she's with you?"

"I can't answer the last question. The answer to the first is that I saw her jump from the jetty, and ran to her help. It's possible your father may have observed us."

The young man strode to his wife and seized her hand.

"Why did you do it?" he cried.

There was anguish in his voice.

Oonagh remained bending over the fire, unresponsive and limp. When he repeated his question, she bowed her head, but she did not answer. The doctor sat down.

"I think I can supply the answer," he said. "Your wife feared that you had played a part in the murder of your aunt."

"I don't understand you."

"Her suicide was sure to be interpreted as a confession of her own guilt. She was shielding you."

Eoghan started.

"Oonagh, is that true?"

There was no reply. The doctor waited a moment and then said to Eoghan:

"It wasn't an unreasonable fear, perhaps. No more unreasonable, certainly, than the fear under which you are labouring at this moment, namely, that your wife's attempt to drown herself was a confession of guilt." His voice became gentle: "What's the use of pretence at a time such as this? The more deeply we love, the quicker must be our fear, seeing that each of us is liable, under provocation, to lose self-control. Why I told you about my examination of your aunt's wound was that you might realize that it cannot have been inflicted by a woman. Your wife did not kill your aunt. Your fear that she may have done so proves, surely, that you, too, are guiltless."

He paused. A look of inexpressible relief had appeared on Oonagh's face. She stretched out her hand to her husband, who grasped it.

"You have reasons, presumably, both of you, for your fears," Dr. Hailey added. "I can only speculate about these; I note, in passing, that you are no longer sharing a bedroom. Whatever your reasons may be, they do not invalidate my argument."

He turned to Eoghan:

"Take John MacCallien's car and drive your wife home. The door of the garage isn't locked."

CHAPTER IX

A HEAT WAVE

DR. HAILEY heard nothing officially about the murder of Miss Gregor for several days after his visit to Duchlan. But news of the activity of Inspector Dundas was not lacking. That young man, in his own phrase, was leaving no stone unturned. He had surrounded the castle with policemen; he had forbidden the inhabitants to leave the grounds on any pretext whatever; and he had commandeered motor-cars and boats for his own service. The household staff, or so it was reported, was reduced to a state of panic. Nor were his activities confined to Duchlan; everyone of the two thousand villagers of Ardmore lay under the heavy cloud of his suspicion.

"And yet," Dr. McDonald of Ardmore told Dr. Hailey, "he hasn't advanced a step. He has found no motive for the murder; suspicion attaches to nobody, and he possesses not even the remotest idea of how the murderer entered or left Miss Gregor's bedroom."

Dr. McDonald made this statement with a degree of bitterness which indicated how grievously he himself had suffered at Dundas's hands.

"The man's a fusser," he added. "Nothing must escape him. And so everything escapes him. He's always trying to hold a bunch of sparrows in one hand while he plucks them with the other."

The Ardmore doctor smiled at his metaphor.

"Lowlanders such as Dundas," he said, "always work on the assumption that we Highlanders are fools or knaves, or both. They invariably try to bamboozle us—to frighten us. Neither of these methods gets them anywhere because the Highlander is brave as well as subtle. Flora Campbell, the housemaid at Duchlan, asked Dundas if he was going to arrest all the herring in the Loch till he counted their scales. The fishermen call herring-scales 'Dundases' now."

"Sometimes that method succeeds, you know," Dr. Hailey said gently.

"Oh, one might forgive the method if it wasn't for the man. Not that he's a bad fellow really. One of the fishermen lost his temper with him and called him 'a wee whipper-snapper' to his face and he took that in good part. But you can't help feeling that he's waiting and watching all the time to get his teeth into you."

Dr. McDonald unscrewed his pipe and began to clean it with a spill of paper, an operation which promised badly from the outset.

"I smoke too much," he remarked, "but it keeps my nerves quiet. Dundas's voice is hard to bear when your nerves aren't as steady as they might be."

He withdrew the spill and tried to blow through the pipe. He looked rather uneasy but seemed to find comfort in his task.

"It's queer, isn't it," he said, "that however innocent you may be you aways feel uncomfortable when you know you're under suspicion?"

"Yes."

"Dundas possesses none of the subtlety which can set a suspected man at his ease and so loosen his tongue. Everybody, even the most talkative, becomes an oyster in his presence, because it's so obvious that anything you may say will be turned and twisted against you. Mrs. Eoghan, I believe, refused to answer his questions because he began by suggesting that she knew her husband was guilty. When he made the same suggestion to Duchlan the old man vowed he wouldn't see him again, and wrote to Glasgow, to police headquarters, to get him recalled."

"He won't be recalled because of that," Dr. Hailey remarked grimly.

"Possibly not. But complaints from lairds don't do a detective any good in this country. Scotland's supposed to be more democratic than England, but that's an illusion. I don't believe there's any place in the world where a landed proprietor has more influence. If Dundas fails he'll get short shrift. He knows that; his nerves are all on edge now and every day adds to his trouble."

Dr. Hailey took a pinch of snuff.

"Frankly," he said, "I rather liked him. If he was a trifle tactless, he was honest and good-natured."

"You're an Englishman."

"Well?"

"Highland people are the most difficult to handle in the world because they're the most touchy in the world. What they cannot endure is to be laughed at, and Dundas began by laughing at them—jeering at them would be a truer description. They won't forgive him, I can assure you."

Dr. McDonald nodded his head vigorously as he spoke. He was a big man, red of face and raw of bone, with a wooden leg which gave him much trouble, a man, as Dr. Hailey knew, reputed something of a dreamer but believed, too, to be very wise in the lore of his profession and in the knowledge of men. His blue eyes continued to sparkle.

"I promised not to interfere," Dr. Hailey said.

"He told me that. He hasn't much opinion of amateur methods of catching criminals."

"So I gathered."

Dr. McDonald's eyes narrowed. He leaned forward in his chair in order to move his leg to a more comfortable position.

"Did you see the old scar on Miss Gregor's chest?" he asked.

"Yes."

"What did you make of it?"

Dr. Hailey shook his head. "You mustn't ask me that, you know."

"Very well. But that's the clue that Dundas has fastened on. Who wounded Miss Gregor ten years ago? He thinks if he can answer that question his troubles'll be over. And the queer thing is that nobody can or nobody will tell him. He's got it worked out that the poor woman was probably at home here when she was wounded. And yet neither Duchlan nor Angus nor Christina seem to know anything about the wound."

Dr. McDonald paused. It was obvious that he hoped to interest his colleague, but Dr. Hailey only shook his head.

"You mustn't ask me for my opinion."

"There's another queer thing: Dundas, as I told you, has paid a lot of attention to the herring-scale you discovered. He found a second scale inside the wound. He argued that the weapon the wound was inflicted with must have come from the kitchen, and, as I said, he'd been giving the servants a fearful time. I believe he found an axe with fish scales on it, but the clue led him nowhere.

"His next idea was that Duchlan himself might be the murderer. He tried to work out a scheme on these lines. Duchlan's poor, like all the lairds, so it was possible that he wanted his sister's money. The old man, I'm glad to say, didn't guess what was in the wind. He's a fine old man, is Duchlan, but his temper's not very dependable nowadays."

A second spill achieved what the first had failed to achieve. McDonald screwed up his pipe and put it in his mouth. It emitted a gurgling sound which in no way disconcerted him. He began to charge it with tobacco.

"Naturally," he went on, "this inquisition has refreshed a lot of memories. And a doctor hears everything. There's an old woman in the village who's reputed to be a witch as her mother was before her. I believe her name's MacLeod though they call her 'Annie Nannie'. Goodness knows why. She remembers Duchlan's wife, Eoghan's mother, well, and she told me yesterday that once the poor woman came to consult her. 'She looked at me,' Annie Nannie said, 'for a long time without speaking a word. Then she asked me if it was true I could tell what was going to happen to folk. I was a young woman then myself and I was frightened, seein' the laird's young wife in my cottage. So I told her it wasn'a true.' However, in the end she was persuaded to tell Mrs. Gregor's fortune. She says she prophesied evil."

Dr. Hailey shrugged his shoulders.

"Married women go to fortune-tellers when they're unhappy," he said. "Possibly Dundas might make something of that."

"Mrs. Gregor's death took place soon after that. It's a curious fact that nobody knows exactly what she died of. But her death was sudden. I've heard that it came as a great shock to the village because people didn't know she was ill. Duchlan would never speak about it, and nobody dared to ask him."

"Where was she buried?"

"In the family vault on the estate. So far as I know nobody was invited to attend the funeral. That doesn't necessarily mean much, because it's a tradition of the Gregor family to bury their dead secretly, at night. Duchlan's father's funeral, I believe, took place by torchlight."

"I would like," Dr. Hailey said, "to know whether or not Miss Gregor attended the funeral of her sister-in-law. If I were Dundas I should make a point of getting information about that."

McDonald shook his head.

"You would find it very difficult to get information. One has only to mention Duchlan's wife to produce an icy silence."

"Did she discuss her sister-in-law with the Ardmore witch?"

"Oh, no. She discussed nothing. She blamed nobody. She merely said that being Irish she believed in fortune-telling. She was very much afraid that her husband might hear of her visit, but he never did."

McDonald lit his pipe.

"Annie Nannie speaks very well of her client, and she's not given to flattery. By all accounts Duchlan's wife was a fine woman. 'It fair broke my heart,' she said, 'to see her sitting crying in my cottage, and her that kind and good to everybody.'"

The doctor took a pinch of snuff.

"It's curious that both father and son should have married Irish women," he said.

"Yes. And women so like one another too. Those who remember Eoghan's mother say she was the image of his wife. Mrs. Eoghan's very popular in the village, far more so, really, than Miss Gregor was."

"How about the servants at the castle?"

"They love her. Dundas has been going into that too; he's got an idea that the Campbell girls didn't like Miss Gregor and he's been trying to find out if either of them went to her bedroom on the night she was killed. There's nothing, as a matter of fact, to show that any of the servants went to Miss Gregor's room after Christina, her maid, had left it for the night."

"Is Dundas still hopeful of being able to solve the mystery?" Dr. Hailey asked.

"No." Dr. McDonald moved his leg again. "In a sense," he said, "I'm here in the capacity of an ambassador. Dundas wants your help; but he's too proud to ask for it—after what he said to you. He suggested that, as one of your professional brethren, I might carry the olive branch."

"I'm afraid not."

"I hope you won't stand too much on ceremony... You have him at your mercy."

"That's not the way to look at it." Dr Hailey took a pinch of snuff. "If I go to Duchlan now I'll be compelled to work along Inspector Dundas's lines. I've no doubt they're good lines, but they are not mine. I should only confuse his mind and my own."

"I see. You insist on a free hand."

"Not that exactly. What I'm really asking is a free mind. I don't want to co-operate. You can tell Dundas that, if he likes, I'll work at the problem independently of him. Any discoveries I may make will belong to him, of course."

"He won't consent to that. He'll give you a free hand only so long as he's with you in all you do."

There was a moment of silence. Then Dr. Hailey made up his mind.

"Tell him," he said, "that I can't accept these terms. I'm an amateur, not a professional, and my studies of crime are undertaken only because they interest me. When I work alone my mind gropes about until it finds something which appeals to it. I follow a line of investigation often without knowing exactly why I'm following it—it would be intolerable to have to explain and justify every step. And Dundas would certainly insist on such explanations. The detection of crime, I think, is an art more than a science, like the practice of medicine."

Dr. McDonald did not dispute this idea; indeed, he seemed to agree with it. He went away saying that he would come back if Dundas agreed to the terms. Dr. Hailey joined John MacCallien under the pine trees in front of the house and sat down in the deck chair which awaited him. The day was insufferably hot and close, so hot and so close that even Loch Fyne seemed to be destitute of a ripple.

"Well?"

"Dundas sent him. But I can't work with Dundas."

John MacCallien nodded.

"Of course not. I was talking to the postman while you were indoors. He says that Dundas has got the whole place by the ears. There's a panic."

"So McDonald suggested."

"Dundas has found out that Eoghan Gregor is in debt. Eoghan's his aunt's heir, so you can guess what inference has been drawn. But there's the shut room to be got over. The man has had an inventory made of every ladder in Argyll."

"The windows were bolted. Nobody can have got into the room through the windows."

"No, so I supposed. But you know what Dundas and his kind are: detail, detail, till you can't see the forest for the trees."

The haze which veiled the loch about Otter and which blotted out the rolling contours of the hills of Cowal seemed to be charged with fire and suffocation. Even in the shade of the trees, a hot vapour lay on the ground. The doctor took off his coat and rolled up his sleeves.

"I never realized that it could be so hot in the Highlands."

He lay back and looked up at the clumps of dark green pine-needles above him.

"Did you know Miss Gregor well?" he asked his friend suddenly.

"Not very well. Since my return from India I've seen very little of her. My knowledge belongs chiefly to my youth. My father always spoke of her as a latter-day saint, and I suppose I adopted that opinion readymade."

He remained thoughtful for a few minutes, during which the doctor observed his kindly face with satisfaction. John MacCallien, he reflected, was one of those men who do not change their opinions gladly and who are specially reluctant to revise the teachings of their parents.

"My father," he added, "had the outlook of the Nineteenth Century on men and women. He demanded a standard of behaviour and made no allowances. Miss Gregor not only conformed to that standard, but exceeded it. Her horror of what was vaguely called 'impropriety' was known and admired all over Argyll. For example, I believe that she never herself spoke of a 'man' or a 'woman', but only of a 'gentleman' or a 'lady'. Ladies and gentlemen were beings whose chief concern it was to prove by their lives and manners that they lacked the human appetites."

"I know."

John MacCallien sighed.

"I suppose there was something to be said for that point of view," he declared. "But I'm afraid it was a fruitful begetter of cruelty and harshness. Anything was justified which could be shown to inflict shame or sorrow on the unregenerate. Besides, these good people lived within the ring-fence of a lie. They were not the disembodied spirits they pretended to be—far from it. Consequently their emotions and appetites were active in all kinds of hidden and even unsuspected ways." He paused and added: "Cruelty, as I say, was one of these ways, the easiest and the most hateful."

"Was Miss Gregor cruel?" Dr. Hailey asked.

"Do you know that's an extraordinary difficult question to answer. Offhand, I should say, 'Of course not'. But it depends, really, on what you mean by cruel. Her code was full, I'm sure, of unpardonable sins, sins that put people right outside the pale. On the other hand she could be extraordinarily kind and charitable. I told you that even tinkers and gipsies used to bless her. She was always bothering herself about people of that sort. Once, I remember, a child got pneumonia in one of the tinker's tents on the shore between here and the north lodge. She nursed it herself and paid for medical attendance. When the parish officer wanted to have it removed to the Poor's House at Lochgilphead she resisted him with all her might because she believed that these people cannot live within four walls. She was told that if the child died, its death would be laid to her charge, but that kind of threat was the least likely to influence her in any way. The case aroused a lot of interest in Ardmore. When the child got well everybody felt that she had saved its life."

Dr. Hailey nodded.

"I see. In that case her personal reputation was at stake, so to speak."

"Yes. And there was no question of sin." John MacCallien sighed. "She was merciless where sinners were concerned," he added, "if their sins were of the flesh. I fancy she might have found excuses for a thief— these tinkers are all thieves, you know."

"Provided he had not sinned?"

"Exactly. Mind you, that view wasn't confined to her. It was my father's also."

"Your father's view was shared by everybody else in this neighbourhood, wasn't it?"

"Yes. By everybody."

MacCallien sat up. He shook his head rather sadly. "When my brother and I were children," he said, "we often met Miss Gregor out driving. Our nurse, on these occasions, always told us to take our hats off and that became a burden. One day, just as the carriage was passing, we put out our tongues instead. I can still see the horror on the dear woman's face. She stopped the carriage, got out, and read us a lecture on good manners We didn't mind that so much but she wrote as well to our father. I remember thinking, while we were being punished, that she wasn't my idea of a saint."

He smiled faintly and then looked surprised when he saw how attentive Dr. Hailey had become.

"How old was Miss Gregor at that time?"

"She must have been quite young. In her twenties or early thirties, I suppose."

"What happened the next time you met her?"

"Oh, we took our hats off, of course."

"And she?"

"I fancy she bowed to us as she had done formerly. Funnily enough, though, I can't remember much about her after that."

"Did you know Duchlan's wife?"

"Oh, yes, rather." MacCallien's voice became suddenly enthusiastic. "She was an awfully good sort. We loved her. I remember my brother saying once that Mrs. Gregor would never have told our father if we had put our tongues out at her. She had a short married life, poor woman."

"Eoghan Gregor's wife is supposed to be like her in appearance, isn't she?" Dr. Hailey asked.

"Yes. I think with reason too, though a child's memory is always unreliable. I know that, when I saw Mrs. Eoghan for the first time, I wondered where I had met her before. And it's certain that I had never met her before. There must be some quality in the characters of Duchlan and his son which draws them to Irish women." He paused and then added: "Not a very robust quality perhaps."

"Why do you say that?"

"I'm afraid neither of these marriages has been conspicuously successful. I suppose the qualities which Miss Gregor represents are the dominants in all the members of her family. Duchlan's wife, like Mrs. Eoghan, was more concerned with men and women than with 'ladies' and 'gentlemen.'"

"It must have been very difficult for her to have her sister-in-law always beside her, don't you think?"

Dr. Hailey frowned as he spoke. His companion nodded a vigorous assent.

"It must have been dreadful. No wife could hope to be happy in such circumstances. As a matter of fact, I believe Miss Gregor did all the housekeeping and management. Duchlan's wife was treated, from beginning to end, like a visitor. Goodness knows how she endured it."

"Was there much talk about the arrangement?"

"Any amount, of course. But nobody could interfere. People older than myself have told me that they saw the poor girl wilting before their eyes. I believe one woman, the wife of an old laird, did actually dare to suggest that it was high time a change was made. She was told to mind her own business. By all accounts Mrs. Gregor was splendidly loyal to her husband and wouldn't listen to a syllable of criticism or even of sympathy. But I haven't a doubt, all the same, that the strain undermined her constitution."

Dr. Hailey passed his hand over his brow.

"What did she die of?" he asked.

"Diphtheria, I believe. She died very suddenly."

Dr. Hailey spent the afternoon in a hammock, turning over the details of the mystery in his mind. He did not disguise from himself that he was disappointed at not having been allowed to attempt a solution; on the other hand such ideas as he had evolved offered no substantial basis of deduction. He discussed the subject again with his host after dinner but obtained no enlightenment.

"I've no doubt," John MacCallien said, "that Dundas has exhausted all such probabilities as secret doors and chambers. He was prepared, I feel sure, to tear the castle to pieces to find one clue. My friend the postman had it from Angus, Duchlan's piper, that he found nothing. There are no secret chambers, no passages, no trap-doors."

"And no other means by which the murderer can have entered the bedroom or escaped out of it?"

John MacCallien raised his head.

"We know that he did enter the bedroom and did escape out of it."

"Exactly. And miracles don't happen."

The doctor took a pinch of snuff. "This is the fourth time that I've encountered a case in which a murder was committed in what seemed like a closed room or a closed space. I imagine that the truth, in this instance, will not be more difficult to discover than in these others—"

A smile flickered on his lips.

"Most of the great murder mysteries of the past half-century," he added, "have turned either on an alibi or on an apparently closed space. For practical purposes these conditions are identical, because you have to show, in face of obvious evidence to the contrary, that your murderer was at a given spot at a given moment. That, believe me, is a harder task than proving that a particular individual administered poison or that an apparent accident was, in fact, due to foul play."

He broke off because they heard a car driving up to the door. A moment later Dr. McDonald came limping into the room.

"You've got your terms, Hailey," he said as he shook the doctor's hand. "Dundas owns himself beaten." He shook hands with John MacCallien, and then turned back to Dr. Hailey. "Can you possibly come to Duchlan to-night?"

CHAPTER X

"DUCHLAN WILL BE HONOURED"

INSPECTOR DUNDAS received the two doctors in his bedroom, a large room situated near that formerly occupied by Miss Gregor and directly overlooking the burn. He was seated on his bed, when they entered, writing notes, and wore only a shirt and trousers. But he did not seem to be feeling the heat.

"It's good of you, Dr. Hailey," he said in grateful tones, "because I wasn't as polite as I might have been at our first meeting. Pride cometh before a fall, eh?"

"On the contrary, I thought your attitude entirely unexceptionable."

The doctor sat down near the open window and mopped his brow. Dundas, he perceived, had lost his air of assurance. Even his sprightliness of manner had deserted him. The change was rather shocking, as indicating a fundamental lack of self-confidence. The man had put all his trust in cleverness and thoroughness and when these failed, had nothing to fall back on.

"Perhaps you would like me to give you an account of what I've done," Dundas said. "A few facts have emerged."

He spoke wearily, without enthusiasm. Dr. Hailey shook his head.

"I should prefer to ask you questions."

"Very well."

The doctor rose and pulled off his coat; before he sat down again he glanced out at the sea, white under the full moon. The exquisite clearness of the north had returned with the falling of night, and the long rampart of Cowal lay like the back of some monstrous creature rearing itself up out of the shining water. He listened to the soft babbling of the burn at his feet, in which chuckles and gurgles were mingled deliciously. The drought had tamed this fierce stream till only its laughter remained. He followed its course round the house to the loch, marking where its water became transformed to silver. The sails of fishing-boats stained the silver here and there and he saw that several of the boats were lying close in shore, at the mouth of the burn. The sound of the fishermen's voices came softly on the still air. He turned to his companions:

"They seem to have shot a net out here."

Dr. McDonald looked out and turned indifferently away.

"Yes."

"I had no idea they fished so close inshore."

"Oh, yes. The shoals of herring tend to come into the shallow water at night to feed. Ardmore has lived on that fact for more than a century. Lived well too. In the best days they used to get £2 or £3 a box and might take 200 boxes at one shot of the net. But not now. The old Loch Fyne herring that the whole country knew and enjoyed seems to have ceased to exist. It was blue and flat; the modern variety is much paler and much rounder."

"So that Ardmore has fallen on bad days?"

"Yes. And with Ardmore, Duchlan and his family. It isn't easy to pay rent if you're making no money."

"Has the depression produced any reactions?"

"Reactions?"

"Hard times tend to separate honest from dishonest men."

A faint smile flickered on Dundas's lips.

"You're thinking of the possibility that one of those fishermen may have climbed in here?" he asked. "That idea was in my own mind. But I feel sure now that there's nothing in it. Nobody could climb these walls."

Dr. Hailey sat down. He polished his eyeglass and put it in his eye.

"I'm afraid I wasn't only thinking of that," he confessed. "Boats, especially fishing-boats, have always attracted me. It used to be one of my boyish ambitions to spend a night with the herring fleet." He leaned forward. "McDonald told me that you observed the scar on Miss Gregor's chest."

"Yes. I tried to work on that clue but I got nothing. Nobody here knows anything about it."

"Isn't that rather strange?"

"Very strange. But truth to tell, doctor, the people here are impossible. They know nothing about anything. When I said to Duchlan that nobody could hide an injury of that sort, he met me with a shrug of his shoulders. What are you to do? The scar is very old. It may date back twenty years."

"Yes. But it represents what was once a severe wound. Long ago, somebody tried to kill Miss Gregor. Since I formed that opinion I've been trying to get information about the lady. I've made a discovery."

"Yes?" The detective's voice rang out sharply.

"Everybody seems to believe that she was a saint and nobody seems to know much about her."

"My dear sir," Dr. McDonald interrupted, "I knew her well. The whole neighbourhood knew her well."

"As a figure, yes. Not as a woman."

"What does that mean?"

"Who were her intimate friends?"

The Ardmore doctor nursed his leg with both hands. He looked blank.

"Oh, the lairds and their families."

"John MacCallien confesses that he used to see her out driving occasionally. He was taught to hold her in great respect. He knows next to nothing about her."

"He's a bachelor."

"Yes. But he goes everywhere. One of his friends told me yesterday that Miss Gregor was looked on as a woman apart. She was full of good works, but she gave her confidence to nobody. She had no woman friend, no man friend. In such a place as this, gossip is passed on from father to son and mother to daughter. It's quite clear that this woman lived her life in seclusion."

Dr. McDonald frowned. "She never impressed me in that way," he declared stubbornly. "On the contrary, there was nothing she was not interested in. Her intrusions in local affairs, believe me, could be most troublesome. Doctors were her special concern and she supervised their work, my work mostly, with tireless zeal. She called it 'taking a kindly interest', but it was sheer interference."

He spoke hotly. Dr. Hailey nodded.

"That's not quite what I mean, you know," he said. "That's impersonal work. The relations between the landed class and their people in this country are so well-defined that there was no danger of familiarity. Miss Gregor helped her poorer neighbours, I imagine, as she cared for her pets. They were remote from her life. Your Lady Bountiful is always the same; she spoils her dependents and avoids her equals."

"There's something in that," McDonald agreed. "I often noticed that the more dependent the person was, the more fuss Miss Gregor made. She got a lot of flattery from her pensioners."

"Exactly."

"Her nephew's upbringing had been the chief business of her life. I can still hear her clear voice saying: 'Doctor McDonald, the knowledge that a young life had been committed to my care overwhelmed me. I felt that I must live and work and think and plan for no other object than Eoghan's welfare in the very highest sense of that word!'"

"Are you not confirming what I've suggested? Miss Gregor's real life was here, in this house, between these walls." Dr. Hailey allowed his eyeglass to drop. "I've been asking myself where her interest was centred before Eoghan was born," he added. "Clever, active-minded women always, believe me, find something or somebody to absorb their attention."

Nobody answered him; Dundas's interest was wholly extinguished. There was a knock at the door. Angus, the piper, entered with a tray on which glasses tinkled together. The gilded neck of a champagne bottle protruded from a small ice-pail, like a pheasant's neck from a coop.

"Duchlan will be honoured, gentlemen," Angus announced, "if you'll accept a little refreshment."

He stood in the doorway awaiting their decision. Dundas signed to him to put the tray down on the dressing-table.

"Shall I open the bottle?"

"Yes, do."

Angus performed this office with much dignity. He filled the glasses on the tray and presented them to the three men. Dr. Hailey took occasion to glance at his face but found it inscrutable. The piper knew how to keep his thoughts to himself. When he had left the room Dundas remarked that a similar courtesy had not been extended to himself.

"I'm getting to know Duchlan," he declared. "This is his way of telling me what he thinks of me. Champagne isn't for a common policeman."

He laughed and flushed as he spoke. It was clear that, under his uncompromising manner, he was exceedingly sensitive.

"This is the hottest night of the year, you know," Dr. Hailey suggested amiably.

"Oh, it's been hot enough every night since I came here."

Dundas emptied his glass at a gulp, an offence, seeing that the wine was good. He made a joke about a farmer at a public dinner to whom champagne had been served, but failed to amuse his companions. Dr. Hailey sipped the liquor, watching the tiny clusters of bubbles on its surface, elfish pearls cunningly set in gold. The wine was excellently chilled and yielded its virtue generously.

"What do you make of Duchlan?" the doctor asked after a prolonged interval of silence.

"He's a Highland laird. They're all alike."

"Yes?"

"Pride and poverty."

"I understood that Miss Gregor was a rich woman."

The policeman's face brightened.

"Ah," he exclaimed, "you know that, do you?"

"John MacCallien told me."

"It's true. An uncle, who made money in business, left her a big sum about ten years ago; why, I don't know. Duchlan got nothing."

Dr. Hailey nodded.

"Has Duchlan helped you?"

"No, he has not."

"What about Eoghan Gregor?"

Dundas shrugged his shoulders.

"Another of the same. But I didn't expect help there after I found that the fellow had just gambled his money away." He leaned forward suddenly. "Eoghan Gregor was ruined on the day of his aunt's death. And his aunt has left him all her money."

He remained tensely expectant, watching the effect of his disclosure. Dr. Hailey denied him satisfaction.

"After all, his aunt brought him up, you know."

"Exactly. He knew that she would leave him her money."

"Wouldn't she have lent him money, if he had asked her?"

"I don't think so. Not to pay gambling debts at any rate. Miss Gregor, by all accounts, was a woman with most violent prejudices against gambling in any form."

Dundas glanced at Dr. McDonald for confirmation.

"She looked on every kind of game of chance as the invention of the devil," the Ardmore doctor declared. "I've heard her myself call playing-cards 'the Devil's Tools'. I'm sure that if she had suspected that her nephew indulged in gambling she would have disinherited him as a matter of principle."

Dr. Hailey nodded.

"I see."

"It came to this," Dundas declared. "Of the three questions that must be answered in every case of murder—Who? Why? How?—I may have found answers to two, namely Who? and Why?" He raised his right hand in a gesture which recalled a bandmaster. "But the third has remained obstinately unanswerable. There isn't a shadow of doubt that the door was locked on the inside. As you know, a carpenter had to be fetched to cut out the lock. He told me that he examined the windows and saw for himself that they were bolted. Dr. McDonald here arrived before the carpenter had completed his work to confirm these statements. In other words that room, with its thick walls and heavy door, was completely sealed up. You couldn't have broken into it without using great violence. And there's not a sign of violence anywhere."

The policeman rubbed his brow uneasily.

"Has the idea occurred to you," McDonald asked, "that the murder may have been committed in some other room?"

"What? But how was the body got into the bedroom in that case? I assure you that you can't turn the key of the door from the outside. I'm an authority on skeleton keys of all sorts. No skeleton key that was ever invented could pick that lock. And the end of the key doesn't protrude from the lock. The locks of this house are all astonishingly ingenious. I'm told they were the invention of Duchlan's grandfather, who had a passion for lock-making."

"Like Louis XVI."

Dundas looked blank: "I didn't know that Louis XVI. was interested in locks," he said in tones which proclaimed his innocence of any knowledge about that monarch.

"He was. And his interest set a fashion. I've little doubt that the Duchlan of those days acquired his taste for mechanics during a visit to London or Paris. Some years ago I made a study of these eighteenth-century locks. Many of them are extraordinarily clever."

"These here are, at any rate." Dundas rose as he spoke and brought the lock which had been cut from Miss Gregor's door for the doctor's inspection. He pointed to the keyhole. "Observe how the key enters at a different level on each side of the door. That precludes the possibility of picking the lock with a skeleton, or of turning the key from the outside with pliers. You would think there were two locks, indeed, instead of only one, but they're connected."

Dr. Hailey focussed his eyeglass on the piece of mechanism and then handed it back.

"I agree with you," he said. "It is absolutely certain that the door was neither locked nor unlocked from the outside."

"That means, remember, that Miss Gregor locked the door."

"I suppose so."

The detective shook his head.

"How can you, or I, for that matter, suppose anything else? Seeing that the windows were bolted on the inside." Again he rubbed his brow. "My brain seems to be going round in circles," he cried. "What I'm really saying is that Miss Gregor inflicted that dreadful wound on herself, seeing that nobody was present in the room with her and that nobody can have escaped out of her room. And she certainly didn't inflict the wound on herself."

"She did not."

Dundas's face had become very solemn. This mystery, which had brought all his efforts to nothing, exerted, it seemed, a profoundly depressing effect on his spirits. He shook his head mournfully as the difficulties against which he had been contending presented themselves anew to his mind.

"What I don't understand," Dr. Hailey said, "is why the windows were shut at all. It was an exceedingly hot night—as hot or hotter than it is now. Nobody in such conditions would sleep with closed windows." He turned to Dr. McDonald: "Do you happen to know if Miss Gregor was afraid of open windows? I mean absurdly afraid?"

"I don't think so. I rather imagine that in summer she usually slept with her windows open."

"In that case she certainly meant to leave them open on the night of her death."

Dundas nodded.

"I thought of that too," he said. "No doubt you're right; but you'll have to supply an answer to the question why, in fact, the windows were shut. Why did she shut these windows on the hottest night of the year? If you can answer that question it seems to me that you'll have gone a long way towards the truth."

"You know, I take it, that Mrs. Eoghan Gregor visited the room immediately after her aunt had gone to bed?" Dr. Hailey asked.

"Yes, I know that. She told me herself. She said that Miss Gregor locked the door in her face."

"Isn't it probable that Miss Gregor shut the windows at the same time?"

"Why should she?"

"Perhaps for the same reason that she locked the door."

"Can you name that reason?" Dundas raised his head sharply as he spoke.

"Mrs. Eoghan Gregor thinks that her aunt was afraid of her."

"What, afraid she would climb in by the window?"

"Panic never reasons, you know. It acts in advance of reason, according to instinct. Instinct's only concern is to erect a barrier against the cause of the panic. A man who was in Russia during the Leninist Terror told me that when he escaped and returned to London he woke up one night and barricaded the door of his bedroom with every bit of furniture in the room. That was in his own home, among his own people."

Dundas looked troubled.

"Do you think," he asked, "that Miss Gregor had been living in expectation of an attack on her life?"

"Yes, I do." Dr. Hailey took a pinch of snuff. "Panic," he stated, "consists of two separate elements, namely, an immediate fear and a remote dread. It's not always conscience which makes cowards of us; sometimes it's memory. Having dreaded some contingency for years, we lose our heads completely when it seems to be at hand."

"But how can this woman have dreaded assassination for years?"

"She had been wounded, remember, years before."

The detective shook his head.

"Time blots out such memories."

"You're quite wrong. Time exaggerates them. One of the leaders of the French Revolution, who had known and feared Robespierre, lived till ninety years of age. On his death-bed, sixty years after the Revolution, he lay imploring his great-granddaughter not to let Robespierre enter his bedroom."

A knock on the door interrupted them. In answer to Dundas's invitation to come in Eoghan Gregor entered the room.

CHAPTER XI

FAMILY MAGIC

EOGHAN WAS PALE and looked anxious. He addressed himself to Dr. McDonald.

"Will you please come to Hamish," he asked. "He's had another slight fit, I think."

He stood in the doorway, apparently unaware of the others in the room. Dr. McDonald jumped up and hurried away.

"That's unfortunate," Dundas remarked, in the tones of a man who resents any deflection of interest from his own concerns. He added: "A fit's the same as a convulsion, isn't it?"

"Of the same nature."

"The child's evidently subject to them. McDonald told me it had one a few days before Miss Gregor's death. He doesn't seem to think they're very serious?"

"No, not as a rule."

"Lots of children get them, don't they?"

"Yes."

Dr. Hailey found himself listening and recognized that, strong as was his interest in detective work, his interest in the practice of medicine was much stronger. He wished that Eoghan Gregor had invited him to accompany McDonald and felt a sudden, sharp disinclination to continue the work which had brought him to the house. It was with a sense of lively annoyance that he heard Dundas ask further if fits were a sign of nervous weakness.

"I have an idea that both Duchlan and his son are very highly strung," the detective suggested in those hushed tones which laymen always adopt when speaking to doctors about serious disease. "I don't mind confessing that I've been working along these lines. Duchlan, as you've probably heard, is a good laird, though a bit queer. His sister,

Miss Gregor, seems to have had notions—what they call hereabouts Highland second-sight. That's the first generation. Eoghan Gregor's the second generation and he's a gambler with the temperament of a gambler. Then there's the boy, the third generation."

He paused expectantly. The doctor was in the act of taking a pinch of snuff and completed that operation.

"Fits in children," he stated coldly, "are usually caused by indigestion."

"Is that so?" Dundas was abashed.

"Yes. Probably the child has been eating berries or green apples."

"McDonald said he was afraid of brain fever."

Dr. Hailey did not reply. Listening, he fancied he heard a child's crying, but could not be sure. He thought that, but for the fact that this mystery so greatly challenged his curiosity, he would have abandoned the attempt to solve it. The picture of Oonagh Gregor, bending anxiously over her child, a picture that came and remained stubbornly in his mind, did not invite to revelations which might possibly add new sorrows to her lot. For an instant the futility of criminal investigations assailed her mind. What did it matter who had killed Miss Gregor, seeing that Miss Gregor was dead and beyond help? Then he recognized the source of that idea in his feelings towards Dundas. The hound is always so much less lovable, so much less interesting, than its quarry.

"I don't think," he said, "that I can go further to-night. I like to sleep on my ideas."

He rose as he spoke; but the expression in Dundas's eyes made him hesitate. The detective, as he suddenly realized, was in great distress.

"The truth is, doctor, that if I can't reach some sort of conclusion within the next day or two, I'll be recalled," Dundas said. "And up till now I've been going ahead from case to case. I'll never get another chance if somebody else succeeds where I've failed. I'm only speaking for myself, of course, but from that point of view there isn't a moment to be lost. I know, because I had a letter to-day from headquarters."

He took a folded sheet of paper from his pocket as he spoke and unfolded it. He read:

"It's obvious that somebody entered Miss Gregor's bedroom, seeing that she didn't kill herself. Your report suggests that you're losing sight of this central fact in order to run after less important matters. Success can only be won by concentration. Ask yourself how the bedroom was entered; when you've found an answer to that question you'll have little difficulty, probably, in answering the further question: Who entered it?"

"That is exactly the method I have always found to be useless in difficult cases," Dr. Hailey said with warmth.

"But you see what the letter means: they're growing restive. The papers are shouting for a solution and they've got nothing to offer."

Dr. Hailey sat down again and leaned forward.

"My method is always to proceed from the people to the crime rather than from the crime to the people. And the person I take most interest in, as a rule, certainly in the present case, is the murdered man or woman. When you know everything there is to be known about a person who has been murdered, you know the identity of the murderer."

Dundas shook his head: "I feel that I do know the identity of the murderer. But that knowledge hasn't helped me."

The doctor rubbed his brow as a tired man tries to banish the seductions of sleep.

"Did you notice," he asked, "that Miss Gregor's room was like an old curiosity shop?"

"It seemed to be pretty full of stuff. Those samplers on the wall..."

"Exactly. It was full of ornaments that most people would have preferred to get rid of. And every one of those ornaments bore some relation to Miss Gregor herself. Are you interested at all in folk lore?"

Dundas shook his head.

"I'm afraid not."

"I am. I've studied it for years. One of the oldest and strongest beliefs among primitive peoples is that the virtue of a man or woman— his or her vital essence so to speak—is communicated in a subtle way to material things. For example, the sword a soldier has carried comes to possess something of his personality. We all make some use of the idea, I admit; but most of us stop short in that use at the point where the material thing serves as a symbol of the spiritual. A modern mother keeps and treasures her dead son's sword; she does not suppose that the sword contains or holds part of her son's personality. But there are still people, probably there always will be people, who do not stop short at that point. Things they or their relations have made or used acquire sacredness in their eyes so that they can't endure the idea of parting with them. The material becomes transmuted by a process of magic into something other than it appears to be. Miss Gregor, clearly, attached such importance to her own handiwork and to the possessions of her ancestors, that she would not willingly allow any of them to be taken out of her sight. Unless I'm very much mistaken that was the dominant note of her character."

He paused. The detective looked mystified though he tried to follow the reasoning to its conclusion.

"Well?" he asked.

"Her character was rooted in the past. It embraced the past, was nourished with it, as with food. But it reached out, also, to the future; because the future is the heir of all things. Her brother Duchlan was of her way of thinking. But could she feel sure that the next generation would hold by the tradition? What was to become of the precious and sacred possessions after her death? That thought, believe me, haunts the minds of men and women who have abandoned themselves to family magic. Duchlan's son, Eoghan, is the next generation. What were Miss Gregor's relations to her nephew?"

"She acted as his mother."

"Yes. So that another question arises: what were her relations to his mother? Duchlan's wife, don't forget, was Irish. That is to say she stood outside of the Highland tradition. If she had lived, and brought her son up herself, would he have inherited the authentic doctrine of the family? In other words, what kind of woman was Duchlan's wife? How did she fare in this place? What relations existed between her and her sister-in-law? I shall certainly try to obtain answers to all these questions."

"You won't obtain them. The old man is determined not to speak about his family. I told you that he professes to know nothing about the scar on his sister's chest. And his servants are as uncommunicative as he is."

"My dear sir, a laird is a laird. There are always people who know what is going on in big houses."

Dundas shrugged his shoulders.

"I haven't found any in Ardmore and I've spared no pains to find them."

Dr. Hailey took a note-book from his pocket and unscrewed the cap of his fountain-pen. He wrote for a few minutes and then explained that he had found that, if he kept a record of his thoughts about a case as these occurred to him, knowledge of the case seemed to grow in his mind.

"The act of writing impresses my brain in some curious way. When I write, things assume a new and different proportion."

He laid his pen down beside the champagne glasses and leaned back.

"Detective work is like looking at a puzzle. The solution is there before one's eyes, only one can't see it. And one can't see it because some detail, more aggressive than the others, leads one's eyes away from the essential detail. I have often thought that a painter could make a picture in which one particular face or one particular object would be invisible to the spectator until he had attained a certain degree of concentration or detachment. This room of Miss Gregor's, for example, seems to us to be a closed box into which nobody can have entered and from which nobody can have emerged. The consequence of that idea is that we cannot conceive how the poor lady was murdered. Yet, believe me, the method of her murder is there, written plainly in the details we have both observed. When I write, I attain a new point of view that is not attainable when I speak. For example..." He leaned forward again and extended his note-book. "I've written here that you found Duchlan and his household exceedingly reticent about past events. When you told me that I merely wondered why it should be so. Now I can see that, in all their minds, a connection must exist between the present and the past. It follows, doesn't it, that the scar on the dead woman's chest is the clue to a great family upheaval, the effects of which are still being acutely felt, so acutely, indeed, that even murder is accepted as a possible or even probable outcome."

"That's possible, certainly."

"I'm prepared to go farther and say that it must be so."

Dundas plucked at his shirt with uneasy hands.

"It's hard to believe," he objected, "that anybody has been waiting for twenty years to murder that poor old woman, or that a man like Duchlan has sat with his hands folded during that time in face of such a danger."

"That isn't what I mean. The beginning of murder, like the beginning of any other human enterprise, lies deep down in somebody's mind—not necessarily in the mind of the person who actually kills..."

"What?"

"We know very little of Miss Gregor's character, but there's no doubt that she was a self-centred woman with a highly developed faculty of domination. People, and especially women, of that type arouse strong opposition. That takes various forms. Weak natures tend to flatter and be subservient; stronger natures are exasperated; still stronger natures resist actively. But though these types of behaviour differ, they have the same first cause, namely, dislike. The subservient flatterer is an enemy at heart and understands perfectly the feelings of the violent opponent. In other words, everybody in this house hated Miss Gregor."

"My dear sir!"

"I know, you're thinking of Duchlan and Eoghan. I believe that both of them hated her."

"Why?"

"Because she was hateful."

Dundas shook his head.

"You'll get no support for that idea in Ardmore."

"Possibly not. The point I was trying to make is that murder has been on the cards for years, so to speak. You get the idea exactly in the popular phrase, 'It's a wonder nobody has murdered him!' which means: 'I feel inclined to murder him myself.' That inclination is the link between the old wound and the new, and the reason why nobody will talk. It's a subject that doesn't bear talking about."

The detective shrugged his shoulders. He raised his hand to his mouth and yawned. Speculations of this kind struck him, evidently, as sheer waste of time. He repeated that he had cross-examined every member of the household about past events.

"Angus and Christina were my chief hope," he complained, "but they seem to think it a deadly sin even to suggest that Duchlan's sister may have possessed an enemy. I simply couldn't get a word out of either of them."

"What do you make of them?"

Dundas shrugged his shoulders.

"I suppose," he said with a bitter smile, "that they belong to a superior order of beings who mustn't be judged by ordinary standards. I'm a Lowland Scot and we all think the same about these Highlanders. They struck me as dull, prejudiced people, without two ideas to rub together. Angus talks about Duchlan as if he was a god. As for Christina, her mind doesn't seem to have grown since its earliest infancy."

He passed his hand over his corn-coloured head. His eyes expressed irritation and perplexity, the immemorial trouble of the Saxon when faced by the Celt. Dr. Hailey thought that a less happy choice of a man to deal with this case could scarcely have been imagined.

"Did they deny all knowledge of the early wound?" he asked.

"Absolutely."

"That only means, probably, that they had no direct knowledge of it."

"Goodness knows what it means."

"I think it should be possible to persuade them to refresh their memories."

Dr. Hailey turned sharply as he spoke. Dr. McDonald had entered the room and was standing behind him. He rose to his feet.

"I'd like you to come and see this boy," McDonald said. "It's one of those puzzling cases that one finds it difficult to name." He hesitated and then added: "It may be only a passing indigestion. On the other hand it may be brain. I've acted so far on the assumption that it's brain."

Dr. Hailey promised Dundas that he would come back in the morning. He took his hat and followed McDonald to the door. He shut the door. When they reached the foot of the stairs leading to the nursery, he remembered that he had left his fountain-pen behind him and told his companion.

"I'll go back for it," McDonald said.

McDonald ran back along the lighted corridor. Next moment Dr. Hailey heard his own name called in accents which proclaimed distress and horror. He strode to Dundas's room.

The detective was lying huddled on the floor beside the bed. There was an ominous stain on his corn-coloured hair.

CHAPTER XII

THE SECOND MURDER

DR. MCDONALD was on his knees beside the man, trying apparently to feel his pulse. He raised frightened eyes as his colleague came into the room.

"He's dead!"

"What?"

"He's dead!"

Dr. Hailey glanced round the room and, seeing nothing, looked again as though aware of a presence that defied human senses. Then he touched the stain on the yellow head. He started back.

"His skull's broken," he cried, "broken like an eggshell. Was the door of the room shut?"

"Yes."

"We met nobody in the corridor. There's no other door on the corridor. There's nowhere anybody could hide."

Dr. Hailey satisfied himself that Dundas was dead. Then he walked to the opened window. The night was very still. He listened, but could hear nothing except the gurgle of the burn below the window and the less sophisticated mirth of small waves on the shingle. The herring-boats were still lying at anchor near the shore. He looked down at the smooth wall which fell even farther here than under Miss Gregor's window, because of the sharp fall of the ground towards the burn. Nobody had come this way.

McDonald had risen and was standing gazing at the detective's body. His cheeks were white, his eyes rather staring. Every now and then he moistened his dry lips.

"There's no sign of a struggle," he said in a hoarse whisper.

Dr. Hailey nodded. The champagne glasses stood where they had been placed and, though the bottle had descended somewhat into its pail, it had not been disturbed.

"You heard no cry?"

"I heard nothing."

"How long do you suppose we were absent from the room?"

"Half a minute. Not more."

"These oil lamps throw long and deep shadows, you know. And we weren't looking for possible assassins…"

As he spoke Dr. Hailey stepped out into the corridor. He lit his electric lamp and directed the beam to right and left. The corridor ended at a window which looked out in the same direction as the windows of Dundas's bedroom, and there was a space of about a yard between this window and the bedroom door—a space evidently big enough to serve as a hiding-place. He extinguished his lamp. The rays of the paraffin lamp near the stairhead, feeble as they were, effectively illuminated the space under the window. He called Dr. McDonald.

"You would have seen anybody there," he said.

"Of course. Nobody could hide there."

"He must have hidden somewhere!"

The doctor's tones were peremptory, like the tones of a schoolmaster cross-examining a shifty pupil.

"Of course. We passed nobody."

"Nobody."

Their eyes met. Each read the growing horror in the other's eyes. They glanced to right and left.

"It's only a question of making a careful enough search," McDonald said. "We've overlooked something of course. Our nerves…"

He broke off. He gazed about him. His mouth opened but no words came to his lips. He walked to the window, looked out, and came back again to his companion.

"Shall I shut the door?" he asked.

"There's nobody here."

"There must be. If we leave the door open he may get away."

McDonald shut the door. He began to prowl round the room like a caged animal. His eyes, Dr. Hailey thought, held the expression which is characteristic of caged animals. He was waiting, expecting. But he was also without hope. He looked into the wardrobe and under the bed and again into the wardrobe. After that he locked the wardrobe door.

"I feel that we aren't alone," he declared in challenging tones.

He kept fidgeting with his necktie. Dr. Hailey shook his head.

"I'm afraid it's useless," he declared.

"Don't you feel that there's somebody beside us?"

"No."

McDonald pressed his hand to his brow.

"It must be my nerves. One doesn't see, though... It's such a long fall to the ground, and I heard nothing."

He continued to make rambling, disjointed comments. His face had lost its accustomed expression of cheerfulness; it revealed the deep agitation which fear and horror were arousing in his mind. "I think," he cried suddenly, "that we ought to go down below and make sure that no ladder or rope was employed."

"Very well."

Dr. Hailey walked back to the dead man and examined his injury again. Then he accompanied his colleague. They found Duchlan and his son waiting for them at the head of the stairs.

"It's good of you to come, Dr. Hailey," Eoghan Gregor said. He noticed the pallor of Dr. McDonald's face and stiffened. "Is anything wrong?"

"Dundas has just been murdered."

Both father and son recoiled.

"What?"

"His skull has been broken..." McDonald faltered over this medical detail and then added: "Hailey and I are going down to... to investigate the ground under the window."

Duchlan seemed to wish to ask some further questions but desisted. He stood aside to allow the doctors to pass. He followed them downstairs and was followed in turn by Eoghan. Dr. Hailey asked them if they possessed an electric lamp and was told that they did not.

Eoghan led the way to the place immediately under Dundas's window. Dr. Hailey lit his torch and swept the bank with the strong beam. The beam showed him nothing. He turned it to light the front of the house and saw that there was a french-window immediately under Dundas's bedroom.

"What room is that?" he asked Duchlan.

"The writing-room."

"You heard nothing?"

"Nothing."

Duchlan put his hand on the doctor's arm.

"I thought I saw something gleam out there just now, to the left of the boats," he said.

"Really?"

The old man stood gazing seawards for a few minutes and then turned again.

"Moonlight is always deceptive," he declared, "and never more so than when it shines on water."

"Yes."

"It seems impossible that anybody can have reached that poor young man's bedroom. Eoghan and I must have seen anybody who tried to descend the staircase."

The doctor nodded. "Nobody left the room," he declared in positive tones.

"Nor entered it."

"No."

Duchlan drew a sharp breath.

"They say there are places in Loch Fyne," he declared inconsequently, "where the sea has no bed. Bottomless deeps about which our local lore is prolific of uneasy tales."

His voice fell to a whisper. "I've heard my father, the late Duchlan, speak of swimmers, half-man, half-fish, whose mission it was..."

He broke off. The awe in his tones sufficiently declared the nature of the fear which was compelling him. He gazed seaward again, expecting, apparently, a further glimpse of the shining object he had already seen.

"The Highland superstition is a byword in the Lowlands," he added after a few minutes. "They mock and jeer at us. But so might blind men mock at those possessed of sight. If our scientists were blind they would, believe me, furnish indisputable proof that sight is no more than an illusion of the simple."

"What was the object like which gleamed?" Dr. Hailey asked in impatient tones.

"Like a fish. A leaping salmon gleams in that way, in moonlight; but this was bigger than any salmon. And it did not leave the water."

"You saw it once only?"

The old man nodded.

"Yes, only once. I've been watching to see if I could catch another glimpse of it, but it has disappeared."

He spoke in tones which left no doubt that he believed that what he had witnessed was no mere reflection of the moon's light on the water. The doctor watched the play of emotion on his features, and realized that he had already reached his own conclusions about the murders. He turned to Eoghan and McDonald and asked them if they had observed anything.

"Nothing," Eoghan said.

"And you, doctor?"

"I've seen nothing at all."

McDonald's voice was unsteady. He stood gazing at the facade of the house as if he expected to gain enlightenment from it. Suddenly he turned and raised his hand to his eyes. He pointed to the herring-boats.

"If they're not all asleep they must have seen something," he declared.

Dr. Hailey was busy with his lamp. He turned the beam on the wall.

There was no sign of any attempt to climb the wall. He walked for some distance to right and left and repeated his examination. The grass was innocent of any mark such as must have been imprinted on it had a ladder been used to reach the window. He turned to Duchlan who was standing beside him.

"The Procurator Fiscal told me that he examined the ground under your sister's window?" he said.

"He did, yes. I was with him. We had the advantage of bright sunlight on that occasion and also of the fact that there's a flower bed under the window. We found absolutely nothing. Neither footprint nor ladder-print."

"There seems to be nothing here either."

"Nothing."

They stood facing each other in silence. The murmur of voices came softly to them from the herring-boats. Dr. Hailey turned and descended the bank to the shore. He hailed the nearest of the boats and was answered in the soft accents of the Highlands.

"Did you see anybody at that lighted window up there?"

"I did not. We've been sleeping. It was your voices that wakened us."

"Did you hear anything?"

"No, sir."

Dr. Hailey felt exasperated at the man's calmness and told him what had happened. The news was received with a stream of exclamations.

"I thought your look-out man might have seen something at the window."

"We have no look-out man when we anchor in-shore. But we're light sleepers, all of us. As I told you, it was your voices wakened us. There was no cry from the bedroom. Not a sound at all whatever."

They returned to the house and entered Duchlan's study. Dr. Hailey told Eoghan Gregor that he wished to see his little boy before they dealt further with the case of Dundas, and he and McDonald left father and son together and climbed the stairs to the top floor of the house. Oonagh met them at the top of the stairs.

"He's had another attack," she cried in anxious tones.

She paused an instant before the word "attack". Dr. Hailey realized that she had meant to say "fit". That short word carried too great a burden of fear. She led the way into a big room, the walls of which were covered with texts from the Bible. The little boy was lying down; as he approached the bed an old woman in cap and apron, who had been bending over the child, stood up and moved aside to let him pass. Her broad, deeply-wrinkled face was streaked with tears. Dr. Hailey lifted the ice-bag from the child's brow and looked into the wide-open eyes. He lit his lamp and flashed it, suddenly, on the small face. When the patient winced, he nodded reassuringly.

"What about the signs?" he asked McDonald.

"They're all negative."

"Kernig's?"

"Yes."

Dr. Hailey patted the hand which lay, closed, on the coverlet beside him. He asked the child to tell him his name and got a clear answer: "Hamish Gregor of Duchlan". Even the babes in Duchlan Castle were taught, it seemed, to set store on their territorial right.

"Who taught you your name?" he asked.

"Aunt Mary."

He bent and drew his nail lightly across the child's forearm, a proceeding watched with careful eyes by the nurse. After a short interval a red wheal appeared on the skin where he had stroked it. The wheal became, rapidly, more marked and acquired a pallor in the middle, which suggested that the arm had been lashed with a whipcord. Both Oonagh and the nurse exclaimed in dismay.

"What does it mean?" Oonagh asked.

"Nothing."

"What?"

"It's a sign of a certain type of nervous temperament, that's all. The attacks belong to the same order. They'll soon pass off though they may return." Dr. Hailey exchanged a smile with his patient, who was now viewing the wheal with astonishment. He added: "There's absolutely nothing to fear, now or later."

Oonagh thanked him with a sincerity that admitted of no question. She seemed to have changed since the night on which he had rescued her but he did not fail to observe that she was strung up to a high pitch. He wondered if it was from her that the child had inherited its weakness, but decided that, in all probability, Dundas's view was the correct one. This girl was physically healthy even if her mind was being severely tried. She listened with an admirable self-control to his direction about the treatment of her boy and emphasized these directions for the guidance of the old nurse.

"You've noticed, I suppose," Dr. Hailey said to the nurse, "that the child bruises easily, and sometimes more easily than at other times."

"Yes, doctor, I have." The old woman's grave, attractive face darkened. "I call him 'Hamish hurt himself' whiles because he always seems to be covered with bruises. There's bruises that come of themselves, too, without his hurting himself. I didna know that it was his nerves."

Her voice was soft and urgent like a deep stream in spate. Its tones suggested that she was only half convinced. Duchlan's descriptions of his servants as friends was evidently fully justified.

"He'll grow out of it."

The nurse hesitated a moment. Then the blood darkened in her withered cheeks.

"I should tell you, doctor," she said, "that Hamish has been losing ground lately. He seems that lifeless and depressed. I think whiles it's as if he was frightened of something or somebody. Children are mair sensitive like than old folk."

She broke off and glanced at Oonagh as if she feared that she had exceeded her right. But the girl nodded.

"I've noticed that too," she said. "He seems what we call in Ireland 'droopy.'"

"Children," Christina repeated, "are mair sensitive than auld folks. They seem to ken when there's anything against them. They're fashed and frightened, like. It doesna do to say that there's nothing in that. What means have we of knowing all that passes through a child's mind?"

She spoke gently without a trace of disrespect. It was obvious that anxiety alone dictated her thoughts.

"I'm afraid," Dr. Hailey agreed, "that we have very small means."

"Aye, verra small means. You, that has the skill, kens that them turns is comin' from the nerves, but what is it that's workin' on the nerves? That's what I would like to ken."

The doctor shook his head.

"That's very difficult to say," he confessed. "Rheumatism sometimes causes this kind of nervous irritability. But undoubtedly other causes exist. I saw a case once that was certainly due to a severe fright and I saw another case which I was able to trace to nervous exhaustion brought on by anxiety. That poor child was terrified of its father, who was a drunkard."

A quick flush spread over the old nurse's cheeks.

"Highland folks," she said, "believes that there's more causes of trouble than any skill can find."

She spoke cryptically but with great earnestness. Dr. Hailey saw a faint smile pass across McDonald's lips. Was this a veiled reference to the relations existing between Eoghan and his wife? Oonagh's eyes suggested that she thought so.

"Do you believe," he asked Christina, "that the feelings of older people are known and understood by children?"

"Aye, that I do, doctor. What's more, I believe that you can poison a mind the same as you can poison a body."

When they left the nursery, McDonald put his hand on his companion's arm.

"You see what Highland people are," he declared. "We haven't changed."

"It isn't only Highland people, you know, who are superstitious about nervous ailments," Dr. Hailey said. "Mankind as a whole is afraid of them. People who bruised easily were looked upon with veneration in the Middle Ages. There are thousands of records of men and women who could, at will, produce the stigmata of the Cross on their hands and feet and brows. It was supposed that these people were in intimate touch with divine beings. Others bore blemishes that were popularly ascribed to the touch of the Devil or the influence of the Evil Eye. It seems, for example, to be true that the real reason why Henry VIII got rid of Anne Boleyn so quickly was that he observed such blemishes on her skin as were reputed to be borne only by witches. He was more superstitious than any of your Highlanders."

They returned to the smoking-room to Duchlan and his son. As they did so, Angus the piper came to the door. He announced that a young fisherman wished to speak to the laird.

"Show him in, Angus."

A tall fellow in a blue jersey appeared. He carried a tam-o'-shanter in his hand. When he had half-crossed the room he stood and began to fidget with his cap in the fashion of a woman unpicking a seam. Duchlan greeted him cordially.

"Well, Dugald, what has brought you here to-night?" he asked, and then before the lad could reply introduced him as the brother of "my two good friends and helpers, Mary and Flora Campbell".

Dugald recovered his self-possession slowly. He stated that he had been told by his friends that the laird was anxious to meet a fisherman who had not been asleep during the last hour and who had therefore been in a position to see what was happening at the castle.

"I wass in the farthest out of the boats," he added, "and I wass not sleeping. I could see the house all the time."

Angus brought a chair and the young fellow sat down. Dr. Hailey asked him:

"Were you looking at the house?"

"Yess, I wass."

"What did you see?"

"There wass a window with a light in it. A big man came to the window and then, after a long time, a little man."

"You didn't see their faces?"

"No, sir. Because the light wass behind them. The moon wass shining on the windows but it wass not so bright as the light in the room."

The doctor nodded his agreement with these just considerations.

"Quite. Now do you remember which of the two men whom you saw remained longest at the window, the big man or the little man?"

"The big man, sir."

Dr. Hailey turned to his companions.

"I looked out of the window after I reached the room. I was feeling very hot and remained at the window a little time. So far, therefore, we seem to be on solid ground." He addressed the fisherman: "Can you describe what you saw of the little man?"

"I saw him at the window. He went away again in a moment."

The doctor leaned forward.

"You noticed nothing peculiar about his coming or going?"

"No, sir."

"Think very carefully, please."

"No, sir, I noticed nothing at all. He came and he went, like the big man before him."

"There was no cry?"

"I did not hear any cry."

"Was that the only window on the floor that was lighted?"

"Yes, sir."

"You're quite sure?"

"Yes, sir."

"What do you say, Duchlan?"

The old man inclined his head.

"He's quite right. I was here with Eoghan. The nursery window doesn't overlook the sea."

Dr. Hailey put his eyeglass in his eye.

"You said the moon was shining on the house? Did you see anything unusual on the wall or the roof?"

"No, sir, nothing at all."

"Do you think that, if somebody had climbed up to the window by means of a ladder, you would have seen him?"

"Oh, yes, I would."

"In spite of the lighted window?"

"Yes. If a cat had climbed up to the window I would have seen her. There wass no ladder."

"You can swear to that?"

"I can swear to it."

"Tell me, Dugald," Duchlan asked, "did you see anything float by your boat about the time when the wee man was at the window?"

A look of fear crept into the lad's eyes. He raised his eyebrows and then contracted them sharply.

"No, laird."

"Something that shone."

"No, laird."

Dugald plucked more vigorously at his tam-o'-shanter. The fear in his eyes had deepened. It was evident that he was well aware of the tales about the fish-like swimmers. He looked inquiringly at Duchlan.

"I thought," the old man said, "that I saw something gleam near one of the boats. But you can't be sure in the moonlight."

Dugald's uneasiness was increasing.

"I saw nothing, laird, nothing at all, whatever. But Sandy Dreich he said that to-night would be a bad night for us because we passed four women when we wass going down to the boats. And, sure enough, there's been no fishin'. Sandy, he saw a shoal a wee bit out from the burn and we shot the net. But there wass nothing in the net."

This information was given with extreme seriousness. It was so received by Duchlan. Laird and fisherman appeared to be in agreement about the probable cause of the poor fishing.

"Is it unlucky," Dr. Hailey asked, "to meet women when you're going to your boats?"

"Yess, sir; there's many as turns back when that happens."

The doctor turned to Duchlan:

"The fishermen of Holy Island, on the Northumbrian coast, won't go out if anybody speaks the word 'pig' in their hearing. They never speak that word themselves. All the pigs on Holy Island are creatures—'craturs' as they call them."

The old man inclined his head gravely. He offered no comment, and it was clear that he thought the subject undesirable in present circumstances.

Angus was told to give the fisherman a drink. When he had gone Duchlan roused himself from the lethargy into which he seemed to have fallen.

"You yourself can testify, Dr. Hailey," he asked, "that nobody entered the room after you had left it?"

"I can."

"So that both door and windows were as effectually sealed as if they had been locked and bolted?"

"It seems so."

"As effectually as were the windows and door of my poor sister's room?"

"Yes."

The old man straightened in his chair.

"Can you suggest any explanation of those two tragedies?" he demanded.

"None."

"They're exactly alike?"

"Yes."

"In conception and execution, exactly alike?"

"Yes."

"The same hand must have struck both blows?"

"It seems so."

Silence fell in the room; they glanced at one another uneasily.

"On the face of it, it's impossible that murder can have been committed in either case," Duchlan said at last.

His voice faded away. He began to move uneasily in his chair. The habit into which he had fallen, of ascribing so many of the events of his life to supernatural agencies, was doubtless the cause of the fear which was expressed vividly on his features.

"It will be necessary," Dr. Hailey said, "to recall Mr. McLeod. I may be wrong but I feel we have no time to lose. What has happened twice may happen a third time."

That thought had, apparently, been present to the minds of his companions. Dr. McDonald glanced uncomfortably about him while Duchlan wiped his brow. There was alacrity too in Eoghan's manner of promising to go at once to the police office in Ardmore.

CHAPTER XIII

"A CURSE ON THIS HOUSE"

DR. HAILEY spent the next morning examining the ground under Dundas's window. The hot weather had hardened the turf so that it was idle to expect that it would reveal much; it revealed nothing. The hardest lawn must have taken some imprint from a ladder that bore a man's weight. He stood looking at the blank slope with eyes that betrayed no feeling; then his gaze moved over the grass, down to the burn; and beyond the burn, to the loch. He shook his head and returned to the castle, where he found Mr. McLeod, newly arrived from Campbeltown, awaiting him. The Procurator Fiscal seemed to be deeply moved by the new tragedy.

"What is this manner of death, doctor," he asked, "which can pass through locked doors?" His tones accused; he added, "Duchlan tells me that you and McDonald hadn't left the poor man more than a minute before he was killed. Is that so?"

"I don't think that a minute elapsed between our leaving him and his death."

Mr. McLeod's big face grew pale. "You're saying that Dundas was struck down, not that he was murdered," he exclaimed in tones of awe.

They had entered the study. The Procurator Fiscal sat down and bent his head. When he had remained in that posture of humility for a few minutes he stated that he had sent to Glasgow for help.

"They'll send their best, depend on it."

"I hope so."

"Poor Dundas!" he moralized in unsteady tones. "This case was to have made his name. How little we know, Dr. Hailey, of the secret designs of Providence." He paused and then added: "I have heard it said that there is a curse on this house."

A kind of paralysis seemed to have affected him, for he sank lower in his chair. He kept nodding his head and mumbling as if he was repeating chastening truths to himself and registering his acceptance of them. Dr. Hailey got the impression that he was greatly afraid lest his own life might be taken at any moment.

"I spoke to Duchlan as I came in," Mr. McLeod said. "He tells me he thought he saw some bright object on the water a few minutes after Dundas met his death."

"Yes."

"He told you that, too, did he?"

"Yes."

Dr. Hailey's tones were not encouraging.

"It's very strange if it's true." Again the worthy man wiped his face. "There's queer stories about Loch Fyne as you may know. The fishermen tell very queer stories sometimes."

"So I believe."

Mr. McLeod roused himself.

"Aye," he exclaimed with warmth, "it's easy to say you don't believe in old wives' tales. But these men are shrewd observers with highly developed and trained senses. Who knows but what they may be able to see and hear and feel more than you or I could see or hear or feel? All the time they are watching the face of the water, which is the mirror of the heavens."

The doctor assented. Mr. McLeod, he observed, was divided, in his fear, between his natural credulousness and his acquired ideas. These ideas were based on gloomy reflections about the trivial character and brief duration of human life derived from the minor Hebrew prophets. No wonder the man found whisky essential to his well-being!

He left him and went up to Dundas's bedroom. The body had not been moved. A shaft of sunlight touched the yellow hair. It was easy to discount the panic of McLeod and the others, but not so easy to escape from the influences which had wrought that panic. He picked up one of the notebooks which the detective had filled with details of his investigation. It made melancholy reading. The pages were crowded with negative observations; everything had been eliminated, door, windows, walls, ceiling, floor. The last note was not without pathos: "It will be necessary to begin again."

He put the book back in its place and polished his eyeglass. He held the glass above the dead man's head where the skull was fractured and marvelled again at the strange, savage violence of the blow. The bedroom, assuredly, did not contain any weapon capable of inflicting this grievous injury. He had already examined such pieces of the movable furniture as might have been made use of. The murderer had carried his own weapon, or rather two weapons; an axe, perhaps, in the case of Miss Gregor, a bludgeon or a knuckle-duster in this case. The first weapon, had it been employed in the second case, must have split Dundas's skull from vault to base. Again he turned to the window and again surveyed the bank between the house and the burn. Autumn was dressing herself in her scarlets and saffrons; already the air held that magical quality of light which belongs only to diminishing days and which seems to be of the same texture as the colours it illuminates. He marked the fans of the chestnuts across the burn, pale gold and pale green. The small coin of birch leaves a-jingle in the wind, light as the sequins on a girl's dress, the beeches and oaks, wine-stained from the winds' Bacchanal, the rowans, flushed with their fruiting. A man might easily from this place throw a tell-tale weapon into that fervent tangle or into the burn even. But no, he had searched diligently and knew that no weapon lay hidden in any of these places. He turned back to the room. He bent forward and then strode quickly to the dead man's side.

The light had revealed a gleam of silver among the golden hair. He recognized another herring scale.

CHAPTER XIV

A QUEER OMISSION

THE DISCOVERY of the herring scale on Dundas's head sent Dr. Hailey down to Ardmore to McDonald. The doctor's house stood on a spur of rock overlooking the harbour. As he ascended the path, which mounted in zigzags to the house, he had a view of the whole extent of this singular natural basin with its islands and bays. The bulk of the fishing-fleet lay at anchor, far up, opposite the town, but skiffs, in pairs, were dotted over the whole expanse of water. He marked the clean, dainty lines of these vessels in excellent accord with their short, raked masts. They looked like young gulls in their first grey plumage, lively, eager. A small coaster was fussing in from the loch. He lingered to watch it enter the narrow mouth of the harbour. As it passed, the fringes of seaweed round the islands were lifted and small waves broke on the shores. The smell of boats and seaweed and fish rose to his nostrils. Soft voices reached him across the still, hot air. He ascended higher and turned again. From this point the drying poles, on which a few herring-nets hung like corpses on a gallows, had a macabre appearance, as of some great ship in irretrievable wreck. But the colour of the nets made very comfortable contrast with the pine-wood on Garvel point, across the bay.

The house was built of red sandstone and had a red roof which stood up sharply against the hill behind it. The windows looked out on the harbour, but their longest view was limited everywhere by rocks and heather, a patchwork of purple and green and grey, very bare and desolate, even in sunlight. He rang the bell and was invited to enter by a young woman whose high colour and dark, shining hair were in the tradition of Highland beauty. She showed him into a big room and only then announced that her master had not yet returned from his morning round.

"But I'm expecting him back at any moment now, so perhaps you'll be able to wait."

She went away immediately, without hearing his answer. He walked to the bookshelf which filled one side of the room and glanced at its contents. McDonald, it seemed, was a reader of catholic taste, for here were most of the classics of European literature, especially of French literature: Balzac, Flaubert, de Maupassant, Montaigne, Voltaire, Saint Beuve. He pulled out one or two of the volumes. They looked distinctly the worse of wear. There were no medical books on any of the shelves. The owner of the library, clearly, was a romantic, though he had tempered his enthusiasm with other fare. Dr. Hailey found it difficult to reconcile his knowledge of the man with the man's books. The room was comfortable as men understand that word; it was supplied with big chairs and the apparatus of reading and smoking. A shot-gun, of rather old-fashioned type, whose barrels were shining with oil, stood in one corner. A vase on the mantelpiece was piled high with cartridges. The walls bore pictures of boats, all of them, evidently, the work of the same artist, all equally undistinguished. Dr. Hailey examined one of them. It was signed by McDonald himself.

He sat down and took a pinch of snuff. The medical profession, he reflected, is full of men who wish, all their lives, that they had never entered it. Yet very few of these doctors succeed in making their escape because, though they possess the temperaments of artists, they lack the necessary power of expression or perhaps the necessary craftsmanship. A practice makes too many demands on time and strength to be bedfellow with any enthusiasm. Since McDonald painted pictures, the odds were that he wrote novels or poetry. It was unlikely that his accomplishment in writing was better than his accomplishment in painting. Why had he not married?

A second pinch of snuff went to the answering of this last question, but before it had been answered McDonald himself strode into the room.

"Annie told me that a very tall man was waiting for me," he exclaimed. "I thought it must be you." He shook hands. "Well, anything new?"

"Not much— There was a herring scale on Dundas's head."

"Good heavens! So the same weapon was used in both cases?"

Dr. Hailey shook his head.

"I don't think that's probable," he said, "though of course the head of an axe might cause such an injury."

McDonald's tone became undecided. He stood in the middle of the floor frowning heavily and tugging at his chin. At last he shook his head.

"These fish scales are mysterious enough," he declared, "but the real mystery, it seems to me, isn't going to be solved by them or by any question of weapons. Until you can explain how these two bedrooms were entered and how escape from them took place you are necessarily working in the dark."

Dr. Hailey considered for a moment.

"It's obvious," he said, "that Duchlan has made up his mind that the murders are due to supernatural agency."

"He was certain to do that in any case."

"Quite. And consequently the temptation, from the murderer's point of view, to supply evidence of such supernatural agency must have been strong. That evidence would tend to paralyse his pursuers."

"I don't follow. What evidence of supernatural agency has he supplied?"

"The fish scales."

McDonald stared.

"What, herring scales on Loch Fyne side! How can they be evidence of supernatural agency?"

"Duchlan thought he saw something which gleamed in the moonlight floating away from the mouth of the burn after Dundas was killed."

The Ardmore doctor whistled.

"So that's it, is it?"

"That?"

"The swimmers. Every time anything which can't be explained happens on Loch Fyne side, it's the 'swimmers' who are to blame. They disturb the shoals of herring and so produce bad catches or they call the fish out of the nets at the moment when the catch seems to be secure. You can point out that such losses are due to carelessness till you're black in the face. Nobody believes you. What can mere men do against such beings?"

Dr. Hailey nodded.

"Ardmore lives by the chances of the sea," he said.

"Most superstitions, as you know, are embodiments of bad luck. In agricultural districts the demons blight the crops and dry up the wells..."

"Exactly."

"The point for us is that these fish scales may have been introduced deliberately into the wounds with the object of suggesting that no human hand was concerned in these murders. If so, we may be able to find our man by a process of elimination. The use of superstition as a cloak for crime is evidence of a fairly high order of intelligence."

"I see what you mean. The servants, for example, would not think of doing that."

Dr. Hailey nodded. He leaned back in his chair. "How long have you attended the Duchlan family?" he asked.

"More than ten years."

"And yet you were unaware that Miss Gregor had been wounded?"

"I was. I've never examined Miss Gregor's chest." McDonald strode to the window and back again. "She often suffered from colds and two years ago had a severe attack of bronchitis, but she would never allow me to listen to her breathing. Duchlan told me, before I saw her the first time, that she had a great horror, amounting to an obsession, of medical examinations and that I must do my best to treat her without causing her distress."

"So he knew about the scar? Dundas said that he denied all knowledge of it."

"It's possible, isn't it, that she had made the same excuses to her brother that she made to her doctors. Duchlan may have believed that she really was averse from any examination."

Dr. Hailey nodded.

"That's true. But you'll admit that it's strange she should have sustained a wound of such severity without allowing anybody in the house to find out that she had sustained it." He wrinkled his brows. "I still think that, when she locked her door, she was the victim of panic. Is there a portrait of Duchlan's wife at the castle?"

"I've never seen one."

"I looked for one in all the public rooms and in some of the bedrooms. I didn't find it. For a man who clings to his possessions so tenaciously, that's a queer omission. Every other event of Duchlan's life is celebrated in some fashion on his walls."

McDonald sat down and drew his wooden leg forward with both hands.

"What are you driving at?" he asked.

"I'm beginning to think that Duchlan's wife was concerned in the wounding of Miss Gregor. That would explain the absence of her portrait and the wish to hide the scar. It might explain Miss Gregor's panic at sight of Eoghan's wife. Both father and son, remember, married Irish girls. Mrs. Eoghan's sudden appearance in her bedroom may conceivably have recalled to the old woman's mind a terrible crisis of her life."

"Miss Gregor, believe me, was a level-headed woman."

"No doubt. But shocks of that sort, as you know, leave indelible scars on the mind, so that every reminder of them induces a condition of nervous prostration."

"Very well," McDonald moved his leg again and leaned forward: "What happened after she locked her bedroom door?"

"I think she shut and bolted her windows. It's only reasonable to suppose that the windows were open on account of the heat."

"And then?"

"Then she was murdered."

The country doctor sighed. He repeated: "Then she was murdered," adding in weary tones: "How? Why? By whom?"

He raised his kindly grey eyes to look his colleague in the face. Dr. Hailey dismissed his questions with a short, impatient gesture.

"Never mind that. Come back to Mrs. Eoghan. She told me that she went to her aunt's room in a blue silk dressing-gown, because, having quarrelled with her aunt before dinner, she now wished to make up her quarrel. A similar order of events may have occurred in the case of Duchlan's wife."

McDonald's face had become troubled.

"You don't suggest, do you," he demanded in tones of impatience, "that that fearful wound was inflicted by a girl?"

"No." Dr. Hailey shook his head. "You go too fast, my friend. Leave the room out of the picture for a moment, entirely out of the picture. Here's a more interesting question: was the quarrel between Mrs. Eoghan and Miss Gregor of the same nature as the quarrel between Duchlan's wife and Miss Gregor? The answer depends, obviously on Miss Gregor. There are women, plenty of women, who cannot live at peace with the wives of their men-folk, women who resent these wives as interlopers, women whose chief object it becomes to estrange their husbands from them, sometimes even to alienate their children. Was Miss Gregor one of these women?"

A prolonged silence followed this challenge. McDonald's uneasiness appeared to grow from moment to moment. He kept shifting in his chair and moving his wooden leg about in accord with the movements of his body. A deep flush had spread over his face.

"She was one of those women," he said at last.

CHAPTER XV

THE REAL ENEMY

McDonald rose and stood in front of the empty fireplace.

"As a matter of fact," he said, "I have reason to know that Mrs. Eoghan's life at Duchlan was made impossible by Miss Gregor's jealousy. Almost from the moment when Eoghan went away to Malta, his aunt began to torment and persecute his wife. The burden of her complaint was that little Hamish, the heir of Duchlan, was not being properly brought up."

The doctor paused and turned to find his pipe on the mantelpiece behind him. He put the pipe in his mouth and opened a jar of tobacco.

"My information comes from Mrs. Eoghan herself," he stated. "I suppose I can count myself one of the only two friends she possessed in this neighbourhood."

He extracted a handful of tobacco from the jar and began to fill his pipe, proceeding with this task in a manner the deliberation of which was belied by his embarrassment. Dr. Hailey saw that his hands were shaking.

"The whole atmosphere at Duchlan, believe me, was charged with reproof and every day brought its heavy burden of correction. Miss Gregor inflicted her wounds in soft tones that soon grew unendurable. She never ordered; she pleaded. But her pleas were so many backhanders. She possessed the most amazing ingenuity in discovering the weak points of her antagonist and a sleepless persistence in turning them to her advantage. Things came to a head a month ago."

His pipe was full. He lit it carefully.

"A month ago, little Hamish had a fit. I was sent for. I haven't had as much experience of nervous ailments as you have had and I confess that I was frightened. I suppose my fear communicated itself to the child's mother. At any rate she told me that she felt sure the trouble had its origin in the state of her own nerves and that she had made up her mind to leave Duchlan. 'Eoghan's work in Ayrshire is nearly finished,' she said, 'and I've told him that, if he won't make a home for me after that, I'll leave him.' I could see that she was at the end of her resources. I tried to calm her; but she was past being talked round. When I came downstairs from the nursery Miss Gregor was waiting for me. 'It's his mother, poor child,' she lamented. 'My dear Oonagh means well, of course, but she's had no experience. No experience.'"

He dropped his pipe and stooped to pick it up.

"I can hear her voice still," he declared. "She shook her head slowly as she spoke and tears came into her eyes. 'We've done everything that love can do, doctor,' she told me. 'But I'm afraid it's too true that our efforts have been resented. Eoghan's father is deeply distressed. I cannot tell you what I feel. As you know I've looked on Eoghan and loved him as my own child.' Then the suggestion for which I was waiting was offered: 'Couldn't you use your authority to insist that dear Oonagh must have a complete rest. She has sisters and brothers who will be so glad to see her, and she needn't feel a moment's anxiety about dear Hamish. Christina and I will devote ourselves to him.' What could I say? I told her that such plans must wait till the child was better."

He paused. Dr. Hailey, who was watching him closely, asked:

"How did she receive that opinion?"

"Badly, that's to say, with an exquisite resignation. 'Of course, doctor,' was what she said, 'we must all bow to your discretion in a matter of this kind. You alone are possessed of the knowledge necessary to a decision. But I do feel that I have a duty to place before you those personal considerations which no doctor can be expected to learn for himself.' In other words: 'If you're on the side of the enemy, I shall make it exceedingly unpleasant for you.' I saw the promise of that in her eyes. And she knew that I saw it."

"You stood your ground, though?"

There was eagerness in the doctor's tones.

"Yes. That old woman roused my fighting instinct. There was a whine in her voice that made my hair bristle. She used to pronounce the word 'dear', 'dee-ah', and she always pronounced Mrs. Eoghan's name 'Una' although she had been corrected hundreds of times. Behind her stubborn nature there was a kind of impishness, a wicked quality, which took joy in hurting the people she didn't like. You looked at the saint or the martyr and you knew that a little devil was watching you out of her swimming eyes."

McDonald's face was red. He shook his head.

"If there had been another doctor here, he would have been sent for. But there isn't. She had to put up with me. Each time we met I felt that her dislike was growing. And she couldn't dislike without disapproving. People who got into her black books were soon described by her as 'not the right thing', a phrase which she knew how to use so that it conveyed an impression of moral obliquity. I was certain I should not have long to wait for some proof of her wish to punish me..."

Dr. Hailey held up his hand.

"A moment, please. Did you continue to visit Hamish?"

"Yes."

"And to refuse to allow Miss Gregor to interfere?"

"I refused to agree that Mrs. Eoghan should leave the child and go to Ireland. One day I said that I thought a child's mother was always the best nurse who could be obtained for him. Miss Gregor winced when I said that, and just for one instant I was sorry for her."

"I see."

McDonald's nervousness increased. He tried to relight his pipe and then abandoned the attempt.

"A week later, three weeks ago," he said, "I heard a knock at this door one night just when I was going to bed. I opened the door. Mrs. Eoghan was standing behind it."

A deep silence fell in the room. It was broken by the pleasant sound of blocks and tackle, the hoisting of sails. Dr. Hailey nodded without offering any comment.

"The girl was in a terrible state, weeping, hysterical, half-crazy. She fell into the hall when I opened the door. I picked her up. Her clothes seemed to have been flung on anyhow. I carried her in here and put her in that chair," with a sudden, jerky gesture he indicated the chair in which Dr. Hailey was seated. "She told me she had left Duchlan for ever. Later on, when she had recovered a little, she told me that she had had a violent quarrel with Miss Gregor. She said Hamish had had another turn. 'Aunt Mary accused me of ill-using him... killing him. I lost all control of myself.'"

"Did it surprise you," Dr. Hailey asked, "that she should have lost control of herself?"

"No, no. What surprised me was that she had endured Miss Gregor so long."

"I didn't mean that. Do you think her a hysterical type?"

McDonald hesitated.

"Not hysterical; highly-strung. She has an extremely quick intelligence and a great honesty of mind. Miss Gregor's hypocrisy exasperated her to delirium. She didn't care what happened. She told me that she didn't care what happened." He covered his eyes with his hand. "I lit the fire here because the night had grown chilly. I boiled the kettle and made tea. After a while she grew calmer and described what had happened. They had all gone to bed. The nurse had called her because Hamish seemed to be breathing badly. She had hurried upstairs to find Miss Gregor giving the child a dose of sal volatile. You can imagine the rest. I had said that stimulants were not to be given."

"Miss Gregor had suggested a dose of sal volatile?"

"Yes. That morning. Mrs. Eoghan ordered her out of the nursery. She obeyed but roused her brother and brought him upstairs to fight her battle for her. Duchlan was clay in her hands; like most cowards he has a cruel streak in his nature."

McDonald broke off. His uneasiness was increasing. He put his pipe down and stood staring in front of him at the pictures on the wall opposite. "Naturally Mrs. Eoghan quoted my order. She demanded that I should be sent for. Duchlan said: 'It seems to me, and your aunt agrees with me, that Dr. McDonald has been sent for quite often enough lately.' There was no mistaking what he insinuated. She wouldn't defend herself. She left them and came here."

"I see." Dr. Hailey moved in his chair. He looked up and saw that his companion was still gazing at the pictures. The muscles of McDonald's neck stood out rigidly; his arms were stiff.

"Miss Gregor had prompted that remark?"

"Of course. She did all her brother's thinking for him. Mrs. Eoghan realized that the prompting hadn't stopped at Duchlan..."

"What?"

"Miss Gregor wrote regularly to Eoghan."

"And yet Mrs. Eoghan came here. Surely that was playing directly into the enemy's hands?"

Dr. Hailey kept his eyes averted without knowing exactly why he did so. A prolonged silence followed his question. At last McDonald said:

"I fancy Eoghan had written his wife an unkind letter."

"Blaming her for sending for you?"

"Accusing her perhaps of being in love with me."

Dr. Hailey sat up.

"Do you mean that she was leaving her husband and child when she came here?" he exclaimed.

"She was."

They heard another sail being hoisted. The sound of rowlocks came up to them from the harbour and then, suddenly and intolerably, the hoot of a steam-whistle.

"Why did she come to you?" Dr. Hailey asked.

"For advice and shelter." McDonald turned and picked up his pipe. His uneasiness seemed to have left him. He lit the tobacco and began to smoke.

"Naturally," he said, "you want to know how much truth there was in Miss Gregor's suggestion. So far as Mrs. Eoghan is concerned the answer is: None at all. But that isn't the answer in my case. I want to tell you," he turned and faced his companion as he spoke, "that I fell in love with Mrs. Eoghan almost as soon as I met her. Her husband was then in Malta. She was hungry for friendship and help and I gave her both. I'm not a child. I knew what had happened to me. And I knew that it was hopeless, in the sense that Oonagh was genuinely in love with her husband. But knowledge about the causes of pain does not help you when you're compelled to bear it. What did help me was to try to smooth her way for her..."

He shook his head.

"She thought that I was acting solely from professional motives. They were there all right, mind you, those professional motives; the girl's nerves were frayed, jagged. But Miss Gregor wasn't so unsuspecting. I had dared to call her behaviour in question. I was an obstacle in her way. Worse, I was a danger. As I told you just now, she hated me." He drew a deep breath. "Do you know, Hailey, there was something big in that wicked old woman's character? I couldn't help admiring her. The busy way she set about discrediting my motives—first in her own mind, then in Duchlan's. What persistence! And mind you, I had sympathy for her too. Eoghan was her child. She meant to hold him and his for ever. I saw that in her little, quick brown eyes. I had more than Highland pride and Highland craft against me. More than a will as strong as buffalo hide. Motherhood, hungry, unsatisfied, implacable was the real enemy. Deep called to deep. I knew her and she knew me. Only one mistake she made and that's not strange in a woman. Oonagh wasn't in love and hadn't guessed, hadn't dreamed what my feelings were. There's the misfortune that nobody could cure. I'm the only doctor in a radius of twelve miles. Oonagh kept sending for me for herself or Hamish and I could plead my duty against my scruples. The old woman's eyes saw every move. When Eoghan came back from Malta the tension reached breaking-point; only his going to Ayrshire prevented a break. He didn't accuse Oonagh then of running after me, but that was in the back of his mind, where his aunt had put it. But he blamed her for her want of gratitude to his people and for her slackness in Hamish's upbringing. They weren't on speaking terms when he went away. The day he went away she sent for me and told me she was afraid of what she might do."

CHAPTER XVI

INSPECTOR BARLEY

His confession seemed to release Dr. McDonald from bondage. His manner, until now gloomy and reserved, changed.

"I've been frank with you, Hailey," he said, "because, sooner or later, you're bound to hear about the suspicions which Miss Gregor instilled into so many minds. I want you to know the truth. Oonagh belongs to Eoghan. Not for a single instant has she swerved from her loyalty to him. Her coming here was a gesture, a protest made when her fears for Hamish and her distress that her husband should have seemed to take sides against her had brought her to the edge of a breakdown."

He seated himself as he spoke and once more arranged his leg in front of him.

"The end of the story, happily, was better than the beginning. I was trying to persuade her to let me take her back to the castle when a car came to the door. It was the old nurse, Christina, who had been sent as a peacemaker, because Duchlan and his sister were genuinely afraid by that time. The old woman was terribly distressed. You saw her last night. She fixed those queer, black eyes of hers on Oonagh's face and told her that Hamish was crying for his mother. I don't know, there was something in her voice, some tone or quality, that made that appeal irresistible. You saw the child's face; heard his voice. Oonagh's resistance broke down at once. Then the old woman comforted her, promising that her troubles would soon be at an end. You couldn't help believing her. But she's a retainer of the Gregors. I felt that, in her heart of hearts, she shared Miss Gregor's suspicions of me. Queerly enough, she awakened a sense of guilt which I hadn't experienced in any of my dealings with Miss Gregor."

He shook his head.

"I wasn't wrong. She had read my secret. She put Oonagh in the car and came back to this room for a shawl that had been left behind.

I was outside at the car, and when she didn't return, I followed her to find out if anything was amiss. She turned and gazed at me just as she had gazed at Oonagh, but with very hostile eyes. 'Whom God hath joined together,' she said in solemn tones, 'let not man put asunder.' Then she picked up the shawl and hurried away."

"Do you know what happened," Dr. Hailey asked, "after Mrs. Eoghan got home?"

"Oh, yes, they received her with relief if without cordiality. That feeling soon passes. What remained was the knowledge that she had disgraced them publicly—the unpardonable sin. I called on the child next morning. Miss Gregor was in the nursery; she told me that Mrs. Eoghan was in bed with a headache."

"She had yielded to them?"

McDonald's eyes narrowed. He shook his head.

"I don't think that is how I should put it. Oonagh isn't an Irishwoman for nothing. She was biding her time. I realized that the real battle would be fought when her husband came back. But I knew also that the period of waiting for that event would be greatly distressing to Oonagh. She's one of those women who can't act alone, who needs a friend to advise her and help her to gather her forces." He raised his right hand, holding the palm horizontal and keeping the fingers extended. "I suppose we all depend to some extent on the feelings which animate us at any given moment. It's only on high emotional planes that we're heroes." He lowered his hand. "Down here is weakness and hesitation. I think the truth is that she came to me for strength. She told me, a few days later, that she only lived when she was talking to me." He leaned forward. "Mind you, it wasn't my strength she wanted; it was her own. I helped her to command her own strength."

Dr. Hailey nodded: "I know. Humanity as well as chemistry has its catalysts."

"Exactly."

Dr. Hailey rose to go. "Am I at liberty to tell the new detective from Edinburgh what you've told me?" he asked.

"Yes."

He held out his hand. Suddenly he turned back.

"Do you know why Eoghan came back so hurriedly from Ayrshire?"

McDonald's face lost its eagerness: a slow flush rose to his cheeks.

"I suppose he came to borrow money. But Oonagh had sent for him."

"To take her away?"

"Yes."

"He refused?"

Dr. Hailey asked the question in the tones of a man who knows the answer.

"I don't know."

"Eoghan's like his father, isn't he?"

McDonald shook his head.

"In some ways. Not in all ways. For example, he isn't superstitious. The terrible logic of the Irish clashes with that Highland element."

"When I met him," Dr. Hailey said, "I realized that he was a difficult man to know. I formed no very clear idea of his character except that he was in love with his wife."

"I have no very clear idea of his character."

"Has his wife?"

"She's in love with him."

Dr. Hailey sighed.

"Sometimes," he confessed rather sadly, "I wonder what that means. Do lovers really see one another truthfully? Isn't it rather their own illusions that they see?"

There was no answer. McDonald passed his hand wearily across his brow.

"Perhaps lovers see everything and forgive everything," he said.

When Dr. Hailey left McDonald he walked up the harbour to the manse. This was a big square house standing back from the road among scrubby trees that looked terribly wind-worn. He rang the bell. The door was opened by a small girl who stated that her father was at home. A moment later a short, stout man in clerical dress came into the hall. He advanced to the door, dismissing his daughter with a genial gesture.

Dr. Hailey explained who he was and was immediately invited to come in. The Rev. John Dugald led the way to his study and shut the door. He moved a big arm-chair by its back and urged his visitor to sit down. After a glance at the formidable array of volumes with which all the four walls were lined the doctor complied.

"What can I do for you?" the minister asked in rich Highland accents. His good-humoured face was grave, but his eyes gleamed with excitement.

"I want you to tell me about Dr. McDonald."

"Really?" With an effort the Rev. John stifled his curiosity. "McDonald is not a member of my congregation," he said. "He's not a member, indeed, of any congregation. But I have always found him to be a good man, aye and a skilful man too. When my wee boy had bronchitis last winter, he saved his life."

Dr. Hailey inclined his head.

"I'm sure he's a good doctor. My concern, frankly, is with his personal character. His character as a man."

"That's a hard question, sir." The minister considered for a few moments. "If you had asked me that question six months ago," he said, "I would have replied that McDonald was a poet and an artist who had lost his way and become a doctor. I would have said that his only interest was his books and his writing."

He broke off. A troubled look appeared on his face.

"And now?"

"Now it's different. There have been rumours. Stories."

"Such as?"

The Rev. John moved uncomfortably.

"I'll be frank with you. The village has begun to talk about the doctor's intimacy with Mrs. Eoghan Gregor. And not the village only."

He leaned forward. His right hand descended to find his pipe on the top of a wooden coal-box which stood beside his chair.

He put the pipe in his mouth.

"The late Miss Gregor was one of my people," he said. "She came to me a few days ago in the greatest distress to ask my advice. It appears that she had surprised her niece walking on the shore, after dark, with McDonald. What troubled her was whether or not she was bound in duty to report to her nephew."

"I see. What did you advise?"

"I advised her to see Dr. McDonald and talk to him."

"Well?"

"She then told me that she was scarcely on speaking terms with him."

Dr. Hailey frowned.

"The suggestion being that McDonald was so deeply in love with Mrs. Eoghan that no plea was likely to be listened to?" he asked.

"Yes."

"What did you advise in those circumstances?"

"I felt that I could not take the responsibility of giving any advice. But I offered to see the doctor myself. That offer was not accepted, and Miss Gregor went away saying that she must consult her own conscience."

"Were you the only person to whom she confided this information?"

The minister shook his head.

"I don't think so."

"In other words a systematic attempt was being made to blacken Mrs. Eoghan's character?"

There was no reply. Again Dr. Hailey leaned forward.

"Tell me," he asked, "whether or not you're inclined to believe the suggestion conveyed?"

"I'm not inclined to believe it."

"You trust McDonald?"

"Yes, and Mrs. Eoghan."

The doctor nodded. Then he asked:

"And Miss Gregor?"

Silence fell in the room. At last the Rev. John said:

"Miss Gregor, as I've told you, was one of my people. I believe that she felt herself justified in what she did and said. At least I hope so. But it has always seemed to me that there was a quality in her character difficult to reconcile with Christian ideals. I've often tried to define that quality in my mind. I can't say I have succeeded. She was not a hard woman; she was not an ungenerous woman. But there was something..."

He broke off. Dr. Hailey rose and held out his hand.

"Jealousy," he remarked, "is neither hard nor ungenerous except in certain directions."

The detective sent from Glasgow to replace Dundas had arrived when Dr. Hailey returned to the castle. He was with Duchlan in the study. He jumped to his feet the moment the doctor entered the room and thrust out his hand like a man snatching a child from danger.

"Dr. Hailey, I presume. My name is Inspector Barley. Thompson Barley."

He seized the doctor's hand and wrung it; at the same time a broad smile exposed his strong, stained teeth.

"Delighted to make your acquaintance, doctor," he cried. "Even at such a tragic" (he pronounced the word traagic) "*contretemps*. Duchlan here has just been telling me of your goodness. What a calamity! What a calamity!" He waved his hand in a gesture which reproached the gods. "What a calamity!"

Dr. Hailey sat down at the table. This most un-Scots-like Scot interested him. Barley, who wore a black-and-white check dust-coat of terrific pattern, looked like a shop-walker and spoke like a decayed actor in a Strand public-house, but he detected another quality and warmed to it. Inspector Barley possessed pleasant grey eyes; his brow was fine, square and massive and he had eloquent hands. What a pity that he had dyed his hair with henna!

"I am going to venture to ask you," Barley cried, "for an outline of the case. After that I hope that we may co-operate in everything." He turned to Duchlan, bowing as he turned. "Doubtless, sir, you are well aware of the great distinction which attaches to Dr. Hailey's name, both in medical and in criminological circles? But let me tell you that it is only among the *élite* of both these professions that his true worth is understood and appreciated. Only among the *élite*."

He gave his head a strong downward movement as he repeated the last sentence. His mouth at this moment was slightly open and his face had a vacant expression which, paradoxically, expressed a great deal. Duchlan gazed at him with lively astonishment.

"No doubt."

Inspector Barley swung round again to face the doctor. He listened with gravity to the story of the two murders, offering no comment, but bowing occasionally as he took a point. His face remained inscrutable. The fact that his features were somewhat broad and coarse and that he wore a bristling moustache added a grotesque touch to his ceremoniousness. When Dr. Hailey finished he leaned back in his chair and closed his eyes.

"Most mysterious. Most mysterious," he exclaimed in quick tones that wholly discounted the meaning of his words. "Apparently murders of a new *genre*. Of a new *genre*. But probably not. Murder, as you know, changes its form only in unessentials. *Plus ça change, plus c'est la même chose*."

His French accent was better than his English and went some way towards explaining his gestures. He rose and walked to the fireplace, seeming to glide across the carpet. He stood with his back leaning on the mantelpiece.

"It must have struck you, of course, Dr. Hailey," he exclaimed, "that there is one person who certainly had the opportunity of murdering poor Dundas."

He paused. He glanced in turn at each of his companions. Neither spoke, though Dr. Hailey frowned.

"I mean Dr. McDonald, who returned alone to Dundas's room to get your pen."

A sound like a groan punctuated the silence.

Duchlan's head had sunk on to his chest. He swayed for an instant and then slipped from his chair.

CHAPTER XVII

"WHAT AN ACTRESS!"

INSPECTOR BARLEY, like Napoleon, who, as he said, he admired
à outrance, knew the value of time. It took him only a few minutes to
ascertain from Oonagh that Dr. McDonald had visited her child on
the night of Miss Gregor's death, a visit which, as Dr. Hailey felt bound
to acknowledge, had been overlooked in all the earlier investigations.

"McDonald has made no secret, of course, of his frequent visits,"
the doctor declared. "And, as I told you, he was present when the door
of Miss Gregor's room was forced."

"Quite. No doubt the circumstance is unimportant." Barley bowed
to Oonagh, who was seated in an arm-chair, apologizing to her, apparently, for the interruption of her narrative. "Pray continue, Mrs. Gregor."

The girl glanced at Dr. Hailey and then lowered her eyes. She
repeated the account she had already given of her behaviour on the
night of her aunt's murder in tones which were so low as to be nearly
inaudible. She looked exceedingly ill at ease. There were dark lines
under her eyes and she kept drawing her hand across her brow.

"In my humble judgement, and you will correct me if I am mistaken," Barley exclaimed when she had finished, "your account amounts
to this. You had gone early to bed because you were feeling indisposed.
You were summoned about 9 o'clock by the nurse Christina, because
your small son had become ill again. Dr. McDonald was sent for and
after he went away you wished to report the result of his visit to your
aunt, Miss Gregor, who had meanwhile gone to bed, where she was
being attended as usual by your nurse, Christina. For some reason
unknown to you, Miss Gregor received your well-intentioned visit to
her bedroom with dismay and locked the door of the room in your face."

He leaned back in his chair and thrust his thumbs into the armholes
of his waistcoat. "Am I right?"

"Yes."

"Dr. McDonald had left the house before you paid your visit to Miss Gregor's room?"

The blood ebbed slowly out of Oonagh's cheeks.

"He remained with Hamish while I paid my visit," she said with an evident effort. "Because Christina had gone to my aunt."

"And then?"

"He was waiting for me at the top of the stairs. We came downstairs together."

"To the study?"

"Yes. Dr. McDonald wanted to give me some directions about the treatment."

Barley swept the room with his eyes, fixing his gaze finally on the ceiling.

"This room is situated immediately under Miss Gregor's room, is it not?" he asked.

"Yes."

There was a moment of silence. Then the detective rose to his feet and pointed his finger at the girl.

"I put it to you," he cried, "that Dr. McDonald accompanied you to Miss Gregor's bedroom?"

"No."

"Take care, Mrs. Gregor."

"He did not accompany me to Miss Gregor's bedroom, Christina will tell you that he did not."

Her eyes were unflinching; her beauty shone with the strength of conviction which animated her face. Barley caught his breath in a gasp of admiration.

"What an actress!" he exclaimed insolently.

He sat down again and appeared to remain unaware of the vigour with which his rudeness had been resented. He dismissed Oonagh with a wave of his hand, then suddenly rose and opened the door for her, bowing as she went out. He rang the bell and returned to his chair.

"Dr. McDonald did accompany her to her aunt's room," he said, "you shall hear."

Angus, the piper, answered the bell. Barley ordered him to sit down in tones so gracious that the Highlander appeared to think himself insulted. His solemn face expressed a lively resentment.

"Did you see Dr. McDonald on the night your mistress was murdered?" the detective asked.

"Yes, sir, I did."

"Where?"

"In this house, sir."

"Where, in this house?"

Angus turned and indicated the door with a gesture superb in its mingling of deference with scorn.

"I opened the front door to him."

"Did you see him after that?"

"I did not, sir. The doctor told me not to wait up for him because Mistress Gregor or Christina would let him out of the house."

"Did you hear him going away?"

"I did not. My room is at the other side of the castle."

"Did anybody hear him going away?"

Angus hesitated. He smoothed his kilt with his big red hand.

"Christina told me that she heard him going down the top flight of stairs, but she did not hear him going down the second flight to the hall."

Barley started and strained forward.

"What do you mean?"

"Dr. McDonald has a wooden leg, sir."

"Ask Christina to come here immediately."

When the door shut, the detective no longer attempted to hide his jubilation. He began to walk up and down the room with his hands clasped behind his back and his head and shoulders thrust forward. He paused at every few steps to throw out a remark, much as turkeys pause to gobble.

"Wooden leg! You didn't tell me that. But, of course, it's a detail… My dear doctor, I believe that the solution of this mystery cannot now be long delayed. The solution may be displeasing, distressing." He shrugged his shoulders. "*Que voulez-vous?* What a point: that thumping of the wooden leg on the wooden stairs! The old woman listening. Hearing the 'thump, thump' down to the first floor. Then silence. A silence more eloquent than words." He came to Dr. Hailey and stood in front of him. "The husband is coming home: there is a story to tell him." He shook his head. "Don't forget that Miss Gregor was Eoghan's foster-mother. *In loco parentis.* Women can endure least of all, in my humble judgement, to see the men they have mothered betrayed in their absence."

He stopped speaking because the door of the room had opened. Christina came hobbling into the room. She was dressed in cap and apron. She glanced at Barley in a manner that was quite frankly hostile and then seated herself on the edge of the chair which he offered her. He came to the point in an instant.

"You heard Dr. McDonald going downstairs from the nursery on the night your mistress was murdered?" he asked.

"Yes, I did."

"Did you hear him go down to the hall?"

"I did not."

"Tell me exactly what you heard."

The old woman clasped her skinny hands in her lap and looked at them attentively.

"I heard him go down to the floor below," she said.

Barley began to nod his head vigorously.

"That means he didn't go down to the ground floor. You couldn't have helped hearing his wooden leg on the stair if he had gone down to the hall."

"I was not listening." The old woman shook her head. "Very likely he did go down to the hall. I had shut the door of the nursery."

A quick frown gathered on Barley's brow.

"A wooden leg makes a deal of noise on a wooden floor," he exclaimed.

"It does, if you are near it."

"Why did you tell Angus that you only heard the doctor go down one flight of the stair?"

"Because I only heard him go down one flight. After that I shut the nursery door."

Christina's face was grave but Dr. Hailey fancied that he detected a grim smile lurking among its wrinkles. The Highlander, he reflected with some satisfaction, has his own sense of humour. Barley did not try to hide his annoyance at the check he had received; but he did not, in his annoyance, abate his eloquence.

"You heard him go down to the first floor. You returned to your duties. *Ca va bien.* Angus, the piper, has told us that he had already gone to bed. The question is: Who locked up the house after the doctor had gone away?"

"I do not know."

"The doctor stayed with the child, did he not, while you went to put your mistress to bed?"

"He and Mistress Eoghan Gregor stayed with Hamish."

"Now be careful how you answer this question: Did Mrs. Eoghan Gregor come to Miss Gregor's bedroom?"

"Yes, and then I went back to the nursery, where the doctor was waiting."

Barley bowed over his waistcoat. He raised his hand in the manner of the conductor of an orchestra.

"What happened," he asked, "when Mrs. Eoghan Gregor entered Miss Gregor's bedroom?"

"I did not see what happened."

"But you were there?"

"I was. But I went away. Mrs. Eoghan took the candle from me at the door. I wished to go back to Hamish."

"Did you hear Mrs. Eoghan come out of Miss Gregor's room?"

Christina shook her head.

"I did not."

"What happened after you returned to the nursery?"

"Dr. McDonald went away down the stair."

"Mrs. Eoghan Gregor says that Miss Gregor ordered her out of her bedroom and locked the door behind her?"

"Yes."

"She told you that?"

"Yes."

Once again Barley gesticulated.

"Dr. McDonald, for all you know to the contrary, may have gone to Miss Gregor's room?"

"Mrs. Eoghan did not say that. She said..."

"Yes, I know what she said." The detective swept away the repetition he did not wish to hear. "Now tell me," he continued, "did you hear Mrs. Eoghan shutting the front door after the doctor left the castle?"

"I did not. I heard Mr. Eoghan's motor-boat coming into the jetty."

"What, so Mr. Eoghan arrived just when Dr. McDonald was going away?"

"Yes, he did."

"Did they meet?"

Christina shook her head. "I do not know if they met."

Barley dismissed her and addressed Dr. Hailey.

"I admit," he exclaimed, "that I have not proved all that I had hoped to prove. But something has undoubtedly accrued from my investigation. Something!" He bit at his words as they escaped from his mouth. Suddenly he took a small comb from his pocket and combed his moustache in short, quick strokes that made it bristle. After the comb he produced a pipe, dark and well-seasoned, which he polished lovingly on the side of his nose.

"Point one," he stated, pointing the stem of his pipe at his companion. "Dr. McDonald is the only person who can possibly have murdered Dundas. Point two. It may very well be that Dr. McDonald entered Miss Gregor's bedroom. We have only the word of Mrs. Eoghan that he did not do so, and her word, in my humble opinion, is suspect. Point three. A link establishes itself between these two associations. What did Miss Gregor know? Here is a young wife, left by her husband in circumstances which doubtless were uncongenial. Her boy is ill. She summons the local doctor who calls at frequent intervals. Acquaintance ripens into a warmer emotion. *A côte de l'amour...*" The pipe made a great circle. "Your Celtic temperament is nothing if not ardent. Emotion rises to full tide in a day, an hour. Nothing else seems to matter. Ah, this is the very quintessence of love!"

The man raised his eyes ecstatically. They were loosely set and moved with a tipsy roll that was full of surprises. Evidently he attached importance to a lyrical quality which he supposed his nature to possess for he quoted some lines about love, the authorship of which he did not disclose. His voice tripped along and stopped and tripped along again like an old maid trying to cross a crowded thoroughfare.

"But there was Miss Gregor to mar these stolen sweets," he went on. "That austere, puritanical nature doubtless burned with cold fire at the spectacle of this doctor and his patient..."

"I feel sure," Dr. Hailey interrupted, "that Mrs. Eoghan's feelings for McDonald were merely those of an anxious mother..."

"Look at the facts. What does our immortal bard tell us?"

"'Facts are chiels as winna ding.'"

"Mrs. Eoghan had fled by night to McDonald's house. Isn't that enough to justify what I've said? 'Love flows like the Solway.' Do you think that Miss Gregor's shrewd eyes had overlooked what was so plainly to be seen?"

"No, but..."

"Oh, my dear Dr. Hailey, your knowledge of that lady is clearly less accurate than it should be. As for me, I've been at pains, at great pains, to inform myself about her. A puritan, believe me, of the most rigid school. In her long life she never touched a playing-card or entered a place of public amusement. How do I know that?"

He stopped. His wide nostrils dilated.

"I have a friend in Glasgow who knew the Gregor family well many years ago. A retired Army man. Excellent family. Delightful, most cultured man. Once upon a time, he told me, he persuaded Miss Gregor—she was a girl in her twenties then—to accompany him to see Sir Henry Irving playing in *Hamlet*. When they reached the theatre the first thing she saw was a notice, 'To The Pit'. After that nothing would induce her to enter the building. That's Miss Gregor for you. What mercy were Mrs. Eoghan and McDonald likely to receive from such a woman?"

Dr. Hailey did not reply. His silence was instantly interpreted as consent. Barley's face stiffened with new gravity.

"The eternal triangle!" he announced magnificently. "With a woman of the hew-Agag-in-pieces-before-the-Lord type in the middle of it. Are not these the lively ingredients of tragedy? Put yourself in McDonald's position, in Mrs. Eoghan's position. Would you not have feared greatly both the husband who was returning and the woman who was waiting to inform him whenever he did return? Believe me, it's that fear which must hold all our attention."

Another gesture called the heavens to witness. Dr. Hailey remained silent.

"As a psychologist," Barley assured him, "you cannot but be aware of the demoralizing effect of fear even on the strongest characters. It corrodes, as rust corrodes iron. It demoralizes. Fear is one of the nursing mothers of crime. Like greed. Like jealousy. McDonald was afraid; Mrs. Eoghan was afraid. They were mice in the presence of the cat. The time was approaching when the cat would pounce..."

He threw himself back with staring eyes and open mouth. His thoughts seemed to coil round his head like smoke.

"In addition," he added, "there was Dundas. Dundas the mole, digging, digging under the surface, piling fact upon fact. What had Dundas discovered? What was he going to tell?"

"I don't think," Dr. Hailey said, "that Dundas had discovered anything. He admitted himself that he had reached a blank wall."

"Dundas, my dear Dr. Hailey, was one of those remarkable men who delighted... delighted to throw dust in the eyes of their rivals. Can it be doubted that he saw a rival in an amateur of your outstanding reputation? No doubt exists in my mind that he called you in only when he already felt sure of success. To employ McDonald as his go-between was entirely in keeping with character."

"It may be so. But I understood him to say that any suspicions he entertained were fixed on Eoghan Gregor, not on McDonald. As I told you, Eoghan has undoubtedly suffered heavy financial losses."

Barley shook his head. He filled his pipe quickly and lit it with an astounding deftness.

"Delightful fellow, Dundas," he exclaimed, "and most honest in all his dealings. But secretive, jealous, *difficile*." He spread out his hands. "My cards, as you see, are on the table. His were under it." Once more the moustache-comb did service.

"'The proof of the pudding is in the eating?' Very well. I shall follow my theory and you, my dear Dr. Hailey, shall be judge of the result. Let us recall Mrs. Eoghan."

CHAPTER XVIII

SECRET MEETINGS

DR. HAILEY found it impossible not to admire Inspector Barley. The man possessed an extraordinary quickness of mind and an excellent imagination which never appeared to escape from the control of his reason. His dramatic instinct, on the other hand, and the thickness of his social skin, enabled him to launch his formidable questions in a way that served his purpose admirably. Either those whom he was examining became resentful or they lost their composure; he knew how to profit by both happenings. His comb, and his method of polishing his pipe on his nose, supplied the element of vulgarity which is necessary to the success of every charlatan.

It was disturbing, nevertheless, to see Oonagh placed at the mercy of such a man. When her cross-examination began the doctor was already sorry for her. Before it had continued many minutes he had become her partisan, for the key-note of the examination was the insult already levelled at her: "What an actress!" Barley continued to discount in advance the sincerity of expression which was the girl's defence.

"I wish you to understand, madam," he gushed, "that the intimate and delicate character of the questions which I am about to put to you is conditioned by no vulgar curiosity. I beg of you, dismiss that unworthy suspicion wholly from your mind. The occasion is so serious, so fraught with momentous consequences, that there is enough justification, in my humble opinion, for any question however embarrassing its nature."

He paused; the sound of his words buzzed about their ears like a May-time swarm. Then, when he judged that the effect he wished had been obtained, he asked quietly:

"What were your relations, madam, with Dr. McDonald?"

Oonagh's lips quivered. A flush of lively resentment mounted to her cheeks. She glanced at Dr. Hailey in the manner of a woman attacked by a bully, who looks to a decent man for help. Then her eyes darkened, and she braced herself to fight.

"What do you mean?" she asked in tones which attacked him.

Barley was much too wide awake to give battle on that ground. He rose to his feet and drew himself up.

"Believe me, madam," he cried, "I am ready, willing, to discount every slander that has been uttered against you. But how can I do that if you refuse me the information I ask for? You know as well as I do that your friendship" (he emphasized the word) "for Dr. McDonald has given rise, in this house and outside of it, to talk, to speculation, perhaps to calumny."

"Dr. McDonald has been very kind to my little boy."

Oonagh measured her words; her face had recovered its calmness of expression. Dr. Hailey realized with a pang that that calmness must soon be disturbed once more. How beautiful the girl looked in her adversity! Barley sat down with the suddenness which characterized all his actions.

"There are only four people who can have killed your aunt," he stated. "Duchlan, the piper Angus, Dr. McDonald and your husband—for that terrible blow was certainly not struck by a woman. Duchlan is a weak old man: I exclude him. There remain Angus, the doctor, and your husband. But we're not dealing only with the murder of your aunt. There's the murder of Dundas to be considered. The only man who can possibly have murdered Dundas, *the only person* who had access to him at all, at the moment of his death is McDonald. In my humble submission, McDonald had access also to your aunt on the night when she was murdered. And the two murders appear to be the work of the same hand."

He broke off and pointed at the girl.

"Why should McDonald have murdered your aunt?" he cried in loud tones.

"I don't know any reason why he should have murdered her."

"Think again, madam."

Oonagh remained silent with her lips tightly pressed together. But her cheeks were losing their colour.

"Miss Gregor was aware of an equivocal relationship existing between yourself and the doctor!"

The challenge was spoken in the tones of a man who offers a suggestion. But its effect was that of an accusation against which there is no defence. The girl wilted visibly.

"Am I right?"

"My aunt misunderstood everything."

The detective's practical mind pounced like a cat.

"Have the goodness to describe the circumstances which your aunt misunderstood," he demanded.

She hesitated a long time before she replied. Then she said:

"I was unhappy in this house. Dr. McDonald was the only friend to whom I could turn for advice. I saw a good deal of him."

"Here?"

"Here and elsewhere."

"Ah!" Barley leaned forward. "You mean that you had private, secret meetings with him?"

"We met privately."

"In the grounds?"

"On the shore. Dr. McDonald has a boat of his own."

Dr. Hailey saw a gleam of triumph in the detective's eyes.

"Miss Gregor surprised one of these meetings, eh?"

"She saw us talking to each other on one occasion."

"I put it to you that she threatened to tell your husband what she had seen?"

There was no reply. Suddenly Oonagh raised her head.

"I've told you," she declared in candid tones, "that my aunt misunderstood everything. She was ready to find evil in all I did, because she wanted to have control of my child and I would not give her control.

Dr. McDonald has never been other than my good friend. If I had to meet him secretly that was only because it was impossible to meet him openly without arousing my aunt's suspicions, or rather giving her the means of making trouble between my husband and me."

"Why should you want to meet Dr. McDonald?"

"He was my only friend."

"What, when you've got your husband!"

"Eoghan was not here."

"He was in Ayrshire. One can write to Ayrshire."

"He would not have understood. Eoghan has always had great faith in his aunt. She brought him up."

Barley's face assumed a grave expression. He smoothed his dull, dyed hair with a careful hand.

"May I ask upon what subject you consulted Dr. McDonald?" he demanded in sarcastic tones.

"I thought of leaving my husband. He tried to persuade me not to do that."

"Most excellent advice, undoubtedly. Most excellent advice. *Les femmes n'ont d'existence que par l'amour*." Barley filled his mouth with the quotation, the equivocal character of which seemed to give him great satisfaction. He paused for a moment and then said: "You thought of leaving your husband because you didn't hit it off with his relations? You'll forgive me, madam, if I say that, in my humble opinion, that is no reason at all for a step of so reprehensible a character?"

"I decided not to leave him."

Oonagh was losing her nerve and no longer seemed capable of offering effective resistance to the detective's bombardment. She plucked at the neck of her dress, creasing the thin fabric in several places. Barley was quick to follow up his success.

"Your explanation is not one which commends itself to reason or to experience," he declared. "Those who seek advice, seek it openly. But I'm prepared to believe that your final decision was to remain with your husband. It is, if I may say so, the final decision of most women in similar circumstances. You know, doubtless, that a doctor who is involved in a divorce suit with the wife of one of his patients is invariably expelled from the medical profession."

He paused to allow this grim truth to sink in.

"When Miss Gregor surprised your *tête-à-tête* with the doctor, she became possessed of the means of ruining him as well as you. Dr. McDonald, at that moment, knew that his existence as a professional man was hanging in the balance. I venture to think that when, on the night of the murder, he heard the sound of your husband's motor-boat approaching across the loch, he realized that the balance had been determined against him." Again the minatory finger was extended. "Why, may I ask, did your husband return at that hour and in that fashion?"

Oonagh shook her head.

"I think," she said, "that you had better ask him that question yourself."

"No, madam. I must ask that question of you. Of you, who, as I have been informed, had already served an ultimatum upon your husband."

"I don't understand."

"You had threatened to leave him unless your terms were agreed to."

"I had told him that I wanted a home of my own."

Barley's body stiffened.

"The Emperor Napoleon used to say that attack is the best form of defence," he exclaimed in tones which suggested that he was speaking of an old friend. "I suggest that you were pressing this demand for a home of your own in order to offset the charge which Miss Gregor had made against you?"

"No."

"You've just admitted that you did demand a home of your own."

"Every mother wants that, surely?"

"No doubt. But you had formerly consented to live here. Your demand for a home of your own was made only when there was danger, great danger, that you might forfeit your right to any home at all, to your husband, to your child."

A sweep of Barley's arm, like a spearman's thrust, speeded this accusation. Oonagh's face grew pale.

"I've always wanted a home of my own," she exclaimed. "Always, since the day I married Eoghan."

"I suggest, on the contrary, that you were quite happy here until you became intimate with McDonald." He thrust out his head towards her. "Do you deny that you offered yourself to McDonald and were refused by him?"

Oonagh jumped up. Her eyes were wild with pain and resentment.

"How dare you?" she cried in tones which betrayed the anguish he had inflicted on her.

Barley bared his teeth.

"You ran away to McDonald in the middle of the night, remember," he said. "Duchlan told me that. And then you allowed yourself to be brought back again. It was after that humiliation, was it not, that your demand for a home of your own became insistent?"

CHAPTER XIX

ACCUSATION

DR. HAILEY had made a few notes during Barley's cross-examination of Oonagh and felt a strong inclination, when the examination ended, to raise some objection to the theory upon which the detective was working. But a glance at the triumphant face of his companion made him decide to postpone the realization of this wish. Barley was transported already to regions of self-congratulation where no whisper of doubt or criticism could penetrate. His eyes were half-closed; his mouth was held slightly open; and his head was poised on one side. He remained in this condition of ecstasy for some minutes and then woke up and combed his moustache.

"We're getting close to the truth, my dear doctor," he said. "I feel it." He frowned and shook his head. "It's most distasteful to me, believe me, to have to question these charming people in this way. But *que voulez vous? Que voulez vous?* Now I must deal with Eoghan Gregor. What a tragedy that it should be necessary to question a young man in his exalted station about the fair name of his wife!"

He rang the bell and flung himself down in an arm-chair, apparently limp with regret.

"I've studied your methods, doctor," he stated. "Most admirable; but scarcely applicable perhaps to the present case. My method as you see is different. You proceed from character to event; I follow a lead, using all my powers of imagination as I go. It seems to me that, in cases where the issue is complicated, you're bound to win; but where there are definite physical obstacles, such as these locked rooms, I have the better of you. 'A nod's as good as a wink to a blind horse'. Opportunity counts for more than character when one person has the chance to kill and the other has not."

He remained in his limp attitude. After he had enunciated his philosophy, he sighed deeply several times. But when Eoghan entered the room, he became immediately as alert as ever.

"Come in, come in," he cried. "Let me see, you're Major Gregor, aren't you?"

"Captain."

Eoghan's indolent good looks had not deserted him. He glanced at Barley and, for a moment, betrayed a flicker of amusement. Then the air of melancholy which he wore with excellent ease removed him from that profane contact.

"I've just been telling Dr. Hailey with what reluctance I'm pursuing this present quest." Barley apologized. "But, 'needs does as needs must'. Let me say that if you resent any of the questions which it is my duty to address to you, you will be within your rights in refusing to answer them."

This with many bows and flourishes.

Dr. Hailey duly noted the difference between the method used in dealing with Eoghan and that used with Oonagh, and felt bound to agree that the characters of husband and wife were Barley's complete justification. Eoghan would be less on his guard if he supposed he was dealing with a fool; Oonagh's weakness was her nervousness.

"Very well," Eoghan said.

"The question I am most concerned to ask you is this: Why did you return so suddenly from Ayrshire?"

"Because I wanted to borrow some money from my father."

"What? You had to come back by motor-boat to do that?"

"I always travel to Ayrshire by motor-boat at this time of year. It's much the quickest way."

"Might you not have written?"

"No."

"You had no other reason for your sudden visit?"

"No."

"Believe me, I don't wish to push my quest beyond reasonable bounds," Barley declared, "but I am compelled to ask for more enlightenment that you seem disposed to accord to me. *Suaviter in modo, fortiter in re.* I have reason to think," he paused suddenly and dramatically, "that you were not entirely easy in your mind about your domestic and family affairs."

Eoghan shook his head. "You're mistaken."

"About your wife's relations with your aunt, and arising out of that, about her relations with yourself."

"Nonsense."

The first note of irritation sounded in Eoghan's voice. Dr. Hailey saw the detective react like a dog making a point.

"Your wife," he said, "has told me that she was scarcely able to endure the interferences of your aunt."

"Indeed."

"Further, that she sought counsel with Dr. McDonald of Ardmore whether or not she should leave you, supposing that you refused to take her away from here."

"Don't be idiotic," Eoghan exclaimed in tones which declared his growing uneasiness.

"My dear sir, if you suppose I'm trifling, or bluffing, you're making a grave mistake. A mistake, I'm afraid, which you will soon have occasion to correct. Your wife has declared unequivocally that she did think of leaving you. Place that fact in the forefront of your mind. The reason she has given is that you had failed to provide her with a home of her own. Very well, it is now necessary for me to ask you when your wife made her first complaint about this failure on your part."

Barley spoke slowly, giving each word due weight. He kept his eyes fixed on Eoghan's face.

"What has this got to do with my aunt's death?" the young man demanded.

"A great deal, believe me."

"What?"

"No, I refuse to be bounced. You must answer my question, or bear the consequences of refusing to answer it." Barley leaned back in his chair. He repeated: "When did your wife first complain about your failure to provide her with a house?"

Eoghan moved uneasily in his chair. He glanced at Dr. Hailey and then let his gaze stray about the room. The doctor had the impression that he was calculating, coolly, the probable effects of different answers. At last, he appeared to reach a decision.

"My wife mentioned quite recently," he stated, "that she thought the time had come for us to set up our own home."

"What does 'quite recently' mean?"

"A fortnight ago."

A gleam of triumph shone in Barley's eyes.

"Do you know that your wife ran away from this house one night?" he asked.

"Yes."

"Who told you?"

"She told me herself."

Eoghan imparted the information in surly tones. But these had no effect on the detective.

"Did your aunt inform you also?" he asked.

"Yes."

"By letter?"

"How else could she inform me?"

Barley nodded. "You told your wife that your aunt had informed you?" he demanded.

"No, sir."

"At any rate, your wife knew that you knew?"

"That doesn't follow, does it?"

Eoghan was recovering his self-possession. It was evident that he had no idea of the object of Barley's questions. Like his wife he had committed the mistake of underestimating his opponent's capacity; like her he was surely destined to pay for his error. Dr. Hailey reflected that the manner of a fool, when it covers the thought of a wise man, is an advantage of incalculable worth.

"I think it does follow," Barley said. "I formed the opinion, after seeing your wife, that she knew how bitterly your aunt disliked her. She was well aware that your aunt would not fail to report to you anything disadvantageous to herself."

"What are you driving at? What does it matter whether or not my wife knew that my aunt had reported the incident?"

"If she knew, her confession to you was made only because she was compelled to make it."

"Well?"

Barley leaned forward.

"Your wife desired to patch up her quarrel with you. She was in a weak position. She adopted the usual method of women in such circumstances. She attacked you because you had not provided her with a home of her own. At the same time she confessed openly what could not, in any case, be hidden. But there was one piece of information, the one essential piece of information, which she did not give."

Silence fell in the room. Eoghan tried to look indifferent but his face betrayed him. He made a small gesture with his right hand.

"I'm afraid," he declared, "that your speculations about my wife's ideas and motives possess very little interest for me."

"On the contrary."

"What do you mean?"

"The essential piece of information which your wife withheld from you was that, when she ran away from this house, it was with the intention of offering herself to Dr. McDonald. McDonald refused her."

Eoghan's cheeks had grown pale. His hands, which rested on the arms of the wooden chair where he was seated, began to twitch.

"Leave my wife out of the discussion," he ordered, in hoarse tones which betrayed the violence of his feelings.

"Impossible. I am very much afraid that it will soon be my duty to accuse your wife of aiding and abetting the murder of your aunt."

"What!" Eoghan jumped up from his chair.

"Of aiding and abetting Dr. McDonald of Ardmore."

A single stride brought the young man to the detective. He seized Barley by the shoulders and fixed his eyes on his face.

"I swear to you that you're wholly mistaken," he cried. "Oonagh had nothing whatever to do with my aunt's death. Do you hear?"

"Have the goodness to unhand me, sir."

"Not until you swear that you'll drop that grotesque accusation."

Barley took a step back, leaving the young man standing alone.

"Sit down," he ordered in tones which revealed a side of his character hitherto undisclosed. His eyes flashed with anger. But Eoghan did not obey.

"I wish you to know," he said, "that it was I who killed my aunt. I'm prepared to give you an account of the murder."

CHAPTER XX

EOGHAN EXPLAINS

EOGHAN'S TONES were so steady, his manner so insolent in its calmness, that even Barley was shaken. He recoiled, and then, collecting himself, sat down and assumed his most judicial attitude.

"Do I understand," he asked, "that you are accusing yourself of the murder of Miss Gregor?"

Eoghan's face had become paler; but he kept so excellent a self-control that this was scarcely noticeable. He bore, Dr. Hailey thought, a remarkable likeness to his father; the harshness of Duchlan's face, however, was softened by a quality which derived no doubt from his Irish mother. The young man looked like an eighteenth century nobleman a little the worse for wear, but with his pride untarnished. His rather girlish cheeks and mouth accentuated, if anything, the firmness of his expression and the cold resolution in his eyes.

"Let me remark at once," Barley declared, "that you made this confession when you heard that I suspected your wife. *Post hoc ergo propter hoc*, may not be good logic in every instance; but the temptation so to regard it in this case is very great." He waved his hand in a gesture of dismissal. "I do not believe that you murdered Miss Gregor."

"No?"

"No, sir."

"Do you expect me to supply you with proofs?"

"Yes, since only the strongest possible proof is going to convince me."

"My aunt has left me all her money. And I need money very badly."

"What does that prove?"

"That her death came most opportunely. Not a minute too soon, believe me."

"Why do you say that?"

"Because it's true. My father, as it happens, has no money. I could not have borrowed from him. And the debts I must meet immediately run into thousands—many thousands."

"Surely you could have borrowed the money from your aunt?"

"Oh! no. My aunt looked on gambling as a deadly sin."

"My dear sir, people's opinions are necessarily conditioned by circumstances."

"Not my aunt's opinions."

"Everybody's opinions. It was Napoleon who said that men are always and everywhere the same."

"Napoleon didn't know my aunt."

Not a flicker of a smile accompanied this statement. Barley gasped, biting at the air in the manner peculiar to him.

"May I say," he remarked, "that, in my humble opinion, the occasion is unsuitable, most unsuitable, for jesting." He leaned forward as judges sometimes lean from the Bench. "May I ask how you entered your aunt's room?" he demanded.

"By the door."

"I have reason to believe the door was locked."

"What reason?"

"Your wife stated that she heard Miss Gregor lock the door."

"Are you prepared to take her word on that point?"

Barley frowned. "Why not?"

"You haven't taken her word on any other point, have you?"

Eoghan raised his eyebrows as he asked this question. The effect on Barley was all that he could have wished. The man scowled and then flushed angrily.

"I must beg leave," he cried, "to accept or reject according to my instinct and experience."

"That means, doesn't it, according to your theory of the crime?"

"It does not. I have no *a priori* theory. I look for facts and am guided by what I find."

"I can only repeat that I entered the bedroom by the door."

"How did you leave the bedroom?"

Eoghan flicked a speck of dust from the sleeve of his shooting coat.

"By the door."

"What!"

"It's obvious, isn't it, that I didn't leave by the window?"

"The door was locked on the inside," Barley stated.

"How do you know?"

Dr. Hailey saw Barley start; but the fellow had excellent nerves.

"There are five witnesses to prove that: Angus, the carpenter who cut away the lock, Dr. McDonald, the maid who took up your aunt's tea, and yourself."

"On the contrary there are no witnesses at all. The door was held shut by a small wedge which I placed under it. The maid naturally thought it was locked; she's young and unsuspecting. When she called me I confirmed that. Angus never tried the door at all. He's old and believes what I tell him. Why should the carpenter disbelieve when I sent for him to cut the lock away? Why should McDonald disbelieve? After the lock was cut out I pulled out my wedge. Then I found an opportunity to turn the key in the lock."

He shrugged his shoulders slightly as he finished his account.

"With what weapon did you kill your aunt?" Barley demanded in husky tones.

"The wood-axe from the kitchen."

Eoghan raised his eyelids and gazed at the detective. "I got it when I took some herring I had bought down to the larder."

The shot told. It was evident to Dr. Hailey that Barley had been keeping the matter of the herring scales up his sleeve for use as a final argument. He threw up his head like an angry horse.

"Were these the methods adopted by you," he demanded in tones of bitter sarcasm, "when you killed my colleague Dundas?"

"Not quite."

"What, you suggest you committed that crime also?"

"It's obvious, isn't it, that both crimes were committed by the same person?"

"You waste my time, sir. You did not kill Dundas." Barley rose and dismissed the young man with a gesture. But Eoghan did not seem inclined to go away. He took a small gold cigarette-case from his pocket.

"May I smoke?"

"I have no more questions to ask you."

He lit a cigarette.

"I think you may have more questions to ask me, however," he said, "when I point out to you that Dundas's bed was provided with a feather mattress and an eiderdown. One of the Duchlan feather mattresses; one of the Duchlan eiderdowns."

There was a ring of triumph in his voice as he spoke. Dr. Hailey felt the blood rise to his own cheeks. Both McDonald and he had looked under the bed after the murder; neither of them had looked in it.

"What do you mean?"

"My aunt possessed the deepest, the most voluminous feather mattresses in a county which holds the world's record in that respect. Her eiderdowns, as you must have seen, are of equal merit. One can lie on such a mattress, under such an eiderdown, without causing so much as a ripple on the bed's surface, provided one has time to settle down and arrange oneself. And I had ample time."

A look of lively horror filled Barley's eyes. He gasped, but no longer solemnly; Dr. Hailey saw that his hands were wet.

"What happened? What did you do?" he cried in tones that showed how small a measure of self-control remained to him. Eoghan took his cigarette from between his lips and looked at the lighted end critically.

"Hit him on the back of the head with a lead sinker," he remarked coolly. "Did it as soon as Dr. Hailey left the room. Only one arm needed, and that was tucked nicely away under the eiderdown before Dr. McDonald got to the room. One got a bit cramped, of course. Still..."

He broke off and replaced the cigarette in his mouth. He added: "Dundas, unlike yourself, Mr. Barley, was on the right track."

He rose as he spoke. His cigarette-case, which he had omitted to return to his pocket, fell clattering to the floor. He stooped down to pick it up.

At the same instant Dr. Hailey sprang from his chair and hurled himself on the stooping figure.

CHAPTER XXI

CHEATING THE GALLOWS

THE TWO MEN rolled together on the floor. Barley sprang to the help of his companion and between them they secured Eoghan. When that had been accomplished Dr. Hailey put his hand in the young man's pocket and took out a revolver.

"Fortunately," he stated, "I saw the bulge it made in his pocket."

Eoghan's face had become flushed and his collar and necktie were dragged out of place; but he did not appear to have lost his self-control.

"Now that you've got my pistol," he said, "you can leave me."

Barley, who was holding down his shoulders, shook his head.

"Certainly not, sir." He addressed himself to Dr. Hailey. "Search all his pockets, if you please. He may have other weapons hidden about his person."

Dr. Hailey was looking after the pistol. He put it down and passed his hands quickly over the young man's body. Then he signed to the detective. Eoghan was allowed to rise.

"You forget, perhaps," he said in unruffled tones, "that as an officer in the Army I'm entitled to carry a pistol."

"But not to use it," Barley exclaimed.

"How do you know that I was going to use it?"

"It's enough, sir, that we have no assurance that you were not going to use it. Are you not a self-confessed assassin?"

The young man shrugged his shoulders. He rearranged his collar.

"What I can never understand about the police," he remarked, "is the tender care with which they surround people whom they know they will have to hang very soon. Why prevent a poor devil from doing himself in, if he has the courage?"

Nobody answered him. He strode to Barley and stood facing him.

"May I ask that you will not tell my wife anything about what I have told you," he requested, "until my arrest has taken place?"

"Why not?"

"Good gracious, man, surely it's better to save people unnecessary suffering! If she knows I'm likely to be arrested she'll move heaven and earth to save me. And she can't save me."

Barley shook his head.

"I make it a rule," he declared, "never to make promises which I may not be able to keep. The chances are that it will not be necessary to tell your wife, but it's too early yet to be sure."

Eoghan shook his head.

"If you people would only adopt the decent and merciful methods of the Army," he exclaimed, "what a lot of distress would be saved."

Nobody answered him. He turned to Dr. Hailey.

"You know that Oonagh suspects that I killed Aunt Mary," he challenged.

"I think she did suspect you."

"Take it from me her feelings haven't changed. She knows about my debts. There was only one way of paying these debts, and not to be able to pay them meant expulsion from the Army."

He broke off and lit another cigarette. Then he added:

"Tell Mr. Barley about Oonagh. It will help him to understand her character and her relations with me."

There was a note of pride in his voice which was unmistakable. He turned to Barley.

"Do you want me here any longer?" he asked.

Barley had returned to the fireside. He looked uneasy and doubtful about his duty.

"Technically you've given yourself up," he stated. "But it remains to be decided whether or not I accept your story. I have not yet accepted it. Far from it. You must remain in the castle till my decision shall have been taken." His manner had become dictatorial; but his mouth was as full as ever of phrases. He waved his hand; Eoghan walked out of the room.

"Do you really suppose, my dear doctor, that he meant to shoot himself?"

"Yes."

Barley took the pistol and opened it.

"It's loaded, anyhow." He emptied it and put the cartridges in his pocket. "It's just possible, I suppose, that he may have murdered his aunt and Dundas. Believe me, your apparently impossible crime always admits of several different explanations. On the other hand the law, as you know, holds confessions suspect. Murderers, cold-blooded murderers at any rate, are not prone to confess their crimes."

"No."

Dr. Hailey considered a moment, and then told Barley about Oonagh's attempt to drown herself and her husband's subsequent visit to Darroch Mor.

"I have no doubt," he added, "that Duchlan knew what was afoot. I don't think Eoghan Gregor knew."

"But this is tremendously important, my dear sir." Barley began to walk up and down the room. "If Duchlan knew, and I share your view that he must have known, then it follows that he had counselled this tragic act. Why should he do that?" A gesture executed with both hands consigned the house of Gregor to bottomless deeps. "Manifestly, because he knew that his daughter-in-law was guilty of playing a part in the murder of his sister. That knowledge, in my humble opinion, would exert on the old man an influence tending to awaken all his most inhuman qualities. He's as proud as Lucifer. He's as cold-blooded as a fish. If the girl was guilty let her drown. Better that than a trial and a public condemnation. Anything to save the sacred name of Gregor!"

Dr. Hailey nodded.

"I reached more or less the same conclusion. Eoghan also gave me the impression of suspecting his wife. I must add, though, that his wife seemed to suspect him. I believe myself that her attempt to drown herself was prompted by the determination to shield him."

"In view of her relations with Dr. McDonald, I confess that that question scarcely interests me. Women do not shield with their lives husbands whom they have already discarded. On the other hand, if Duchlan knew that she was accessory to his sister's murder, her fate was sealed. With his son's name at stake that old man would not spare her; from his point of view she was better drowned than hanged."

He clapped his hands. "I shall question the old man. I had meant to send for Dr. McDonald, but Duchlan shall come first. Now I understand why he nearly fainted when I said that McDonald was the only man who could have murdered Dundas."

That idea formed the basis of the first questions which Barley addressed to Duchlan. The old man looked pale and more wasted than usual but his eyes had not lost their quickness. He seated himself like a king about to give an audience and disposed his hands on the arms of his chair according to his habit. His head kept moving backwards and forwards. The detective showed him a deference which he had not accorded to any earlier witnesses.

"My investigations," he explained, "have made it necessary that I should inquire closely into the behaviour of your daughter-in-law both before and after the death of your sister." He paused. When he spoke again his voice had assumed a grave tone. "I have reason to believe that you were a witness of certain incidents which you have not, so far, seen fit to mention to the police."

"For example?"

"Mrs. Eoghan Gregor was in the habit of meeting Dr. McDonald at night on the shore."

Duchlan closed his eyes. The wrinkles in his face deepened as his muscles contracted. He looked like a mummy recalled suddenly to affliction.

"You are aware that your daughter-in-law met Dr. McDonald in this way?"

"Yes."

"You were the witness of one, or more, of these meetings?"

"Yes."

"Was Miss Gregor with you on these occasions?"

"Yes."

Barley leaned forward.

"Was your presence observed by your daughter-in-law and the doctor?"

The old man bowed his head.

"Yes."

"That was the reason why Mrs. Eoghan retired to her bedroom at such an early hour on the day before your sister was murdered?"

"My sister felt it to be her duty to warn my son's wife. Unfortunately her kindness was misunderstood and resented."

Duchlan spoke in low tones, but his voice was perfectly clear. It was obvious that he suffered greatly in being forced to recall the incident. But Barley was inexorable.

"I'm afraid," he stated, "that I must ask for details. For instance, did Miss Gregor utter any threat?"

"She said that, as Eoghan's nearest relation, she must tell him about what was going on."

"Ah."

"As a matter of fact she had already written to Eoghan, hinting that things were not in a satisfactory state. She took that action, believe me, after long and most anxious consideration and after very many attempts to recall my daughter-in-law from the dangerous course on which she was embarking."

"I see." Barley closed his eyes and nodded gravely. "*Facilis est decensus Averni, sed revocare gradum,*" he quoted insolently.

The rest of the quotation was lost in his moustache. Duchlan sighed.

"We had both done all that lay in our power to preserve Oonagh from disaster," he said. "The time for warning had evidently gone by, though in my weakness, as I now recognize, I was prepared to accord one further chance."

"You were against telling your son?"

"Perhaps I feared to tell him." The old man glanced up rather timidly. "My son is quick-tempered. And he is devotedly attached to his wife."

"Miss Gregor over-ruled your fear?"

"She anticipated it. I was not aware that she had written to Eoghan. When I heard that she had done so I recognized the wisdom of her action."

Dr. Hailey had been leaning back in his chair. He intervened to ask:

"When Miss Gregor wrote to your son did she know about the meetings with Dr. McDonald at night?"

"No. In point of fact neither she nor I knew about these meetings until the night before she met her death. What we did know was that my son's wife was in constant communication with the doctor."

"So the question on the fatal day," Barley exclaimed, "was whether or not a definite accusation was to be made as soon as your son returned?"

"Yes."

"And whereas you favoured mercy, your sister was determined to punish?"

"Please don't express my dear sister's attitude in that way," Duchlan pleaded. "Goodness and mercy abounded in her heart. Her one, her only concern, believe me, was the welfare of this misguided and rebellious girl. She felt, I think, that her own influence was exhausted; Oonagh had defied her and made cruel and untrue accusations against her. My dear Mary wished that the strength of the husband might be made available to rescue the wife. Naturally her thought and care went out, too, to Eoghan, for she had been more than mother to him, and to Eoghan's child, exposed meanwhile to these lamentable influences."

Barley shook his head.

"No mother, in my humble judgement," he declared, "can endure the thought that her child is to be taken away from her."

"You misunderstand, sir. My dear sister's plan was not to remove Hamish from his mother's custody, but to place his mother under some measure of restraint. She felt that if Oonagh could be influenced by herself, the girl's good qualities of courage and cheerfulness might be developed in such a way as to effect a change of character."

Barley shrugged his shoulders and spread out his hands. Then his business-like manner reasserted itself.

"Did your daughter-in-law complain to you or your sister," he asked, "that her husband had failed to provide her with a home of her own?"

"She did, yes. She made many bitter and unjust complaints against Eoghan. These, as you can imagine, were very difficult to bear and it needed all my dear sister's self-restraint and kindness of heart to bear them. We pointed out to her that she was fortunate in possessing a good and kind husband whose sole desire it was to make her happy and to make provision for her boy. The pay of an Army officer is small. Eoghan's resources were slender and had it not been that his aunt and I, but especially his aunt, gave him some financial help..."

Barley interrupted with a sudden gesture.

"So," he exclaimed, "your son and his wife were dependent to some extent on your sister's bounty?"

"To a very great extent. The pay of a Captain in the gunners approximates to £1 a day. Eoghan's personal expenses absorb all that. My daughter-in-law has been living here at the expense of myself and of my dear sister." Duchlan paused and raised his eyes. "Not that we have ever begrudged her anything for her good."

"You made your son no regular allowance?"

The old man raised his hand and moved it in a circle which indicated and presented his estate.

"How could I? You've seen these heather hills. What is there to yield an income? Believe me, it has been as much as I could do to make ends meet these many years. When Eoghan told me he was going to marry, I had to warn him that he must make provision for his wife out of his pay. Then my dear Mary came to his rescue. She possessed a considerable fortune of her own."

Barley's face expressed both doubt and some indignation.

"It appears to me," he said, "that your late sister made a mistake in her manner of giving. Your daughter-in-law must have felt like a charity boarder in this house. Does she, tell me, possess any means of her own?"

"Oh, no. None."

"What did she do for pocket money, pin money, whatever it's called?"

"My dear sister allowed her to buy her clothing at certain shops…"

"What, do you mean to say she had *no* money that she could call her own?"

"I think Eoghan sent her such sums of money as he could spare."

"Her position was worse than that of your servants?"

Duchlan did not reply for a few minutes. Then he said:

"She had no expenses so long as she remained here with us."

"I see." Barley leaned forward suddenly. "Tell me please: At what period of her stay did your daughter-in-law begin to complain of her husband?"

"She has never seemed to be really satisfied. But these last weeks have been much more trying than any earlier period."

"Since she became friendly with McDonald?"

"Yes, I think so."

"It was during the last few weeks, was it, that she began to demand a home of her own?"

Duchlan inclined his head.

"After she ran away from this house," he stated in low tones. "That evening saw the crisis of her relations with my sister. She told my sister that she would never again be indebted to her for a crust of bread. She said she was going away to earn her own living by any means that offered, even if it meant going into domestic service."

"Did she talk in that way after she came back?"

Barley asked the question in tones which thrilled with excitement. He thrust his body forward as if he feared to miss a syllable of the reply.

"Not quite in that way. After she came back she expressed a determination to have a home of her own, with her husband and child."

There was a short period of silence. The cackle of a seagull fell unseasonably on their ears. Then Barley waved his hand.

"It boils down to this, I venture to think," he remarked, "namely, that Miss Gregor suspected your daughter-in law and was determined to expose her to her husband, doubtless from the highest motives. That, believe me, was likely to be a serious affair both for Mrs. Eoghan and for Dr. McDonald. As Mrs. Eoghan is not possessed of any private means, her position as a divorced wife, deprived of her child, must have been sufficiently melancholy. As for the doctor, he ran a great risk of being removed from the Medical Register and so completely ruined. It's obvious therefore that both the woman and the man had strong motives for wishing that your sister might be removed from their paths."

Duchlan did not reply. Even his fingers were still. The detective rose and struck his hands together.

"I suggest," he declared in tones that were menacing, "that it was these considerations which led you to suggest to your daughter-in-law, after the murder of your sister, that she had better take immediate steps to cheat the gallows?"

"What! You accuse me..."

"Pardon me, Duchlan, but the facts as I know them admit, in my humble opinion, of no other explanation. You believed that your daughter-in-law was party to the murder of your sister by Dr. McDonald. His fate did not concern you; hers did. She is your son's wife, the mother of your only grandson, of the heir to Duchlan. You knew very well that if she drowned herself there would be silence not only about her share in the crime but even about the manner of her death. There is no Coroner's Court in Scotland. Moreover, only you knew about her meetings with Dr. McDonald. So long as she lived there was the dreadful fear that these relations might continue and so be discovered. Her death promised safety for everybody, for you and your son and your son's son, for your house and your name."

The silence fell again and deepened so that the chiming of a clock in the hall outside was an intolerable burden. Duchlan's head began to nod like the head of one of those cunning ivory toys which react for long periods to the slightest touch.

"Your daughter-in-law," Barley added, "yielded to your compulsion. Acknowledgment, surely, of her guilt."

CHAPTER XXII

TORTURE

When Duchlan had gone away, Dr. Hailey gave the detective an account of his interview with Dr. McDonald.

"You can, of course, question him yourself if you wish," he added, "but I think that if you do, you will waste your time. He admitted quite frankly that he had fallen in love with Mrs. Eoghan; he denied and went on denying, that she has ever, in any degree, given him encouragement."

"Did he?" Barley's expression showed how much importance he attached to such a statement. "It's curious, if he's telling the truth, that Mrs. Eoghan should have tried to drown herself; indeed, that these murders were committed at all. Innocent people never commit crimes to escape from unjust accusations."

"I agree. But innocent people sometimes sacrifice themselves to preserve those they love."

"Why should Mrs. Eoghan have thought that her husband had killed his aunt?"

"I feel sure she did think so."

"Yes, but why, why?"

"If one loves one fears. There was a strong motive, remember."

Barley frowned.

"That's saying that she believed her husband capable of murder."

He stared at Dr. Hailey as he spoke. When the doctor shook his head he frowned again.

"It may mean that, of course. But does it necessarily mean that? Knowing that a strong motive exists one may be seized by a dreadful fear, a fear that does not shape itself in words, scarcely even in thoughts; that is a feeling rather than an idea. And one may act on that feeling..."

"Still, the basis of the idea is murder."

"No, I think the basis of the idea is sympathy, the knowledge of human nature which we all derive from the fact of our own humanity. Is there a single crime that you or I might not commit in certain circumstances? You remember: 'But for the grace of God there goes John Bunyan.' I feel sure that only very stupid or very vain people are so entirely sure of themselves as to believe themselves immune from temptation. Saints and sinners have more in common than is usually supposed."

Barley leaned back in his chair. His face assumed a gracious expression.

"Your method, believe me," he declared, "is rich in attraction for me. If I could believe that Mrs. Eoghan cared for her husband, I might even be persuaded. But what are the facts?" He shook his head. "Can you doubt, speaking as man to man, that she cared for McDonald? Does a woman run away at night to a man in whom she is not specially interested? Does she meet that man in secret? Women, believe me, are not easily got rid of when their affections are engaged. But she was shrewd. If she couldn't have the doctor, she did not mean to lose her husband. Remember that Miss Gregor's death served the purposes of three different people: It rescued Dr. McDonald, it saved Eoghan Gregor, and it gave back her husband and child to the woman."

"Even so, McDonald struck me as being an honest man."

Barley did not reply. He had made up his mind to question Dr. McDonald and was not the man to be turned from such a resolution.

Assuming his singular dust-coat, which made him look like a chess-board, he drove to Ardmore with Dr. Hailey during the afternoon. They found the doctor at home. He took them to a small room at the back of the house, which smelt faintly of iodoform. The room contained a number of glass cases full of instruments and numerous jars in which lints and gauzes were stored. Though the cleanliness and order of this surgery were beyond reproach, it had a desolate aspect. The spirit somehow was lacking.

Dr. McDonald opened a drawer in the desk which occupied the end of the room and took out a box of cigars.

"You'll smoke, Inspector?"

"No, thank you." Barley sat down on a leather-covered couch and crossed his legs. He got to business immediately, explaining that the questions he was about to ask were likely to tax both memory and observation.

"Let us go back, in the first place, to the night of the murder of Miss Gregor. You were, I understand, summoned on that night to see Mrs. Eoghan Gregor's little boy?"

"Yes, I was."

"About what time?"

"About half-past nine."

"Did Mrs. Eoghan Gregor receive you?"

"She was in the nursery. The child had had another of his hysterical attacks and was rather weak. I..."

"Excuse me interrupting you, but how was Mrs. Eoghan Gregor dressed?"

"She wore a blue dressing-gown."

"Was the maid, Christina, in the nursery?"

"Yes. But as soon as I arrived she went away to attend to Miss Gregor. She came back before I left."

"So that you and Mrs. Eoghan Gregor were alone?"

"With the child, yes."

"Did Mrs. Eoghan seem to be unduly excited?"

McDonald raised his head sharply. A look of anxiety appeared on his face.

"She was distressed about the child."

Barley thrust out his hands.

"I shall be frank with you," he declared. "Duchlan has just told me that Mrs. Eoghan and her aunt quarrelled violently during the evening, for which reason Mrs. Eoghan retired early to bed. What I want to know is whether or not Mrs. Eoghan discussed this quarrel with you."

"She told me that she was upset with the attitude her aunt was adopting towards her."

"Did she tell you that her aunt accused her of being in love with yourself?"

Barley's voice rang out. But the impression he produced was less than he seemed to expect. McDonald nodded.

"She told me that, yes."

"That Miss Gregor was determined to impart all her suspicions to her nephew on his return?"

"Yes."

The detective thrust his head forward:

"That meant ruin both for Mrs. Eoghan and yourself?" he demanded.

"Possibly, if Eoghan Gregor believed his aunt."

"Have you any reason to suppose that he would not have believed her?"

McDonald wiped his brow.

"Eoghan Gregor," he said in quiet tones, "is in love with his wife, and she is in love with him."

"Nevertheless his wife was meeting you each evening after dark?"

"Did Duchlan tell you that too?"

"He did."

"It's not true. We met on one or two occasions only, because Mrs. Eoghan wished to ask my advice." Suddenly McDonald's voice rang out: "You can have no idea of the torture inflicted on that poor girl by her father-in-law and her aunt."

"Torture! Torture!" Barley exclaimed in tones which rebuked such extravagance of language.

McDonald rose and began to stump about the room. His powerful body seemed too big for its narrow limits. Dr. Hailey was reminded of a young tiger he had seen pacing its cage at the Zoo.

"Yes, torture," he cried. "That's the only word that applies. You didn't know Miss Gregor; I did. A woman without a flicker of compassion; devoured by jealousy and family pride. She had not married, I believe, because the idea of losing her name of Gregor of Duchlan was intolerable to her. It may seem a grotesque idea, but I am convinced that it was her instinct to be the mother as well as the daughter of her race. Fate, as it happened, had allowed her to realize that instinct in the case of Eoghan. Mrs. Eoghan, however, robbed her of its complete fulfilment. She dared to assert her wifehood and her motherhood. Eoghan loved her more than he loved his aunt. It was obvious that as soon as the slender thread of Duchlan's life was broken, Miss Gregor's reign at the castle would end for ever." McDonald paused and then added: "Unless, in the meanwhile, husband and wife could be estranged from one another and separated permanently. In that case Hamish would fall into his aunt's hands just as his father had done before him. Miss Gregor would remain the mistress of Duchlan."

He turned as he spoke and faced his accuser. Barley was too good a student of human nature not to be impressed, but he was also a practical man, well able to judge of the motives underlying any process of reasoning.

"You are telling me, remember," he warned, "that neither you nor Mrs. Eoghan could expect any mercy from Miss Gregor. That is exactly what I believe myself."

"What does that prove?"

"It supplies a strong motive for the crime which, as I believe, you committed between you."

The doctor started.

"What? You think I murdered Miss Gregor?"

"With the help of Mrs. Eoghan."

McDonald's face darkened. He wiped his brow again. Dr. Hailey saw him glance out of the window as though an impulse to escape had come to him. Then he began to laugh.

"You must be crazy. Crazy! How do you suppose I got into the woman's bedroom?"

He wiped his brow again. He sat down and disposed his leg with the most attentive care.

"By the door."

"What? Do you mean to say you don't know that the door was locked?"

"Eoghan Gregor says it was not locked."

The doctor stared. He repeated in tones of bewilderment:

"Eoghan says it was not locked? Why I saw the carpenter cut out the lock."

"Did you try the handle?"

"No."

"So your knowledge is at second-hand."

"The carpenter tried the handle."

"He told you that?"

"Good gracious, no, I saw him do it. He tried it several times."

Barley blinked his eyes. "That, however, was in the morning. What I am suggesting is that the door was unlocked when you left the nursery at the end of your visit on the night before?"

"It was locked then too. Mrs. Eoghan heard her aunt lock it."

"Forgive me, Mrs. Eoghan's evidence is of no value on that point."

McDonald laughed again. "I see. It's a case of heads I win, tails you lose, is it?"

"My dear sir, Miss Gregor was murdered. Somebody, therefore, entered the room and escaped from it. And human beings do not pass through doors and windows. It's easier, in my humble opinion, to assume that Mrs. Eoghan and yourself have given an untrue account of your doings than to believe that the laws of nature have been set aside."

"How do you suggest that I killed the old woman? With my wooden leg?"

"No, sir. I believe that Mrs. Eoghan brought an axe from the kitchen. The servants had gone to bed."

"I see." The doctor drew a deep breath. "And the herring scale that was found in the wound, where did that come from?"

"Possibly from the blade of the axe."

"You have still to explain how the door locked itself on the inside, haven't you?"

"I believe I can explain that too."

Barley had recovered his suavity; like a huntsman whose quarry has turned at bay, he seemed to be making ready to deal a final blow.

"I shall be surprised," he declared, "if positive proof is not soon forthcoming that you did murder Miss Gregor. Very greatly surprised! I go farther than that. I know where to look for that proof and I know that, when I do look for it, I shall find it."

He spoke with complete conviction.

Dr. Hailey experienced a sense of bewilderment, which, he saw, was shared, fully, by McDonald. How could it be proved that the doctor had entered the bedroom? Or that he had escaped from it again without passing through the door?

"There's one further point," Barley said, "on which I am seeking enlightenment. Do you remember who was the first to enter Miss Gregor's room after the lock had been cut from the door?"

"I was."

"Were the blinds in the room drawn?"

"Yes."

"Did you open them?"

"Yes."

"Very well. Now tell me, was the amputation which made it necessary for you to wear a wooden leg a high or a low amputation?"

"A high amputation."

"So that you walk with difficulty?"

"Oh, no."

"I mean you're always in some danger of slipping or falling?"

McDonald shook his head. He raised his wooden leg from the floor, using both hands in the work.

"As you see," he remarked, "I wear a special shoe in this foot. These nails in the sole are guaranteed to grip anything."

On the way back to the castle, Barley asked Dr. Hailey if he had noticed that no mention of the murder of Dundas had been made by McDonald.

"Every moment I expected to hear him advance that second murder as proof of his innocence."

"Why?"

"Because guilty people always overstate their cases."

"I see. Does that mean that you harbour some doubts about his guilt?"

"Not doubts exactly. I believe my case is good; good enough to secure a unanimous verdict from any jury. But it's a case in logic rather than in personal conviction. Frankly, McDonald doesn't seem to me to fill the part assigned to him."

"I agree with you."

"And the same applies to Mrs. Eoghan?"

"Yes."

"And yet the choice undoubtedly lies between them and Eoghan Gregor. And we know now that Eoghan Gregor lied to us."

"About the locked door?"

"Exactly. The carpenter did try the door." Barley lay back on the cushions and combed his moustache. "I left a message that he was to be called to the castle. We shall hear his own story."

"You didn't ask any questions, I noticed," Dr. Hailey said, "about Mrs. Eoghan's flight to McDonald's house?"

"No. He would have told me what he told you. Frankly, since I've seen him, I feel less sure about the circumstances of that flight. I begin to think that he is in love with her. In that case it's certain that he didn't reject her."

"And therefore unlikely that she offered herself."

Barley shook his head in his most emphatic manner.

"No, no; that doesn't follow. Women in love seldom or never count the cost, and therefore act as a rule with extreme rashness. But it's quite another matter with men in love. A man, happily, never loses his social sense, no, not even when he seems to be ready to abandon himself. The ages have branded it upon the male mind that work that is service must have first place. McDonald, I believe, suggested the secret meetings which afterwards took place. But he sent Mrs. Eoghan home that night. He was not ready to immolate his professional being."

CHAPTER XXIII

FOOTPRINTS

THE CARPENTER awaited them. He was a tall lean man with big features and clear, bright eyes. He made short work of the idea that the door had not been locked when he opened it.

"It was locked," he declared. "I tried the handle mysel'. What is more I tried to force the lock. But that's not possible with these doors. I dare say that you knew that Duchlan's father was a locksmith."

Barley nodded. "You're prepared to swear, are you," he asked, "that the key had been turned on the inside?"

"I am."

The detective dismissed the man and told Angus to bring a pair of bellows from the kitchen. Then he invited Dr. Hailey to accompany him.

"I promised you positive proof of McDonald's guilt," he said. "And will now furnish it. I warn you to be prepared for a surprise. As you've just heard, Eoghan Gregor's story is a fabrication."

They left the house and walked to the flower-bed which lay under the window of Miss Gregor's bedroom. The detective took the bellows from the piper.

"Observe," he said, "that Miss Gregor's room is immediately above the study. Also that the earth in this bed is quite dry. Mr. McLeod, the Procurator Fiscal, examined the bed on the morning after the murder and found it undisturbed." He turned to Angus: "Am I right?"

"Yes, sir. I was with Mr. McLeod, sir, when he examined the ground. It looked exactly as it looks at this moment."

"Very well."

Barley applied the snout of the bellows to the surface of the earth and began to blow gently. As he blew dust was driven away in semi-circles, leaving a more or less even surface. He continued to work for a few minutes and then stood erect. There was a puzzled look on his face.

"Well?" Dr. Hailey asked.

"You see, there's nothing. Frankly I don't understand it." He glanced up at Miss Gregor's window. An exclamation broke from his lips. He pointed to an iron spike sticking out from the wall just above the window.

"What's that?" he demanded of Angus.

"It was put there long ago to carry a sun-blind, sir. But Miss Gregor did not like the blind."

"You could reach it from the window-sill?"

"Yes, sir."

The detective measured the distance from the spike to the ground with his eye. Then he stepped on to the border and applied his bellows to a spot immediately under the spike. A few vigorous strokes of the bellows revealed a footprint under the loose dust of the surface. A moment later a second footprint, on which the marks of heavy nails were clearly visible, was disclosed. Barley stood back and pointed to these signs.

"You see. Footprints, one of which is studded with nails."

A gleam of triumph shone in his eyes. He turned to Dr. Hailey.

"You saw McDonald's shoe," he exclaimed. "Do you doubt that this print was made by it?"

"No. There's no doubt that it was made by it."

"Notice: right under the spike. He had a piece of rope apparently. He must have dropped only a short distance because these footprints are not deep. I feel sure that, as soon as he landed, he climbed into the window of the smoke-room; there are no other footprints. No doubt she was waiting for him there, ready to throw a few handfuls of loose earth on his tracks."

Dr. Hailey nodded: "It must be so, of course," he said. "I congratulate you."

They returned to the house and mounted to Miss Gregor's room. Barley climbed out on the window-sill and satisfied himself that the spike was within reach.

"We may as well complete our job," he declared, "by inspecting the spike from above. The iron is rusty and it's long odds that the rope he used has left some trace of its presence."

This expectation was confirmed. Looking down from the window of the little pantry, which served the nursery on the top floor, Dr. Hailey had an excellent view of the upper surface of the iron spike. The thick rust on the surface had been broken away at one place and the metal was visible.

"Are you satisfied, now, that a rope was used?" Barley asked.

"Yes."

"That must be the explanation, because, as you see, nobody can possibly have reached the spike from above, the drop is too great. Nobody reached it from below because there are no signs of the use of a ladder. It was reached therefore from the window-sill, which as I've just proved, is easy."

Barley leant against the dresser, which occupied one side of the room, and on which were standing jugs of milk and dishes of various kinds.

"What I think happened was this," he said. "When Mrs. Eoghan realized that her aunt was determined on her ruin and the ruin of her lover, her first idea, as you know, was to run away. But neither she nor McDonald has any money. He saw the folly of that course. Did he not exert himself to get the girl home again when she escaped to his house? From what you told me about that incident, I think it's a just inference that he had become thoroughly alarmed by her violence and by the reactions to her violence in this house. He was specially afraid of Miss Gregor, whose character he knew only too well. But to get rid of a headstrong woman with whom one has become compromised is no easy task. *Facilis est decensus Averni, sed revocare gradum, hic labor, hoc opus est!*"

The quotation broke gorgeously from his lips. He swept the air with his hands, making the plates behind him rattle.

"Mrs. Eoghan could summon him whenever she wished, because of her child. She compelled him in addition—and perhaps he needed no compulsion—to visit her unofficially in his boat. He learned that matters were going from bad to worse here. Then came discovery, and the immediate prospect, almost the certainty, of ruin. Duchlan might perhaps be induced to forgive and forget, but not so Miss Gregor.

"And so the murder was planned. The exact nature of these plans can only be guessed at; I admit that gaps still exist in our knowledge. But the outline is clear. After the doctor's arrival on the night of the murder, Mrs. Eoghan went to her aunt's room and told her that she was much alarmed about her child. That prepared the way for Dr. McDonald's coming to the bedroom. When he came, Mrs. Eoghan went downstairs to the study. The doctor must then have struck his blow. As you know it was a blow of terrific violence which, nevertheless, was not mortal. But the old woman's heart failed. He locked the bedroom door on the inside, assured himself that she was dead, fixed his rope in a single loop over the spike and let himself down from the window, which he had closed behind him. The rope was not long enough to bring him to the ground. There was a short drop. As we saw, it only remained to climb into the smoke-room, coil up the rope, get rid of the weapon, and cover the footprints. McDonald then left the house by the front door. He knew that he would be sent for as soon as the crime was discovered. Things fell out so well, as you know, that he was actually afforded the opportunity next morning of bolting the window without being observed, thus placing a most formidable barrier between his pursuers and himself."

Barley spoke with a pride which, in the circumstances, was pardonable. His case was complete; there remained only the work of rounding it off.

"I hope," he added, "that you will criticize me without mercy."

Dr. Hailey shook his head.

"The only criticism I could make has been made already by yourself. The facts and the people seem to be ill-mated. On the other hand, so far as I can see, the people, in this case, must yield to the facts. There is no other possible explanation."

"No." Barley made the plates rattle again. "The murder of Dundas is incredible if Dr. McDonald did not commit it. Think of it; you were on guard, so to speak, at the door of his room; that young fisherman was watching the window. You're ready to swear that nobody entered by the door; he's ready to swear that nobody entered by the window. And we know that Eoghan Gregor's story is an invention."

"We presume that, at any rate."

"No, sir." Barley smiled suddenly. "You noticed perhaps that I left you on the way up to this room. I looked into Dundas's bedroom. The mattress in his bed is a hair mattress, a hard hair mattress at that. I presume that he must have asked that the feathers might be taken away. Eoghan was unaware of the change."

There was a knock at the door of the pantry. Christina entered and asked Dr. Hailey to come into the nursery for a moment.

"It's Hamish," she explained. "He looks queer again."

She led the way, but turned back to close the door of the nursery behind the doctor. He walked to the cot where the child was lying asleep and bent over him.

"What happened?" he asked.

"His face was twitching."

"I don't think there is anything to be alarmed at."

He listened to the child's breathing for a few minutes and then turned to the old woman who stood behind him plucking nervously at her apron.

"What he wants is sleep, rest."

Christina's eyes were troubled. She shook her head in a fashion that expressed melancholy and resentment.

"Where is the poor lamb to find rest in this house?" she asked in her rich tones. Suddenly she took a step forward; she raised a skinny hand.

"Will you tell me: is it true that the detective from Edinburgh will be suspecting Hamish's mother?"

"I... I don't think I can discuss that."

The old woman uttered a cry.

"Oh, it will be true then, if you will not tell me." She put her hand on his sleeve and raised her black eyes to his face. "She is not guilty," she declared in tones of deep conviction. "I know that she is not guilty."

Dr. Hailey frowned.

"How can you know that?"

"Mrs. Gregor would not hurt a fly."

He shook his head. He had no wish to argue the case with this old woman and yet there was something in the passionate earnestness of her voice which challenged him.

"I hope you're right."

She continued to clutch his arm.

"I know what the man from Glasgow will be saying," she declared. "That it was Dr. McDonald who killed Miss Gregor, him being helped by Hamish's mother." She released him and stood back from him. "Will you please sit down? There is something that I must tell you."

He hesitated a moment and then did as she asked. She sat down opposite to him in a low chair that he guessed had been used for generations in the Duchlan nursery. Her face was dark and drawn and the muscles round her mouth were twitching.

"Did you see the scar of a wound on Miss Gregor's chest?" she asked him.

"Yes."

"I will tell you about it."

She pressed her hand to her brow and remained for a moment as if praying. Then she faced him.

"I came to Duchlan," she said, "the year that the laird was married. When Mr. Eoghan was born, his mother asked me to be his nurse. Many's the time I've sat on this chair and bathed him before the fire there. His mother used to sit where you are sitting now."

She covered her eyes again. An uneasy silence filled the room. Dr. Hailey found himself listening attentively to the soft breathing of the child.

"Well?" he asked.

"She was one of the angels; very beautiful too. The laird he was mad for her. I can hear his step on the stair now, coming up to sit beside her while I bathed Mr. Eoghan. Ah, he was a different man in those days from the man he is now, full of jokes and laughter. But Miss Gregor was the same always and he was afraid of her. Do you know she stayed in this house all the time that the laird was married?"

Again she paused. When her eyes were shut she looked like some very old bird moulting its last feathers.

"Miss Gregor had not a good word for her brother's wife. And she was clever and cunning to wound the poor lady. Every day she was making hints and finding faults. The food was not fresh; there was waste going on in the kitchen; the laird's clothes were not aired for him; Mr. Eoghan was not gaining weight. Everything. She did not complain to her sister-in-law; only to the laird. 'You must speak to her' was what she said always and he did not dare to disobey.

"The laird's wife was an Irishwoman and she had a quick temper. Because she loved her husband it was an affront to her the way Miss Gregor was carrying on. One day, after her husband had complained of her bad housekeeping, she ran to her sister-in-law and told her that she knew where these complaints were coming from. She was so angry that she did not care that I could hear her. 'Surely I am entitled to speak when I see my brother and his child neglected?' Miss Gregor said in her soft, gentle voice. 'You are not entitled to make trouble between me and my husband, nor to try to take my child away from me,' Mrs. Gregor said. I saw the blood come boiling up in her cheeks and her eyes. She cried out: 'Ever since I married, you have tried to steal my happiness from me. You are stealing my husband. Then you will try to steal my child. Other people may think you a good woman but I know what you are.' Miss Gregor smiled and said she forgave everything, as a Christian woman should. Then she went, her eyes red with crying, to her brother to tell him about his wife's temper."

Christina's toothless jaws snapped. Her eyes glowed.

"Oh, she was cunning. Have you seen a cat waiting for a mouse? The laird began to think that his wife was unjust to his sister. There were dreadful quarrels between them and Miss Gregor was waiting always to take his side. He did not come here any more when his wife was here, but he used to come with his sister. Mr. Eoghan was afraid of Miss Gregor, who was never no hand with children, but his father made him kiss her. Doctor, doctor, I knew that there was sorrow coming, and I could not do anything to help the poor young lady. Do you know I could see madness growing and growing in her face."

She bowed her head. When she spoke again her voice had fallen almost to a whisper.

"It was like that, too, with Hamish's mother, only Mr. Eoghan was away from her most of the time." She clasped her knees and began to sway backwards and forwards. "Hamish was afraid of Miss Gregor. The first time he took one of them turns was after she was here trying to give some medicine of her own. His mother she came to the room and took the poor laddie in her arms because he was screaming with fear."

She broke off suddenly and a look of anxiety came into her face.

"I mind the day Duchlan's lady did the same thing," she exclaimed. She remained silent for a few minutes and then added:

"The night Duchlan's lady was drowned, his sister was taken ill."

CHAPTER XXIV

BY THE WINDOW

Dr. Hailey's face expressed the horror which this information caused him.

"Drowned!"

"Yes. In the burn there, at the high tide."

"What was the nature of Miss Gregor's illness?"

"I do not know. The doctor, Dr. McMillan, brought bandages with him every day when he came to see her. I saw the bandages myself in his bag."

Her voice faded away.

"What explanation did the laird give?" Dr. Hailey asked.

"He did not give any explanation. The Procurator Fiscal from Campbeltown, not Mr. McLeod, but the gentleman who was Procurator Fiscal before him, came here once or twice. When Miss Gregor was better she and the laird went away for a trip to England."

"I see." He shook his head. "Did he, the laird I mean, seem... Did you think he was distressed at his wife's death?"

Christina sighed deeply. "Maybees he was; maybees not. I could not say."

"Did he come to the nursery much?"

"No, he did not. But Miss Gregor she came every day. Mr. Eoghan was hers and she would have it that he would call her 'Mother'. When he was older Miss Gregor told him that his mother had died from a cold."

Dr. Hailey rose.

"Do you remember what kind of a dressing-gown your poor mistress used to wear?" he asked suddenly.

"Always a blue dressing-gown like the one Hamish's mother wears. They was wonderful like each other, Mr. Eoghan's mother and his wife."

She rose also. "Will you tell me," she pleaded, "why they are blaming Hamish's mother now?"

He started slightly. Had she not been giving him the very information which was lacking to Barley's case? He was about to refuse her request when an impulse to reward confidence with confidence made him change his mind.

"Only Dr. McDonald can have committed these murders," he said. "He and Mrs. Gregor are friends."

"Why do you say: 'Only Dr. McDonald can have committed these murders?'"

Again he hesitated. But her distress overcame his reluctance. He gave her an outline of the case.

"I don't think that Dr. McDonald went into the bedroom," she declared.

"If you could prove that! Unhappily I saw him myself going into Mr. Dundas's room."

"They are going to arrest Hamish's mother?"

Dr. Hailey shook his head sadly.

"I suppose so."

"No, no. They must not. Hamish's mother did not do it. She did not. I am sure."

The child began to cry. Dr. Hailey watched him awaken and then descended to the ground floor. The heat wave continued and the afternoon was heavy with distant thunder. He left the castle and walked towards Darroch Mor. The woods, he thought, looked like a gipsy child he had seen once winding red leaves about her limbs. He came to an open space where was a view of the loch and the great mountains beyond Inverairy. The turf, set with thyme on which heavy bees lingered, invited to rest. He sat down and took out his snuff-box. The bees on the thyme made music for him till he fell asleep.

A woman's voice awakened him. He sat up and saw Oonagh. He jumped to his feet.

"I'm afraid I was sleeping."

She nodded.

"Yes. It was unkind of me to wake you."

She looked weary and anxious but he noticed how well dressed she was. Less observant eyes than his might have failed to recognize, in the simplicity of her frock, and in the way she wore her clothes, an attitude of mind and spirit denied to the vulgar. Most women in this crisis of fate would have relaxed their self-discipline.

"I want you to help me if you will," she said. "That I need help very badly must be my excuse for waking you. I've seen Dr. McDonald and heard about your visit to him this morning."

She broke off as if she felt that she had explained herself with enough clearness. He stooped to pick up his snuff-box, which had fallen to the ground.

"You've been so wonderfully successful in other cases, haven't you?" She caught her breath. "If murder will out, so will innocence, don't you think?"

"Yes."

"Very well, I give you my word that Dr. McDonald did not murder my aunt. Now, how can we prove that he didn't?"

Her face had become animated and her beauty, in consequence, was enhanced. In spite of himself Dr. Hailey felt the influence of that potent magic.

"I don't know how we can prove that he didn't," he said.

"At any rate it's got to be tried, hasn't it?" She came to him and put her hand on his arm: "You will help me?"

"On one condition."

"Yes?"

"That you will tell me the whole truth from the beginning, and answer any questions I may ask you."

Oonagh nodded. "Yes, I promise." She seated herself on the grass, inviting him to do the same. Tall bracken, becoming yellow, framed her face.

"Where shall I begin?"

"I want, first of all, to know about your relations with your aunt."
She frowned.

"We were rivals I suppose."

"Rivals?"

"I am Eoghan's wife and Hamish's mother. But I am not a Gregor
as they are." She plucked a piece of thyme and gazed at it. "Perhaps I
did not attach enough importance to that." Suddenly she raised her
head and looked him in the face. "Being a Gregor, after all, was my
aunt's chief interest in life. The Gregor family was her husband and
children, all she had to live for."

"You would not say that, would you, if she was still alive?"

"Perhaps not. But if not, I'm sorry. I think now that there was
something very sad, very lonely, in that woman's position. She was
so bitterly hungry for the things I had, Eoghan's love, my child's love,
perhaps even Duchlan's love. She wanted..." Oonagh broke off, her
lips remained parted as if waiting the word she needed to explain
her thought. "She wanted to have a hand in the future of the family.
To belong to the future as women do who have children of their
own. Because she couldn't bear children who would be members
of her family, she wanted to steal the children other women had
borne so that she could stamp her personality and ideas on their
minds. Behind that too, I think, was the ordinary need of every
woman for a child."

Again she broke off. Dr. Hailey nodded.

"I see."

"I feel that I'm being horribly cruel. It's like talking about a
deformity."

"Deformed people, you know, have ways of their own of forgetting
their afflictions."

"I suppose so."

"Family pride, I imagine, was Miss Gregor's way. I noticed that her
bedroom was full of all sorts of rubbish that she had made at different
times in her life."

"Yes, I often noticed that too. She was horrified once when I wanted to give an old coat of Hamish's to a child in the village. The coat disappeared and Christina told me that my aunt had burned it. Whereas she didn't mind in the least when I gave some of my own clothes to the child's mother. Duchlan's cast-off clothes were always put away in a wardrobe upstairs to be sent to a missionary in China."

"To be dedicated."

Oonagh raised her eyebrows sharply.

"Yes, that's exactly what she told me, and that was the Duchlan atmosphere."

She pulled the thyme to pieces and scattered the pieces. "After I realized what was happening I began to grow resentful. My nerves got jagged. One day I lost my temper and told my aunt that she was not to interfere with the way I was bringing up Hamish. She wept and became hysterical. Poor woman, I can hear her protesting that she had no wish to interfere in any way. But I was afraid of her. There was a look in her eyes. She told my father-in-law too that I had been cruel to her. After that the very air I breathed seemed to grudge itself. Every day things got worse. Dr. McDonald told you, didn't he, that I ran away?"

"Yes."

She shook her head. "Did he tell you why I ran away?"

"Yes."

"I suppose I ought not to have lost my temper as I did. I don't think it was for myself I was so angry; it seemed so horrible that they should suspect Dr. McDonald. I was upset too for Eoghan's sake and Hamish's sake."

She caught her breath sharply.

"Once I got out of the house I felt different. But I felt, too, that I couldn't go back again. It was like waking up out of a dreadful nightmare. In that house neither my husband nor my child belonged to me; it was only when I got away that I felt myself wife and mother again. I meant to go back to Ireland, to my people. I meant to write to Eoghan from there telling him that if he wanted me he must give me a home of my own..."

She broke off. Her voice, when she spoke again, was rather faint.

"It's not easy to be independent when you've got no money. The truth is that I was completely dependent on Miss Gregor. Eoghan hasn't enough to keep a wife and child in any kind of comfort."

"Did she make you an allowance?" Dr. Hailey asked. He watched her closely. It was just possible that Duchlan's account of the financial arrangements at the castle had been inaccurate.

"No. She had a system by which I could buy clothes at certain shops. She paid the bills. They were the kind of shops I wouldn't have gone to of my own accord. You know, good, old-fashioned places with no liking for modern ideas. It really meant that everything I got was regulated and controlled." She broke off and added:

"Very rarely Duchlan gave me a few pounds. But when he did, he always kept asking what I meant to buy with his money."

"Your husband gave you nothing?"

She raised her head sharply. Her eyes flashed.

"How could he? Eoghan really had no right to marry when he did. He wasn't in a position to keep a wife. He wasn't in a position to have a home of his own. He knew from the beginning that the girl he married would have to live with his people. To be just, though, I'm sure he had no idea what that meant. Men never understand what one woman can inflict on another woman."

"Did you talk in this way to Dr. McDonald?"

"Yes."

"What did he think?"

"He told me he felt sure that Eoghan loved me and that, in time, it would all come right."

"Did he say that on the night when you ran away from Duchlan?"

"Yes." She hesitated a moment and then added:

"Dr. McDonald begged me to return to Duchlan," she said. "He had persuaded me before Christina came."

Dr. Hailey nodded.

"How did the old people receive you when you returned to the castle?"

"Not very well. They were furious, but they tried to pretend that they were more hurt than angry. That didn't prevent them from spying on me next day."

Her cheeks flushed as she told how she had asked Dr. McDonald to meet her where they were not likely to be disturbed.

"I felt that if I was left entirely alone I might do something desperate. My nerves were in that condition. A friend with whom you can talk things over is the greatest blessing in such circumstances; besides, Dr. McDonald knows what life is like at Duchlan." She frowned and bit her lip.

"My aunt followed me from the house. When I returned, just before dinner, she came to my room and told me that she had seen us. Nothing happened then, but the next afternoon Duchlan spoke to me in her presence. My self-control broke. I told them that my mind was made up to leave Eoghan if he refused to take me away."

Her eyes more than her words revealed the extreme tension at which she had been living. She plucked at the thyme, scattering its small flowers about her.

"I didn't appear at dinner. But the evening post brought me a letter from Eoghan which changed everything. He told me plainly that he had lost a huge sum of money and was coming to Duchlan to try to borrow it from Aunt Mary. He said that, if he failed to borrow it, he would have to leave the Army in disgrace. The letter ended with an appeal to me to put my feelings on one side and help him, for the sake of Hamish." She looked up and faced the doctor: "That was why I went to Aunt Mary's room after Dr. McDonald had seen Hamish."

Dr. Hailey had been polishing his eyeglass. He put it to his eye.

"McDonald was still in the nursery when you went to Miss Gregor's room?" he asked.

"Yes. I left him there."

"When did you meet him again?"

"In the smoke-room. He had come downstairs. I told him that I had decided to make the best of things for Eoghan's sake. The window was open because of the heat. My aunt's room as you know is directly above. We heard her walk across her room to the windows and shut them."

"McDonald told me nothing of that?"

Dr. Hailey's voice challenged. He saw the girl blush.

"He wouldn't, for my sake."

"Because you had been alone together in the smoke-room?"

"Yes. As a matter of fact just after we heard Aunt Mary close her windows we heard the engine of Eoghan's motor-boat. My father-in-law must have heard it too because, a minute later, we heard him coming downstairs. Dr. McDonald didn't wish to meet him. He climbed through the open window and went away round the house to his car. I put the light out and waited till my father-in-law had opened the front door..."

"What? McDonald climbed out through the window?" Dr. Hailey's eyeglass dropped.

"To avoid meeting my father-in-law. I had told him about the scene with my father-in-law before dinner. The door of the smoke-room was shut and the front door was locked. If he hadn't gone out by the window he would certainly have met my father-in-law."

"I see."

"It was really the only thing to do in the circumstances. I was glad he thought of it, because it was so important not to give my father-in-law any further cause of complaint against me."

"What did you do after that?"

"I went back to my room. Eoghan came to my room..."

She broke off. Tears she could not restrain, filled her eyes.

CHAPTER XXV

A PROCESS OF ELIMINATION

"I THINK you must tell me," Dr. Hailey said in gentler tones, "exactly what happened between your husband and yourself."

Oonagh had recovered her self-possession but her busy fingers still plucked at the thyme.

"Eoghan told me about his loss," she said.

"Did he come straight to your bedroom?"

She gazed in front of her, at the brown sails of a pair of herring-boats which were lying becalmed far out in the loch.

"No."

"He went to Miss Gregor's room before he came to you?"

"Yes."

"He told you that he had been to her room?"

"Yes."

Her voice was scarcely audible. Dr. Hailey watched her for a moment and then asked:

"He told you that her bedroom door was locked?"

"Yes."

"And that, though he had knocked at the door, she had refused to open it?"

"He said she hadn't opened it."

"Nor answered him?"

"He said she hadn't answered him."

"Was she a light sleeper?"

"Very light."

"So he thought she hadn't answered him because she was angry with you?"

The girl drew a sharp breath.

"Yes."

"He was angry with you?"

"He was upset."

"Did you tell him that you had decided to apologize to your aunt?"

"Yes, I did."

"Well?"

"He was too upset to... to believe me. He... said I had ruined him..." She turned suddenly. "I had told Dr. McDonald about Eoghan's losses and he offered to lend me money. Eoghan was upset about that too..."

She broke off and covered her face with her hands.

"You mean that such an offer from such a quarter aroused your husband's suspicions?"

"My aunt had written to him."

"Telling him that you were in love with McDonald?"

"Hinting at it."

The doctor's eyes narrowed.

"The fact that he found Miss Gregor's door shut against him and the fact that you had received an offer of money from McDonald, taken together, convinced him that he had been correctly informed?"

"Yes, I think so."

"He accused you of being in love with McDonald?"

"Yes."

"And then?"

She raised her head; he saw that she was trembling.

"He was so dreadfully distressed."

"He didn't try to excuse himself for his gambling, then?"

"Oh, no."

Dr. Hailey hesitated.

"I kept my promise to you," he said, "about those bruises on your throat. I've mentioned them to nobody. But I think that, now, you must tell me how..."

"Please, no."

Oonagh's eyes quailed. She raised her hands suddenly, as if warding off an assailant.

"You promised complete frankness, remember."

"I can't tell you."

"That means that your husband inflicted..."

She covered her face with her hands.

"You mustn't ask me."

He frowned slightly but did not pursue the subject.

"Tell me," he asked, "didn't you think that it was strange that Miss Gregor had refused to answer your husband?"

"I thought it very strange."

"Almost incredible?"

"Yes. Aunt Mary loved Eoghan."

"Do you still think it strange?"

Oonagh started.

"What do you mean?"

"Do you still think it strange that your aunt refused to speak to your husband?"

She shook her head.

"No, not now."

"Why?"

"I think she was dead."

The words were spoken with evident distress. The doctor's face became anxious.

"If she was dead," he said, "then either Dr. McDonald or your husband had killed her?"

"Oh, no."

"Is it or is it not true that, when you heard of her death, you feared that your husband had killed her?"

She hung her head and did not reply.

"It is true?"

Suddenly she faced him.

"I can't answer directly," she said, "because my feelings weren't direct. It's as you said at Darroch Mor. If you ask me do I think Eoghan capable of murder, I say 'no'. But if you tell me murder has been committed, I become afraid. Suppose that in some terrible, unguarded moment..."

"Your husband has confessed that he murdered his aunt."

"What!"

Oonagh's eyes dilated. She put out her hands, as if to ward off some great danger. Her body began to sway as the colour ran out of her cheeks. Dr. Hailey put his arm round her shoulders.

"Let me say at once that I don't believe him," he assured her.

She tried to pull herself together and managed to regain her balance.

"Why don't you believe him?"

"Because, though it's just possible he may have got into Miss Gregor's bedroom, it's certain that he did not get out of it. The door was locked on the inside."

She gazed at him with vacant, fearful eyes.

"Somebody got out of the bedroom?"

"Yes."

She shook her head. It was obvious that, whatever her heart might suggest, her reason had pronounced judgement.

"I know," she declared in positive tones, "that Dr. McDonald did not go into my aunt's room. That idea is wrong, whatever evidence there may seem to be in favour of it." She shook her head: "And somebody did go in."

"There were other men in the house in addition to your husband remember, namely Duchlan and Angus, the piper."

"Duchlan didn't kill Aunt Mary." She put her hand on the doctor's wrist. "It's certain, isn't it, that Aunt Mary and Mr. Dundas were murdered by the same person?"

"Nearly certain."

"How can Duchlan have killed Mr. Dundas?"

Dr. Hailey shook his head. "I don't know." He added after a moment, "Your husband confessed to that murder also. But, again, there's evidence enough that he did not commit it."

"What evidence?"

"The fact that he was not in the room when I left it. He says he was hidden in the bed; he was not."

"Dr. McDonald was in the room with Mr. Dundas when you left it, wasn't he?"

"He returned to the room."

She pressed her hand to her brow.

"I know that Dr. McDonald didn't kill my aunt. So he didn't kill Mr. Dundas either."

Dr. Hailey readjusted his eyeglass. His kindly face looked troubled.

"Duchlan must have found out that Dr. McDonald left the smoke-room by the window?" he stated.

"Why do you say that?"

"Because it's obvious that he thinks McDonald killed his sister—with your help."

He watched Oonagh closely as he spoke. To his surprise she accepted his suggestion.

"He saw Dr. McDonald's footprints on the earth under the window next morning. He covered them up."

"He told you that?"

"Yes."

"What conclusion did he draw from the footprints?"

"He knew that they were Dr. McDonald's, because of the difference in the two feet. One of them..."

"Yes. I know that. That's not what I mean. How did he think that McDonald had left the house?"

She hesitated. Then her expression grew resolute.

"He thought that Dr. McDonald had jumped from my aunt's window," she said in low tones.

"That means that he thought you were guilty of a share in her death?"

"Yes."

"He told you that?"

"Yes."

"And suggested that you had better anticipate the fate in store for you?"

"Yes."

"Please tell me what he said."

"He said he knew that Dr. McDonald had killed Aunt Mary to prevent her fulfilling her threat to tell Eoghan. Then he said that he had covered up the doctor's footprints to save Eoghan and Hamish from the shame of my complicity in the murder. 'There is only one thing left for you to do,' he said, 'namely, to make an end of a life that is already forfeit. That will at least spare your husband and son the horror of your death on the gallows.' He added: 'High tide is at 2 a.m.!'"

Her tones had not faltered. She seemed to be recounting events far removed from her present state.

"And you," Dr. Hailey said, "feared, if you didn't believe, that the real murderer was your husband?"

"I did fear that."

"I was right in thinking that your death would divert suspicion from him?"

Oonagh inclined her head.

"It would have done, wouldn't it?"

The doctor shook his head. "Perhaps. But it would also have fastened suspicion on Dr. McDonald."

She started.

"Oh, no. Duchlan had covered up these footprints. He would never have told what he had discovered, for Eoghan's sake."

"Forgive me; Inspector Barley discovered the footprints for himself. Your death would have hanged McDonald."

She frowned and bit her lip.

"I don't think," she said deliberately, "that Dr. McDonald could have been suspected at all if Inspector Dundas had not been murdered. Inspector Dundas did not suspect Dr. McDonald."

Dr. Hailey nodded; the point was a good one.

"I thought it all out carefully before I decided," she went on. "I'm a physical coward and I was terribly afraid. I had fearful visions of what it would be like down among the seaweed at the burn's mouth. There's a lot of ugly green weed there which I've always hated to look at. Rank, slimy-looking stuff. But I thought that, if I kept struggling, I might drift out into the loch before the end because the force of the burn carries its water out a good way from the shore. The one sure thing seemed to be that my death would put an end to all the bother for everybody. And I knew that Eoghan was terribly disappointed in me... I thought he had ceased to care for me. If I lived Hamish would see my distress and be forced to take sides between his father and me. What was there to live for?"

She shook her head sadly as she spoke.

"I talk as if all that lay in the past," she added. "But it's here now, with me. If Eoghan accuses himself, perhaps that's only because he's a brave man and belongs to a class in which, as a matter of course, the man sacrifices himself for the woman and child. With his upbringing he must think of me as a wayward and discontented child unfit to be either wife or mother. If I live, our troubles will begin all over again. He'll never understand me or forgive me and I'll never be able to make him the kind of wife he wants and needs."

"That, if I may say so, is the wrong way of looking at your trouble. I feel sure, too, that you're wholly mistaken. The truth is that whereas you tried to give up your life for your husband and child, your husband is trying at this moment to give his life for you. In other words your husband shares his father's dread that you may be guilty. That, as I said before, is presumptive evidence, that neither you nor McDonald nor your husband nor your father-in-law is guilty. By a process of exclusion, therefore, we come to Angus."

They heard steps on the carriage-way behind them. Dr. Hailey turned his head and saw Duchlan approaching.

CHAPTER XXVI

ONCE BITTEN

DUCHLAN HAD AGED in these last days; he walked feebly, finding his steps. But his features retained their habitual expression. He came to Dr. Hailey, who rose at his approach.

"I have been looking for you," he stated in breathless tones, "because Inspector Barley tells me that he has received a confession from my son."

His head shook as he spoke. He kept his eyes fixed on the doctor, ignoring his daughter-in-law utterly.

"Your son made a confession," Dr. Hailey said.

"It's nonsense. Eoghan never killed his aunt."

The old man's voice rose in a shrill crescendo. Fear and anger were mingled in his expression.

"I can prove his innocence," he cried. "Do you hear, I can prove it."

He continued to avoid directing even a glance at Oonagh. But that abstention did not lessen the menace with which his words evidently threatened her. Dr. Hailey readjusted his eyeglass.

"I don't think," he said, "that Inspector Barley is the least likely to treat your son's confession seriously."

"Eh? What do you say?"

The doctor repeated his statement. He was surprised to observe that it failed to reassure the anxious father.

"Don't talk nonsense," Duchlan cried. "If a man confesses to murder, a man in my son's responsible position at that, his confession is bound to be taken seriously."

"Why?"

"Why? Because the presumption must be that he has spoken advisedly." The old man's eyes flashed. "The truth is that he is shielding others whose guilt can be proved and who are wholly unworthy of the sacrifice he is making on their behalf." He turned his back on Oonagh. "I should like to talk to you alone."

Dr. Hailey shook his head.

"Much better to talk here openly. Your daughter-in-law, unless I am wrong, has just been telling me all that you propose to tell me."

"What's that?"

"About your discovery of Dr. McDonald's footprints on the earth under your sister's bedroom window."

Duchlan started. But he kept his back resolutely turned on Oonagh.

"I did find his footmarks: the one smooth, the other studded with nails. Nobody could misinterpret that sign. So you see the fellow jumped from my poor sister's window after he had committed his horrible crime. It was I, myself, who covered the footmarks lest my daughter-in-law's association with the murder should be discovered." He drew a deep breath, nodding his head all the while. "What a mistake I made. What a mistake I made. But she is the mother of my grandson, who will be Duchlan one day. Can you blame an old man because he has tried to deliver his son and his son's son from ineffaceable shame and dishonour? But God is just; murder will out. This Quixotic chivalry of my son has, perforce, unsealed my resolve to keep silence. Am I to stand by and see an innocent man, my son, led out to death while I possess knowledge that will save him? Those who have shed the blood of the innocent must bear the punishment of that dreadful crime."

His voice shook. A faint tinge of colour had mounted to his cheeks. But that common hue of living men brought with it no suggestion of human kindness. A cold, unmerciful gleam filled the black eyes. Dr. Hailey stepped back that he might see Oonagh. She remained seated; her fingers continued to pluck at the thyme. "Is your belief that Dr. McDonald murdered your sister," he asked in calm tones, "founded exclusively on your discovery of these footprints?"

"It is not indeed."

Duchlan sneered. He raised his hand and seemed to clutch at the air in front of him.

"Is it possible that my daughter-in-law's candour has not extended to her relations with McDonald?"

"On the contrary, sir."

"Why ask, then, if the footprints are the only evidence of guilt?"

"You have assumed that the relations between your daughter-in-law and Dr. McDonald are improper relations."

The old man started.

"I have drawn the conclusion which the evidence of my senses compels me to draw."

"What, because a mother whose child is showing alarming symptoms sends for the doctor..."

"No. Emphatically no. Because a wife who has flouted her husband's nearest relatives is found to be meeting a man, clandestinely, after the fall of darkness."

"You had already, before such meetings took place, made accusations which must have driven any woman to secrecy."

"We had our reasons, believe me."

"What reasons?"

Dr. Hailey's voice had grown as hard as Duchlan's. He allowed his eyeglass to fall and faced the old man.

"The doctor was summoned on the most frivolous pretexts. My dear sister was not permitted to be present during these visits..."

"I see. On that evidence, you were ready to believe that your son's wife was untrue to him?"

"Both Mary and I were jealous of Eoghan's honour."

"Because Miss Gregor was excluded from the consultations with Dr. McDonald, she, and you too, became suspicious that these consultations were not, in fact, what they appeared to be?"

"McDonald was sent for on every conceivable occasion..."

"By a mother whose child was taking convulsions."

Dr. Hailey spoke these last words slowly and with emphasis. When no reply was forthcoming he asked:

"Is it not obvious that both you and your sister were inclined to suspicion in the case of your daughter-in-law?"

"I don't understand you."

"I mean that, in her case, you were ready to suspect, perhaps even determined to suspect."

"Nonsense."

"On your own showing, you found the natural anxiety of a young mother a cause of uneasiness?"

"No."

"My dear sir, when your daughter-in-law kept sending for the doctor, both you and Miss Gregor accused her of unworthy motives."

The old man frowned, but this time offered no comment. The doctor proceeded:

"And, meanwhile, on your own showing, you were forcing her to receive your charity. You were using every means to hurt her pride and humiliate her wifehood. Men do not desire such punishments for women. I can only conclude therefore that you have acted throughout at the dictation of your sister."

"My sister, as I told Inspector Barley, possessed means of her own. I have nothing but this estate." He indicated the woods and the loch. "My sister was under no obligation whatever to give my son or his wife a penny. Eoghan married without consulting our wishes."

"Why should he consult your wishes?"

"Why should my sister give him her money?"

Dr. Hailey shook his head.

"An outsider," he said, "sees most of the game. It's obvious to me that your sister, having got your son's wife at her mercy, adopted every method she could think of to make her life intolerable. My personal view is that that was a policy undertaken with a definite object, namely, to separate husband and wife. The policy failed. Your daughter-in-law remained here, enduring everything. It began to seem probable that she would have a home of her own. A change of policy was necessary;

an immediate change of policy. Your sister managed, I don't know how, to persuade you that the visits of Dr. McDonald were more than ordinary medical visits."

"I saw for myself that they were more than ordinary medical visits. Their duration…"

"My dear sir, nobody thinks anything of a prolonged doctor's visit when the case is a serious one."

Duchlan's face was pale with anger.

"I tell you," he exclaimed, "I did think something…"

"Exactly."

Dr. Hailey looked him straight in the face. He added:

"I assume, therefore, that this wholly commonplace behaviour of McDonald was distorted in your eyes by some earlier experience. Once bitten, twice shy."

The words were spoken in a low tone. But their effect could not have been greater had they been shouted. Duchlan swayed on his feet.

"No, no," he ejaculated hoarsely.

"Some earlier experience in which a young wife…"

There was no reply. The muscles of the old man's face were unloosed. His jaw fell. After a moment he moved away a few paces and leaned against a tree.

"You are speaking about the death of my wife?" he gasped.

"Yes."

"She…" A fit of coughing shook Duchlan's body. He turned and grasped one of the branches of the tree against which he was leaning. Dr. Hailey came to his side.

"I am aware of the circumstances of your wife's death," he said. "And of the events which preceded it, the wounding of your sister."

"Mary was guiltless."

"No doubt. But her accusations…"

Duchlan made a peremptory gesture.

"Her accusations were just," he declared in tones that vibrated with pain.

"At least you chose so to regard them. It comes to the same thing. What is certain is that Miss Gregor employed against your wife the methods she employed recently against your daughter-in-law, namely, a perpetual and persistent interference, a merciless criticism, and a diligent misrepresentation. These methods expressed, I believe, her jealous hatred of a rival whose presence in the castle threatened her position. She drove your wife to violence; you, doubtless, completed the work of destruction by exhibiting the callous spirit which made it possible for you the other day to suggest suicide to your daughter-in-law."

Dr. Hailey's voice thrilled with an anger which was not cooled by the spectacle of the old man's distress.

CHAPTER XXVII

MAN TO MAN

DR. HAILEY returned alone to the castle. He found Barley awaiting him.

"My case is complete," the detective assured him. "I've found the axe with which the murder of Miss Gregor was committed."

He led the way to his bedroom and produced a small axe from a drawer of the dressing-table. He handed it to his companion.

"Observe, my dear Hailey," he pointed out, "that there are herring scales on the handle. The axe is nominally used to chop wood but the cook admits that she employed it the other day to break up a big bone for the stock-pot. She had been cleaning some herring just before she did this."

Dr. Hailey sat down and took snuff.

"Don't forget," he said, "that there were herring scales on Dundas's head."

"Quite. I feel sure that that blow was struck with a lead sinker. I've seen Dr. McDonald's boat. It's plentifully endowed with scales. He's a keen deep-sea fisherman and often uses herring as bait."

Barley hooked his thumbs into the arm-holes of his waistcoat and spread out his fingers.

"I confess," he declared, "that I have great sympathy—the greatest possible sympathy—with Mrs. Eoghan. Poor woman, her life has been made unbearable by her aunt, who deserved perhaps no better fate than that which has overtaken her. At the same time, let us not deceive ourselves, murder is murder. Deliberation of a most calculating kind is revealed by the use of that axe, which had to be fetched from below stairs and by the fact that a rope was kept in readiness to enable the murderer to escape. Once he had bolted the windows of Miss Gregor's bedroom, on the morning after her death, McDonald must have felt that he was secure against detection."

Dr. Hailey described his talk with Oonagh and his meeting with Duchlan and, as usual, received a careful and courteous hearing.

"More collateral proofs, in my humble judgement," Barley exclaimed. "Duchlan's discovery of the footprints seems to me of crucial import. What a feeble defence to say that a doctor left his patient's house by the window rather than face a poor, distracted old man!"

"McDonald, remember, didn't cover up his tracks. He left those footprints to tell their tale, surely an act of gross carelessness in a murderer."

Barley shrugged his shoulders and then spread out his hands.

"Yes, a point. I admit it. But how small after all! I apologize in advance for using a bad argument, an argument which, generally speaking, I deprecate; but if McDonald didn't commit this murder, who did? Again surely we are entitled to ask *Cui bono*? McDonald undoubtedly. He had access, he alone, to the murdered persons. He was able to escape, he alone, from the rooms where the murders were committed. He has left traces, unmistakable, damning, of his escape. I confess that, so far as I am concerned, not a shadow of doubt about his guilt exists."

He broke off and remained for a few minutes in silent contemplation of the carpet.

"An hour ago," he said, "I applied for warrants for the arrest of Dr. McDonald and Mrs. Eoghan Gregor. It is my purpose to effect these arrests, at the latest, to-morrow morning."

"Your case will necessarily be founded," Dr. Hailey said, "on the assumption that McDonald and Mrs. Eoghan were lovers?"

"Yes."

"Have you any real evidence to support that charge?"

"Circumstantial evidence. Besides, if Mrs. Eoghan's motives in meeting McDonald were strictly correct, the effect of the meetings remain. Both man and woman knew that Miss Gregor would report to her nephew; both had a clear idea what the effect of that report would be. The motive for murder remains therefore and is, I submit,

by no means invalidated by assuming that these meetings were absolutely *en règle*."

"Innocence does not kill."

Barley frowned. He began to comb his moustache with unusual
vigour.

"Exactly," he declared, "and therefore I presume that the relationship was not innocent."

"Do you believe seriously that McDonald is that type of man?"

A curious expression came upon Barley's face. He seemed, for a
moment, to take off the policeman and become his ordinary, human self.

"I think, my dear doctor," he exclaimed, "that you mustn't ask me
such a question. It's like..." He raised his hand. "It's like asking a surgeon
if he doesn't think it cruel to wound people. I may like McDonald, I
may pity him. But the one thing I can't do, the one thing I mustn't do,
is to import my personal feelings into my case against him."

Dr. Hailey shook his head.

"Why not?"

"Because a detective is primarily an observer. You know very well
how apt the personal equation is to obtrude on scientific observation.
It's the same in this kind of work. If you begin by finding heroes and
heroines and villains you won't end by finding your murderer."

"You admit that if McDonald's relationship with Mrs. Eoghan was
innocent, your case is weakened considerably?"

Barley shrugged his shoulders.

"That's a debating point," he declared in brisk tones. "And I must
ask to be excused the task of debating it." He rose and took the axe
which the doctor had placed on a table beside him. He laid it back in
its drawer. Dr. Hailey left him and went to his own bedroom. He lay
down on the bed and was soon asleep. When he woke, the night was
marching across the sky. He watched the changing colours of the clouds,
wondering vaguely what time it was; then his critical faculty asserted
itself. The fault in Barley's theory as he now recognized was its disregard
of the character of Miss Gregor. That woman had been ready to sow

hate and suspicion between husband and wife; but the idea that she was concerned to effect a public breach of their marriage was certainly mistaken. Such women look on divorce with lively horror, and will exert their whole strength to preserve their kin from the disgrace attending it. McDonald must have known this, and known, consequently, that he had nothing to fear. Why then commit murder? He had discovered no answer to this question when he heard light footsteps approaching his door. A moment later Oonagh burst into the room.

"Eoghan's gone off in the motor-boat," she cried.

Her face was quick with foreboding. Her eyes beseeched help. She grasped the rail of the bed and stood trying to recover her breath.

"I feel terribly anxious about him."

Dr. Hailey jumped up.

"When did he go?"

"I suppose about half an hour ago. Nobody seems to have seen him. I went to his room to talk to him. He wasn't there. I searched the house. Then I noticed that the boat had disappeared. The wind is off-shore; I imagine he let her drift from her moorings so as not to excite attention."

She gazed at the doctor as she spoke, but his face remained expressionless.

"Where can we get a motor-boat?"

"In Ardmore."

She put her hand on his arm.

"Do you think that... that he's in danger?"

"Perhaps."

She mastered herself. They went downstairs.

"I haven't told Duchlan," she said.

"Much better not."

They left the house and hurried towards the village. Once they stopped to listen; the night held only murmurings of winds. Oonagh did not speak, but the glimpses which the moon gave him of her face showed how acutely she was suffering. McDonald had not lied when he said that this woman loved her husband.

The boat hirer had ended his day's work and did not seem eager to resume it. He stood in the doorway of his cottage, from which the smell of frying herrings emerged, and expounded the many weaknesses of his motor-boat and the unwisdom of sailing in her in the dark. His round, red face grew melancholy as he emphasized this danger.

"I'm ready to run any risk, Mr. McDougall," Oonagh said.

"But surely Mr. Eoghan can be in no danger? He's a good sailor, whatever."

The tones were challenging. She shook her head.

"His engine must have broken down. We couldn't hear it; on a quiet night like this you should hear it five miles away."

"The weather is very settled. He will not come to no harm before the morning."

"I can't wait till the morning. Not another hour. Sandy Logan has a motor-boat, hasn't he?"

"Aye, he has."

The Highlander spoke stiffly. He was not concerned to enter into rivalry with anyone. Let them go where they would. He took a step back, preparatory, apparently, to shutting the door when the beat of a motor engine came faintly but distinctly to their ears. Mr. McDougall strained forward to listen.

"Yon's Mr. Eoghan's boat," he declared with assurance. "She's coming into the harbour."

He waved his hand in a gesture that absolved him from any further responsibility.

"How can you be sure?" Dr. Hailey asked.

"By the sound, sir. There's no two engines make the same sound. That one of Mr. Eoghan's is the newest and best between Rothesay and Inveraira."

The beating of the engine grew louder, more insistent.

"I think it is Eoghan's boat," Oonagh said. She pointed seaward. "I can see it."

They left the cottage and walked to the shore. The motor-boat was coming in fast and seemed to be making for the jetty under Dr. McDonald's house. Dr. Hailey touched his companion's arm.

"You realize where he's going?"

"Oh, yes." She turned to him in distress. "I feel that something terrible is going to happen."

He considered a moment.

"I think that you must leave this business to me," he said at last. "If we remain together the chances are that we'll fail."

"Oh, I can't go back to Duchlan."

"Not for your husband's sake?"

She did not reply. They could see the motor-boat clearly now in the wake of the moon. Eoghan was standing up in the stern. She grasped his arm.

"Very well." She moved away a few paces and then came back. "Promise that you'll keep him from doing anything... terrible."

"Yes."

She disappeared away among the shadows. He waited until the motor-boat had been brought to the jetty and then walked in the direction of Dr. McDonald's house. He reached the gate in time to see Eoghan ascending the steep footpath to the door. He followed, going slowly and with great caution. When he reached the top of the path he crouched down. Eoghan had been admitted to the house and was standing in the study, the windows of which were wide open. His face was very pale; even from a distance, it was obvious that he was labouring under great excitement. McDonald entered the room. The men did not shake hands. Dr. Hailey moved into the deep shadows which lay beyond the beam of light cast by the windows. He approached the house and crouched again. He heard Eoghan's clear, well-bred voice say:

"The position is this: I've done my best to persuade them that I'm the man they're looking for. I've failed. Barley has made up his mind that you and Oonagh killed my aunt between you and that you killed

Dundas." He paused for an instant and then added: "Don't misunder-stand me when I say that I think he's got a strong case."

"Against me, perhaps; not against your wife."

"My dear sir, his case fails unless he can associate my wife with you. He believes," Eoghan's voice hardened in spite of himself, "that you and my wife were in love with each other. My aunt thought so too; she wrote me to that effect. My father is convinced of it. So, also, I think, is Christina."

He paused. Dr. Hailey heard McDonald move across the room. Then he heard the doctor ask:

"And you?"

"No, I'm not convinced."

"Thank you."

Dr. Hailey stood erect; he took a step near to the beam of light and then retired to a point from which he could see the two men. Eoghan's expression was less friendly than he had expected.

"I don't want to sail under false colours," he told Dr. McDonald. "No man can be grateful to another for bringing suspicion on his wife. What I mean is that, although the case as others see it, is damning enough, I don't choose to be damned by it. But if I believe Oonagh against the weight of evidence, I'm not fool enough to suppose that the weight of evidence is thereby lightened. Barley has asked for war-rants to arrest you and her. He means to execute them to-morrow."

His features were grim. He stood facing McDonald with clenched fists and tense muscles so that, for a moment, Dr. Hailey thought he was about to attack him.

"Your wife is innocent, Gregor," McDonald cried. "I swear it."

"I'm afraid, my dear fellow, that that isn't likely to help much; whatever you or I may swear Oonagh will be tried with you for murder. The odds, frankly, are enormous that you'll be convicted, both of you. Barley, I understand, has discovered footprints under my aunt's window. His case is that nobody but you can have committed this murder and 'pon my word, I can't see any other solution myself."

"There must be another solution."

"Can you suggest one?"

"No, but..."

"The murders are a man's doing. They've excluded me. The only other possibilities are Father and Angus." Eoghan paused and then repeated. "Father and Angus."

He stood gazing at McDonald who faced him courageously.

"Why on earth should I murder your aunt?" the doctor asked.

"I've told you. As Barley points out your professional life was at stake."

"Only if you divorced your wife." McDonald took a step forward. "I do not believe that you would ever have done that."

Eoghan did not reply for a moment. Then he said:

"I'm afraid that, from Barley's point of view, what I might or might not have done is of no consequence. I'm not here because I believe in anybody's guilt. I'm here because the evidence in the possession of the police is so strong that they're bound to succeed against you and my wife. They will ask the jury to consider what must have happened if I had got a divorce, not whether or not I was likely to petition for one. After all, no man can be sure what another man will do in such circumstances. Barley is entitled to assume that divorce was on the cards."

Eoghan's manner was very grave. He added:

"I've tried to think what my own attitude would be if I sat on the jury that will try the case. I'm afraid I should be compelled to take the view that you were in a dangerous position."

His voice challenged. He had come to make demands, the righteousness of which shone in his eyes. Dr. McDonald seemed to shrink from him.

"What do you want me to do?" he asked in the tone of a man who speaks under strong compulsion. Eoghan frowned; a moment later, however, his face cleared.

"I'm afraid," he said, "that I want you to die."

CHAPTER XXVIII

"READY?"

DR. HAILEY strained forward to catch McDonald's reply. He saw the doctor square his shoulders.

"Very well."

"The position is that, if you and I are out of the way, they'll drop the case against Oonagh. You can't try a dead man and no man is guilty till he's been convicted. Lacking a conviction against you, they could scarcely hope to succeed against her."

McDonald nodded.

"Yes." He threw back his head in a gesture of defiance. "Why do you say," he demanded, "'if you and I are out of the way'? What difference can it make whether you are out of the way or not?"

"I've accused myself, remember."

"Since they don't believe you, that counts for nothing."

Eoghan shrugged his shoulders.

"Possibly not. Still, my death will give substance to my confession. In face of it, and with your death added, Oonagh should be safe."

He took his cigarette-case from his pocket and opened it. He began to tap a cigarette on the side of the case.

"I've got the motor-boat in the harbour," he added. "I propose that we go sailing."

He put the cigarette in his mouth and lit it. His coolness was admirable; but there was a quiet strength in McDonald's face that was not less striking. Dr. Hailey felt regret that Barley was not with him to see how the man he called murderer behaved in face of death.

He left his place at the window and hurried down the path to the road. The motor-boat was lying at the jetty. He reached it and stepped aboard. The bow was decked to make a fo'c'sle. He opened the door of this and entered, closing the door behind him, except for a small aperture. He struck a match. The fo'c'sle contained only a few coils of rope and a canvas bucket. It was unlikely that the two men would have occasion to enter it.

They came after the lapse of a few minutes. Dr. Hailey noticed that neither spoke a word as they cast off. The noise of the engine soon made it difficult to hear any speech. The little craft was lively and rushed out of the harbour in a few minutes. Through the small opening in the door he could see the lights of Ardmore receding behind the tops of the pine trees on Garvel point. What was Eoghan Gregor's game? Every now and then he caught a glimpse of the young man's face. The moonlight had blanched it; but it had lost nothing of its resolution. McDonald's expression was far less determined and he looked up, sometimes, at the sky in a way that was rather pitiful. After the lapse of about half an hour, Eoghan stopped the engine. The rush of water on the boat's sides and the gurgle under her stern mingled pleasantly; little by little the wide, lively silence swallowed them up.

"We must leave them guessing," Eoghan said. "This isn't necessarily suicide, or murder; it may be just an accident. Loch Fyne is so deep out here that it holds its secrets for ever."

"Yes."

"Are you a swimmer?"

The question came sharply, like an order to fire.

"I can swim, but I tire very easily."

"So do I."

The moonbeams were reflected on a long, dull barrel. Dr. Hailey saw Eoghan raise a shot-gun, of the heavy type used for duck, to his shoulder.

"I'm going to blow the bottom out of her," he said, and then pronounced the word "Ready?"

"There's just one thing, Gregor. I'd like you to know that, though your wife has never cared for anybody but you, I cared for her." McDonald's voice broke. But a moment later he added: "She never knew, of course."

"Thanks, old man... Ready?..."

Dr. Hailey flung open the door of the fo'c'sle.

"Put that gun down, Gregor," he ordered in stern tones.

CHAPTER XXIX

PAINFUL HEARING

EOGHAN OBEYED HIM so far as to lay the shot-gun across his knees.

"What the devil are you doing in my boat?" he demanded.

Dr. Hailey did not answer. He left the fo'c'sle and came aft where the two men were seated.

"This is madness," he declared. "Nothing has been proved." He addressed himself to Eoghan: "Oonagh guessed your plan. She accompanied me to Ardmore. She's waiting now for news of you."

"Barley has a warrant for her arrest." The young man's voice was cold and hard.

"What does that matter? A warrant is not a verdict."

"I believe they'll get their verdict."

"I don't."

Dr. Hailey's voice rang out with an assurance which surprised himself and which astonished his companions.

"What!" Eoghan exclaimed. "In face of those footprints on the flower-bed?"

"Which your father covered up the next morning."

"Well?"

"A murderer asking for punishment."

"It's easy to make a slip."

"Would you have made that particular kind of slip yourself?"

Eoghan considered a moment.

"Perhaps not."

"That, in McDonald's case, means certainly not."

"Why?"

"Because he has a wooden leg. People with artificial limbs are more aware of their footsteps than ordinary people and they seldom jump."

Eoghan did not answer. He bent suddenly and laid his gun on the bottom of the boat. His hands reached out to the starting-handle on the engine.

"Wait a minute," McDonald exclaimed. He turned to Dr. Hailey:

"My reason for coming here," he said, "was that Barley's case seemed to me so well buttressed by circumstantial evidence that a conviction was certain. So far as I can see you are in no position to disprove that evidence. If we go ashore with you, therefore, Mrs. Gregor and I will be arrested to-morrow, taken to Edinburgh, convicted and hanged. I prefer to drown."

He spoke with deliberation, solemnly, as a man speaks who has paid a price for his words.

"You say that, knowing that you are innocent?" Dr. Hailey asked.

"What does that signify?"

"Everything."

The Highlander moved his wooden leg to a more comfortable position.

"In actual practice innocence that cannot be substantiated," he declared, "is no better than guilt. I don't deceive myself. In Barley's place I should think and act as he has done. After all, what alternative has he got? He can prove that Gregor here didn't commit these murders; he can prove that Mrs. Gregor and I were friends; that we had reason to fear Miss Gregor; that we had access to her bedroom. If I didn't know that I hadn't killed the poor lady, I swear I would be convinced that I must have killed her."

Dr. Hailey shook his head.

"Did you fear Miss Gregor?" he asked.

"No."

"Then why do you say 'we had reason to fear Miss Gregor?'"

"I meant, that's what the jury will think."

"You know as well as I know that there was never, at any time, any question of divorce. That can be proved."

"How?"

"By reference to Captain Gregor here and to his father." Dr. Hailey turned to Eoghan:

"Did you threaten your wife with a divorce?" he asked.

"Of course not. But I'm afraid I agree with McDonald that that doesn't matter. Barley is entitled to assume that the threat of divorce existed; the jury will make the same assumption."

"I don't think the jury will do anything of the kind. Even juries have to take cognizance of human character. Is it likely that your aunt would have wished a divorce? Or your father? Divorce is still looked on by old-fashioned people as a disgrace. Any Scottish jury will understand that, I can assure you. Besides, you can go into the box and state that at no time did the idea of divorce enter your mind. You never spoke about it to your wife. You threatened nobody. What a fool McDonald must be if he committed murder in order to escape from a danger which had no existence."

"My dear sir," McDonald interposed, "the prosecution will counter that by saying that a guilty mind loses its judgement. 'The wicked flee when no man pursueth.'"

"No. My point is that this idea of divorce can be shown to have originated in Barley's mind. His whole case is founded on it. No jury, let me repeat, is going to believe that these murders were committed by a doctor who had nothing to gain by committing them and nothing to lose if they were not committed. Again, why kill Miss Gregor since Duchlan lived, since Mrs. Gregor's husband lived." Dr. Hailey found his eyeglass and put it in his eye. "That's the weak spot in Barley's case. Miss Gregor was no more dangerous to you, McDonald, than her brother, and both she and her brother were less dangerous than her nephew, who had already been informed about what was happening. Far from being a murder with a strong motive this was a wholly senseless murder if its object was to prevent a divorce. I feel sure these arguments will make a strong appeal to any jury."

Eoghan nodded; he started the engine.

"There's no doubt you're right," he declared. "We've got a fighting chance."

The boat began to move. He pulled the tiller over and set her course for Duchlan. The lights in the castle winked at them. Nearer, to the left, they saw the flares of a herring-boat which had secured a catch and was calling the buyers. Red and green lights announced the approach of the steamers of these merchants, which everywhere follow the fishing fleet. Oonagh was standing on the jetty awaiting them. She bent and caught the gunwhale, holding it till Dr. Hailey and Dr. McDonald had stepped ashore. Then she jumped into the boat. They saw her throw her arms round her husband's neck.

"I think I had better see Barley," McDonald said in hurried tones.

They found the detective in the smoking-room with Duchlan who seemed to be on good terms with him. Dr. Hailey waited till Eoghan and Oonagh came to the room and then expounded his objections to Barley's theory.

"It boils down to this," he declared. "McDonald knew that Miss Gregor had written to her nephew. The mischief was done. Murder in the circumstances was senseless."

Barley had accorded his habitual courtesy to the criticism. He bowed his head in silent acknowledgment of its weight. Then, with a gesture, he swept it aside.

"This gathering, as you know," he stated, "is not of my summoning. If what I say makes painful hearing, you cannot charge that to my account. My case does not, as you appear to think, rest primarily on motive; it rests on ascertained facts and on observations, each of which has been carefully checked." He rose and stood in front of the fireplace. "There are three separate methods of approach to this case," he declared. "The first of these is the method of observation. It can be shown that Dr. McDonald jumped on to the flower-bed under Miss Gregor's window. Again, marks which suggest the use of a rope can be shown on the iron spike above that window. You can suggest that Dr. McDonald left the house by the window of the study, which is situated under that of Miss

Gregor's room. That suggestion does not explain the marks on the spike, whereas my suggestion, that these marks were made by a rope used as a means of descent from Miss Gregor's window, explains both marks and footprints. Any actuary will tell you that the odds in favour of my theory are, consequently, very long. But that is not all."

He leaned forward. The habitual good-humour of his expression had faded. He looked, Dr. Hailey thought, like an actor who has, suddenly, thrown off his mask.

"The method of deduction must also be used. Miss Gregor's death followed immediately a violent quarrel between her and Mrs. Eoghan Gregor, which quarrel was about secret meetings with Dr. McDonald. Miss Gregor had written to her nephew about his wife's behaviour; had she written about these secret meetings?"

The question was addressed to Eoghan. He flushed as he answered it in the negative.

"You see. The worst, or at any rate, what looked like the worst, had not been told. Again, the murder took place before Captain Eoghan Gregor reached home."

"How do you know that?" Dr. Hailey asked.

"I know that Captain Eoghan Gregor went to his aunt's room as soon as he landed. He was not admitted. The proof that he was not admitted is that the door was locked on the inside. The carpenter's testimony on that point is clear and final."

"Yes."

"So that the murder occurred within a few hours of the discovery and reproof of a young wife and a few minutes before the return of her husband. Who can say what secret Miss Gregor will carry with her to her grave?"

He gazed at Eoghan as he spoke. The young man's face had grown grave, but he continued to hold his wife's hand. He drew her closer to him. McDonald bent and moved his wooden leg.

"The third method is that of elimination, admittedly the least satisfactory of the three. If Dr. McDonald did not commit this murder who did? Not Captain Eoghan Gregor. Not Duchlan. Not Angus..."

Dr. Hailey interrupted: "On what grounds do you exclude Angus?"

"If, as Mrs. Gregor has told me, she and Dr. McDonald, while they were in this room, heard the windows of Miss Gregor's room being shut, then they must immediately afterwards have seen the murderer drop to the ground. Look for yourself. These windows were open then as they're open now; you can see the whole extent of the flower-bed. Do you suppose that if they had seen Angus drop from Miss Gregor's room they would not have reported the fact?"

"You're assuming that the murderer must have left the room by way of the window?"

"We know that he cannot have left by the door." He waved his hand. "You can't have it both ways. In my humble judgement if Dr. McDonald and Mrs. Gregor are speaking the truth, they must have seen the murderer making his escape. That, it appears to me, was a consideration overlooked by them when framing their story. Their story fails therefore on two separate counts: It doesn't explain the marks on the spike and it ignores completely the descent of the murderer from the window he had just closed. I reject their story, and in rejecting it, exclude Angus from the case. Somebody closed the windows; some-body descended from them. There is only one person who can have accomplished these acts. As it happens, he is also the only person who can possibly have killed Inspector Dundas, seeing that there is ample evidence that nobody entered or descended from Dundas's window."

Barley's voice had fallen to a low pitch. When he ceased to speak a chill fell on the room.

"Had Dundas not been murdered," he added, "the case against Dr. McDonald would have been overwhelmingly strong; as things are, it is irresistible."

They heard a car approaching the house, a moment later it reached the door. Everyone in the room knew what this coming portended and even Duchlan shrank in horror. He put his skinny old hand on his son's arm but Eoghan remained indifferent to him. Eoghan had his arms about his wife. A dull glare burned in his eyes. Dr. Hailey turned away; the spectacle of McDonald's distress made him avert his eyes a second time. Angus's heavy, shuffling steps crossed the hall to the front door. Then they returned, at the same pace, to the door of the room. The door opened. A policeman in uniform entered.

"Inspector Barley?" he asked.

"Yes."

The man saluted. He presented a long blue envelope.

"I'm Sergeant Jackson, sir, and these are the warrants for the arrest of Mrs. Gregor and Dr. McDonald."

CHAPTER XXX

THE GLEAM OF A KNIFE

OONAGH ROSE.

"May I go upstairs to the nursery for a minute?" she asked Barley in tones which revealed an excellent courage.

"Certainly."

She hurried out of the room. Barley signed to the policeman to accompany him and followed her. They heard him talking to the man in the hall. Dr. Hailey approached Eoghan:

"I'm certain," he declared, "that a frightful mistake has been made. We must fight this case to the last."

The young man did not answer him. But his eyes were full of bitter reproach. Duchlan, who still held his son's arm, muttered something about resignation to the will of Providence. Duchlan's face wore a look of melancholy, but the doctor saw that his eyes were bright. All he cared about was his own blood. Barley returned to the room. He wore his black-and-white dust-coat and looked a garish, incongruous figure. He walked to McDonald and handed him a large sheet of blue paper.

"It is my painful duty," he said in hurried, formal tones, "to arrest you on the charge of having wilfully murdered Miss Mary Gregor and Inspector Dundas. I warn you that anything which you say from now onwards will be used in evidence against you."

He turned away and immediately left the room again. They heard him go out to the front door and speak to someone in the waiting car, the engine of which had been kept running. Was he about to arrest Oonagh? Eoghan jumped up and would have opened the door had not Dr. Hailey reached it before him.

"For your wife's sake, Gregor."

"I wish to go to my wife."

"Don't put a further strain on her courage at this moment."

The young man stretched out his hands like a blind man, groping. "You don't understand."

The glare was still in his eyes. Dr. Hailey stood his ground, urging in conciliatory tones that Oonagh should be left free to stay away or return as she chose.

"My dear doctor, she asked me to follow her. Our child's upstairs, remember."

He opened the door as he spoke. He was about to leave the room when a young woman in a police uniform appeared in the doorway. She was gasping and her cheeks were bloodless.

"Oh, quick," she cried, "Inspector Barley has been murdered."

She caught at the jamb of the door and leaned against it. Dr. Hailey supported her.

"Where is he?"

"Outside, on the grass."

Her voice failed. He brought her to a chair beside Duchlan. McDonald had already left the room with Eoghan. He followed them and found them bending over Barley, who lay stretched out on the bank above the burn. The headlights of the car shone on the man's face. It was streaked with blood; but the blood flowed no longer. McDonald knelt and put his ear to the chest.

"Well?"

"I can hear nothing. There's no pulse."

Dr. Hailey lit his electric lamp and turned the beam on to the detective's head. An exclamation broke from his lips. Barley had been killed as Dundas had been killed.

"He's dead, McDonald."

"Yes."

"Since you were with us in the study his death disproves his theory."

The wardress who had called them, joined them. She had recovered enough to give an account of what she had seen.

"I accompanied Sergeant Jackson from Campbeltown," she explained, "because of the female prisoner. Sergeant Jackson told me to stay in the saloon till I was wanted. He left the engine running and the side-lights on. After a few minutes he came back and told me Inspector Barley had ordered him to watch the female prisoner, who had gone upstairs to say good-bye to her child. After the sergeant went away, Inspector Barley came out. I knew him because I had seen a photograph of him in that queer coat. He walked along here and stood looking up at the house. I thought he was going to try to open that window—" (She pointed to the french-window of the writing-room) "because he seemed to put his hands on it. Just as he did that he cried out and turned round. I saw his face in the moonlight. Then he seemed to stumble. He sank down. I turned up the headlights of the car as soon as I could find the switch, but by that time the man that stabbed him had escaped."

"Why do you say 'the man that stabbed him?'" Dr. Hailey demanded in hoarse tones.

"Because I saw the gleam of a knife just before he fell."

CHAPTER XXXI

THE INVISIBLE SLAYER

Dr. Hailey turned to Eoghan.

"Might I ask you to send Sergeant Jackson here?" he asked. "I fancy he's standing guard over your wife."

The young man walked away to the house. The doctor put his hand on McDonald's arm.

"What is it?"

"Who knows?"

The words were spoken in tones that carried a burden of fear.

"Dundas was killed in exactly the same way."

"Yes."

The wardress asked if she might return to the car. Dr. Hailey accompanied her, giving her his arm.

"You saw nothing beyond the flash of the knife?" he asked.

"Nothing."

"But it was dark, was it not? Sidelights are feeble."

She agreed: "Still, I saw Inspector Barley clearly enough. I'm sure I should have seen anybody else."

"If there was a knife there must have been a man to use it. Did you hear anything?"

"The engine was running, sir."

They reached the car. The doctor switched off the headlights, leaving the sidelights burning. McDonald's figure stood out clearly enough and even Barley's body was visible.

"You see," the girl remarked, "it isn't so dark..."

"There are heavy shadows close to the window."

"Yes. I thought the man had come out through the window."

Dr. Hailey walked back to McDonald and then examined the french-window. It was open.

"He must have come this way?"

McDonald did not reply. They saw Sergeant Jackson approaching. Dr. Hailey went to meet him and told him what had happened. He illuminated Barley's face that the policeman might see the nature of the injury.

"Dr. McDonald," he stated, "was with me in the smoking-room. I take it you can answer for Mrs. Gregor. This is exactly the same type of blow as that which killed Inspector Dundas." An exclamation broke from his lips. "Look. The herring scale."

He bent down and pointed to a shining scale which adhered to the scalp over the seat of injury.

"Oh, dear!"

"You know, of course, that herring scales were found on Miss Gregor's and Inspector Dundas's bodies?"

"Yes, sir."

"These three people have died by the same hand, Sergeant."

The policeman glanced about him uneasily.

"I went upstairs with Mrs. Gregor as directed by Inspector Barley," he stated in the manner of the police court. "She entered the nursery and I heard her and the nurse crying. Not wishing to intrude further than was necessary on their trouble I came downstairs to the first landing. Nobody passed me on the stairs going up or going down."

"Where was Angus, the piper?"

"The old man that opened the door?"

"Yes."

"I think he was in the hall. Leastways, he was there when I went upstairs."

They returned to the house and went to the little writing-room at the window of which Barley had been struck.

"It's possible that the murderer was waiting here," Dr. Hailey said. "If that is so he must have escaped back into the house. We know exactly where everybody in the house was at the moment of the Inspector's death—with the single exception of the piper."

"Ah."

"No, I confess I feel no confidence in that theory." He passed his hand across his brow. "Let me see, the front door was open and the wardress was in the car. She must have had a good view of the hall all the time. Ask her to come here, will you?"

Sergeant Jackson went away. The doctor walked back into the hall where McDonald was awaiting him. A moment later the wardress entered the house. He asked her if she had seen anybody in the hall at the time of the murder.

"Only the butler."

"You saw the butler?"

"Yes, sir. He was standing where you are standing now. When I saw Inspector Barley fall I called to him, but he didn't hear me. As you know I ran into the house."

"Where was the butler then?"

She pointed to the foot of the stairs.

"He was standing over there. I didn't notice much."

"You are quite sure," the doctor asked in deliberate tones, "that you saw him standing here a moment after Inspector Barley fell?"

"Quite sure. And a moment before he fell too."

"What I am really asking you is whether or not it is possible that the butler could have reached the french-window from the inside of the house, and got back to the hall again in the few minutes during which you were watching Inspector Barley."

The girl shook her head.

"Oh, no."

"It doesn't take long to go from here to that writing-room."

"I'm sure he couldn't have gone anywhere in the time."

Dr. Hailey turned to McDonald.

"Where is Gregor?"

"He's gone upstairs to his wife."

"And Duchlan?"

"He went upstairs a few minutes ago. Angus was with him."

They entered the study with Sergeant Jackson. The doctor closed the door.

"I fancy," he said, "that we can exclude Angus. It is incredible that he had any part either in the murder of Miss Gregor or in that of Inspector Dundas. This third murder is more mysterious, if that is possible, than its predecessors. I confess that I haven't the slightest idea how it was committed."

He gave the policeman a careful and detailed account of Barley's work adding:

"His own death, as you see, disproves his case. But it leaves us under the necessity of explaining how this murderer entered and left a locked room, how he entered and left a room the door and windows of which were under constant observation, finally how he killed in the open, in the presence of a witness, without betraying himself further than by a gleam of his weapon. We must explain, too, why that weapon, on each occasion, carried herring scales into the wounds inflicted by it."

Sergeant Jackson had nothing to say except that he must report immediately to headquarters, so that another detective officer might be sent. When he had gone, Dr. Hailey helped himself liberally to snuff, an indulgence which appeared greatly to soothe him.

"Three murders," he said at last, "and not a shred of evidence, not a breath of suspicion against anybody. This case, my dear McDonald, must be unique in the history of crime."

"Yes."

"I've experienced nothing like it. Think of it: that girl actually saw the weapon that killed Barley; you reached Dundas within thirty seconds of his death; Miss Gregor was shut off from the world by locks and bolts!" His eyes narrowed: "Barley was reasoning soundly enough when he said that you ought to have seen Miss Gregor's murderer drop from the window, eh?"

"Yes. But we didn't see him."

Dr. Hailey shook his head. "The wardress ought to have seen Barley's murderer, and she didn't," he said. "You ought to have seen Dundas's murderer. You didn't." He glanced about him. "This assassin kills but remains invisible."

"And moves about," McDonald added, "without leaving any trace of his movements. Presumably he descended on the flower-bed out there. But only my footmarks are found on the bed." He remained silent for a few minutes. Then he asked:

"Do you wonder, in face of all this, that stories such as that about the fishlike swimmers who come out of the deepest parts of the loch get widely believed?"

"No." The doctor started. "That's a clue that we've neglected," he declared. "I had meant to follow it up but Barley's theory made that impossible."

McDonald sighed. He had aged in these last, terrible moments and his features were haggard. He pressed his hand to his brow.

"What an immense difference there is," he remarked inconsequently, "between thinking about a thing and actually experiencing it. No wonder novelists write about what they know." He seemed to shake himself out of a lethargy. "Poor Barley," he exclaimed. "How upset he would be if he was still alive!"

"Yes."

"He was very able, I thought."

"Yes."

Again McDonald sighed. "It's queer that the detectives should have been chosen as victims. After all, too, Dundas had failed. He wasn't killed because anybody had cause to fear him."

Dr. Hailey nodded.

"I was just thinking that. Barley tried to make out that Dundas was bluffing when he said that he had failed."

"He was not. You saw him yourself. The man was at his wit's end. He told me again and again that this case was likely to ruin him with his superiors. The papers were saying nasty things at the time."

"That was my impression."

"It was everybody's impression. Even the servants here knew that no progress had been made. The fishermen, as I told you, jumped at once to the conclusion that no murderer would ever be found. They drove poor Dundas to distraction with their superstitious ideas. He wouldn't listen to them and yet he had nothing to advance against them. In this atmosphere of credulity, Dundas represented reason at bay. Why anybody should have wanted to kill him I cannot imagine."

The room was silent and the whole house seemed to have become partner in its silence. Dr. McDonald, who was standing at the fireplace, with his elbow on the mantelpiece, looked uneasy.

"Things which happen in houses frighten me more than things which happen in the open," he said. "I can say honestly that I wasn't afraid in the motor-boat."

"You're afraid now?"

The Highlander turned sharply to the window and then faced his companion again.

"Yes."

He smiled as he spoke. Dr. Hailey nodded.

"So am I."

CHAPTER XXXII

MOTHER AND SON

DR. HAILEY had reached the age when a man knows, and is inwardly convinced of his knowledge, that life is short. That is a time when imagination loses something of its power. The vigour of his apprehensiveness in face of these murders, consequently, surprised him. He was punished, it seemed, for his discounting of Highland superstition. He took more snuff and rallied his thoughts.

"I abandon the search for the method of these crimes," he told his companion. "And I shall not concern myself any more with their occasions. There is left only the strictly human business of motive. After all, it takes two to make a murder."

McDonald nodded: "One can perhaps understand the murder of Miss Gregor," he said. "But the murderer can scarcely have had any personal feeling against Dundas and Barley."

"No. Especially as Dundas had failed to discover anything and Barley had built up a strong case against innocent people. But it seems to me quite useless to trouble about that aspect of the case. I mean to concentrate on Miss Gregor. I believe I know enough now about her character to warrant certain broad conclusions." He leaned forward in his chair. "Don't forget for a single instant that Miss Gregor narrowly escaped being murdered long ago. The healed wound on her chest was inflicted by Duchlan's wife. Here is a woman who knew how to drive her sister-in-law to madness, to death, without losing her brother's regard. Duchlan isn't a fool. We may very well ask by what alchemy of persuasion he was held during all these years."

McDonald agreed fervently. "As I told you," he said. "My own impression of Miss Gregor was one of inhuman perseverance. She had a way of restating the most cruel slanders in the kindest terms, assuring you that she had forgiven faults which existed only in her own invention and pleading with you to be equally generous. When she spoke about Mrs. Eoghan in that way I wanted to tear her to pieces. She knew; she understood; and she persisted."

Eoghan entered the room. His face expressed profound relief, but he looked, nevertheless, very grave.

"Has the policeman gone?" he asked Dr. Hailey.

"Yes. He said that he must report at once."

"I've been with Oonagh in the nursery. What courage that girl has shown." Suddenly he held out his hand to Dr. Hailey. "I want to thank you for what you did to-night in the boat."

He sat down and covered his face with his hands. He exclaimed:

"Shall we ever come to the end of this horror? It's worse than death." He raised his head. "I'm a coward, I know, but I've never been so frightened before. I was frightened to come downstairs just now. I swear I looked for a murderer at every step."

He pronounced the word murderer like a personal name, a manner which neither of his companions found odd.

"That's exactly how I feel," McDonald confessed. He stretched out his arm in a vague, uncomfortable gesture. "Murder is here."

Dr. Hailey put his eyeglass in his eye.

"We had better stop this kind of thing," he declared firmly, "and get to work, to business. If murder is here, let us try to find and end it." He turned to Eoghan. "I want you to tell me," he asked in earnest tones, "exactly what your feelings were towards your aunt."

His voice recalled the young man sharply.

"She brought me up."

"That isn't what I want information about. What did you feel towards her?"

The question wrought a silence which became uncomfortable.

"One hates to speak about such things," Eoghan said at last.

"I beg that you will speak."

"I suppose I didn't feel as grateful as I ought to have felt."

"You disliked her?"

"In a way. Yes."

"Why?"

Eoghan shook his head.

"I don't know. She was very, very kind to me."

"Did you quarrel with her?"

"Yes, I did. Very often."

"About your mother?"

The young man started.

"Yes."

"Although you had never known your mother?"

"I don't remember anything about my mother."

"So that what upset you was the picture of your mother which your aunt gave you?"

Eoghan started again.

"I suppose it was."

"Children are always conventional. Other boys had mothers whom they liked; you naturally wished to believe that your mother had been as good and lovable as theirs. It seems that such an idea was not welcome in this house."

Dr. Hailey's earnestness was such as to disarm resentment.

"A child," he added, "usually goes straight to the heart of things. I take it you told your aunt that she hated your mother?"

"Yes."

"She denied that?"

"Yes."

"Did you ask your father about your mother?"

"No. I was afraid of my father." Eoghan took out his pipe and tried to fill it. "As a matter of fact I was a solitary sort of kid. I was happiest when they left me to myself in the nursery. I used to pretend that my mother came and played with me there and that we were both frightened of Aunt Mary and father. I don't know where I got the idea but I always thought of my mother and myself as the Babes in the Wood."

"Your aunt was the oppressor?"

He nodded. "My head was full of fairy tales. My mother was Red Riding Hood and Goldilocks and Cinderella in turn."

"And your aunt the wolf and the bear and the ugly sister?"

"Perhaps, yes. It was vague, you know."

"Your mother was Irish?"

"Yes."

Dr. Hailey allowed his eyeglass to drop.

"Do you possess a picture of your mother?" he asked. "Only a small photograph." He flushed as he said this.

The doctor held out his hand.

"May I look at it?"

There was a moment of silence. Eoghan had stiffened in his chair, resentful apparently of the fact that it should have been guessed that he carried his mother's photograph about with him. But his resentment was soon lost in confusion. He took a small leather case from his pocket and handed it to the doctor.

"My mother gave the photograph to Christina," he said in hurried tones which revealed how deep was his hurt that his only relic of his mother had come to him thus, at second hand.

There were two photographs in the case. One faded, inscribed to "my dear Christina", the other new, of Oonagh. Oonagh bore a likeness to Eoghan's mother that was unmistakable. Dr. Hailey handed the case back without comment.

"You're a poor man?" he asked gently.

"I am."

"Was that why you left your wife and child here, in this house?"

The question seemed to cause the young man acute distress.

"I don't think that was the only reason," he said in hesitating tones.

"May I ask your other reason?"

"I didn't realize that Oonagh would be so unhappy here. I felt that I would like her to be here, where I had lived so long."

"I see." Dr. Hailey nodded several times. "Just as you would have liked your mother to be here?"

"Perhaps that is part of the reason, although I didn't think of it at the time. I wanted Hamish to have Christina as his nurse and I knew she would never consent to leave my aunt even if my aunt consented to part with her."

"Were you gambling to make money?"

The question came abruptly. But it produced very little reaction.

"Yes."

"To have enough to set up a home of your own?"

"Yes."

"So you realized that your wife's position was hopeless in this house?"

"Yes."

"Your aunt knew that you meant to have a home of your own?"

"She may have known."

"What do you mean by that?"

"I had told her that I thought a married woman ought to have her own home." Eoghan hesitated again. "I suppose I knew that she was opposed to the idea, because I didn't develop it."

"You were afraid of her?"

"I think everybody was a little afraid of her. My aunt had a way of making people who disagreed with her feel guilty. I can't tell you how she did it, but I often noticed the effect. I think her secret lay in her absolute conviction that whatever she thought or felt must be right. She was a deeply religious woman in rather a superstitious way. Perhaps it's necessary to be a Highlander to understand exactly what that means."

The doctor nodded again.

"Without being a Highlander," he said, "I had guessed that."

"She was kind in making me an allowance. I couldn't have married Oonagh when I did but for that allowance."

"It was paid to you?"

"Oh, no. It was paid chiefly in kind. My aunt dressed Oonagh and Hamish. She contributed to their board because my father is very poor. In addition she was constantly giving little presents."

Eoghan broke off. Dr. Hailey gazed at him in silence for a few minutes.

"I want you to tell me quite frankly whether or not your wife's responses to those gifts seemed to you ungrateful," he said.

"Sometimes they did seem to me a little ungrateful."

"You told your wife that?"

"I tried to explain to her that my aunt's up-bringing and her up-bringing had been entirely different. Oonagh's people live a care-free sort of life. They have no money but they hunt and go about a great deal. Oonagh never knew what it was to be restrained till she was married. And she never knew what it was to lack money because she possessed everything she wanted. Coming here was like coming to prison. I tried to make her realize that Aunt Mary couldn't be expected to understand this and that, consequently, it wasn't fair to judge her as one might have judged a younger woman."

He passed his hand across his brow. He, too, looked haggard and weary.

"Your wife wasn't persuaded?"

"No, she wasn't. She said she would prefer one room of her own anywhere. I had made up my mind to take her away from here no matter what it cost."

"You mean, no matter whether or not your aunt refused to help you if you did?"

"Yes. Unfortunately I made a bad break in trying to get money quickly. I had to fall back on Aunt Mary."

Dr. Hailey frowned.

"Surely that was an extraordinarily foolish thing to do?" he said.

"Yes, it was. But I was getting desperate." Eoghan glanced at McDonald and then braced himself to tell the truth. "The truth is I felt I was losing Oonagh. Aunt Mary hinted that I had lost her. When she wrote me about Oonagh's flight from this house, I nearly went mad. If I could have got leave I would have rushed back here. Then I thought of blowing out my brains, so that she could be free. That moment of madness passed. I told myself it was a punishment for my not having got Oonagh a home of her own. I determined to try my luck there and then, because I felt somehow that a miracle would save me. I felt that it was impossible that Oonagh could be taken away from me. I could scarcely think. I hadn't slept for nights. All my thoughts were whirling in my brain like peas in a drum. I plunged and plunged till my friends were aghast. And I lost..."

He broke off. A bitter smile curved his lips.

"Lost. So that I hadn't a bean left in the world. I went back to my quarters and took my pistol out. There was nothing for it now but a quick ending. I think I would have shot myself if my best friend hadn't found me. He sat with me all night, listening while I talked. And I talked till dawn. Talked and talked. I told him everything, about my mother and my aunt and Oonagh. About you, McDonald. At the end he swore that Oonagh was in love with me. 'Go back to her,' he begged, 'and raise the money you owe somehow, anyhow. It'll come right in the end.'

"I was calmer and I saw what a fool and coward I had been. I asked for leave and got it."

"You meant to borrow from your aunt?"

"Yes. I had a tale ready that my friend concocted for me—about losses on shares. Aunt Mary had no objection to gambling on the Stock Exchange."

"That was business?"

"That was business."

Dr. Hailey shook his head. His eyes expressed the wonder which so many human prejudices and misunderstandings caused him.

"You had written to your wife?" he asked.

"Yes. I had to appeal to her to keep on good terms with my aunt. I know now that it was that letter which sent her to Aunt Mary's room. When I arrived here I went straight to my aunt's room. My madness had returned on the long, lonely journey across the Firth. I was terribly worked up and felt I must get an answer immediately. Her locked door and her silence convinced me that she had made up her mind to have nothing more to do with me. Naturally, murder never entered my head. I rushed off to Oonagh's bedroom."

He paused again. He shook his head sadly.

"I don't want to excuse myself in any way. But you had better know the facts. I suppose I was half-crazy with anxiety and worry and loss of sleep. I accused Oonagh of ruining me—not perhaps in those words, but she knew very well what I meant. I said I would have to leave the Army and go abroad. There was no hope now because Aunt Mary was against me. 'There was only her money,' I cried, 'between me and ruin. That's gone. I must go too.' I saw a terrible fear in Oonagh's eyes. She jumped up and tried to put her arms round my neck. She told me that you, McDonald, had offered to lend me money...'"

He drew a sharp breath.

"That was like a wound in my heart. 'Do you know,' I said very quietly, 'that I would rather rob my aunt, cheat her, murder her if need be, than touch a penny of that swine's money.' Suddenly everything seemed to go red in front of my eyes. I sprang at Oonagh. I seized her by the throat. 'Tell me,' I shouted, 'exactly what has happened between you and that man.' I believe that, for one awful moment, I was prepared to strangle her."

He covered his face with his hands. The room grew so still that the voice of the burn reached them, gurgling in its immemorial delight. Dr. Hailey saw that McDonald's face had grown stiff, like a mask.

"Yes?" the doctor asked.

"Oonagh swore that nothing had happened. She swore that her love for me had not wavered. I had the feeling that she was pleading for her life. I wasn't convinced. But the first gust of my rage had passed. I began to tremble. The tension of my nerves gave way suddenly and I broke down. She told me that she didn't care whether we were rich or poor. She said she was able to work and ready to work and that between us we would make enough to keep Hamish. I don't know why, but when she spoke in that way my troubles seemed to get less. I began to believe her."

His voice faded away. Dr. Hailey waited for a few moments and then said:

"It was your statement that you would rob or kill your aunt sooner than borrow from McDonald which made your wife fear that you had murdered her?"

"I suppose so. That, and my attack on herself. I believe I was mad for a few minutes."

"She was ready to die for you?"

Dr. Hailey's voice was low but his tones thrilled with admiration. Eoghan raised his head sharply.

"God knows," he cried, "I never was worthy of Oonagh. I never will be worthy of her."

Eoghan drove McDonald home. When they left the house Dr. Hailey went out to the place where Barley had been killed. The fear, which had oppressed him indoors, lost its power as soon as he crossed the threshold. He stood listening to the voices of night, softly-moving winds, the gurgle of the burn and, louder than these, the fall of waves on the shingle. He walked to the spot where Barley had fallen. His lamp revealed nothing. The tide was ebbing but remained high, so that the mouth of the burn resembled a tiny harbour. He descended the steep slope to the water's edge, and stood there for a few minutes. Then he climbed the bank again. It was obvious that, at the moment of his death, Barley had been concerned about the murder of Dundas, whose bedroom was immediately above the spot where he had been standing. The doctor wondered what doubt or question had sent the poor man on this fatal errand. If Barley really believed that McDonald had killed Dundas, why should he trouble about the ground under Dundas's window?

He returned to the house and went upstairs to his bedroom. The more he thought about it, the stranger this last act of Barley's seemed.

The only possible explanation seemed to be that the detective had begun to doubt his theory that McDonald had killed Dundas; but if so, why had he arrested McDonald? Barley was an honest man and as such would certainly have delayed making an arrest so long as any substantial doubt remained in his mind. But he was a practical man who would not have gone out of his way except for a reason. It seemed certain therefore that a reason why he should examine the ground under Dundas's window must have occurred to his mind or been forced upon his mind after he had effected the arrest of McDonald. The doctor frowned. How could any such reason have arisen at the time? He mastered his fears and walked along the corridor to Dundas's bedroom. Barley's body lay on the bed, under a sheet. He removed this and searched the dead man's pockets. He found nothing except a diary, in which notes of the progress of the case had been made from time to time. The last of these notes consisted of a summing-up of the evidence against McDonald and Mrs. Gregor. He replaced the book and went downstairs. Eoghan had just returned and was in the smoke-room pouring out a whisky-and-soda. The young man looked relieved when he saw the doctor.

"I heard you coming downstairs," he exclaimed, in tones which betrayed the anxiety that sound had occasioned him. He added: "When I was outside I felt all right. This house seems to have become different."

He offered Dr. Hailey a drink and poured it out.

"People can say what they like about whisky," he declared, "but there are times when it's the most sobering drink in the world."

He lit his pipe and carried his glass to an arm-chair. He sat down and put the glass on the floor beside him. The doctor told him about his difficulty in accounting for Barley's last excursion.

"Can you think of any reason," he asked, "why he should suddenly have developed a fresh interest in Dundas's murder?"

"No."

"You saw him arrest McDonald. Did it strike you that he had any doubts about the justice of what he was doing?"

"What, after the lecture he had given us? 'Pon my soul, doctor, he made out a strong case, a terrible case."

"Exactly. And then, apparently, hurried off to test its merits. It seems absurd on the face of it."

"Possibly he had some other reason for going..."

"Yes, but what other reason? Barley was a man who knew how to economize his efforts. I feel absolutely certain that it was no trivial cause that sent him along that steep bank at that moment."

Eoghan shook his head. Among so many mysteries, this one, he seemed to think, was too small to deserve notice.

"I'm sorry for Barley," he declared, "but the big fact about his death, so far as I'm concerned, is its effect on Oonagh. When I heard that last summing-up I thought..." His voice broke; he gulped the remains of his whisky. "They'd have been convicted," he concluded in hurried tones.

Dr. Hailey started slightly. He leaned forward.

"So the reason which sent Barley to Dundas's window was an essential element in their salvation?"

"As it happened, yes."

"My dear sir, it did happen. How can we say that in this case cause and effect are unrelated?"

Eoghan frowned: "You don't suggest, do you," he asked, "that McDonald or Oonagh supplied a reason for Barley's going to that place?"

"Of course not. But somebody else, who was interested in them, may have supplied that reason."

"Who? My father was here, so was I."

"The murderer perhaps."

"The murderer?"

"Angus was in the hall when Barley left this room."

Eoghan drew a sharp breath.

"What! My dear doctor, if I may say so, that's the most absurd suggestion I've ever heard in my life. If you knew Angus you would realize just how absurd it is."

"Possibly."

"If Angus murdered Barley, he murdered Dundas and my aunt also. Can you imagine him dropping from my aunt's window, or Dundas's window? How did he get into my aunt's bedroom? How did he get into Dundas's bedroom? How did he kill Barley, seeing that he remained in the hall?"

The questions came sharply, like the rattle of machine-gun fire. Dr. Hailey shook his head.

"No. I can imagine none of these things," he confessed. "But in a case like this one is driven to ask every possible and impossible question." He pressed his hand to his brow. "Surely no theory can be dismissed as ridiculous in respect of a series of events each of which is itself ridiculous to the point of utter impossibility." He helped himself to a pinch of snuff. "And so I return to Angus. He is the only person who can have spoken to Barley after Barley left this room. He is consequently the only person who can have supplied a motive for that sudden, and in the circumstances, amazing visit to the bank under Dundas's window..."

Dr. Hailey broke off. Footsteps were approaching the door.

CHAPTER XXXIII

THE SWIMMER

THERE WAS A KNOCK at the door; Eoghan jumped up and opened it. Dr. Hailey saw Angus standing with a lighted candle in his hand which shook so that the flame danced. The man's face had a sickly green complexion. Behind him, half-hidden among shadows, were two women in hats and coats.

"You'll forgive us, sir," Angus said in a shaky voice, "but we cannot sleep in this house."

He came a little way into the room as he spoke and the women also advanced. The women's faces were tear-stained and one of them, the younger, was whimpering.

"Why not?"

"Because, sir, we cannot."

"That's no reason, Angus."

The old man glanced behind him suddenly as if he expected to be stabbed in the back. His mouth opened.

"It's down in the burn, sir," he ejaculated wildly.

"What?"

"It's down in the burn, sir."

"Down in the burn? What's down in the burn?"

Again the piper glanced behind him. He tried to speak but his voice failed.

Eoghan drew himself up.

"Pull yourself together man and don't talk nonsense," he ordered.

Fear gave the old man courage of a sort. He faced his master.

"I heard It myself, sir, splashing in the burn this night before Mr. Barley was killed," he declared. "And Mary, she heard It too. And she heard It when Mr. Dundas was killed…"

"Rubbish."

"It is not rubbish, sir. To-night, after Mr. Barley was killed, Mary saw It swimming away from the mouth of the burn to the loch. And she called Flora and Flora saw It too, a black head It had, like the head of a seal, and It was swimming slowly…"

Angus began to shake. The candle he was holding swayed in its socket and fell to the floor. Eoghan snatched the candlestick out of his hand and made him sit down. He gave him a stiff glass of whisky. Then he turned to the women, who seemed to find his energy reassuring:

"What is he talking about, Mary?"

"It's the truth, sir, he's been telling you," the elder of the two girls declared. "I saw It with my own eyes, swimming out of the burn's mouth and I heard the splashing It made when It came up out of the water and went back to it… I called to Flora 'Oh, look, look,' I cried to her, and she jumped out of her bed and came to the window and there It was swimming away."

"What was?" Eoghan cried irritably.

"The thing that is covered with fish's scales…"

"Good gracious, girl, are you crazy?"

"I saw It, sir, and Flora saw It. It was black, like a seal, till It came to the place where the moon was shining on the water. And then we saw the scales on Its head shining like the body of a fish." Her voice fell. "You know, sir, that there was fish's scales…"

She broke off, overwhelmed by fresh fears. Eoghan turned to her sister.

"Well?" he asked.

"Yes, it's true, sir. I saw It as Angus and Mary has told you. Its head was shining like the body of a fish…"

"Are you trying to tell me that a fish climbed up to my aunt's bed-room?" Eoghan exclaimed in mocking tones.

"Oh, no, sir."

"That's what you're saying."

"Oh, no, sir."

"What are you saying, then?"

The girl gathered her courage. "The Evil One," she declared in shaking tones, "can take any form he wishes to take."

"Oh, so it was the Devil you saw?"

There was no answer. The young man glanced at Angus:

"What do you mean by saying that you can't stay in this house?" he demanded sternly.

"There is something wrong with this house, sir."

Fear and whisky had combined to excite the old Highlander. He rose to his feet; his eyes, lately so dim, began to flash.

"God is my witness," he cried in solemn tones. "It was into that very water that your mother threw herself."

He stopped, suddenly afraid. Dr. Hailey saw the blood rush into Eoghan's cheeks and then ebb out of them again suddenly.

"Angus, what are you saying?"

There was no answer. Both the women drew back.

"What are you saying, Angus?"

Eoghan's pale face expressed a degree of emotional tension which brought Dr. Hailey to his side.

"I shouldn't trouble..."

The young man interrupted with a quick, peremptory gesture. He took a step towards his father's servant.

"You said my mother threw herself into the burn?" he cried. "Is that true?"

Angus had recovered from the first shock of his boldness; he was still in close enough touch with the emotions which had driven him to the room and enough under the influence of the whisky he had drunk to be unwilling to recede.

"It's the truth, Mister Eoghan," he declared. He thrust out his hands. "It was these hands which helped to carry her back to this house."

"You are saying that my mother drowned herself?"

The piper bowed his head.

"Well?"

"Yes, Mister Eoghan."

A queer, wild light shone in the young man's eyes. But his features remained stiffened in immobility.

"And now you think that this... this thing which splashes and kills... is come to avenge her?"

Angus's excitement was abating. He stood gazing at his master with sorrowful eyes, already remorseful because of the pain he had inflicted. Eoghan turned to the doctor.

"Do you know anything of this?" he asked.

"Yes."

"You too. Everybody except me." He addressed the servants. "Go where you like," he cried. "I've no wish to keep you here. In this house. I've no wish to keep you in this house." He waved his hand, dismissing them. "Why should you suffer in this house for other men's crimes?"

He sank into a chair. Dr. Hailey approached him.

"May I take them into another room and ask them some questions?"

"No. Ask your questions here. Let me, as well as everybody else, be informed this time."

Eoghan's tones rang out full of bitterness and derision. He gripped the arms of his chair with fingers the joints of which blanched. His lips moved up and down on his strong teeth. Dr. Hailey signed to the servants to sit down and sat down himself. He turned to the girl Mary.

"You say you heard a splash on the night when Inspector Dundas was murdered?" he asked.

"Yes, sir. But I didn't think at the time what it might be. There were fishing-smacks lying off the burn that night, sir."

The doctor nodded.

"I know. And your brother was on one of these smacks?"

"Yes, sir."

"Your brother came here to report what he had seen that night. He didn't mention hearing any splash."

"No, sir. Please, sir, it wasn't till to-night that I thought anything about the splash." She fumbled with the buttons on her coat. "There's often splashes when the fishing is going on," she added. "If my brother heard the splash, he would think it was made by somebody on one of the other boats throwing something overboard."

"I see."

"It was not a very loud splash."

"Where were you when you heard it?"

"I was going to bed, the same as I was when I heard the first splash to-night. Flora was sleeping."

Dr. Hailey leaned forward eagerly:

"You heard two splashes to-night?" he asked.

"Yes, sir."

"Loud splashes?"

"They were not very loud, sir."

He adjusted his eyeglass.

"Why should you have troubled about them to-night when you didn't trouble before?"

"Because there were no smacks fishing to-night. I thought it was very strange that I should be hearing a splash when there was nobody to make it."

She glanced over her shoulder as she spoke.

"Did you hear anything between the splashes?"

"No, sir."

"Did you see anything?"

"No, sir."

He leaned forward again:

"Tell me exactly what you saw after the second splash."

"I have told you sir. There was something swimming out of the mouth of the burn. It had a head like a seal, that looked black till the moon shone on it. Then I saw that it was shining like the body of a fish."

She repeated the words mechanically but her voice shook.

"It was then you called your sister?"

"Yes, sir. 'What is it?' she said to me. 'I don't know what it is, Flora,' I said, 'but it's what I heard splashing in the water and maybe it's what I heard splashing when Mr. Dundas was murdered.' When I was speaking we heard voices below the window and somebody said 'He's dead' and Flora caught hold of my arm and began to cry. We went down to the kitchen and there was Angus sitting in a chair as white as death. I told him what we had heard and he said, 'Mr. Barley's been murdered, too, I heard the splashes when I was standing in the hall!'"

The girl shook her head when she finished speaking, and then again glanced behind her. She added:

"Angus was crying and saying..."

"Never mind that." Dr. Hailey's voice was stern. "How long did you watch the thing you saw swimming?"

"Until we heard the voices."

"So you didn't see where it went to?"

"No, sir, we did not."

The doctor turned to Angus.

"You were standing in the hall when you heard the first splash?" he asked in sharp tones.

"Yes, sir. I was waiting in case Duchlan might require me."

"Where was Inspector Barley at that moment?"

"He had just gone out of the house. He was standing at the front door, near to the motor-car."

"Do you think he heard it too?"

"Yes, sir, I think he did, because he walked towards the burn."

"You saw that?"

"Yes, sir."

"Did you hear anything after that, before you heard the second splash?"

Angus's face stiffened with new fear. He bent forward in his chair.

"I heard a sound, sir," he whispered, "that I know was the rattle of death."

CHAPTER XXXIV

"SOMETHING WRONG"

THE SWEAT GLEAMED on the old man's brow. He wiped it away with his hand. Eoghan rose and gave him more whisky.

"You were standing near the door of the small writing-room, were you not?" Dr. Hailey asked him.

"Yes, I was."

"And the window of the writing-room was open?"

"Yes, it was open."

"So that you were bound to hear everything that passed between Inspector Barley and his murderer?"

"I did not hear anything except the sound I have told you about."

"What you call the death-rattle?"

"It was that, sir; I have heard it before."

"The second splash followed?"

"Yes, sir. And when I heard it I knew that..."

"I don't want to hear what you knew, only what you heard and did. What did you do?"

"A young woman who was dressed like a policeman came running into the house."

"I know that. Please answer my question: What did you do yourself?"

The piper shook his head.

"I went back into the kitchen."

"Because you felt afraid?"

"Because I knew that the day..."

Again the doctor interrupted sharply. He rose and announced that he had no more questions to ask. He glanced at his watch.

"You had better go back to the kitchen. You can keep two or three candles burning till dawn," he said.

He waited until they had gone. Then he turned to Eoghan.

"At least we know now why Barley went to the place where he was killed," he said in eager tones. "The next step, clearly, is to discover the truth about this swimmer."

"I suppose so."

The young man rose and walked to the fireplace. He stood leaning with one elbow on the mantelpiece, a dejected figure.

"I understand your questions about my childhood now," he said in low tones. "I understand everything now."

"Your father was very much under your aunt's influence," Dr. Hailey said in the accents of a man who feels it incumbent on him to be special pleader.

"Yes."

"From what I could gather it was such another case as that of your wife and McDonald. The atmosphere of this place broke down your mother's nervous strength."

"You mean it broke her heart?"

The words came with extraordinary vehemence.

"No, I don't mean that. I feel sure that your father loved your mother in his own, strange way. But he was held in a kind of bondage by your aunt. He could not prevent himself from seeing and feeling what his sister willed that he should see and feel…"

Eoghan started and took a step towards his companion. His face had flushed suddenly:

"Dundas told me," he exclaimed, "that my aunt had a healed wound on her chest. A wound that must have been inflicted long ago by someone…"

His voice broke. He covered his face with his hands. But a moment later he recovered his self-control.

"You know that it was my mother who inflicted that wound?" he asked in level tones.

Dr. Hailey drew his hand across his brow. "My dear fellow," he said gently, "your mother was no longer in her right mind."

"They had driven her mad!"

"Perhaps not intentionally."

He clutched at his brow with both hands.

"Horrible, horrible," he cried. "And to think that I was taught to call my aunt 'Mother'... that I called her 'Mother'."

A strong tremor passed over his body.

"That was why my father thought that Oonagh had killed her," he added. "Because Oonagh is like my mother."

Suddenly a cry broke from his lips. He seized Dr. Hailey's arm.

"Did he, did my father make the same suggestion to Oonagh as he made to my mother? That she should drown herself?"

"He believed her to be guilty, remember."

"Oh, I might have guessed it."

"My dear fellow, as you know the evidence was very strong."

The rebuke was spoken gently but exerted its effect. Eoghan's eyes fell. He shook his head.

"Angus was right," he said, "there's something wrong with this house."

CHAPTER XXXV

THE CHILL OF DEATH

A MOMENT LATER both men started and remained tense, listening. Shuffling feet were approaching the open window of the room. Dr. Hailey walked to the window and reached it just as a tall figure in a black dressing-gown emerged from the darkness. It was Duchlan.

"Is Eoghan with you?" the old man asked.

"Yes."

"I desire to speak to him. I'll come round by the writing-room."

He gathered his gown about him and disappeared. Then they heard him crossing the hall. As he stood in the doorway the colour of his dressing-gown made painful contrast with the faded whiteness of his cheeks. His features were haggard and his long eyelids had fallen over his eyes, as if he might no longer face a world that had overthrown him. His son rose at his coming.

"Sit down, Eoghan."

The withered hand made a gesture that was a plea rather than a command. Duchlan sat down himself and leaned his head on the back of the chair exposing his stringy, vulture-like throat.

"Sleep has gone from me," he said. "To-night I cannot rest."

The slight affectation of his tone and language did not hide his agitation. Dr. Hailey glanced at Eoghan and saw that the son shared fully the distress of the father.

"You have no idea, I suppose," Duchlan asked the doctor, "how this man Barley met his death?"

"None."

"These murders are inexplicable, is it not so?"

"We have not yet discovered the explanation of them."

The long eyelids closed.

"You will not discover any explanation. And if you go on seeking, sorrow will be added to sorrow."

Duchlan's fingers began to beat on the arms of his chair. The muscles round his mouth were twitching.

"God is just," he declared in tones of awe. He turned to his son. "I feel that my end is approaching; before it comes there is something that I must tell you."

He raised himself in his chair as he spoke. Eoghan recoiled.

"I know it already," he said.

"That's impossible."

"Why and how my mother met her death."

Silence filled the room. The song of the burn, now in the ebb became a deep crooning like a mother's song to her babe, came up to them.

"Your mother," Duchlan said at last, "died of diphtheria."

"You know, sir, that my mother drowned herself in the burn?"

The old man did not flinch.

"That is the other part of the truth."

"What do you mean?"

"There was an epidemic of diphtheria, during which many children died, Christina's son among them. Your mother insisted on helping with the nursing and contracted the disease herself. As you know, diphtheria sometimes attacks the brain..." Duchlan sighed deeply. "What followed, therefore, was due to the promptings of a disordered mind."

He paused. His breathing had become laboured. Eoghan remained in a posture of tense expectancy.

"But that is not all. Far be it from me at such an hour as this to hide from you any longer the burden of guilt which lies upon my heart. If it was disease which finally wrought your mother's death, there were other causes, operating through weeks and months of sorrow, which led up to that tragedy. I am here to confess that my own weakness was the chief of these causes."

"Please don't go on, father."

Duchlan raised his hand.

"I beg of you to hear me." He tugged at the neck of his gown, opening it wider. "From my childhood, I suffered a weakness of character which I found it impossible to overcome. I was timid when I would have been brave, fearful when resolution was required of me. It was my calamity that the qualities I lacked were possessed in fullest measure by my sister, your Aunt Mary. In consequence, she acquired, from the beginning, a dominion over me which I was unable to resist. She is dead; that dominion lives so that now I feel powerless to conduct my life without her. Your mother possessed an excellent strength of mind, but her strength was inferior to that of my sister; our marriage consequently was doomed."

He paused. His fingers continued their ceaseless drumming.

"When she was eighteen your aunt became engaged to be married to an Englishman and I felt myself suddenly and terribly alone. I went to stay with an old friend in Dublin and there I met your mother."

The old man sighed deeply.

"She was a lovely girl, as lovely as Oonagh. Her people had a small place in the west, by the sea. A lonely, desolate place where the bogs stretched for miles like a desert under the wild skies. She had been brought up there and had lived free of all restraint with her dogs and horses. The sea was in her eyes, and the love of the sea was in her heart. I felt as I looked at her that she had discovered the secret which, all my life, I had been seeking, namely, release from spiritual bondage. If I could only capture this wild, wonderful creature, she would teach me the way of her strength and courage and deliver me from my fear. I tried to tell her what was in my heart and I saw that she pitied me. It seemed so easy, in that land of hers, to possess one's own soul and live out one's dream. We fell in love with each other…"

He broke off. They saw a shiver pass over his body.

"She called me her 'dour Scotsman' and promised to make a wild Irishman of me. I stayed on at her home, week after week, forgetting everything but my love of her. This place and its associations became a dim memory, like the evening memory of a distressful dream. We needn't, I thought, spend very much of our time at Duchlan. I can let the place and we can come and live in Ireland."

His voice had developed a rhythmic quality. As he bent and swayed in his chair he looked, Dr. Hailey thought, like some old bard singing of times long buried in the earth's womb. Tears had gathered in his eyes; they crept down his cheeks, going from wrinkle to wrinkle.

"That was treason; because my father had vowed that no stranger should ever dwell in Duchlan. But even my father had lost his power over me in that wilderness. I had fallen under the spell of your mother's folk, who cared nothing for the ideas which live in this place. Your grandfather and your grandmother, your uncles and aunts were all of the same way of thinking. They belonged to life, to the present, to the Nature which surrounded and nourished them, and to each other. They were as generous as they were brave and their hospitality had no end. It never occurred to one of them to ask questions and whatever I said about myself was accepted as the whole truth. I ceased to feel lonely. I began to be thankful that my sister had got engaged. In other words, I surrendered myself completely to your mother's influence.

"We were married a few months later. When we returned from our honeymoon your aunt's engagement had been broken off. She begged that she might be allowed to remain here for a few months until she was able to find a home elsewhere. I will not hide from you that, when I yielded to that request, I knew that I was making a sacrifice of your mother."

He sighed again. "And so it proved. My sister had broken off her engagement, as she confessed to me, because she could neither endure to leave this place nor to enter another family. Naturally, your mother resented her intrusion on our married life and wished to be quit of her. A duel began between them, of which I was the helpless and unwilling spectator. Both appealed to me daily. Soon, very soon, the strongest character asserted itself.

"Your mother had a quick temper but with it a fatal generosity. Mary possessed neither the one nor the other. I used to marvel at the way in which she achieved her ends. She was as sleepless as a spider and as calculating. Everywhere, webs, webs, webs, until her victims were bound with gossamer that was stronger than steel. Violence could gain nothing against that subtlety."

He leaned forward. His voice grew louder.

"For I was violent too; it is the way of the weak. I loved your mother and sometimes I dared to rebel. Sometimes I stormed and raged against the tyranny which threatened us; it was like the rage of a young child against the nurse who takes away its playthings. Then you were born."

Duchlan's eyes closed again. He remained silent for a few minutes, motionless, like a figure carved out of old ivory. Then his fingers began to drum once more on the carved wood.

"Your birth," he continued, "made everything much worse because you are the heir. Your mother felt that you belonged to her; your aunt that you belonged to the Gregors. Your aunt was determined to take you away from your mother and in addition she wanted you because she had no child of her own. Thus all the furies which dwell in the hearts of women were unleashed." He made a despairing gesture. "The tide of hatred flowed and submerged me. I felt that my marriage was drifting to utter catastrophe and yet I possessed no power to save it. Your mother grew to hate and then to despise me. Her natural goodness was turned to a scorn that stung without stimulating. One day she threatened to leave me unless I ordered your aunt out of my house. Her anger and bitterness were terrible and for the moment they prevailed. I told my sister that a new arrangement was imperatively necessary. She took to her bed and became ill so that the doctor had to be summoned. He told me that she was very ill and that, if I persisted in my plan to make her leave her home, he would not be responsible for the consequences. By that time your mother's anger had cooled and her generosity had asserted itself. Your aunt stayed; our marriage was wrecked."

He held up his hand, forbidding interruption.

"At the moment when my wife's body was carried into this room a chill of death struck my heart. I had heard the splash of her fall into the water. They laid her body on that couch." He pointed to the piece of furniture and continued to keep his finger stretched towards it. "There were little pools of water on the floor and they grew bigger and became joined to each other. Water was running in thin streams from her hair and from her elbows, because they had crossed her arms on her breast. Angus and the men who had helped him to carry her up from the burn went away and left me here, alone with her. But I felt nothing... nothing but curiosity to watch the little streams and pools of water. I counted them; there were eleven streams and seven pools. Eleven and seven. Then I thought about the last moments we had spent together the night before, after the wounding of your aunt, and I repeated aloud what I had said to her: 'You have killed my sister, you have ruined my life and my son's life. There is only one thing left for you to do. It will be high tide at...' Well, she had done it. But it seemed unreal and far away like something one has read about long ago and forgotten and remembered again. So I called to her to open her eyes..."

His head shook, nodding assent, perhaps, to some remote voice of his spirit.

"I thought: is she dead? And I kept repeating that word, 'Dead', over and over again so as to recall the meaning of it. But it had no meaning. Then it occurred to me, suddenly, that all the difficulties and troubles of my life were ended. If Mary got well, and the doctor expected her to get well, because the knife had missed her heart, we should have the house to ourselves again, as in the old days. You see, I had given my mind and my will wholly to my sister. It was with her eyes that I was looking at my wife's dead face." He plucked again at the neck of his gown. "Now I have no eyes but hers, for you, for this house, for our family. When I thought that Oonagh was a partner in Mary's death I spoke the same words to her as I had spoken to your mother: 'You have killed my sister... It will be high tide...'"

"Stop, father!"

Eoghan had jumped to his feet. He stood with quivering features and clenched fists. The old man bowed his head.

"I ask your forgiveness."

"Why should you tell me this? Why should you tell me this?"

Dr. Hailey saw a shudder pass over Duchlan's body. The old man faced his son.

"To give you back to your mother," he said simply. "That is all that is left to me now; to give you back to your mother."

Duchlan rose as he spoke. Again he pointed to the couch.

"I killed your mother; I would have killed your wife. What are these other crimes compared to my crime?"

He walked to the couch and stood gazing down at it as if he saw his wife once more as he had seen her with the water dripping from her hair and her elbows. But his face expressed nothing. He had spoken the truth when he said that the chill of death was entered into his spirit. Eoghan followed him with horrified eyes until he left the room.

CHAPTER XXXVI

THE MASK

DR. HAILEY put his hand on Eoghan's shoulder.

"Have pity," he said gently.

"Pity?"

The young man spoke the word mechanically as if its meaning had escaped him. He continued to gaze at the door through which his father had just passed.

"For a mind in torment."

Eoghan turned suddenly and faced the doctor.

"You call that a mind in torment?" he asked bitterly. He strode to the fireplace and stood looking down into the empty grate. Dr. Hailey followed him.

"Men whose faces have been dreadfully disfigured," he said, "are condemned to hide them behind a mask. It is the same when the disfigurement is spiritual."

"What do you mean?"

"When your father yielded his will to your aunt, he condemned himself to a punishment that is exacted in shame and despair. The only refuge of the weak is another's strength. To escape from the hell of his own thoughts and feelings it was necessary that he should adopt completely and blindly those of your aunt. Moral cowardice has used that mask from the beginning. But the face behind the mask still lives."

"I see."

"Your mother found something to love in that weakness, remember. She allowed your aunt to stay here. She was even ready, perhaps, to endure the bitterness of that arrangement when illness deprived her, momentarily, of her reason. I feel sure she would have wished that you should not be less generous and forgiving. Your father is stricken because you had nothing to say to him. As you heard, he looks on these murders as supernatural occurrences, the expression of Heaven's anger against himself. The man is utterly forsaken."

Dr. Hailey spoke in very gentle tones which were free of any suggestion of reproof. He added:

"At least he didn't spare himself."

Eoghan stood erect.

"Thank you," he said. "I'll go to him."

He strode out of the room. When he had gone, Dr. Hailey sat down and helped himself to snuff. He remained for some minutes with his eyes closed and then rose to his feet. He left the room and ascended the stairs, going as quietly as possible. When he reached the first landing he stood, listening. The house was silent. He began the second ascent, pausing every few steps. As he neared the top of the stairs he crouched down suddenly. A faint sound of voices had reached his ears.

He waited for a few minutes and then completed his ascent. He could hear the voices distinctly now. They came from the nursery and he recognized Oonagh's clear, well-bred accents. He hesitated for a moment and then decided to continue the enterprise which had brought him upstairs. He crossed the narrow landing and put his hand on the door of the pantry from the window of which he and Barley had examined the spike in the wall above Miss Gregor's bedroom. He turned the handle and opened the door. At the same moment the nursery door was thrown open by Oonagh. She uttered a little cry of dismay and drew back a step. Then she recognized him.

"Dr. Hailey! I... I thought it was..."

She broke off and came towards him. He saw that she looked pale and strained but there was a new light of happiness in her eyes.

"Hamish has been rather restless," she said. "Christina and I have been trying to get him to sleep."

She led him into the nursery as she spoke. In spite of the heat of the weather there was a peep of fire burning in the grate and on this a kettle simmered. The room possessed an air of repose which affected him the more graciously in that it contrasted in so sharp a manner with the unease of the room he had just quitted. He walked to the cot and stood for a moment looking down at the sleeping child. Its small face had that flower-like quality which is childhood's exclusive possession; its features expressed an exquisite gentleness. Christina joined him at the cot. She pointed to a number of small red spots on the child's brow.

"I think he's had a little touch of the nettle rash," she said in her soft accents.

"Yes. That's the real origin of his trouble."

Oonagh was standing at the fire.

"You can't think," she exclaimed, "what a relief to me your view of his case has been. That was the one bright spot in all our troubles."

She crossed the room as she spoke.

"Is there any light on the death of that poor man?"

"None." Dr. Hailey polished his eyeglass between his finger and thumb. "Were you here when his death occurred?" he asked in earnest tones.

"Yes."

"The window was open?"

She started and then nodded assent.

"Did you hear anything?"

There was a moment of silence.

"It's strange but I thought I heard a splash... two splashes." She spoke with hesitation as if the sounds had troubled her.

"Did you look out of the window?"

Again he saw her start.

"Yes, I did, after I heard the second splash." A note of fear crept into her voice. "The moon was shining on the water where the burn flows into the loch. I saw a black thing, like a seal's head, swimming down the burn, but when the moon struck it it flashed and glimmered."

"Like a fish's body?"

"Exactly like that."

The doctor put his eyeglass into his eye.

"Other people saw the same object," he stated in deliberate tones. "And put their own interpretations on it. What did you think it was?"

"I couldn't think what it was."

Dr. Hailey turned to the nurse.

"Did you see it?"

"No, sir, I was getting the baby's milk at the time. But Mrs. Gregor told me about it."

"Has anything of the sort ever been seen here before?"

"Not that I've ever heard, sir."

Christina's hands were locked together. She kept wringing them. A lively fear had come into her eyes.

"The fishermen do say," she exclaimed in awe-struck tones, "that sometimes there be them that splashes round their boats at night."

"Yes?"

"They will be afraid when they hear the splashing..."

Dr. Hailey shrugged his shoulders.

"Loch Fyne is full of porpoises, you know," he said. "A school of porpoises can make a lot of noise."

The old woman did not answer. She continued to wring her hands and shake her head. He stood looking at her for a moment. His eyeglass fell.

"One of the maids says that she heard a splash on the night when Inspector Dundas was killed. Did you hear anything that night?"

"No, sir."

"The windows were open on that night also?"

Christina assented. "I've kept them open," she said, "ever since this spell of heat began."

Dr. Hailey walked to the window and stood looking out. The moon had travelled far since the time of Barley's death but its light still fell on the water in intermittent gleams as clouds, newly come from the west, moved across its face.

"One ought to hear a splash from any of these windows," he commented in tones which seemed to carry a rebuke. He turned back to face the occupants of the room. "The weather seems to be breaking. I thought this heat could not last much longer."

Again he surveyed the water. His face was troubled as if some important decision was toward in his mind. It seemed that he was in doubt how to explain himself because he frowned several times. At last he left the window and returned to Oonagh.

"That splash may be more important than you suppose," he said in guarded tones. "I feel that we ought to know everything about it that can possibly be known."

He paused. The girl's clear eyes looked into his. She shook her head.

"I felt dreadfully afraid," she confessed, "when I heard the splashes. It was a strange, eerie sound at that hour of the night. But perhaps my nerves were overwrought because of what was happening."

She made a little gesture of apology for herself, adding: "When one knows there is a policeman waiting at the foot of the stairs."

"The other people who heard the splashes were terrified so that they wanted to leave the house."

She shook her head again. "I think I would have felt the same wish myself in other circumstances." He saw her glance at the cot as she spoke. Her eyes filled with tears and she turned away.

"You can help me," he told her gently, "by listening again during the next few minutes. I'm going downstairs to carry out an experiment, the results of which may or may not clear up this horrible business." He paused and considered for a few moments. "The points I wish to determine," he resumed, "are these: can you hear doors and windows being opened; can you hear every splash at the mouth of the burn; are small objects on the surface of the water clearly visible from these windows? I won't explain myself further because I want your judgement to be unbiased, but I will tell you that I mean to go out of the house by the french-windows in the little writing-room. I shall cough rather loudly just before I come out of the room and I wish specially that you will listen for this cough. A splash will follow, perhaps several splashes."

He watched Oonagh closely as he outlined this programme. She showed no sign of any deeper interest in it than the facts warranted.

"There is one other point. I want these observations made in this room. Can I therefore ask you to remain in this room until I come back?"

He had emphasized the words "in this room" each time that he spoke them. He saw a look of surprise in her face but she offered no comment.

"I shall not leave this room," she said, "until you come back. Do you wish me to stand here or beside the window?"

"Here at first. If you hear a splash go to the window at once and watch the mouth of the burn."

He walked to the door, treading softly so as not to disturb the child. At the door he turned again.

"Remember," he said in a loud whisper. "You will hear a cough just before I come out of the french-window. I will leave this door ajar. So you may hear the cough either through the door, that is through the inside of the house, or through the window, that is from the outside. Try to discriminate between these two ways."

He descended the stairs to the ground floor. The only illumination of the hall came from the study which remained empty. He listened and heard voices in the gun-room behind the writing-room. He knocked on the door of this room and was invited by Duchlan's shrill voice to enter.

Duchlan, still in his dressing-gown, was seated in an arm-chair, the only chair in the room. His son stood beside him and the old man had his hand on Eoghan's arm. There was a look of such happiness on Duchlan's face as caused the doctor to regret that he had intruded. But the old man showed no resentment at his coming.

"Forgive me," Dr. Hailey said, "but at last there is a gleam of light. I am anxious to act quickly in case it should be extinguished and I need help."

Both men stiffened to hear him; he saw anxiety in both their faces.

"A gleam of light." Duchlan repeated in the tones of a prisoner who has abandoned hope and now hears that hope remains.

"That, or an illusion, perhaps. I won't raise false hopes by entering into any details, and besides, time is short." He glanced at the window as he spoke. The deep, transparent blue of the night sky was unchanged in colour but the outlines of the clouds had become sharper. He turned to Eoghan. "Will you come with me?"

"Of course."

"What about me?" Duchlan asked.

"We will report to you at the earliest moment."

They left the old man with his happiness and crossed the hall to the study. Dr. Hailey shut the door.

"I am about to keep an appointment," he stated. "May I ask that, if you agree to accompany me, you will obey implicitly any directions I may give you, and not ask any questions?"

"With whom is the appointment?"

The doctor hesitated. Then a slight frown gathered on his brow.

"With murder," he declared in laconic tones.

CHAPTER XXXVII

THE SWIMMER RETURNS

"I WANT YOU to obtain a reel of black cotton and some pins." Dr. Hailey spoke sharply. "You must find them downstairs, possibly in the servants' quarters. On no account are you to set foot on the stairs."

Eoghan did not try to hide his surprise, but his Army training instantly discounted it.

"Very well."

He left the room. The doctor followed him and went to the little apartment opening off the hall, where hats and coats were hung. He took his own hat from its peg and carried it into the study. He glanced out anxiously at the night and then looked at his watch. The outlines of the trees below the window were dimly visible. After about five minutes Eoghan returned with the thread and pins. He handed them to his companion without comment.

"Wait here," Dr. Hailey told him. He left the room, closing the door gently behind him. When he returned he was wearing an overcoat and carried a second overcoat over his arm.

"Put this on, please," he ordered Eoghan, "and turn up the collar, then follow me."

He extinguished the lamp and climbed out of the window on to the bed of earth on which McDonald's footprint had been discovered. He glanced up as he did so at the window of Miss Gregor's room, shut now, and lighted by the moon. The gravel crunched under his feet and he stood still, in sudden hesitation. When Eoghan joined him he urged that the utmost care was necessary to avoid noise.

"The slightest sound may betray us. Ears are strained at this moment to catch the slightest sound."

They crossed the gravel path, passing the front door. When they reached the grass bank the doctor told his companion to lie down and remain without moving. He threw himself on the grass as he spoke and crept forward towards the window of the writing-room. Eoghan lost sight of him among the shadows and then fancied that he could see him again near the window; but a moment later he gave up this idea. The air was still heavy with heat and felt oppressive and damp. He thought that it was true that the darkest hour comes before the dawn, perhaps the eeriest hour also, since the clear lines of night are blurred by mists and shadows. What had happened to the doctor and what was he doing?

A cough, short and dry, came from the darkness. Then Dr. Hailey's voice rang out in accents that vibrated with fear and distress:

"Don't come out!"

There was a gleam, as of steel, Eoghan thought he heard a thudding sound. Then something that went heavily came galloping down the bank towards the place where he lay. He wiped his brow with his hand as it passed. There was a splash in the water below. He turned and looked down at the water.

A black object, like a seal, was swimming quickly out to sea. He felt sure that it was a seal.

The moonlight touched it. It gleamed.

Eoghan wiped his brow again. He could hear his heart thumping against his ribs.

A groan, low and piteous, came to him from the direction of the french-windows. He heard his name pronounced in feeble tones.

CHAPTER XXXVIII

THE FACE IN THE WATER

EOGHAN ROSE and ran to the window. As he approached it he saw the large form of Dr. Hailey bending over someone who lay on the ground on the spot where Inspector Barley had fallen. The doctor lit an electric lamp and illuminated the face of the man. A cry broke from Eoghan's lips. It was his father.

The old man spoke his name again. He threw himself on his knees beside him.

"Here I am, father—Eoghan."

The long withered eyelids opened wide. A smile of wonderful contentment appeared on the thin lips.

"Give me your hand..."

Eoghan took his father's hands in his own. He bent and kissed the old man on the brow.

"I'm killed, boy..." A fresh groan broke from Duchlan's lips and his features became convulsed. But the spasm of pain passed. "He struck me on the head... as he struck the policeman." He broke off, gasping for breath. Dr. Hailey bent forward.

"Please don't try to talk, sir, it's only wasting your strength."

Duchlan shook his head. His grip of his son's hands tightened.

"It was my fault," he whispered, "from the beginning. But you've forgiven me. Tell me again, Eoghan, boy, that you've forgiven me?"

"Yes, father."

He smiled again. His face, Dr. Hailey thought, looked younger. But suddenly they saw the light in his eyes grow dim. A cold rigidity spread over his features, fixing them in an expressionless stare. He moved convulsively, like a man who tries to break strong bonds; he managed to raise himself on his elbow.

"This must be death..."

Suddenly his voice rang out clear and full of passion. He pronounced the name "Kathleen". A moment later he was dead in Eoghan's arms. Dr. Hailey opened his dressing-gown and put his ear to his chest.

"He's dead."

"What happened, doctor? What is this frightful thing?"

Eoghan's voice was hoarse with emotion.

"Your father came out through the window. I wasn't able to warn him in time. He came on in spite of my shout."

The young man's breath had become laboured. He bent his head.

"It passed close to me going down to the burn. If I hadn't promised you to obey orders I could have prevented It. I saw It swimming away."

His voice faded in horror.

"We must carry him into the house," the doctor said. "Unhappily there's something that remains to do. You must prepare your courage."

"What do you mean?"

"Come—"

As he spoke Dr. Hailey passed his hands under the old man's body and after a moment of hesitation Eoghan followed his example. They lifted the body and began to walk slowly towards the french-window.

"We had better take him to the study."

They moved very slowly in the darkness and several minutes elapsed before they found the couch. As they laid Duchlan on this bed, on which his wife had been laid, a sob broke from Eoghan's lips. Dr. Hailey struck a match to light the lamp. He saw the young man kneeling beside the couch, with his arms outstretched over his father's body.

The sound of a thud, dull, sickening, came to them through the open door.

Eoghan jumped to his feet.

"What was that?"

He strode out into the hall and stood listening. Dr. Hailey joined him. The sound of heavy breathing came to them through the open window of the writing-room. The doctor lit his torch. Suddenly a shrill cry rang out. It was followed by a splash. Eoghan gripped his companion's arm so that the beam of the torch was turned on to his face. His face was bloodless and his brow shone with sweat.

"There it is again."

They rushed to the french-window. The first breathing of dawn showed them the mouth of the burn, black as old pewter. The surface of the water was troubled though no wind blew.

They ran down the bank to the water's edge. The troubling had ceased and the surface of the little estuary lay, mirror-like, under the lightening sky. Dr. Hailey plunged into the water, which reached above his waist, and then bent down. Eoghan saw a white object, which he recognized suddenly as a human face, emerge from the water.

CHAPTER XXXIX

DR. HAILEY EXPLAINS

AN HOUR LATER Dr. McDonald came limping into the study where Oonagh, Eoghan, and Dr. Hailey awaited him. He sat down and arranged his wooden leg.

"Well?" Dr. Hailey asked.

"I agree with you. Duchlan was murdered exactly as Dundas and Barley were murdered. Christina died from drowning but her arm had been broken. There are herring scales on Duchlan's wound and on one of Christina's hands." McDonald's face expressed a lively horror. He added: "And still we remain without an explanation."

"I don't think so. I know the explanation." Dr. Hailey put his eyeglass in his eye as he spoke. He turned to Eoghan: "The first gleam of light," he said, "came when your father told me that during the epidemic of diphtheria here your mother nursed Christina's son through his last illness and so gave her life for the boy. I know the Highland character. Gratitude is one of its strongest elements."

He rose and stood in front of the fire.

"Christina from that hour, I feel sure, gave you all the mother-love which had belonged to her son and, in addition, all the kindness which your mother's sacrifice had awakened in her warm heart."

"She did," Eoghan exclaimed. "She was my real mother."

There were tears in his eyes. He brushed them hastily aside.

"For which reason her feelings towards your aunt cannot have been other than bitterly hostile. In fact she admitted to me that they were hostile. She knew to what distresses your aunt had subjected your father's bride, she knew that your mother's happiness had been ruined by a process of exhaustion against which no happiness could be proof and she knew that, in a sense, at any rate, Miss Gregor was directly responsible for your mother's death." The doctor leaned forward. "But she was a Highland woman, a member of this household, in whose faithful eyes duty to your father, her master and chief, overshadowed every other duty. Since your aunt was Duchlan's sister, she must continue to serve her.

"That attitude endured right through your childhood, till your marriage. Christina's behaviour towards your aunt was respectful and solicitous until the illness of your little son began. But Hamish's illness effected a great change…"

The doctor broke off. He readjusted his eyeglass.

"That illness was undoubtedly most alarming both to nurse and mother. To a superstitious mind, and Christina shared the mental outlook of her race, fits, even the mildest and least serious fits, always seem to partake of the supernatural. It is for that reason that epileptic children are called 'fey' in so many country villages all the world over. Christina undoubtedly felt that some evil influence was at work. She did not need to look far in order to discover it. Your aunt was already behaving towards your wife as she had behaved towards your mother. The tragedy of your father's marriage was being re-enacted before the eyes of the woman who loved you as only a mother can love. To the strong emotions of motherhood was added, therefore, that fear which haunts superstitious minds and, sooner or later, compels them to action. Your aunt, in Christina's eyes, was become the deadly enemy of the Duchlan family in that she was secretly, by evil influences, destroying the health of its youngest heir, possibly even threatening his life. Thus the reason which had existed for serving your aunt faithfully was changed into a reason for opposing her by every means. Motherhood and loyalty to this family were joined against the enemy of both."

Dr. Hailey allowed his eyeglass to drop. It touched one of the buttons of his waistcoat and the sound struck sharply on the silence which filled the room.

"Christina told me," Oonagh said, "that she was sure some evil influence was at work against Hamish's health. She said the child would not recover until that influence was destroyed."

"Exactly."

"She repeated it again and again."

Dr. Hailey readjusted his eyeglass.

"Bearing this in mind, let us come to the night of Miss Gregor's death. That event had been preceded by two important happenings, namely, your flight from this house, Mrs. Gregor, and the discovery of your meetings with Dr. McDonald on the shore. In the first instance Christina was sent as an ambassador to bring you home and from what you, McDonald, told me I conclude that, though Christina exonerated her young mistress from all blame, she was less ready to pardon you. You told me that she quoted the words: 'Whom God hath joined together...'"

"She did, yes, as she was leaving the house."

"Note how jealous she was of the Duchlan honour. That jealousy was certainly re-awakened when she learned about the meetings on the shore. Hers was not a mind, I think, able to understand the need of asking advice in a difficulty. Her own feelings compelled her so powerfully that she could not imagine the state of mind in which such compulsion is absent." He turned to Eoghan. "Consequently she foresaw the immediate disruption of your marriage if news of what was afoot reached you. Here again the danger was your aunt." Oonagh had flushed hotly. She put her hand on her husband's hand.

"Christina told me," she stated, "that she was very much afraid of Eoghan's return, because his aunt was going to poison his mind."

"Did she urge you to see as little as possible of Dr. McDonald?"

"Yes. I told her Eoghan was incapable of misunderstanding."

"Which she did not believe?"

"Which she did not believe."

Dr. Hailey nodded. "Very well, now we come down to the night of the murder. The important fact to grasp is that, on that night, you, Mrs. Gregor, had gone early to bed after a severe quarrel with your aunt. But you were roused because Hamish was ill again. You put on a blue dressing-gown to go to the nursery. Incidentally you received a letter from your husband in which he told you of his financial loss and begged you to keep on good terms with Miss Gregor. This letter was the cause of your going downstairs, while Dr. McDonald was busy with Hamish, to report to Miss Gregor on the boy's condition. Christina was coming out of Miss Gregor's bedroom candle in hand. As soon as she saw you your aunt showed the liveliest terror and drove you from the room, locking the door behind you."

He glanced at Oonagh for confirmation. She nodded.

"Yes."

"Why should Miss Gregor have reacted in that extraordinary way? I believe the answer is that, standing in the dim candlelight, in your blue gown, you looked exactly like Eoghan's mother. So, years before, Eoghan's mother had come into that room, knife in hand, and with the light of a feverish insanity in her eyes."

Dr. Hailey's voice fell to a whisper.

"That insanity, the result of a fatal attack of diphtheria, had momentarily deprived its victim of her self-control, Miss Gregor was stabbed over the heart and severely wounded. The memory of that hour remained, quick and terrible, in her spirit. Panic seized her. In her panic she locked herself in, closing the windows as well as the door." He turned to McDonald: "You heard the windows being shut?"

"I did."

"She was therefore shut up in her bedroom. There is no question that the door was locked. Now consider the case of Inspector Dundas. That poor man made one important discovery, namely, that you, Captain Gregor, had just suffered a heavy loss at cards and must, if possible, obtain money from your aunt. I take it that you told your wife that Dundas had learned of this necessity?"

"Yes, I did."

"Where did you tell her?"

Eoghan looked surprised. He frowned and then his brow cleared.

"I remember. I told her one night while we were sitting in the nursery."

"Was Christina present in the room?"

"Yes, she was. I remember it all quite distinctly now. Christina said she didn't trust Dundas who, she was sure, would give us great trouble. She had suffered cross-examination at his hands, and in addition he had dared to order her about like a servant."

"I see. Dundas threatened your safety. There could be no greater crime in Christina's eyes. Barley's case resembled that of Dundas except that the threat in this instance was to your wife." Dr. Hailey turned to Oonagh. "Was Christina in the nursery when you heard the splashes and saw the black, shining object swimming down the burn?"

"No, she wasn't. She'd gone into the pantry..."

"Was she in the nursery when Dundas was killed? You were there then, if you remember, awaiting my coming to see Hamish?"

Oonagh started; fear dawned in her eyes.

"She was going back and forwards to the pantry that night too," she said.

The eyeglass fell. Dr. Hailey sat down and took out his snuff-box.

"In each of these wounds, as you know, one or more herring scales have been found. Throughout this investigation, therefore, efforts have been made to find a weapon likely to bear such scales. They have been unsuccessful. No weapon was found in Miss Gregor's room; none in Dundas's room; none near Barley's body, though the wardress in the car says she saw the gleam of steel." He addressed Eoghan. "You say you saw the gleam of steel when your father was struck down?"

"I'm certain I saw it."

"Yet there was no weapon in that case either?"

The young man shook his head.

"No."

"Your aunt's wound was of a terribly severe nature but it was not mortal. In these circumstances one would have expected very severe bleeding. In fact there was very little bleeding. Only two explanations are possible; either she died of shock the moment she was wounded or the weapon remained impacted in the wound. She did not die the moment she was wounded because there is a trail of blood from the window to the bed. Nobody escaped from her room. That is certain, not only because your wife and McDonald were in the room below when the windows were shut and had a clear view of the only place to which an escaping murderer could descend but also because the windows were bolted on the inside. We arrive at the apparently absurd conclusion that the weapon which killed your aunt vanished away as soon as that lady's heart had stopped beating, that is to say as soon as her blood had ceased to flow."

He took a pinch of snuff.

"In each case the weapon vanished after the blow had been struck. Come back to the murder of the lady. You, Mrs. Gregor, were the last person who saw her alive. She was then stricken with panic. I imagine that her first impulse was to return to bed and hide there. But soon the open windows attracted her notice. What if an attack was made from that direction? Panic does not reason; it acts. She jumped up and shut one of the windows. She was about to shut the other when she heard, far away, the sound of Captain Gregor's motor-boat. That sound, with its promise of safety and triumph, reassured her. She leaned out of the window the better to hear it. As she leaned there was a crash above her and she was wounded. She staggered back, shocked and panic-stricken. One arm was helpless but she managed to close and bolt the window with the other. She staggered across to her bed and sank down... Her heart stopped..."

The doctor leaned forward.

"You all know how much importance Barley attached to that spike in the wall above Miss Gregor's window. He observed, from the pantry on the top floor, that the rust on the spike had been rubbed away at one place and concluded that a rope had been used. There is another explanation. The weapon which struck Miss Gregor as she leaned out of the window may have struck the spike in the course of its descent. And that, in fact, is what happened."

He rose and resumed his place in front of the fire.

"When Miss Gregor leaned out of her window, Christina, in the pantry above, saw her. The sound of the motor-boat reached Christina's ears also. That faithful, superstitious woman heard in the sound the doom of all those she loved, of you Captain Gregor, of you Mrs. Gregor, of your child. Of Duchlan himself. In a few minutes Miss Gregor's evil influence would be exerted to blast your marriage as it had been exerted to blast your father's marriage, as it was being exerted to destroy your son's health."

Dr. Hailey paused and then added in quiet tones.

"At the moment when she heard the sound of the motor-boat, Christina was engaged in chipping ice from a large block to refill the ice-bag on Hamish's brow."

CHAPTER XL

THE END

THE SILENCE in the room was broken by the first clear notes of a blackbird. A moment later the chorus of the birds, that immemorial song of the dawn, broke on their ears. A look of great gentleness appeared on Dr. Hailey's face.

"Christina in that moment," he said, "heard the call of her gods to action. She seized the block of ice and dropped it out of the window. It struck the spike and was shattered into several jagged daggers. One of these struck Miss Gregor and was wedged firmly into the wound it had inflicted. In this hot weather it soon melted; she was dead before that occurred.

"The effect on Christina was exactly what might have been foreseen. Those who feel themselves called by Heaven to take action against the powers of evil, and who are greatly successful, develop immediately a spiritual pride that is nearly, if not quite, insanity. Christina constituted herself the protector of the Gregor family. When she heard that Dundas suspected you, Captain Gregor, she marked him down for destruction. The room above his, as you know, is empty. All she had to do was to wait there till he leaned out of his window and he did that no doubt at very frequent intervals on account of the heat. She knew that McDonald and I were coming upstairs; she heard Dundas wish us good night. He appeared below her. The block of ice was not shattered in this instance, for there is no spike above Dundas's room. It rolled down the bank and went splashing into the burn. The current carried it out into the loch. The procedure was the same in Barley's case except that a bait was necessary to induce him to walk under the window. It was supplied by the dropping of a preliminary block of ice, the resulting thud and splash, heard at the moment when he was about to arrest you, Mrs. Gregor, naturally excited his liveliest interest."

He stopped and bowed his head.

"I planned, to-night," he said in tones of deep regret, "to excite Christina's fears and direct her hostility against myself. That was the object of my visit to the nursery and of the directions I gave. I succeeded too well. I had arranged my hat in such a way that, when I pulled on a thread, it would swing out from the french-window. If Christina was guilty I felt sure she would strike again. Then, as I coughed to give the signal, Duchlan appeared. As you know, I shouted, but it was too late."

He drew a long deep breath.

"The knowledge that she had killed her master was sentence of death to the woman at the window," he added. "Her fall did not kill her; as soon as she knew herself alive she rushed headlong down the bank to the water."

The chorus of the birds filled all the spaces of morning. McDonald rose stiffly, dragging his leg.

"I believe," he said, "that the ice comes from the Ardmore fishmonger. There are herring scales on every square inch of his walls and doors."